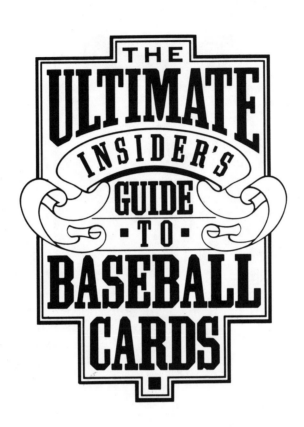

THE
ULTIMATE
INSIDER'S
GUIDE
· TO ·
BASEBALL
CARDS

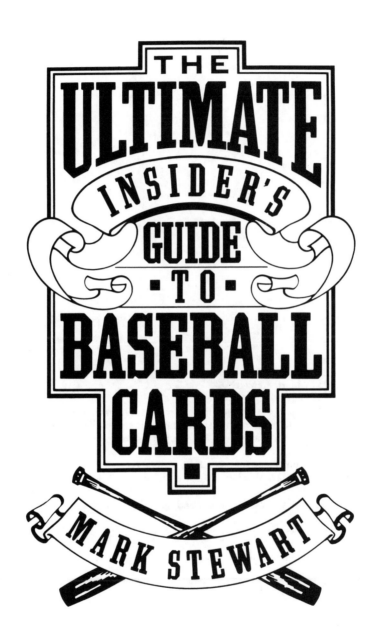

# THE ULTIMATE INSIDER'S GUIDE ·TO· BASEBALL CARDS

## MARK STEWART

CROWN TRADE PAPERBACKS, NEW YORK

Published by Crown Publishers, Inc., 201 East 50th Street,
New York, New York 10022. Member of Crown Publishing Group.

Random House, Inc., New York, Toronto, London, Sydney, Auckland

Crown Trade Paperbacks™ and colophon are trademarks of Crown Publishers, Inc.

Manufactured in the United States of America

Library of Congress Cataloging in Publication Data

Stewart, Mark.
    Ultimate insider's guide to baseball cards / by Mark Stewart.
      1. Baseball cards—Collectors and collecting—United States.
    2. Baseball cards—Prices—United States.  I. Stewart, Mark.
    II. Title.
    GV875.3.S74    1993
    796′.49796357′0973—dc20                  92-33645
                                               CIP

ISBN 0-517-88035-0

10  9  8  7  6  5  4  3  2  1

First Edition

# CONTENTS

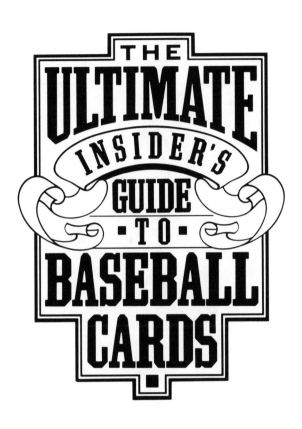

# INTRODUCTION

What is the single most valuable thing a baseball card buyer can own? A 1952 Mickey Mantle? A 1968 Nolan Ryan? Neither. The answer is *knowledge*. Why? Because knowledge is power. Granted, it's an overused cliché, but consider for a moment the fact that the baseball card business is one of the only consumer-based industries where the consumers don't have any real power. Given that the commodity is cardboard, doesn't it seem strange that the people who produce it, sell it, and evaluate it determine what you should pay for it? If it doesn't, it *should*.

Who has all the money? Buyers. Who creates the demand? Buyers. So why is it that when you go into a shop and see a card you like, you're at the mercy of a dealer who shoves a price guide in front of you and tells you that the price he's asking is fair? Worse, why have you no power to argue otherwise? Because, as a typical card buyer, you have no knowledge of the inner workings of the business.

This book provides you with the knowledge to handle yourself in such a situation—and then some. Think of it as a textbook, an educational tool that will expand your mind and open your eyes. Use the information in this book to make money, save money, or spend money—that's entirely up to you—just use it to your advantage. If you are a beginner, this book is perfect for you, for its goal is to make sense of an extremely complex market. If you are an intermediate buyer, the value of this book lies in many of the buying, selling, and evaluation techniques that are covered in great detail. If you are an advanced buyer, you can see how well you've fared thus far and make course corrections as you go forward.

Finally, if you are one of those people who buys a card for the "pure pleasure" of owning it, read this book twice. If you paid too much for that card, the pleasure of owning it isn't as pure as you'd like to believe.

"A card's only worth what you're willing to pay for it." You'll hear this statement from time to time around card shops and shows. If you think it sounds like a pretty profound philosophy, however, think again. Just because you feel an Eddie Murray rookie is worth only $15, that doesn't change the fact that everyone else feels it's a $50 or $60 card. Nor does it mean that you have even the remotest chance of finding one at your price. Conversely, if you pay $150 for a Murray rookie, that doesn't change its value either—unless you plan to spend about $20 million buying up every single card. A card has value, yes. And that value does have something to do with what someone's willing to pay for it. But value is not determined by *you*—it's determined by *everyone* who buys cards.

The more you know about what other buyers feel cards are worth, the more accurately you'll be able to gauge the marketplace. That's important, because when it comes right down to it, you're basically spending your hard-earned money on cardboard. You have to be aware of how many people want a particular card and why they want it. Is it as easy as looking up a card in a price guide? No, although that's a start. Ultimately, you have to understand the dynamics that make card values fluctuate, and that means understanding the collective mind-set of all card buyers. The better the "feel" you develop for what it is people want (and don't want), the more fun and profitable your experience with cards will be. It takes time, however, and you're never going to be right 100 percent of the time. But you should, at the very least, have a solid starting point. Well, that's what this book has been designed to be.

Unless you have a long temper and a lot of money, you cannot start from ground zero and expect to truly understand what makes the card business go. Even if you've been building a collection for a few years, you may not fully appreciate what makes card values rise and fall. From the vagaries of human performance to the laws of supply and demand, there is an awful lot going on—more, in fact, than even most full-time card dealers are capable of digesting. The problem is that the "players" in the card business—the card companies, dealers, buyers, collectors, and commentators—suffer from a severe case of tunnel vision. What should be a cohesive, smooth-running multibillion-dollar industry is, in reality, a completely uncalibrated collection of gears that grind horribly against one another whenever they come into contact.

That's hardly surprising. The card business, in its current incarnation, is relatively young—no more than a quarter of a century old. It's a real mixed bag. There are dealers who collect, collectors who deal, buyers who have no idea what they're buying—and card companies that would just as soon keep it that way. Those are the so-called professionals. Add to that about a million kids, a million price guides—and millions more cards than there are people to buy them—and what you get is a market that is something less than stable.

Ah, but that's the fun of it. The less stable the market, the more room for profit and, more to the point, the more valuable every piece of information you acquire. Given the fact that there are a lot of profoundly stupid people at every level of this business, a little intelligence can go a long, long way.

This is a book about value. And value is a function of supply and demand. Hopefully, this is not a revelation. But what you may not realize is that in the card business, those two factors are nearly impossible to calculate. That makes the concept of value a very gray area, which is far and away the most negative thing that can be said about cards. What are the positives? The major one is that cards are a conduit to fantasy—the fantasy of reliving the simplicity and innocence of the past. Baseball and baseball cards were more than threads in the social fabric of childhood—in many cases they were the strongest part of the weave. Everyone was more or less equal back then (whenever "back then" was), if not on the playing field then in the candy store, where one kid's nickel held just as much promise as the next kid's. Even today, a card buyer on a $20-a-month budget has the same chance of pulling a Ken Griffey card out of a given pack as does a well-heeled investor who buys by the case.

That's part of the fantasy of *possibility*, which, sadly, tends to evaporate from other aspects of life as the years roll on. Cards, however, offer that fantasy every day, as the living, breathing young men depicted on those little pieces of cardboard strive to fulfill their potential. If you own a Juan Gonzales card, in a way Juan is working for you—as he hits and throws and runs the bases, he is trying to become the player you've always hoped he could be. That's a nice feeling, especially if you've got a few hundred of his cards.

What this all adds up to is intrinsic value. When you buy a card, you're essentially buying a dream. That's what buoys the market; that's what keeps the foundation relatively solid.

But can you put a price on dreams? No. You need something a little more tangible. That's where the nasty business of supply and demand comes into play. And don't think for a moment that, in the world of cards, it isn't nasty.

# SUPPLY

The concept of supply is a tricky one when you're talking about cards. Since cards aren't "used" for anything, the only time the supply is truly diminished is when cards are destroyed. When a parent throws a child's card collection away, those cards are gone forever. When kids bend cards in half or spill something on them, those cards, though not "gone forever," are worth no more than the cardboard on which they are printed, which means they have ceased to be "cards" in a market sense. And, of course, when cards are purposely destroyed—as they were in 1952, when the owners of Topps dumped a huge quantity of unsold cards into the ocean—they are gone forever, too.

There is no way to calculate how many cards have been destroyed over the last hundred years, although it can be safely said that most cards issued prior to the emergence of the hobby in the 1970s have gone up in smoke. On the other hand, it's also safe to say that—as the value and popularity of cards have become widely recognized in recent years—a significant majority of the cards issued over the last decade still exist. No one, in other words, has been throwing cards away. So, assuming that 80 or 90 percent of newer cards still exist somewhere, it should be relatively easy to cal-culate the total supply—*if* you have information from the card companies on how many cards they printed.

That's a big if. Topps, Donruss, Fleer, Score, Upper Deck, and other manufacturers guard those numbers closely. How closely? Very closely. It's as if they fear the earth might spin off its axis were those numbers ever to be made public. Meanwhile, everyone's left guessing. Are there 5 million 1993 Cal Ripken cards out there? Are there 10 million? There could be 20 or 30 million for all anyone knows. All those figures are well within the realm of possibility, which raises some scary questions, given that there are, at most, only 2 million card buyers in this country.

If there were indeed 30 million Cal Ripken cards made this year, does that mean each card buyer has to own fifteen before they are worth anything? And if that's true, what is a 1993 Craig Shipley worth? If only 1 million buyers want one Craig Shipley apiece, what happens to the other 29 million cards? Where do they go? Who has them? What will they ever do with them?

We're not talking about pencils here. Pencils get used up. Even though, at any given time, there may be 29 million more pencils than people need, they're going to need them sooner or later, so there's nothing to worry about. A card buyer, however, *should* worry about who's using up all the Craig Shipleys.

Given the enormous supply of new cards, the difference in price between Ripken and Shipley is worth looking into. When you see a 1993 Ripken priced at 20 cents, and a 1993 Shipley priced at 2 cents, that relationship seems reasonable. Ripken is easily ten times more desirable than Shipley, so no one raises an eyebrow. What buyers patently ignore, however, is the question of why Ripken is worth 20 cents to begin with. Granted, the card costs a penny or so to license, print, and ship, but the 1,000 percent premium for a card whose supply may never dry up is a little mystifying. In other words, before the issue of *demand* is even addressed, there's something terribly wrong with the *supply* of the card equation.

The question is What's going on? The answer is that the people holding the Ripkens—collectors, investors, dealers, and high-volume wholesalers— are unwilling to let them go below a certain price. It's sort of a silent, unorganized conspiracy. Everyone senses that if they don't "hold the line," something awful might happen. Well, in a way they're right. Assuming the selling price of a 1993 Ripken would have to drop to, say, 4 cents before *every single one* was absorbed by the card-buying public, that would not leave enough room for dealers to make money. Remember, they're paying about 3 cents each for Ripken's card, plus a prorated share of their other business expenses.

For the sake of argument, say that everyone *didn't* hold the line; say that a lot of people decided to *take* 4 cents for their Ripkens. You know what? It would probably be a good turn for the card business as a whole. The dealers would be forced to confront the card manufacturers and say: "Hey, we can't make money unless we sell your Ripkens at 20 cents. We're tired of shilling for your overproduced product. How about cutting back your print runs so that the supply actually meets the demand at that price?"

The response of the card companies would probably be "What are you guys complaining about? You're making money, aren't you?"

And the dealers would probably back down.

What's wrong with this picture is that it assumes that more and more people with more and more money will continue to buy cards. If that's the case, then everything will be fine. The 1993 Ripkens will be absorbed at 20 cents in 1994, 1995, and 1996. But given a queasy economy and the fact that the card companies plan to release even *more* sets in the coming years, it would seem that all involved, not just the dealers, are headed for a big fall. Already, buyers are becoming disenchanted with the sheer quantities on the market, a couple of the card companies are less than healthy, and many small dealers are being crushed—both literally and figuratively—under the weight of their unsold cards. Thus the more cards that are produced in the coming years, the riskier it is for everyone, top to bottom, to continue on in the business in its present state. The ill effects of overabundance could come to roost much more quickly—and much more severely—than people think.

Whether or not a cardboard Armageddon is on the horizon doesn't change the fact that the supply of cards that have already been printed is pretty much set. As stated, the supply of new cards is overwhelming. But what about slightly older cards—cards from the 1980s, for instance?

Some overproduced sets from the past decade— such as the 1988 Donruss—have yet to sell at retail, meaning there are countless cases hanging around in job lot warehouses. By and large, though, the cards of the 1980s have been pretty much absorbed. Interestingly enough, card companies and dealers alike are fond of pointing this out whenever someone suggests that far too many cards are being issued in the 1990s. They say, "Don't worry about a glut—the buying public will eventually suck up anything that comes on the market." What they forget is that the print runs for cards in the 1980s, though of mind-boggling quantities, pale in comparison with the number of cards being produced today.

They are also ignoring the fact that those cards were absorbed in large part by *new* buyers, who entered the fray in the last few years and were making up for lost time. The sets these new buyers went after were the 1984, 1985, and 1986 Donruss; 1984, 1985, 1986, 1987, and 1988 Fleer; and 1989 Upper Deck—all of which turned out to have relatively short print runs. The supply of cards from those sets has pretty much dried up. However, the supply of all Topps cards from the 1980s—with the possible exception of 1980 itself—is still quite plentiful. Will the new buyers of the 1990s absorb the remaining cards of the 1980s *and* all the new stuff issued in this decade? So far, that hasn't been the case.

Once you get into the 1970s, however, estimating supply gets a little trickier. The number of cards in collectible condition definitely drops as you hit the middle of the decade. Why? The main reason is that until 1974 or 1975 few if any cards coming right out of the packs commanded a significant premium. A 1972 Hank Aaron—the Rolls-Royce of cards from that set *at that time*—sold for about a quarter. Bench, Seaver, Carew (yes, the high-number Carew), and other stars fetched only a dime. In other words, the vast majority of new cards weren't worth selling. And, unfortunately, that meant they weren't worth protecting, either. So you find a lot of bad corners and minor creases from sets predating 1974. And those cards just aren't considered collectible.

As you get into the 1960s, the supply of cards in collectible condition gets even smaller. There were no shows, no mail-order ads, and not much interest in purchasing single cards, so no one had the foresight to protect them in any way. At least in the 1970s there were plastic sheets available. In the 1960s the most advanced storage unit was a plastic "locker," which was little more than a corner-crushing carrying case. As a rule, the farther back you go into the 1960s—and 1950s, for that matter—the smaller the supply of cards in collectible condition. As you move toward 1948—the first year of significant postwar card production—you find that fewer cards were printed and fewer survived.

There are a couple of interesting exceptions. There seems to be an unusually high percentage of 1952 Topps cards in collectible condition. One explanation that has been offered for this anomaly is that these were the first "big" cards ever issued, and kids did different things with them than they had with the smaller Bowmans. For instance, the Topps cards didn't fit in back pockets quite as easily, so more must have gone right into shoe boxes. Also, the bigness of cards made them a little more special, which might have translated into a few more kids taking better care of them. The 1953 Topps, by contrast, were not really novel in any way and did not fare very well in terms of condition. Another exception to the supply rule is the 1954 Bowman set. That year competitor Topps came out with several innovations, including two photos on the front of its cards, and a little cartoon on its bright red-and-green back. Bowmans, by contrast, were butt-ugly, with washed-out photos and boring statistics. Apparently, kids looked at their Bowmans once and then put them away for good. Thus there exists a relatively healthy supply of 1954 Bowmans in collectible condition.

So supply is far from an across-the-board constant. In recent years—with the emergence of premium card sets, updates, and the like—gauging supply has become especially frustrating, as the relationship between age and scarcity is even less strong than it used to be. The *most* frustrating aspect of supply, however, is that its effect on card values pales in both significance and complexity to that of *demand,* which drives the business with the force of a cyclone.

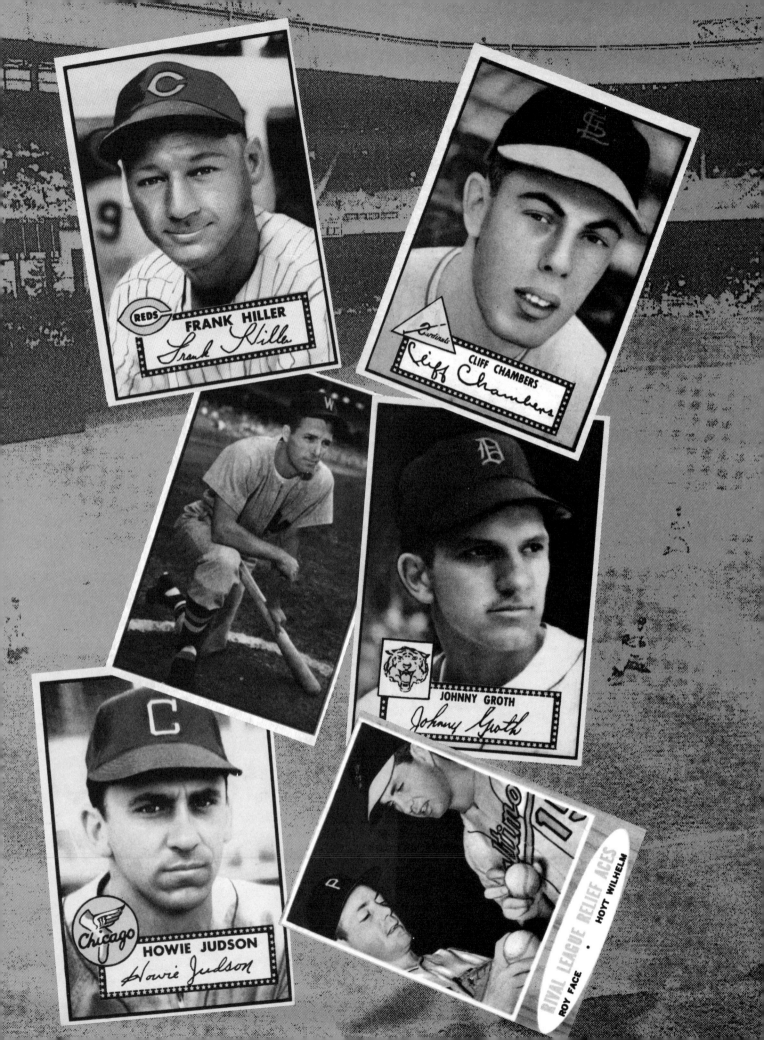

FRANK HILLER

CLIFF CHAMBERS

JOHNNY GROTH

HOWIE JUDSON

RIVAL LEAGUE RELIEF ACES

ROY FACE · HOYT WILHELM

# 2

## DEMAND

In 1990, a young Dodgers hurler by the name of Ramon Martinez got off to a lightning-fast start and caused quite a stir in the industry. In May and June he was dominating batters and racking up wins at an impressive rate. By mid-season, Martinez looked like a lock for the Cy Young Award and—best of all—he was only twenty-one. You could smell a Hall of Fame career in its embryonic stages. Not surprisingly, everyone was scrambling to acquire his 1989 rookie cards.

The Topps, Score, and Donruss Martinez cards, overproduced as usual, were not hard to come by, yet in some areas they were selling for $3. The Fleer card, also produced in great quantity, was selling for as much as $4 (due mainly to the fact that many '89 Fleer boxes had not been opened by the collectors who had originally purchased them in hopes of acquiring the notorious Billy Ripken error card). Dealers were gladly paying $1 to $2 for these common issues, while the much-tougher '89 Upper Deck Martinez was hovering around $5 retail.

Martinez did not win the Cy Young Award, having faded a bit down the stretch, but all in all he still had a terrific year. That was enough to keep demand fairly constant over the winter, especially for the Upper Deck card, which broke the $10 barrier. After a so-so 1991 campaign and a miserable

1992, however, collectors cooled to Martinez. And that's when everyone began to recognize just how many of his rookie cards were out there. The four common issues sank well below a buck, while the selling price of the Upper Deck card was cut in half. Meanwhile, as millions—yes, *millions*—of Martinez rookies were changing hands in 1990 and early 1991 (pretty much regardless of price), the infinitely less-abundant and older cards of Hall of Famers were sitting around in showcases collecting dust.

Put simply, the demand for a particular card—or, more to the point, the demand for a particular player—has a greater effect on a card's market value than supply does. This dynamic should not be taken lightly, as it goes far in explaining why prices for relatively abundant cards can skyrocket at a moment's notice. Since no one can really put a number on the availability of a given card at a given time, collectors and dealers tend to adopt a rather provincial outlook when it comes to determining the relationship between supply and demand for a "hot" card.

The Martinez case, however, is a little more complex than it seems. A lot of people, you see, sized up this situation in the following way: Why spend $3 on one of the perhaps 10 million cards that existed of this unproven phenomenon, when for that same $3 you could pick up one of the fifty thousand or so 1974 Jim Hunters, 1975 Willie Stargells, or 1976 Brooks Robinsons that were on the market at the very same time? All three players were among the greatest ever to play their positions—something it might take another decade for anyone to say with any certainty about Martinez. In other words, why take a chance on a high-supply card of an unproven player when relatively low-supply cards of "sure things" can be had at the same price? Those people had a valid point, but where they failed in their analysis was in their attempt to apply logic to a completely illogical marketplace.

The question isn't Why do this as opposed to that? The question is Why is the marketplace like that to begin with? Why is demand such a dominant factor when supply almost always outstrips it? Why is a 1957 Early Wynn the same price as a 1987 Ruben Sierra? The answer goes right to the heart of value and pricing.

Consider the universe of card buyers. The vast majority never saw Wynn pitch and rarely heard his name mentioned. To them, he is a few lines of agate in the back of *The Baseball Encyclopedia*—which, by the way, most card buyers don't even own. That he won three hundred games and was elected to the Hall of Fame is almost immaterial, for there is no *connection*. Even a forty-year-old would be hard-pressed to recall seeing Wynn on the mound, much less to associate him with an enjoyable experience—no connection, no demand. Buying a card, remember, is like buying a dream. And Martinez and Sierra are a lot easier to dream about than Early Wynn.

What of Wynn's credentials? Do they count for anything? Well, he's been retired for three decades, he's already in the Hall of Fame, and the chances that he might resurface—in body or name—are, to say the least, remote. Thus a buyer looks at Wynn and sees a player whose card has "topped out." Indeed, there is almost no upside at all. The only future demand for his cards, in fact, will come from the odd buyer who wants a cheap Hall of Famer, or someone who happens to need Wynn's card to fill

in a particular set. So the supply of Wynn's cards (or Stargell's or Hunter's or Robinson's), while hardly plentiful, barely makes a dent in the almost nonexistent demand. The only reason Wynn's cards cost as much as they do is that dealers refuse to let a Hall of Famer go for the price of a "minor star." Even the fact that there are probably fifty beat-up examples of a 1957 Wynn for every one in collectible condition makes little impression on buyers who have $15 to spend.

*The first rule of demand,* then, is that just because a player was great, it doesn't mean that his card will *ever* be in demand. There are several "great" players who, for one reason or another, just haven't clicked with card buyers. Some are in the Hall of Fame, some are not. The important thing is to be aware not of how these players are judged by baseball, but of how they are judged by people who spend money on cards. In other words, cards of these players are not worth what *you're* willing to pay for them; they're worth what the going price is to *everyone else*.

*The second rule of demand* is something of a corollary to this confusing situation, in the sense that a player clearly does *not* have to be great to be in high demand. The value of Bob Uecker cards, for instance, increased tremendously as he gained recognition as a sitcom star.

*The third rule of demand* concerns the profit motive. If enough buyers believe that a card will jump in price, they can actually *force* it to do so. It can happen to a new card or an old card, although the dynamics for each differ considerably. The thing to keep in mind is that if you play the market correctly, these largely artificial swings can be extremely profitable.

It's fascinating to watch this third rule in action, as it feeds off a sort of mob mentality. When this happens to a new card, the player is usually a rookie with little or no major-league experience. And it usually starts before the rookie has even reported to spring training. The ball gets rolling when dealers break down their cases in January and February and separate rookies from their other cards. Then they look for cards of players between the ages of twenty-one and twenty-five, who seem to have good minor-league statistics. They also look for players who have performed for a week or two at the major-league level and who hit a couple of homers, won a couple of games, or went 4 for 10 as late-season fill-ins.

If they spot a young outfielder with flashy numbers in A or AA ball—and the team that owns him is hurting at that position—they put a few of his cards out for their customers at 25 or 50 cents. Card buyers, meanwhile, see the same flashy stats and decide to spend a couple of dollars on those cards, thinking that the dealers know something that they don't. The dealers (who knew absolutely nothing), suddenly fear they've sold these cards too cheaply, so they either put out a new bunch at a higher price or just hang on to what they've got left until they know what's going on.

The effect of these decisions hits card buyers like a one-two punch. Since half the dealers are no longer offering the card to their customers, the illusions of scarcity and high demand are created. And since the other half of the dealers have jacked up the price of the remaining cards, the illusion of a rising price is created, too.

What happens next is that this young outfielder arrives at spring training with his flashy stats and catches the eye of the news media. Always looking for an interesting angle in February, the media can't resist a twenty-two-year-old who's hustling and smiling and crushing the ball in batting practice. It really doesn't matter that this youngster can't hit a curve or a cutoff man—a story's a story. So the name of this young outfielder finds its way into the papers, especially if there's a malcontent or underachieving millionaire playing the same position. Card buyers read these stories and think, "Hey, this kid might make so-and-so tradable . . . He'd be perfect for that team's ballpark . . . He's everything so-and-so isn't." Meanwhile, the team's manager, anxious to get his millionaire motivated, starts telling the reporters that this kid may play his way onto the team, that he's the center fielder of the future, or that, gee, he's no longer the team's best-kept secret.

That's usually enough to start the feeding frenzy. Card buyers snap up whatever they can, and dealers start raising the prices of what they have left. When April comes around and this amazing young talent is sent back to AA ball, buyers are left holding the bag.

What's important to recognize here is the fact that this demand is based on little else other than greed. Since less than one in ten buyers of these cards has any real information on the player in question, the *potential for profit* is driving the price of the card up all by itself. The demand is not based on player performance—and it's certainly not based on supply, since the supposed scarcity of these cards occurs at a time when less than 25 percent of all new cards have even been *opened*. It's a simple matter of an industry driving itself. If you know your history, you know that that's how the stock market crashed in 1929. Well, every year the market for these rookie cards crashes in at least nineteen out of twenty cases.

*The fourth rule of demand* is that it can be created. This process is also driven by the profit motive, but it requires a number of other things to happen, such as one or two players having outstanding seasons. It also relies on the mass hysteria of dealers and buyers, who, of course, are ready, willing, and quite able to lose all objectivity at a moment's notice.

The creation of value begins with a basic fact about the card business: no matter what happens during a season, the industry cannot survive without at least one player to "obsess on." There has to be at least one player whose name is on the tip of everyone's tongue for at least a few months. It has happened every year for two solid decades. Sometimes it's more than one player; sometimes it's one player for the first half of the year and another for the second half. It has happened to players like Mickey Mantle, Pete Rose, George Brett, Steve Carlton, Ryne Sandberg, Nolan Ryan, and Cal Ripken.

So far, so good. But in the past twenty years it has also happened to the likes of Fred Lynn, Kevin McReynolds, Kirk Gibson, Eric Davis, Mike Greenwell, Fernando Valenzuela, and Bob Horner. They're not bad guys if you're building a team, but they were absolute death if you were building a portfolio. Here are a few other names that devoured hard-earned dollars: Jim Kaat, Steve Rogers, Ken Landreaux, Joe Charboneau, Leon Durham, Von Hayes, Kevin Seitzer, Kevin Maas, and Pete Incaviglia. In the case of each player, there was a prolonged period during which otherwise reasonable humans were possessed by the unreasonable urge to buy as many of his cards as was humanly possible. Yet the business never learned from its mistakes, and buyers continue to go on hog-wild buying sprees every single season. Why? Who "creates" this demand?

Well, in a sense, everyone does. For dealers and card buyers, there is a built-in mechanism that is triggered largely by boredom. Boredom? Yes. Taken purely at face value, the card business isn't all that exciting. Less than 5 percent of all existing cards are in demand at any one time, and many of the cards that *are* in demand are extremely pricey. Thus the typical dealer or buyer is looking at an incredibly stagnant inventory, despite what all the little arrows in the price guides say. This in turn creates the feeling that there's nothing to buy or sell, which, for a business that paints itself as fast-moving and highly profitable, is an intolerable situation. At this point, the desire for "demand for the sake of demand" becomes so intense that everyone is just dying for something interesting to happen.

And something always does. It can be a breakthrough year by a young player, a surprising season by an established star, or a big-name, blockbuster trade. If nothing significant is happening on the playing field, then the business turns inward for its inspiration and either looks for an unappreciated older set or a flashy new release. Whatever the trigger, the reaction is fast and furious.

How does this created demand differ from demand that is driven by speculation? They *can* be one and the same. One distinguishing factor, however, is the base of knowledge that surrounds the player whose cards are suddenly in high demand. Ask a buyer why he's hoarding cards of an unknown rookie, and the best answer you'll get is that he's taking a chance that the card will go up. Ask the same buyer why he's snapping up cards of a player about to hit his four hundredth home run, and you get that player's life history, current stats, and the odds of his making the Hall of Fame. In other words, the people chasing after these cards have convinced themselves that there's virtually no risk.

The same is true when sets are involved. Ask a buyer why he's plowing money into a newly released set produced in unknown quantities, and the best answer you'll get is that he believes the set will be in demand and therefore will rise in value. Ask the same buyer why he's buying a four-year-old set, and he'll tell you how hard it's been to find at shows, which rookie cards show promise, and how it stacks up against other sets that were printed during the same year.

Because created demand feeds off actual known performance, it can last a very long time. It can also end very abruptly. It all depends on what else is out there and how quickly buyers get a grip on reality. The point is not that demand doesn't always follow a logical path—that should be obvious by now—but that *created* demand is a powerful factor when it comes to card values.

*The fifth and final rule of demand* is that it inevitably subsides. In and of itself, demand in the card business is simply a gauge of what people *feel* like buying. If a player does badly, demand for his cards dries up. If the price of a card or set rises dramatically, it is no longer in demand by people who suddenly can't afford it. And if buyers merely prefer to spend their money on something else, that cuts into demand as well. Regardless of which dynamic originally generates high demand for a particular card or set, *something* will eventually start working against it. In twenty years, no single player, card, or set has been immune to this process.

# 3

# PRICE GUIDES

Logic should tell you that if a card is not widely available and depicts a popular player, it has a good chance of holding or increasing its value. Likewise, if a card is widely available and depicts a player who is *not* particularly popular, logic should tell you that its chances of holding or increasing its value may not be all that good. It's the logic of supply and demand, of course, and in the case of cards that meet either of these two extremes, the various monthly price guides that are available reflect these dynamics in terms of the selling prices that they "report."

And well they should. There's no trick to reporting what 1963 Sandy Koufax cards are selling for, because they are in relatively constant demand at around $125. Nor is it difficult to report what 1983 Al Cowens cards are selling for, because common cards from that year are not in high demand and generally fetch no more than a penny or two. However, in terms of reporting the selling prices for the millions of cards that fit somewhere in between these two extremes, the price guides play a very dangerous game.

Before delving further into the pros and cons of the monthly price guides, consider for a moment the difference between what they are meant to be as opposed to what they have become. Price guides

for cards became available back in the 1960s. At the time, they included all cards—sports and non-sports—and did not make a distinction between individual cards, other than saying that "stars" were worth a premium. That all changed in the early 1970s, when detailed price guides started appearing on a regular basis in hobby publications and, later, as entities unto themselves. Stars were listed separately, along with their prices, an innovation that was greeted with great enthusiasm by those who didn't like all the guesswork involved in buying and selling. The prices, which moved up and down as they do now, were derived from a rather unscientific survey of dealers at the few shows that were being held at the time, and were weighted toward players who were popular in the regions from which these guides emanated.

Despite the obvious problems with this system, these publications were quickly adopted by both buyers and dealers—not as bibles, however, but as guides in the literal sense. The prices quoted were assumed to be relatively accurate reflections of what individual cards were selling for, but everyone knew that there was room for negotiation. Because there were far fewer cards available back then, most people in the business were familiar with what they were really worth. Everyone knew,

Hank Aaron | OUTFIELD

BROOKS ROBINSON • 3B

ORIOLES

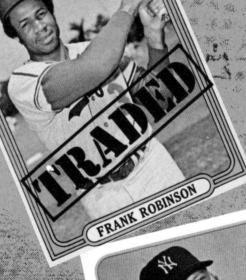

TRADED

FRANK ROBINSON

YANKEES OUTFIELD

MICKEY MANTLE

for instance, that a 1967 Hank Aaron was worth around $5 in 1974. If the price guides said it was worth $4 or $5.25 or $6.50, no one really took offense—there wasn't enough money involved to make much of a difference. The seeds of manipulation, however, had been sown.

In 1979, things began to change when the business started to wake up to the world of rookie cards. Long ignored because a good player often had to share space with a marginal one, rookie cards quite suddenly became high-demand items. Tom Seaver's rookie card jumped from a couple of dollars to more than $50. Rod Carew's rookie card shot up to $25. And Pete Rose, who became the talk of baseball that year when he signed a huge deal to play with the Phillies, climbed toward the $100 mark. These developments took everyone by surprise, given that a year earlier these cards were all plentiful and reasonably priced.

Things began to happen very quickly. Cards would literally double in price from one weekend to the next. At shows, you could find a 1963 Willie Stargell priced at $3 at one table and $15 at another—a huge difference, considering how low card prices were back then. In this time of chaos, the price guides seemed to be the only source of reason.

And that's when the card business changed forever. There developed, on the part of buyers and dealers, a collective willingness to accept—*without question*—the prices published in monthly guides. It didn't seem to matter that some prices were clearly too high and that others were far too low; that there was a "definitive" source for value made up for those shortcomings.

Those shortcomings, however, may have been carefully planned. The publisher of one widely used price guide—who also happened to be a card dealer—was accused of manipulation, first by other dealers and then by the authorities. This individual allegedly dropped the prices of cards he wanted to stock up on and raised the prices of cards of which he had a large supply. Needless to say, this gave him an unfair advantage when dealing with unsophisticated buyers and sellers. He reportedly would set up at card shows and sell the cards he marked with "pluses" at "bargain" prices, while buying cards he marked with "minuses" at artificially low prices from panicked sellers. It was the first real scandal in the card business.

The name of the publisher and of the publication aren't important; he eventually got what he deserved. What was important was that this ridiculously simple scam clearly showed how easy it was to manipulate prices and, therefore, the market itself.

Predictably, there was a downswing in the card business. But was it a reaction to price manipulation? Not entirely. As it so happened, this lull in buying and selling, and subsequent drop in card prices, took place during an economic downturn, when interest rates were very high, unemployment was on the rise, and inflation was taking a bite out of many card buyers' budgets. Within a few months it was business as usual, card prices recovered, and the whole incident was forgotten.

The main beneficiary of this turmoil was a monthly guide called *Current Card Prices,* or CCP, which for several years went unchallenged as the final word on what cards were really worth. In 1986, Dr. James Beckett, whose annual card guides had been among the most popular in the business, decided to enter tne monthly fray with *Baseball Card Monthly,* or Beckett's, as it is commonly known. CCP and Beckett's, along with at least a dozen other hobby publications, now carry updated prices every month.

With so many guides on the market, you would think that there would now be enough checks and balances to prevent the kind of price manipulation that occurred in the formative years of the card business. And with the many thousands of card shops and shows in operation, you would think that the sheer volume of information on what cards are actually selling for would ensure a fair amount of accuracy. But that may not be the case.

From a card buyer's standpoint, the situation may be even *worse.*

Here's the problem: The prices in these monthly guides are supposedly reflections of what cards are currently selling for. How do the guides get that information? First, they claim to "observe" actual sales at shops and shows. Second, they rely on regular reports from dealers as to which cards they are selling and what those cards are selling for. You don't have to be a genius to see what's wrong here.

In terms of "observing" sales, it is highly unlikely that a publication with an information-gathering staff of ten or so people can get its personnel around the country to "observe" a sufficient number of actual sales to arrive at an accurate price for each of the thousands of cards it lists. What if they go a month without "observing" the sale of a particular card? Is it worth less than the month before?

And what of the sales they do observe? If a price guide person "observed" you buying a 1962 Red Schoendienst, a 1974 Willie Stargell, and a 1957 Luis Aparicio from a single dealer for $65, what would that person report? Would the prices be $35, $3, and $27, respectively? Or $30, $4, and $31? What if the dealer had marked the Schoendienst at $35 and the Aparicio at $30 and threw in the Stargell for free? Does the Stargell card's value plummet to $0? Do they average the $0 price in with the other Stargell sales they "observe"? The whole idea of "observing" actual sales, while in theory the best way to determine definitive prices, is in practice preposterous.

With insufficient data from observed sales, the price guides have to rely on reports from dealers. Some claim to accept information from card buyers as well, but whether or not they put much stock in that information is unclear. Most guides have a panel of "experts" or "analysts," which is a fancy way of saying that an unspecified number of dealers have agreed to report the prices of the cards they sell. These reports—which vary in detail from a full accounting of sales to comments such as "Everyone wants 1989 Upper Deck"—are collated each month, with unusually high or low selling prices discarded to provide something of a safety margin. If the average reported selling price of a 1988 Fleer Jose Canseco turns out to be $1.75, that is the price listed in the next issue. If it is different

from the price in the previous issue, this is indicated by adding an upward or downward arrow, or a plus or minus, next to the $1.75 price.

What's wrong with this picture? Plenty. First of all, by making such a big deal about how they arrive at their prices, these guides, both individually and collectively, have convinced card buyers that these prices are accurate reflections of what cards actually sell for. Although each publication prints a disclaimer to the effect that it is "only a guide," the reality is very different. The vast majority of buyers judge the value of the cards they own and the cards they intend to purchase based solely upon these prices, and the people who publish these guides know it. Some, like Beckett's, print a high and low price for each card, which is commendable, but the reality is that no one—neither dealers nor buyers—pays much attention to the lower price. In short, buyers regard the information in the price guides as more than accurate and reliable—they consider these publications to be unimpeachable.

For kids, this unquestioning acceptance is perfectly natural and quite understandable—they have little else to go on. But why educated, free-thinking, and presumably intelligent grown-ups feel this way requires a little explaining.

Adult card buyers suffer from something of an inferiority complex. They spend a lot of time and money on something that they know the rest of the world considers pretty childish. They worry that others consider them to be arrested in their intellectual development. Rarely, if ever, will they discuss their passion in social situations, fearful of what others will think. (The irony, of course, is that adult card buyers have consciously *chosen* to arrest their intellectual development, and there's not a damn thing wrong with that! Who would quibble with the merits of recapturing one's youth? If an adult who loved camping and backpacking as a child chooses to spend his vacation tromping through the woods, he's admired by his peers for his pioneer spirit and love of the outdoors. The fact that he blows thousands of dollars a year doing so doesn't make people think any less of him. Well, if *you* spend thousands of dollars a year reliving *your* childhood passion, what makes that so different? The profit motive? Certainly not! That you pursue personal fulfillment *and* have something to show for it is a pretty neat trick!) The fallout from these insecurities, however, goes far in explaining why card buyers place so much faith in the price guides. Their need to legitimize participation in the card business is facilitated by *a legitimization of the card business itself*. And since the card business revolves around what cards (i.e., commodities) trade for, the model with which everyone aspires to equate the card business is the stock exchange.

The parallels certainly exist: the daily blur of buying and selling, the chaotic nature of supply and demand, the real-life performance of the entities whose paper is being exchanged. Beyond those fundamental similarities, however, is where card buyers get in trouble. They start seeing things that just aren't there.

For instance, a card buyer will insist that the card business mirrors the stock market in that owning a card of a player is like owning a share of stock in a company. It can be, in an abstract way, but the reality is that possessing a share of stock means that you actually own a part of a company, while possessing a player's card means you own a piece of cardboard. (If you want to "own" part of a player, buy stock in his team). A card buyer will also assert that wheeling and dealing in the card market is just as difficult, if not more difficult, as buying and selling stocks. That may be true, but that doesn't make the two pursuits any more similar than apples and oranges. Finally, there is the contention that the card business and the stock market mirror each other in that after a specified trading period, an accounting is rendered, in black and white, of what the respective commodities are trading for. In the case of the stock market, it's the daily "bid" and "ask" listings in the financial pages of the newspaper. In the case of the card business, it's the price guides.

This is where the two fundamental problems with price guides—that they are not really empirically researched and that buyers consider them to have the final, up-to-date word on values—meet with the destructive force of a high-speed collision. And this is why buyers who use price guides are worse off now than they were ten or fifteen, or twenty years ago. Price guides make no pretense—not overtly, at least—of reporting what buyers are willing to pay for each card, nor do they reflect the prices at which sellers are willing to let each card go. They merely publish prices at which unspecified dealers, in unspecified locations, at unspecified times, have sold specific cards. That's it. Nothing else! What countless buyers read into those prices, however, ranges from scientific data to the word of God. What they never read into those prices, despite common sense, human nature, and the lessons of the past, is that a subtle form of manipulation may be taking place.

Step back for a moment and apply what you now know about supply, demand, and price guides to what you've experienced at shops and shows. You may not like what you see.

As integral to the card business as the price guides are, they are separate in one important respect: they are independent entities, owned by individuals who publish them to make money. For that to happen, people must buy them. This is accomplished in part through subscriptions, but the real profit comes from over-the-counter sales at card shops, card shows, and newsstands. Those sales not only generate revenue from the vendors who order the guides every month, but also, by increasing overall readership, they increase the amount the publishers can charge for advertising space. (There are only one or two guides that do not accept advertising.)

In order to stay in business, a price guide has to keep two groups happy: dealers and buyers. If the pricing information in a price guide helps dealers to turn a profit on the cards they sell, dealers in turn will be willing to sell the guide to their customers. And if the pricing information makes buyers feel they got a fair deal on the cards they've purchased, then buyers will continue to buy the guide. What would happen, though, if a price guide sent its research staff out to purchase a large sampling of cards, and the prices they were able to negotiate were far lower—by 20 or 30 or 50 percent—than those published in all the other guides? And what would happen to that guide if those prices were actually printed?

For starters, dealers wouldn't let that guide into their stores. They would stop selling it immediately. Why would they make a guide available to their customers that basically said, "Hey, the cards I'm trying to sell you are worth a lot less than I'm trying to get for them"? In-store sales would dry up and circulation would decline, forcing the guide to reduce the amount it charged its advertisers. The advertisers, meanwhile, would likely pull out altogether, given that they often advertise cards for sale at prices comparable to those quoted in the guide. As for buyers, they wouldn't mind having a guide that enabled them to buy cards for less, but these lower prices would also devalue their past purchases. Given the basic insecurities card buyers harbor already, the last thing they need is a guide that tells them their portfolio is worth less than they paid for it! In other words, if a price guide took the position that the majority of cards on the market are worth significantly less than everyone thinks, it would go out of business!

The question, then, is whether the prices for cards quoted in existing guides are true reflections of what you can actually go out and buy those cards for. If not, if the real prices are actually lower than what you find in the guides, then the market is being manipulated and you, the buyer, are paying the price.

Are the prices in the guides accurate? In the sense that someone sold a particular card at a particular price in the not-too-distant past, they are. But that's not how people use the guides. When they see a Von Hayes rookie card listed at 50 cents, they assume that the guide has received a flood of reports that the card has been selling at that price for the last thirty days. If that price has been unchanged for a year, they assume that the card has been experiencing steady sales at 50 cents over that time. What it really means, of course, is that no one has been buying Von Hayes rookie cards at all, and

that there is no mechanism in place to record this! Remember, the price guides claim they arrive at their prices either by witnessing actual sales or by compiling data from sales that have been reported to them. Well, how do you "witness" a card that just doesn't sell? And how do you come up with a price for a card that no one reports as having sold?

It kind of blows the whole deal for the price guides, doesn't it? If, as many buyers insist on believing, the guides collected pricing information the same way the stock exchange does, then the price for that Von Hayes card would reflect what buyers were ready and willing to pay for it, as well as what it most recently fetched on the market. What would that price be? Fifty cents? Not in a million years. Von's closest friends probably wouldn't shell out 50 cents for his rookie card! The price at which that card would actually sell might be as low as 10 or 15 cents. The price, in short, would have to sink until demand for it finally covered the available supply. At the current price, the supply of Von Hayes rookies is so far beyond demand that a 50-cent price is a joke. That the guides continue to publish this price is a travesty, and it's costing people money.

The same "non-reporting" problems affect older and more expensive cards, too. Look up any set of cards in a guide and see how the individual card prices break down. The 1972 Topps set, for instance, has about a dozen cards that are in high demand at any given time. Those cards *will* sell at, or even above, the prices quoted. But the other 775—including major stars, rookies, and Hall of Famers—are not presently in high demand and can be had for a lot less than the prices quoted. Why isn't this reflected in the guide? Because a dealer who's been holding a 1972 Jim Hunter for two years isn't going to report that he hasn't been able to sell it for $5, and, more importantly, is not going to report that he did, could, or would sell it for $2.75.

Consider what that says about price guides. If dealers know they can't sell a card at the price quoted in the guides, but are willing to sell it for less, that means that (*a*) they know that many of the prices in the guides are incorrect, and (b) as the primary source of price information, they have no intention of doing anything about it. They know that the 1972 Hunter card *will sell* at $2.75—as long *as the price in the guides remains at $5.* If they report what they know to be the true selling price—$2.75—and the price in the following month's guide plummets to that level, they're afraid that they won't be able to get $2.75 for the card anymore. What this all adds up to is price manipulation on a massive scale.

It also adds up to something else: experienced dealers use a price guide that is completely different from the ones their customers are using. This guide has the real card prices—namely the prices at which the dealers *know* individual cards will sell. If you doubt for a moment that this "insider pricing" exists, offer to sell a dealer two different cards whose values are equal according to the price guides, such as a 1973 Tom Seaver and a 1960 Harmon Killebrew. You'll probably get offered 50 percent more for the Seaver. That's because the dealer knows that the actual selling price for the Seaver is $25, while the price for the Killebrew would have to drop well below $20 before it walked out the door.

So where is this "dealer's" guide published? It's not published at all—it's in their heads. How accurate is it? It's right on the money. It changes every day, taking into account supply, demand, player performance, buying patterns, the economy, and the mood in the card business as a whole. It goes by past performance and doesn't pretend to predict the future—it's a ruthless, dollars-and-cents evaluation of every card in a very complex and chaotic marketplace. And the more experienced the dealer, the more comprehensive his guide is. Sound familiar? It should. This is the card business's version of the daily stock market report!

Unfortunately, this is what buyers believe they are getting when they purchase their price guides each month. Needless to say, what buyers are actually getting is vastly different. Do dealers use the monthly price guides? They sure do. If they see a card price that is far too high, they will put that card in their showcases at a slightly lower, "bargain" price. And if they see a card that is far too low, they either try to buy that card based on the low price or try to sell it at a premium by saying that the price in the guide is "already a month behind"—which, by the way, is often the truth. In short, experienced dealers use the price guides as a tool, in the hopes that their naive customers will use it as a crutch.

That there is price manipulation within the guides seems rather obvious. In the inner circles of the card business, some dealers laugh about it while others just shake their heads. Certainly, few would disagree with the observation that were the card business regulated as strictly as the stock market, a lot of people would be sorting their commons in eight-by-ten cells.

The question is Who's doing the manipulating? The guides? Indirectly, perhaps. Ironically, it's more a case of buyers incorrectly using the information the guides publish than it is a case of the guides doing something wrong. The dealers? By omission—by not reporting the real prices—it could be said that they are manipulating the market, but there are no laws or rules that dictate their conduct when it comes to reporting prices, nor is there a moral obligation for them to do it more accurately. Are buyers manipulating themselves? Sure they are, but that's just another definition of "demand."

No, you can't pin price manipulation on anyone in the card business—it's merely a result of the way the business is run. Everyone is guilty, everyone is to blame. And that's what makes it such a hurtful situation, because the only people who are really damaged by it are buyers—the people who generate the capital that keeps the business going. How can this change? The price guides aren't going to change. Can you imagine the havoc that would be created if suddenly without warning 90 percent of the card prices in these guides were accompanied by downward arrows or minuses? And, for the same reason, the dealers on whom the guides rely for pricing information aren't going to change, either. The only element of this "house of cards" that can change are the people who buy the cards. They can start using the price guides to *supplement* what they know about the card business and spend accordingly, rather than letting the guides *dictate* how much they spend.

The purpose of this chapter is not to beat up on these publications—price guides are necessary and they are useful. There also happens to be one later on in this book, although, as you'll see, it's more in line with the aforementioned guide the dealers keep in their heads. No, the purpose of this chapter is to beat up on card buyers who just don't get it, who don't understand what a price guide's supposed to be. By the way, if you're wondering whether you fit this description, think back to the last time you bought a card and ask yourself if you would have purchased it had you not looked it up in a price guide. If the answer is no, you've got some homework to do!

# POWER

Who has the power in the card business? The answer to that question may surprise you. But does it have any bearing on what you, as a card buyer, are going to do today, tomorrow, or a year from now? It could—that's really up to you. But until you understand how the various parts of the card business interact, you'll never know.

Here are some basic facts:

1. The card business is a pretty good microcosm of the capitalist system, in that everyone is basically out to make money off someone else.
2. Because a card cannot continue to rise in value indefinitely, someone will eventually pay more for that card than it will ever be worth.
3. There are two distinct card markets. The *primary* market—which starts with the production of new cards and ends when those cards have reached the hands of retail buyers—and the *secondary* market—which is everything that happens after that point.
4. Because the primary and secondary markets absorb all of the dollars pumped into the business, they affect each other greatly.
5. Power in the card business is a function of how much money is controlled, either directly or indirectly.

With the ground rules laid out, it's a little easier to determine who's really in control. To begin, take a look at everyone's favorite group, card dealers. Dealers are middle men. They buy up a very large percentage of new cards and disperse them to their customers, so they are important to the primary market. They also purchase older cards from the public and resell them, which is important to the secondary market. Do they produce anything? No. They are go-betweens, connecting the card manufacturers with retail buyers, and connecting retail buyers with one another through the purchase and resale of older cards. For this service they take a cut of the action, and for this cut of the action they take risks: they spend money on rent for shops and/or shows; they spend money buying cards from manufacturers, the public, and one another; and they often do so at the expense of building a career in a more traditional line of work. Are they necessary? They are a convenience, albeit a valuable one, for people who would otherwise have a hard time finding the cards they want to purchase.

How much power do they have? Their mere existence elevates the price of a card every time it passes through their hands, so in that sense they exert a lot of force on the market. But in terms of power, they are subject to both the whims and demands of buyers and manufacturers, and are fur-

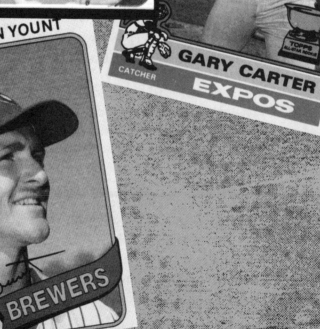

ther affected by what the economy is doing and what other dealers are doing. In short, they have no power at all. They are sitting on piles of cardboard that have no real value until someone is actually willing to exchange money for it. *Could* dealers have power? Theoretically, they could. But they would need to function as a single entity, much like the Federal Reserve, tightening or loosening the supply of specific cards in response to the economy and buyer demand. That won't happen, nor should it.

Next, look at the card companies. Around 60 percent of all the money spent on new cards each year goes directly into their pockets. Their licensing, production, distribution, and advertising costs are known quantities, so in order to gauge the appropriate print run for a set, the only thing they must calculate is how many cards can be sold in a given year. A decade ago, the card companies had a tough time figuring this out; they had to guess how much money would be spent on cards in candy stores that year and then determine what their slice of the pie would be. Often they got stuck with tons of unsold cards. But with the proliferation of card dealers in the mid-1980s, the card companies found the perfect patsies. "Why not let the dealers do the figuring," they decided, "and let us know before we start the process?" Well, that's just what they did. Today, when card companies sell their products to dealers and other retailers, they usually demand that orders and *payment* be sent months in advance of delivery. This gives them a huge edge, for they know how many cards to print, they know they can sell *all* the cards they print, and if they've printed too many for the market to absorb immediately, it doesn't matter because they already have their money.

How much power do the card companies have? They, too, exert a lot of force on the market, in that their products soak up a huge chunk of the money that is spent on all cards each year. And so far, the more they've printed, the larger their share has been. In the last two years, Topps, Donruss, Score, Fleer, and Upper Deck have each come out with more than one set. They have regular sets, update sets, premium sets, super premium sets, novelty sets—some of which have sold extremely well, some of which have not. What they have succeeded in doing, however, is increasing the percentage of dollars that buyers devote to new cards, which has cut the demand for many older cards.

The power of the card companies, however, though considerable now, is tenuous at best. If card buyers feel that a company has printed too many cards, or that its cards are ugly or too expensive, they can exercise their right not to purchase those cards. That has happened with increasing frequency since 1988, when the Donruss set got a resounding thumbs down from card buyers. When this happens, the dealers are left holding the bag. But they in turn can exercise their right not to purchase the following year's cards in large quantities, and have done so on occasion. Initially, the reaction of the card companies to this little uprising was to cut production. The 1983 Fleer and Donruss sets were such poor sellers that their 1984 sets saw a huge drop in pre-orders from dealers. So those two companies short-printed their sets for the next four years. This was a crucial time for dealers—had they held their ground, they stood to gain a strong voice in how the primary market was run. Indeed, legitimate power was actually within the grasp of dealers during the mid-1980s, but, not surprisingly, when they put their heads together, they ended up shooting themselves in the foot.

Ironically, it was the successful marketing by dealers of non-baseball sports cards that gave the card companies the weapon they needed. The sudden—and largely contrived—demand for football, basketball, and hockey cards in the late-1980s spurred several companies to issue non-baseball sets on a limited basis. To get the allocations of non-baseball cards they wanted, dealers were afraid to cut their orders on baseball cards. There was an implied threat on the part of the manufacturers that if dealers refused to order a lot of what they didn't want, then they might not get a lot of what they did want. And that pretty much ended the threat.

What was revealed by that situation, however,

was a chink in the armor of the card companies. They had subjugated the dealers, all right, but had done nothing to address the issue of responding to the likes and dislikes of card buyers. They did not have the power to produce cards in limitless quantities, despite the fact that they could strong-arm the dealers into buying them. They recognized that eventually this approach would blow up in their faces. With more and more new buyers entering the market, however, they didn't want to cut production. The decision was made to create additional, limited-run sets that would only be available through card dealers. The plan looked as if it might work; in theory, dealers would have something that the candy stores, supermarkets, and department stores didn't, and card buyers would have something other than those dreary wax packs to spend their money on.

But the plan didn't work. In fact, it never got off the ground. Upper Deck came along in 1989 with the novel approach of actually giving card buyers what they wanted: an attractive, high-quality, limited-run set with a few bells and whistles added for good measure. The other companies stood by their regular product, which retailed for about half of Upper Deck's price, until they finally woke up to the fact that card buyers were willing to pay more for what they wanted, and that they had better make some changes. In 1992, Fleer and Donruss vastly improved the quality of their regular issues, Topps started using four colors on both sides of its cards, and Score, which had entered the market in 1988 with what it *thought* was a premium card, made no changes at all. The five card companies continued to strong-arm dealers, of course, but they also supplied those dealers with enough super-premium sets that the dealers could at least recoup what they had spent on any unsold boxes of regular-issue cards.

When you look at what has transpired over the past year or two, it's tempting to say that the power in the card business has shifted to the card buyers. After all, they finally spoke out, and all of the major card companies listened. On the other hand, you could say that the card companies have increased their power, for just about everything they pro-

duced in 1992 created excitement in the market when issued, and most of it sold immediately. In fact, buyers spent more money, and a higher percentage of their money, on new cards in 1992 than ever before. Clearly, a case could be made for either the buyers or the companies controlling the business.

But the reality is that the price guides, for all their imperfections, wield enormous power over the business right now. And it all comes down to the prices that they are reporting on three specific sets: 1989 Upper Deck, 1990 Leaf, and 1991 Topps Stadium Club.

Why? The enormous demand for the premium and super-premium cards from 1992 and 1993 has invigorated the business and kept both the card companies and the dealers fat and happy. Card buyers are scrambling to acquire these cards at very high prices, based on what they mistakenly believe to be past history—specifically, that if enough people are willing to pay a little more for high-quality cards, then their value is "guaranteed" to skyrocket. The reason they believe this theory to be true, of course, is the collective performance of the three aforementioned sets.

The 1989 Upper Deck, 1990 Leaf, and 1991 Stadium sets have all increased in value by around 500 percent. In the card business, it's not unusual to see this caliber of short-term performance for cards of individual players, but until these three issues came along, movement like this was unprecedented for entire sets. What distinguished these sets from the other cards produced in 1989, 1990, and 1991 was that they were higher in quality, scarcity, and price. Each set represented the zenith of card making at the time it was issued; each set was totally original. After the initial run on each set, there was a secondary run, as card buyers, looking to obtain quantities of relatively recent cards, felt that the ground-breaking aspects of these sets gave them good investment potential. That's when demand was at its highest for cards in these sets, and when the prices really started to climb. That's also when a lot of buyers began to draw the wrong conclusions.

The mistake they made was to ignore what distinguished these sets in the first place. What created such high demand was that these were "firsts," not that they were expensive, short-printed, and high-quality. Yet buyers insisted upon gobbling up all of the 1992 premium and super-premium cards, despite the fact that everything about them was derivative of earlier issues. The price guides dutifully reported this phenomenon but, as they are wont to do, did not pick up on the fact that much of the money being spent on the relatively plentiful 1992 Fleer Ultras, Topps Stadiums, and Score Pinnacles was being diverted away from the "already-too-expensive" 1989 Upper Deck, 1990 Leaf, and 1991 Stadium sets! So as far as anyone who read the price guides was concerned, this misguided buying strategy was really paying off! Now, in 1993, the same thing is about to happen: much of the money earmarked for this year's super-premium cards will be spent at the expense of the 1992 super-premiums, as well as the 1989 Upper Decks, 1990 Leafs, and 1991 Stadiums. If this diverting of capital is not recorded in lower prices for those cards, then the super-premiums will continue to drive the business and dramatically affect spending patterns for all other cards.

As long as the price guides continue in their failure to more accurately reflect downward trends, they control to a great degree how money in the card business is spent. As explained in the previous chapter, the mechanism to achieve this level of accuracy will likely never be in place. And meanwhile, the guides cover themselves—as well they should—by reiterating that they are just "guides," despite the fact that card buyers use them as "bibles." Until this situation changes, much of the power in the business rests in the hands of the people who publish the price guides.

Think about how extraordinary this is! In a multibillion-dollar business, the people with the most power are stuck in a position where they can't do anything with it! If you owned a price guide,

how would you wield this power? You might want to take steps to ensure better accuracy, but why bother? It would cost a lot of money to institutionalize the price-reporting process, not to mention that the result of this effort would be lower prices for many cards, which in turn would kill your business! There are two great ironies at work here. The first is that the price guides have stumbled into their position of power because the people who use them use them improperly. The second irony is that the people who use them are the ones who used to—and should—have the power!

Card buyers have all the money, yet they control none of it. Why? Because, as a group, card buyers are totally out of control. They trust everything but their own instincts when it comes to making purchases. They lap up information from card companies, dealers, and price guides—all of whom, by the way, are in business to relieve them of their money—without considering whether or not that information makes any sense. Worst of all, card buyers make most of their purchases based on what they think other card buyers will purchase. In just about any other major secondary market—antiques, art, coins, rare books, and of course, the stock market—this strategy makes perfect sense. But in none of those markets is there more of the actual commodity than there are people to absorb it.

Can this situation change? Possibly. Although any change would have to be triggered by an outside force, such as the economy. The problem is that card buyers are kids. There are hundreds of thousands of kids who buy cards, and even the older buyers are kids at heart. They're buying dreams, remember? Without reiterating all the psychology, suffice it to say that this lack of sophistication—which is, and always will be, the most charming thing about the card business—just about precludes the level of independent thinking that would return power to where it rightfully belongs.

A. LEAGUE 1966 HOME RUN LEADERS

**FRANK ROBINSON**
BALTIMORE ORIOLES

**HARMON KILLEBREW**
MINNESOTA TWINS

**BOOG POWELL**
BALTIMORE ORIOLES

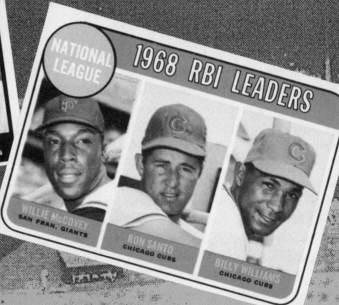

NATIONAL LEAGUE 1968 RBI LEADERS

**WILLIE McCOVEY**
SAN FRAN. GIANTS

**RON SANTO**
CHICAGO CUBS

**BILLY WILLIAMS**
CHICAGO CUBS

**BOB GRIM**
pitcher NEW YORK YANKEES

**ERNIE BANKS**
shortstop CHICAGO CUBS

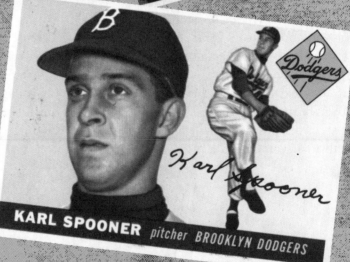

**KARL SPOONER** pitcher BROOKLYN DODGERS

Dodgers

# 5

# DEALERS

Have you ever stopped to consider what it would be like to be a card dealer? Who are they? How do they think? What kind of life do they live? Should you care? Yes. As is true in any business, the more you know about the people with whom you're dealing, the better you're likely to make out.

There are thousands of card dealers across the United States, and they come in quite a variety of flavors. There are young ones and old ones, rich ones and poor ones, smart ones and dumb ones, full-timers and part-timers, business owners and table renters—and just about any combination of the above. They become dealers for a number of reasons, but they do so primarily to make money. A few truly understand the market—and where they fit into it—but most just cruise along blindly, blundering into profits and losses without ever formulating much of a plan.

The dealer you run into at a typical card show is between eighteen and thirty-five years old and is there to supplement his income. His weekdays are spent working at an average-paying job; his weeknights are spent sorting, pricing, and arranging his cards for the weekends, which are spent behind a table waiting for buyers to drop some cash in his lap. He eats badly, his back and neck hurt from

hunching over his inventory thirty hours a week, and he gets virtually no intellectual stimulation. In other words, he is a fanatic.

That is not to say, however, that he is passionate about cards. He may have his own collection, he may have a favorite player or team, but eventually he reaches a point where cards simply represent the best way he knows how to make a little extra money. How little? The typical show dealer rarely clears more than $800 a month. Considering that he devotes thirty hours a week—and that those hours take the place of "leisure" or "quality" time—the pay isn't all that good. So if a show dealer isn't passionate about the cards *and* makes less than $10 an hour, what's the attraction? Being his own boss. Controlling his own destiny. Building his self-image. Turning *his* time and *his* knowledge into cold hard cash. *That's* what he's passionate about.

Does he actually want to own a legitimate business? Well, he already does in a way, although as far as the IRS and the state are concerned he's anything but legitimate. The answer for most show dealers—who don't keep books or pay taxes, and who, if money's tight, have the option of not shelling out cash to rent or restock—is that going full-time is just a bit too scary. It takes someone with a little more confidence to give up a full-time job and make that quantum leap—someone who either knows about the ups and downs of running a business or is confident and bright enough to learn what it takes. It also requires a very different mentality.

A card shop dealer is typically a little older, twenty-five to fifty. He is capable of looking at things over the long haul, as well as sizing up opportunities on a short-term basis. For him, the selling process is not compacted into a few hours in the ballroom of a Holiday Inn—it's broken down into months, weeks, and days. Because his buyers know they can visit him at their leisure, they are more pensive, more selective, and far less urgent, as is he, for individual sales can and often do develop over time.

Card shop dealers—if they want to be successful, that is—must have a plan. They have to know exactly what it will take to generate enough cash flow to pay the rent, restock, and turn a big enough profit to make the whole venture worthwhile. In order to succeed, they must have a realistic view of supply, demand, competition, and the potential of their customer base. They must know how to market their shops, their cards, and, most importantly, themselves, for buyers have a lot of options these days, including mail order, shows, auctions, and other shops. When a customer walks through the door with money in his pocket, a successful card shop dealer must know more than how to make him spend that money—he has to know what will make him feel good about coming back and spending more. In the end, this is what makes or breaks the business.

Think back to all the card shops you've visited since you started buying cards. What percentage of those shops made you feel good about spending your money the first time you walked in? What percentage made you think, I can't wait till I come back here again? Unless you live in Utopia, about one in three. Now think back again. How many of the card shops you've visited are still in business? Probably about one in three. If you consider the fact that over the last decade more money has been spent on cards during each year than during the

year before it, that should tell you that the owners of the card shops that went belly-up were doing something wrong.

Whatever mistake they made, you can be sure it wasn't charging a little less for their cards, or being too nice to their customers. (In some markets, that's all it takes to *stay* in business!) The point here is that far less than half of card shop dealers know what they're doing, or at least the rest of them don't know what it is they're doing wrong, which is another way of saying that they shouldn't own shops at all.

Is a card shop dealer's life better than a show dealer's? That depends. If he treats "down time" as an ally—if he uses it to organize, learn more about the business, market his shop, and explore creative buying and selling opportunities—then those hours when no customers are in his store have a positive effect on his bottom line. If, on the other hand, he treats "down time" as an enemy—fretting over the pressures of business, wondering if he should be doing something more productive with his life, agonizing over cards he sold too low or bought too high—then those idle hours will cost him when he takes out his frustrations on his customers. If it's true that life is what you make it, then it's doubly true for the card shop dealer.

A mail-order dealer may own a shop or do shows, but he really falls somewhere in between. Like a show dealer, he has the luxury of tinkering with when, where, and how often he makes himself available to buyers; like a shop dealer, he does his business from a central location. He does have one important advantage over his peers, however: he doesn't have to interact on a face-to-face basis with his customers. Why is this an advantage? Because most people in the card business have rather poor social skills—in most selling situations they say or do the wrong thing, or hurt themselves in some other way. A mail-order dealer can be the most insufferable boor on the planet, but if his prices are competitive, his grading is fair, and his service is reliable, he can count on a lot of return business. Another advantage he has is that he displays his wares in a forum where buyers can comparison-shop without leaving their homes: the trade publications. If he has what buyers are looking for and prices his merchandise fairly, he stands to do very well with people who don't mind doing business through the mail.

How do dealers, in general, feel about themselves? Well, they feel powerless a lot of the time. When they have good cards and good prices but aren't doing any business, they can't help wonder what external forces are conspiring to rob them of their livelihood. They hate having no leverage with the card companies, and they don't like the fact that much of their life is spent dealing with children. Some are able to put what they do into the proper perspective; they provide a service, they educate, and they sell dreams. That helps (and it's certainly better than thinking of themselves as middlemen in a world of cardboard), but by and large most dealers would prefer to go to cocktail parties and say they were lawyers or surgeons or even plumbers. Why do they stay in the business? The money and the sense of independence.

For those who cannot be lawyers or surgeons or plumbers—which is most of us—there's always a home in the card business. Technically, being a dealer is no more complicated than buying a case of cards, opening it, and then offering the cards for sale at a show or flea market. All you need is a price guide, some plastic sheets, a pen, and some little white stickers. What happens from there, however, is what separates the men from the boys.

How do dealers feel about people who buy cards? That depends on the dealer—and gives a good indication of how successful he's likely to be. Some feel jealous. They are envious of the buyer who can spend $500 on cards—even if he happens to spend it on their cards! Why? Because when a buyer drops a bundle on cards, the dealer presumes quite rightly that it is disposable income—in his eyes, that buyer could just as well spend it on a vacation, a color TV, or anything else. Once the dealer takes possession of that $500, he has to pay rent, buy new cards, and take care of bills, which may not leave much in the way of fun money. The dealer who thinks this way sometimes treats a well-

heeled buyer very strangely. He will spout some completely uninvited theory about cards, or politics or the economy, in order to show the buyer that he's more than just a lowly card dealer—often to the point where he actually drives that customer away! Meanwhile, the next buyer who comes along could be looking at $2 or $3 cards, yet that same dealer will have a perfectly normal conversation with him or, better yet, keep his mouth shut entirely. As a buyer, you can gain an edge by letting this type of dealer talk. Feign interest in what he's saying. Compliment him on his powers of reason, on his knowledge of the world outside of cards. You'll make his day and probably get another 10 percent off your purchase.

Some dealers think of customers as patsies. They chuckle to themselves when people blindly purchase their overproduced new cards or low-demand stars just because some price guide says it's a smart investment. They can't believe that people are so dumb as to pay them two, three, and four times what they paid for cards that can easily be restocked. They adore the fact that unloading their unwanted cards on customers is as simple as cutting prices that are far too high to begin with. And they are tickled to death when they can really shaft a customer who offers his cards for sale. In other words, some dealers like to feel superior at the expense of others. They derive more joy from making $10 off something they know to be worthless than they do from making $20 helping a customer to complete a set. They are also fond of disagreeing with their buyers' opinions just to make them feel less informed. In fact, if you do business with a character like this, let him disagree with something you say, then say exactly the opposite the next time you run into him and watch him contradict you—and therefore himself—again. Then point this out to him, watch him squirm, and walk away.

Most dealers, though, feel pretty good about their customers. They are realistic enough to recognize that without buyers they would be unable to sell anything. They attempt to fill the role of middleman without getting bent out of shape about it, and without harboring too much resentment or insecurity. Being a dealer is not easy, it's not glamorous, and it's not the least bit fulfilling. But it's a service that someone needs to provide. The best dealers come in all shapes and sizes, but they have one thing in common: they accept who they are, what they are, and what they do—and do the very best they can with what the good Lord gave them.

The task of finding a good dealer—whether he does shows, owns a shop, or does business through the mail—should not be taken lightly. If you know what you want and what you're willing to pay for it, he's the guy who is going to get it for you, so leave no stone unturned. How do you know a dealer's good? It's really a gut feeling more than anything else, but there are a couple of tip-offs.

First of all, a good dealer listens. When you articulate your approach to the card business, he tunes in and responds immediately. He talks, too, of course, asking questions to gain a better understanding of what you want and what your spending patterns are, and he makes suggestions. Listen to those suggestions.

Is he pushing something you'd been thinking of buying? That's usually a good sign. Is he offering something that perhaps you hadn't thought of before? That could be good, too—a good dealer makes you think. What if he tries to sell you some-

thing you have no interest in? Tell him you don't want it and *why* you don't want it, and listen to his response. If he considers your objections carefully and says something like "You may be right," or "My customers seem to be divided on that," you've probably found a gem of a dealer.

What about prices? Obviously, one thing that makes a dealer good is good prices. But that's superficial. You should be more interested in his approach to dealing cards. Is he interested in moving his inventory, or is he paranoid about selling cards too cheaply? If you make reasonable offers on several cards and get turned down on every one, ask the dealer why he won't sell you those cards. If he says he'd prefer to wait for some unknown customer to waltz into his store sometime in the future and pay top dollar for the cards in question—or if he claims to have too much tied up in those particular cards—ask him which cards he can be more flexible on. If he says none, clear out.

In short, a good dealer is one whose goal is to keep his merchandise turning and keep his customers happy. If he's bought right, he'll pass the savings on to his clientele. He grades accurately, he prices his cards fairly, and he's willing to work with you in a number of different ways. If you find someone like this, don't let him slip through your fingers.

# 6

## CONDITION

The key to buying real estate is location, location, location. . . . The key to buying cards is condition, condition, condition." This annoying little saying hit the card business a couple of years ago, and you still hear it around shops and shows. It's true, of course, for once you've decided to obtain a particular card, it *is* best to buy it in the nicest possible condition.

But don't card buyers already know that? Sure they do—they just have a problem remembering it.

They will look at a card that's almost, but not quite, in the condition they had hoped for, and then somehow talk themselves into believing that it really is in that condition! Granted, the grading process, though supposedly objective, is inherently subjective. No one looks at the same card in exactly the same way. But subjectivity has nothing to do with ignoring what your eyes are telling you. That's called denial. Perhaps the new saying for the card business should be "Be your best friend . . . by being your worst enemy."

What does this mean? It means that if you learn how to be tough when grading the cards you own—the ones in which you have already invested time, money, and emotion—you'll sharpen your ability to grade cards you do not own. This reevaluation process can be costly, both to your ego and

to what you have previously assumed to be the value of your collection. But if you are making mistakes—if you are talking yourself into buying overgraded cards—you can put an end to the problem and save yourself a lot of money down the road.

First, you must understand something very important about the entire grading process. When grading a card, the typical person—be it a dealer or a buyer—takes that card right down the line: "Is it mint? No. Is it near mint? Well, it seems to fit the description pretty well. Okay, it's near mint." Well, this is part of the reason that so many cards are overgraded—if you start from the best condition and work backward, you can't help but elevate a card's grade! Instead, work from the bottom up, or merely invert the typical grading guide. Don't be surprised if you find that as many as a third of the cards you thought you'd graded accurately turn out to be of slightly lesser condition.

Why don't buyers grade this way? Partly because every grading guide ever printed seems to start with *mint* and continue down from there. Think about it: as you grade a card, you compare it to the description of the best possible condition and work down toward *near mint, excellent,* and so forth. You try to be objective, but there's this voice in your subconscious yelling, "Stop! Stop! You're losing

money! That card looks fine!" That is why the following condition guide is presented "upside down." And by all means use it that way. You may not like how it changes the condition of the cards you own now, and you may feel like you're becoming your own worst enemy, but just think—the next time you spend money on cards, you'll have a new best friend!

*Poor (P):* Your card has clearly been adulterated. The only way it could get any worse is if you tore it in half or dipped it in paint. Under no circumstances should you buy a card in this condition if you ever plan to resell it.

*Fair (F):* Your card has some redeeming quality but is still not even close to being in collectible condition. A pinhole in an otherwise decent card is an example of a card in *fair* condition.

*Good (G):* Your card is either well worn or has some sort of major defect, such as a cockeyed cut or extremely poor centering. Also, if your card has an obvious crease, stop right here. Some dealers will tell you that cards in *good* condition are collectible as fillers for sets. Forget it. If you're spending the time and money to put a set together, wait for something better. If you must buy a *good* card, just remember that it's a buyer's market—don't pay more than 5 to 10 percent of the *near mint* selling price.

*Very Good (VG):* Your card probably looks *excellent* at first glance, but upon closer inspection has too many little things wrong with it. *Very good* cards generally have a ding or two, slightly rounded corners, a hairline crease, or poor centering. Be very tough with this grade—about a third of the cards out there that are graded *excellent* are actually very good. Serious buyers won't touch cards in *very good* condition, even if the price is right. The right price? 15 percent of the *near mint* selling price for "weak" VGs; 25 percent for "true" VGs; 35 percent for "strong" VGs.

*Excellent (EX):* Your card is in collectible condition. It is clearly not *mint*, nor does it grade *near mint*. What's the cutoff? If your card has any *two* of the following flaws, it doesn't grade any higher

than *excellent:* a visibly dinged corner, dented edges, slight discoloration, light rounding, or centering worse than 60/40. Cards in *excellent* condition move at around half of the *near mint* selling price. Given the sometimes minuscule differences between the two grades, it pays to check any card graded *near mint* thoroughly. Some dealers cover themselves by grading cards *excellent-to-mint* (EXM). Don't be fooled—this is a grade left over from the 1970s, when the concept of *near mint* did not exist. It has about as much meaning as *uncirculated* has in the coin business, which is to say it is meaningless. If you come across a card that is clearly better than *excellent,* but not quite *near mint,* it's okay to pay up to 70 percent—as long as you are aware of the problems you'll have reselling it in this in-between grade.

*Near Mint (NM):* Your card is just shy of perfect. It may have a barely perceptible ding at one corner, a little unevenness on a border, 45/55 centering, or some other flaw that is not readily apparent upon first glance. The best way to approach this condition is to listen to that little voice in the back of your head—if it keeps telling you to back off, follow the advice. Most *mint* cards are in *near mint* condition, so you'd better know what you're doing before you pay a *mint* premium.

*Mint (M):* Perhaps the greatest irony in the card business is that just about everyone is confused about something that is quite easy to understand: what makes a card *mint.* This is a real no-brainer, yet each year millions of dollars are thrown away by buyers who believe they are purchasing cards in *mint* condition. A mint card—regardless of what a dealer or another buyer may tell you—is a card that is perfect in every way, back and front. Anything less bumps the card's condition down to *near mint* or worse.

A *mint* card has four sharp corners, with absolutely no dents or layering whatsoever. A *mint* card has four razor-sharp edges, with no flaking, no dents, and no "fuzzy" cuts. A *mint* card is perfectly centered, both top and bottom, and its image lines up perfectly parallel to its edges. A *mint* card has an even gloss, its image is in perfect register, and the colors are what they should be. And, obviously, a *mint* card has no blotches, specks, pits, scuffs, holes, wrinkles, creases, or tears.

The definition of a *mint* card is absolute. If you are looking at a card that you feel is not perfect, then it's not perfect—*period.* If a dealer tells you, "Sure, it's not *absolutely* perfect, but it's still *mint,*" or "Hey, it looks the same as it did the day it came out of the pack," don't necessarily assume he's trying to cheat you—but you can go ahead and assume he's an idiot. Conversely, if you look at a card that you feel is not perfect, and talk yourself into buying it at the *mint* price, then go ahead and assume you're an idiot, too. The fact is that there are very few *mint* cards on the market. Every time a card is handled, however carefully, some damage is done. Thus, the older it is—i.e., the more it's been handled—the less likely it is to stay in perfect shape. That is why there is such a huge premium attached to older cards in *mint* condition.

What kind of premium? It depends not only on the year, but also on the card. Up to and including 1973—the last year cards were issued in monthly series—commons and minor stars command premiums ranging from 10 percent to 50 percent in *mint* condition. That premium is added to their selling prices in *near mint* condition, which is considered by most to be the highest obtainable grade for the vast majority of older cards. Thus a *mint* 1970 Topps Wes Parker, a very plentiful common card that sells for around 75 cents in *near mint,* would be worth around 10 cents more than that in mint. However, a *mint* 1953 Topps Eddie Pellagrini, a much scarcer common card that sells for around $20 in *near mint,* would command an additional $8 or $10.

Now, buyers don't normally spend their lives hunting for *mint* Eddie Pellagrini cards—nor does Wes Parker interest them very much—so there is relatively little money thrown away on improperly graded commons and minor stars. (The only people who are actually looking for older *mint* commons are those who are trying to put "perfect" sets together, and they quickly learn the difference between *mint* and *near mint.*) Where the money is thrown away is on the "big" cards.

The premiums attached to *mint* examples of players like Mickey Mantle, Willie Mays, Jackie Robinson, and Sandy Koufax can reach 100 percent and more. When you consider that the demand for these players is high to begin with—and that less than 5 percent of their cards in collectible condition could be graded as *mint*—it makes perfect sense; if someone wants and can afford the very best, he should be willing to pay the price. For all the top players "in between" the Mantles and the Pellagrinis—Killebrew, Clemente, Carlton, Kaline, etc.—the premiums shrink to between 25 percent (for cards in the late 1960s and early 1970s) and 50 percent (for cards in the early to mid-1950s. A 1954 Topps Whitey Ford—close to $100 in *near mint*—commands around $140 in *mint,* while a 1969 Willie McCovey—normally a $9 or $10 card—would easily fetch $12 or $13. The point here is that the more popular the card, the higher the stakes when it comes to knowing what's *mint* and what isn't. True *mint* 1953 Mantles have sold for over $4,500 at auction, establishing a price that the rest of the business has followed. Unfortunately, people have paid that much for 1953 Mantles that were just a little bit "off," and ended up with $2,500 cards. A similar mistake on the 1954 Ford card might not seem devastating by comparison, but these mistakes are made every single day.

The rule of thumb is be careful, double-check every aspect of an older card, and if you're still not sure whether or not it's *mint,* then walk away. If, however, the card is being offered to you at the *near mint* price, go for it—even though your doubts are probably well founded, you're still getting a card you wanted in collectible condition and at a fair price.

As for newer cards, you can't afford *not* to buy *mint.* This may seem a little frivolous—after all, new cards are pretty cheap—but if you think about it, it makes a lot of sense. Why do you buy new cards? Because they are affordable, and down the road, some may rise dramatically in value. Fine. Let's say you guess right on a player like Juan Gonzales. You buy up several hundred of his 1990 rookie cards, and in the year 2010 he makes the Hall of Fame. Let's say those cards sell for $50 each in *mint*. What will the *near mint* price be? No one has a crystal ball, but it's probably fair to say that it will *not* be just a few dollars less. Remember, those Gonzales cards were printed in 1990, when cards were being printed by the tens of millions and almost everyone in the card business recognized the value of keeping cards in nice condition. In the year 2010—assuming that we haven't all killed one another by then—there will be an awful lot of Gonzales rookies around, and a very high percentage of them will still be in perfect shape. The price for a *near mint* Gonzales could be less than $25.

In fact, the condition-to-value ratio for non-*mint* cards produced in the 1990s may differ very dramatically from that for cards produced in the 1950s, 1960s, 1970s, and most of the 1980s. Interestingly, the condition-to-value ratios for those older cards probably *won't* change—a *near mint* card will always be worth around twice what an *excellent* example is, and so forth. Why? Because most of the older cards in circulation right now are in the hands of people who appreciate them and know how to take care of them. Even though a majority of all the older cards ever printed have been damaged or destroyed over time, that process has halted in the last few years as everyone, it seems, knows that a card loses its value if it's not protected in some way. In other words, because people both inside and outside the business have wised up to the value of cards, the supply of older cards today is pretty close to what it will be in 2010.

But back to Gonzales. There are, at this very moment, millions of his rookie cards available. And

it's probably fair to say that around half of them are still in *mint* condition. The rest are almost all *near mint*—some have incurred a very minor amount of damage, while others were simply printed off-center. The percentage of cards that have been badly damaged or destroyed is minuscule. So if you are planning to stockpile Gonzales rookies, why settle for a card that's just a little bit "off," especially when true *mint* cards are available at the same price? That's right—the price for a *mint* Gonzales carries little or no premium over a *near mint* Gonzales, because they're so new that no one's really paying all that much attention! If Gonzales is indeed destined to become a $50 card, why lose $25 down the road when all it means is being a little selective now?

If this seems like nitpicking, think back to the spring of 1990, when 1983 Cal Ripken cards were selling for $2. A lot of people started buying them up that year, but few people were being finicky about condition. About one in three 1983 Ripkens were available in *mint* condition, so buyers who blindly bought, say, thirty cards ended up with ten in *mint* and twenty in *near mint*. Boy, are they sorry now. A *mint* 1983 Ripken brings well over $20, while its *near mint* counterpart has yet to really crack the $20 mark. Needless to say, that difference will only widen as the card's value continues to climb.

So learn how to determine whether a *mint* card is really *mint*—you'll avoid getting taken for a ride when purchasing older cards, and you'll get the most bang for your buck when you buy new ones.

# 7

# CATEGORIZING CARDS

A 1959 Sandy Koufax is worth roughly the same as a 1969 Tom Seaver, yet each has different characteristics that can affect its value down the road. Likewise, a 1987 Jose Uribe is worth the same as a 1992 Tim Wallach, yet each has different characteristics, too. Naturally, the longer you've been in the business, the more you know about individual cards. If you're a relative novice, you've got a lot to learn. But either way, it's nearly impossible to understand what makes *every* card unique. The best shortcut, especially for the purposes of buying, is to establish a number of "categories."

The cards in each category, though not exactly the same, should share key characteristics. In other words, they should have enough in common that if there is an across-the-board trend in the business, all the cards in that category will be affected in much the same way. Each category, meanwhile, should differ from the others in characteristics that are *not* shared. In other words, cards of certain Hall of Famers, such as Eddie Murray and Rickey Henderson, might be grouped together in a Blue Chip category, while cards of aging, non–Hall of Fame stars, such as Willie McGee and Kal Daniels, might be grouped together in a Wanna-Be category. Obviously, the more cat-

egories you use, the more accurate your take on the market will be.

It may seem a little simplistic to divide all cards into "good and bad" categories, but actually that's a pretty decent start. The next step is to look at the cards you feel are "good," and try to determine what makes each card attractive. Are some of these cards rookies with potential? Are some of them Hall of Famers? Are some of them players who you feel will blossom in a year or two? If you can find similarities among the cards you consider "good," then group them according to those similarities. Then see if you can break down those groups a little bit more. What you'll end up with is five or ten or twenty categories that will help focus your efforts when buying or selling cards. Too often, buyers don't think about what kind of card they're getting, only about what they're paying for. That's a mistake that can hurt you down the road, especially if you use the prices quoted in the monthly guides as a barometer of a player's ultimate worth.

Here's the important thing to remember: in the short run, every card increases and decreases in value—sometimes dramatically, sometimes not. But over the long haul, it's the cards of Hall of Famers that are *always* in demand, often at a premium price. The players who fall short *never* pay off. If you're considering the card of an active player or a retired non–Hall of Famer, your main concern should not be price. It should be *potential.* Simply put, ask yourself if that player is going to make the Hall of Fame.

Here are some basic categories that address different types of players and their cards, with particular attention paid to potential:

## PREMIUM CARDS (PC)

These are the special cards of the special players. The early Mantle cards, the Seaver rookie, the Ryan rookie, the T-206 Honus Wagner—cards, for lack of a better definition, that have gained recognition *outside* the business and are thus subject to demand from people who buy things like classic cars, diamonds, and football teams. You can throw away the price guide on these cards—they just seem to keep climbing.

## BLUE CHIP CARDS (BC)

These are cards of players who either have made the Hall of Fame or would be elected if their careers were to end today. Eddie Murray, Roger Clemens, Kirby Puckett, Cal Ripken, and Nolan Ryan are players typical of this group, as are players who have already made it to Cooperstown. In terms of value, these cards are fairly stable; they don't experience sudden drops unless they have made sudden and dramatic increases, and they tend to increase in value with age. An investment in Blue Chip cards is like buying mutual funds—essentially it's an investment in the market itself. Don't expect to make a killing on any of these cards, for although demand will remain fairly constant, there should always be a plentiful supply.

## ON-THE-FENCE CARDS (OTF)

This is a category that could be divided in two, as the players it encompasses are at different stages of their careers. As a group, though, these players are "on the fence" where the Hall of Fame is concerned.

Some have put in brilliant careers, but their numbers may not be overwhelming enough to ensure enshrinement. Jack Morris, Paul Molitor, Bert Blyleven, Tim Raines, Dave Parker, Alan Trammell, Lou Whitaker, Dennis Eckersley, and Don Mattingly are players typical of this group. Most will make the Hall of Fame, but some will not. Solid performances over the next few years could move them into the Blue Chip category.

Others have put up big numbers but haven't played enough years to qualify for the Hall—if their careers ended today, they would not be eligible. The odds of any of these players making the Hall of Fame are pretty good now, but not so much that their card prices have peaked. If you guess right, you'll be rewarded. If you guess wrong, you'll get creamed. Jose Canseco, Ruben Sierra, Joe Carter, Eric Davis, Barry Larkin, Barry Bonds, Fred McGriff, Bobby Bonilla, Will Clark, and Roberto Alomar are players typical of this group. Remember, more than a few players who looked like shoo-ins for immortality suddenly stopped producing and withered on the vine. Bo Jackson would have made this OTF list two years ago.

## VOLATILE CARDS (VC)

This is the high-risk category. It is comprised of players like Frank Thomas, Juan Gonzales, Ken Griffey, Dave Justice, Tom Glavine, Eric Karros, Ron Gant, and Dave Fleming. The newer the set, the more Volatile cards there are, as there are more promising young players in the early stages of their careers. This is where most of the action is in the day-to-day card business. Card buyers treat the players in this category like gods. And why not? They are the gods of profit! There is little question that the next century's first bunch of Hall of Famers will come from this group, which means that this is where the money is. The law of averages, however, says that only a handful of these players will actually have what it takes to be considered for induction; an awful lot can happen to these guys over the next decade, both good and bad. Deep down, card buyers know this. And they also know that none of these players has a truly rare card. There are no 1967 high numbers here, no 1953 Bowmans—so there is absolutely no chance that a $1,000 card is going to emerge from this group. Still, with whatever inflation lies ahead, a 1989 Upper Deck Gary Sheffield rookie could conceivably clock in at $100 in ten years if he turns out to be the next Mike Schmidt. The hope for these cards, of course, is that they will vault into the On-the-Fence group, and eventually become Blue Chip cards. For now, these cards are considered Volatile for their potential to increase significantly in value over the next couple of years—or to come crashing down.

There are some things you should know about Volatile cards:

1. Card buyers have snapped up a sufficient amount of them that if a player hits fifty homers or wins twenty-five games, the ensuing demand will not be met by the supply at the current price. That means that as long as the player is "hot," buyers will gladly pay over "book" price to obtain more, and in turn, dealers will pay up to 75 percent of that amount.

2. Given the money and emotion buyers have tied up in these cards, there is an understandable backlash when one of these players has an off year or suffers an injury. The moment one of these guys slips off the fast track, most buyers cease purchasing his cards and many try to sell them off at 30 to 50 cents on the dollar while the prices in the monthly guides are still artificially high. Dealers, who suddenly find themselves overstocked with cards that used to be impossible to keep in stock, tend to panic, too, and often attempt to unload the cards of these "underachievers" at a discount.

3. A "Volatile" player can *afford* an off year or two—or even three!—before he no longer has a credible shot at Cooperstown. In that sense, it's best to think of a Volatile player as a cat with three lives. Of course, some of the players in this category have used up a life or two already, so you have to watch them closely. But look

how many of these young men have gone from "hot" to "cold" back to "hot" again: Ventura, Gant, Grissom, Sheffield, Avery, Smoltz. In the case of each player, the actual selling prices of his cards dropped at least 50 percent from their initial peaks, only to bounce back even stronger when he recovered from an off year or two. Don't give up on these cats if they've only used up one or two lives.

4. A Volatile card, by definition, is one with the potential to become one of the most valuable cards in a set—or become a common. When you pay a premium for a card in this category, never forget that you are taking a significant risk.

5. If you still don't get it, here's what many buyers consider to be the ultimate Volatile card: the 1992 Topps Brien Taylor gold card. Enough said.

There are a number of players out there who, for one reason or another, do not fit into any of the above categories. Brett Butler, Willie Randolph, Brian Downing, Lance Parrish, Jack Clark, Bill Madlock, Bill Buckner, Ron Cey, Jim Kaat, Al Oliver, Cecil Cooper, George Foster, Frank White, Dave Kingman, Don Baylor, and Buddy Bell, for instance, don't really fit anywhere here. Since these categories were configured in such a way as to include anyone with a shot at Cooperstown, you'd think that any player who doesn't fit, doesn't have a shot. And you'd be right. Thus, if you're considering buying a card of a player who doesn't squeeze into one of these categories, ask yourself why you're buying it. If it's for future appreciation, you're better off spending your money on someone else, because these guys don't have a ghost of a chance of being enshrined. Also note that cards of these players have been omitted from the price guide in Chapter 9.

Besides the aforementioned categories, some other distinctions are worth making, too. You should understand what a rookie card is, for instance, and you should know what makes a card common.

There is a fair amount of confusion among card buyers as to which card qualifies as a player's rookie card. Is it the first card ever issued? Is it the first card issued by a "major" manufacturer? Is it the first card to appear in a "regular" set? These are important questions, but they kind of skirt the issue. Indeed, people who get hung up on what a rookie card is or is not often miss the whole point of the buying process.

Once you've decided to buy the cards of a particular player, you should be looking for his *best* card—the card for which other buyers will someday be shelling out the most money. Whether it's that player's minor-league card, a card from a non-mainstream set, a short-printed insert, a card from an updated or extended set, or a card from a regular set makes little difference as long as it's that player's *best* card. Only when you've accepted this idea should you start to delve into the nomenclature.

## ROOKIE CARDS

At the moment, most people in the business consider a player's rookie card to be the first one ever issued by a major company, namely one of Topps, Score, Donruss, Fleer, and Upper Deck. If a player's first card is issued in a specialty or premium set issued by these companies—Bowman, Stadium Club, O-Pee-Chee, Pinnacle, Leaf, Triple Play, Studio, Ultra, and whatever else comes down the line—it is also considered a rookie card. Likewise, a player's first card, if issued in an updated, extended, "rookie," or "traded" series, is also considered a rookie card.

The price guides complicate things by creating varying "degrees" of rookie cards. For instance, a player's first card in a *regular* set is called his "rookie" card, even if his first card was actually printed a year or two earlier in some sort of special update series. If that's the case, then his actual first card is called an "extended rookie" card, while his first card in a regular set is still his "rookie" card. If that's not confusing enough, many guides call the first card a company prints of a player his "first" card, even if the other companies

have already issued a dozen cards of that player.

These distinctions—these "degrees of rookiness"—are no more than ads for card dealers, as the information they provide buyers is designed to get them interested in cards that are not really "first" cards at all. There is no real market, for example, for a 1986 Topps Tom Henke card—his first card was issued by Donruss two years earlier. Yet a lot of guides go to the trouble of listing Henke's 1986 Topps card as his "First Topps Card." Who cares? The number of buyers who collect only Topps cards is smaller than the number of buyers who'd want Henke's cards in the first place! What the inclusion of this type of information accomplishes, however, is to make naive buyers think there's something special about the card, that it's "worth" a quarter, and that it would be a great deal for a nickel or a dime. In other words, this information is not included as a service to buyers—it's a service to dealers who would like to get a few extra pennies for what is essentially a common card.

Confused? Well, it gets worse. The proliferation of minor league cards since the late 1980s has further clouded the issue of what a rookie card is. Although legal and licensed, these sets are considered to be "underground" issues by most buyers. Most of the nationally distributed sets were overproduced, and there are still huge quantities sitting in warehouses all over America. Less plentiful regional sets—often sold or given away at minor league ballparks—are of poor quality and design, and there's no guarantee that the original plates have been destroyed. In other words, the means and incentives for reproducing or counterfeiting these cards are already in place, while the means of preventing this from happening are not. For these reasons and others, a player's minor league card, even if it's his first, is not considered his rookie card.

Things have gotten even *more* complicated since the major manufacturers started printing cards of college and minor league players. At the moment, these cards, because they have been issued in regular or updated sets, *are* considered bona fide rookie cards. Why might that change? It won't. But a lot of buyers are intimidated by the prospect of having to determine the potential of untried eighteen-year-olds, and many decide to steer clear. However, when these young players start making an impact on the major-league level in a couple of years, those same buyers will be buying up those cards as rookie cards.

Finally, there are cards being produced by card *dealers* who hope to capitalize on the rookie craze. The most notable is Scoreboard, Inc., which issues Classic cards. For the past couple of years, the company has produced high-quality sets of draft picks in relatively small quantities. Are these cards rookie cards? No, not at the moment. But the jury's still out. Buyers seem hesitant to consider Classics "regular" cards—some people, in fact, won't buy them at any price—but if the company one day joins Topps, Fleer, Score, Donruss, and Upper Deck as a major manufacturer, buyers will probably be scrambling to get the cards they passed up in the late 1980s and early 1990s.

## BEST CARDS

Now that you're thoroughly confused about what is, is not, might be, should be, and could be a rookie card, let's look at what's really important: what makes a player's card his *best* card? Think back to what you know about the relationship between supply and demand in the card business. Demand has an inordinately large bearing on the selling price of a card, while actual supply is almost immaterial. All that has to happen is for buyers to *believe* the quantity of a card is low and things will start to happen. If you can figure out which card everyone believes is a player's scarcest, then you're halfway home.

Sometimes, however, you can figure wrong. When Will Clark broke in with the Giants in 1986, the consensus was that his 1986 Donruss Rookies card was his best card. By 1987, however, it had become clear that Donruss—as well as Topps and Fleer—had produced a lot of postseason sets in 1986, and buyers switched allegiance to Clark's supposedly scarce 1987 Donruss card. It wasn't until 1988 that it finally dawned on buyers that

Clark's best card was actually the 1987 Fleer—if you went with the flow from 1986 to 1988, you took a real roller-coaster ride! This brings up two important points about determining a player's best card. First, a "best" card is not always a "first" or "rookie" card. Second, doing as the crowd does in the card business is about as safe as following the lead lemming.

In defense of card buyers in 1986 and 1987, they did have the right idea. It's just that their execution and judgment were poor. It's happened before. Nobody knew, for instance, that Don Mattingly's best card would be his 1984 Donruss rookie until a year after it was issued—everyone was stockpiling his Topps cards. Which card will be Brian McRae's best card? His 1991 Upper Deck, 1991 Stadium Club, or 1992 Donruss Diamond King? Maybe it will be his first minor league card. How about Dave Fleming? Will it be his 1991 Bowman card, his 1992 Upper Deck, one of the cards issued in the super-premium sets, or his Pinnacle insert? You can never be sure.

The best strategy for picking a player's best card is to go with your instincts. If you visit a lot of card shops and attend card shows regularly, pay attention to which *sets* are moving as opposed to which individual players people seem to want. If you notice a set selling fast, find out why. Is it because the players in the set are in high demand? If so, this doesn't tell you anything about its scarcity—even if the cards are being snapped up as fast as dealers get them, there's no guarantee that they won't be coming out of the woodwork a year or two later. But if it appears that a set is selling out quickly because dealers did not get a large allocation of cases from the manufacturer, that is usually a good sign that the production run was fairly low. In a year or two, buyers will be zeroing in on the individual cards in that set. If a player's first card happens to be included in that set, chances are good that it will turn out to be his best card.

Something that may further complicate the process of determining which card is a player's best card is the move toward limited-run super-premium sets. Last year, for instance, Fleer's Ultra set included a scarce subset of "award winners," which included cards of Chuck Knoblauch, Tom Glavine, and Matt Williams. By mid-summer, each of these 1992 cards was selling well between $4 and $5. At the same time, however, the "previous" best cards of these players—Knoblauch's 1991 Stadium, Glavine's 1988 Fleer, and Williams's 1987 Donruss—were all selling for about the same price. What does that mean? Does it mean that these players have "new" best cards? It would certainly appear that way. The answer may not come until these players show that they can sustain their Hall of Fame numbers for more than a couple of years. Only then will their "old" best cards and "new" best cards truly be put to the test.

## COMMONS

What makes a card a common? It's very simple. A card falls into the common category when its supply is greater than the number of buyers willing to purchase it at a premium price. This, of course, is largely a function of the player depicted on the card. If no one "wants" a particular player, then it stands to reason that no one would "want" to pay a premium to obtain that player's card. Therefore, the card commands no premium and becomes a common.

Indeed, each set of cards produced during the last century has commons. In fact, every set has its own "threshold"—a price above which buyers will not purchase a *near mint* card unless there is something special about the player on that card. For example, the T-206 tobacco series (issued from 1909 to 1911) has a threshold of around $45. Once cards are priced above that level, demand tails off dramatically unless a card depicts a star, Hall of Famer, rare variation, or scarce minor leaguer.

Whichever cards do not sell above that threshold are, for all practical purposes, *commons*. Likewise, the 1975 Topps set has a threshold for cards of around 25 cents. Cards that don't sell briskly above that price should be considered commons, too.

What's the threshold for newer commons? Most price guides list commons from the last few years at a nickel or so. Well, here's a shocker: in reality, the actual selling price is more like a tenth of that amount. Half a cent apiece? That's right. Commons are essentially fill-ins for incomplete sets. But since the mid-1980s, ready-made factory and hand-collated sets have been available pretty cheaply to anyone who wanted them. That means the commons that are still out there on the market are of almost no interest to people making up sets.

Let's look at the 1990 Topps Alvaro Espinoza card. There are well over a million sitting in commons boxes around the country and that's where they'll stay. Forever. Are there a million people who want one? No. Will there be a million people who, over the next decade, feel compelled to slap together a 1990 set? No. So where do these cards go? Nowhere. Unless the price is right. And right now, the right price is two for a penny. With few exceptions, that is the bulk selling price for recent commons.

Why is the 1990 Espinoza listed in the monthly guides for a nickel? Because, for the rare buyer who actually needs one, a dealer must charge that amount to offset the time it took to sort that card and place it in numerical order. And that's a fair price—if you're buying commons one at a time. But should you ever be possessed to purchase recent commons in bulk, don't get snookered. The price for a thousand commons is not $50. It's more like $5.

# 8

## PICKING A WINNER

The $64,000 question in the card business has always been How do you spot the rookie card that will skyrocket in value someday? The second half of that question, though rarely articulated, is How do you *avoid* spending money on rookie cards that end up amounting to nothing? The answer to both questions is that there is no sure way of maximizing the dollars you spend on new rookie cards. You can, however, improve your odds.

First, you must recognize that what you're after is not necessarily a card that has a chance to rise quickly in price. You want a card with "staying power." If you play the card business like the stock market—buying low and selling high—that's okay; you'll win some and you'll lose some. But ultimately the rookie cards you want in your portfolio are those of the truly great players—the Hall of Famers. That means being scientific and being selective. It means that when the 1993 and 1994 cards come out, you have to determine which players stand the best chance of turning in Hall of Fame–caliber careers. That's a tall order, of course, but it can be done. How? Well, if you believe in past performance and statistics—and put stock in the laws of probability—there's an awful lot to be learned from the rookie cards of the 1980s.

What are the odds of there being, somewhere in this year's sets, the rookie cards of future Hall of Famers? Pretty good. In every year from 1980 to 1985, each regular set of cards issued contained at least one rookie who is now a strong Hall of Fame candidate. And from 1985 to 1989, each regular set issued contained at least one rookie who looks like a pretty good candidate already. Thus, in order to increase your odds of identifying those cards in *this* year's sets, it makes sense to see what the top rookie cards of the 1980s had in common.

In order to do that, it's necessary to create a "universe" of the top rookie cards from that ten-year period. Defining which cards are considered "top," however, can be a little tricky. You don't want to limit yourself to the half dozen or so sure Hall of Famers, because that's too small of a group from which to derive any usable information. Instead, create a universe consisting of players whose *second-year* cards have experienced relatively constant demand over the last few years. In that way you eliminate "faddish" or "flash-in-the-pan" rookie cards, while gaining a large sampling of very good, consistent stars—most of whom have, at this very moment, at least an outside shot at enshrinement in Cooperstown.

Going just by steady demand for their second-

'74 Highlights

Hank Aaron

NL ALL STAR
Outfield

AARON SETS HOMER MARK

Topps

DAVE STEWART
PITCHER
DODGERS

A.L. ALL STAR
OF

Yankees
REGGIE JACKSON

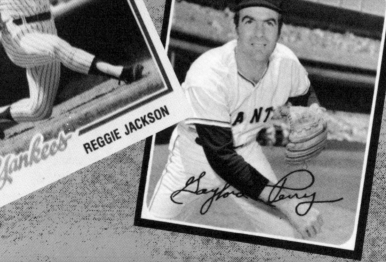

GIANTS
gaylord perry • pitcher

Gaylord Perry

year cards, the players who make up this universe are Jim Abbott, Roberto Alomar, Steve Avery, George Bell, Andy Benes, Wade Boggs, Barry Bonds, Bobby Bonilla, Jose Canseco, Joe Carter, Will Clark, Roger Clemens, Vince Coleman, David Cone, Eric Davis, Len Dykstra, Tony Fernandez, Cecil Fielder, Julio Franco, Ron Gant, Tom Glavine, Dwight Gooden, Mark Grace, Ken Griffey, Jr., Mike Greenwell, Kelly Gruber, Tony Gwynn, Rickey Henderson, Orel Hershiser, Kent Hrbek, Bo Jackson, Gregg Jefferies, Howard Johnson, Felix Jose, Barry Larkin, Greg Maddux, Ramon Martinez, Don Mattingly, Jack McDowell, Fred McGriff, Mark McGwire, Kevin Mitchell, Hal Morris, Rafael Palmeiro, Kirby Puckett, Tim Raines, Jeff Reardon, Cal Ripken, Bret Saberhagen, Ryne Sandberg, Benito Santiago, Steve Sax, Gary Sheffield, Ruben Sierra, Lee Smith, John Smoltz, Darryl Strawberry, Danny Tartabull, Fernando Valenzuela, Andy Van Slyke, Robin Ventura, Frank Viola, and Matt Williams.

Again, the two criteria for this universe are a player's rookie card having been issued in a regular set between 1980 and 1989, and his second-year card having already seen steady demand, at least since the end of the decade. You can quibble with some of the players on this list—and you can certainly argue that a few others should be added—but for the purpose of gathering information on rookies and rookie cards, it will do just fine.

## HITTERS

Take a look at the hitters first. What can be said about them? For starters, there are forty-six of them, which means that any major similarities cannot be chalked up to mere coincidence. Here are three important questions to ask about these players:

1. How old were they when their rookie cards were first issued as part of a regular (non-update) set?
2. How old were they when they first broke into the majors?

3. How old were they when they first established their abilities on an everyday basis: at what point did the fast players start stealing bases, the high-average hitters start to drive the ball consistently, and the power hitters start hitting home runs?

| Age When Rookie Card Was Issued | Number of Hitters |
|---|---|
| Age 20 | 4 |
| Age 21 | 11 |
| Age 22 | 13 |
| Age 23 | 10 |
| Age 24 | 7 |
| Age 25 | 1 |
| Age 26 | 0 |

| Age at Major-League Debut | Number of Hitters |
|---|---|
| Age 19 | 3 |
| Age 20 | 10 |
| Age 21 | 15 |
| Age 22 | 9 |
| Age 23 | 9 |
| Age 24 | 0 |
| Age 25 | 0 |

| Age When Skills Were Established | Number of Hitters |
|---|---|
| Age 20 | 4 |
| Age 21 | 10 |
| Age 22 | 9 |
| Age 23 | 15 |
| Age 24 | 4 |
| Age 25 | 3 |
| Age 26 | 1 |

Before delving into the numbers above, consider the importance of the questions that generated them. They are concerned with three pieces of information that are available to anyone who buys cards. That means that you can take whatever information you derive from these numbers and apply it to other players when evaluating their cards.

Now take a look at the numbers. Any surprises? Well, if you've been buying cards of twenty-five-, twenty-six-, and twenty-seven-year-old rookies, you just learned something. Where hitters are concerned, the odds of a twenty-five-year-old rookie paying off in the long run is one-in-a-decade! And the odds for older rookies are nil! Who was the twenty-five-year-old rookie? Kevin Mitchell. What are his chances of making the Hall of Fame? In a word, "remote." Has any twenty-five-year-old rookie hitter *ever* made the Hall of Fame? Only one—Cap Anson—and that was because there was literally no league to be a rookie in until he was twenty-five. In Mitchell's defense—or rather, in the defense of his card—he was twenty-four during his rookie season and had actually played a few games the year before. But as the lone twenty-five-year-old on a 1980s regular-issue rookie card, his case is nonetheless compelling.

Equally compelling is the fact that every single one of these players had major-league experience by the age of twenty-three. Since this group consists more or less of the forty-six best hitters to come up during the last decade, it's safe to assume that if a team did not feel a player was worth bringing to the bigs by age twenty-three, they probably didn't see anything that would suggest that player had the potential to become a Hall of Fame—caliber performer. Obviously, teams don't actually think that way, but again the numbers are rather convincing.

Also interesting is the fact that all but eight of these players had established themselves by the age of twenty-three. No less than thirty-eight were already full-time players by that time, starting to do the things for which they would be recognized a couple of years later. Four—Henderson, Sierra, Alomar, and Griffey—had done so before their twenty-first birthdays. Equally interesting is the fact that the four players who did not get rolling until twenty-five or twenty-six—Morris, Carter, Gruber, and Fielder—were all special cases. Morris was stuck behind a bunch of Steinbrenner's mil-

lionaires in Yankee Stadium and flourished the moment his old manager, Lou Piniella, brought him to Cincinnati. The Cubs held Carter back while trying to squeeze every last drop out of Gary Matthews, Keith Moreland, and Bob Dernier. Gruber got plenty of playing time in 1986 and 1987 but was not given a full shot at third by the Blue Jays until the platoon of Rance Mullinicks and Garth Iorg proved untenable. And Fielder . . . well, you probably know that one already.

Obviously, from these basic observations, a definite pattern begins to emerge. You start to increase your odds of buying into prime rookie cards if you *avoid* buying cards of rookies who are older than twenty-four, who played their first major-league games after the age of twenty-three, and who have not established themselves—for whatever reason—by the age of twenty-five. Gee, you say, that means I would have missed out on Cecil Fielder. No. You would have bought his cards in 1986. Had you decided in 1989 to go back and pick the best unheralded rookies from the 1986 set—or had you decided to jettison all of your "lost-cause" 1986 rookie cards in 1989—then yes, you would have missed out on Fielder.

By the way, if that's what you glean from this universe of players, you're missing the whole point. What these three very basic sets of statistics should tell you is that choosing rookie cards is *not* a matter of predicting who's going to do well—it's a process of predicting who's not. In keeping with this thought, let's break down this universe of players in some other ways.

Let's look at the breakdown by position. Of the forty-six hitters, fourteen came up to the majors as either first or third basemen, including Sandberg and Ripken, who were soon shifted to the middle infield. Eleven came up as middle infielders, including Raines, Sheffield, Williams, Tartabull, and Gant. And twenty came up as outfielders, all of whom, except Mattingly and Palmeiro, remained there. That's forty-five out of forty-six, which means that of the countless catchers who came to the majors during the 1980s, only one—Santiago—managed to make a lasting impression on card buyers. So add to your list: Avoid buying catchers.

Of the fourteen players who came up as corner-men, twelve arrived with minor-league power credentials. Boggs and Ventura did not, but the former had batted .320 in four minor-league campaigns, while the latter established an all-time best NCAA batting streak against good college pitching at Oklahoma State. So add this to your list: Avoid cornermen with no power, unless they consistently bat over .300 in the minor leagues.

Of the twenty outfielders, the common denominator was speed—even for the sluggers. The two notable lead-foots of the group—Mattingly and Morris—were projected to be first basemen all along. Of the other less-than-swift players, you might be surprised to learn that Bell managed 10 steals during his last full year in the minors, Palmeiro swiped 15 bases in his last year, and Greenwell tallied 9 thefts while scoring 70 of the 155 times he reached base in his last year. So add this to your list: avoid outfielders who show no signs of speed, regardless of their other numbers, unless you know they are projected as cornermen.

Of the eleven middle infielders, every last one had solid minor-league batting stats. In their final bush-league campaigns, Raines batted .354 with 77 steals; Sax hit .346 with 34 steals; Franco batted .300 with 21 homers and 33 steals; Larkin batted .329 with 10 homers and 19 steals; Alomar batted .319 with 12 homers and 43 steals; Fernandez batted .300 with 35 steals; Tartabull hit .300 with 43 homers and 109 RBIs. Jefferies hit .367 in his second-to-last season and then .282 with 32 steals the next; Williams hit 6 homers in a third of a season before hitting another 8 after being called up to San Francisco; Gant hit 27 homers his last two years, drove in 190 runs, and stole 59 bases. These were not Punch-and-Judy numbers, even for the minor leagues. That Tartabull, Raines, Williams, Sheffield, Gant, and Jefferies lacked the defensive skills to nail down middle infield jobs in the majors was of little consequence, for all were good enough hitters that their teams found new positions for them. So add this to your list: Avoid middle infielders who

don't put up gaudy numbers, even if they come with terrific defensive skills.

You can break these numbers down endlessly, of course, but this should be enough to narrow your choices of rookie cards. Remember, evaluating rookies is like determining the condition of cards: you should always look for reasons *not* to grade a player too high. Follow these parameters and the odds should be in your favor—and remember, these only apply to hitters:

Don't buy a position player's rookie card if . . .

1. The player is twenty-five or older when the card is issued.
2. The player has not appeared in the majors before his twenty-fourth birthday.
3. The player has failed to establish himself before his twenty-fifth birthday.
4. The player is a catcher.
5. The player is a first or third basemen and doesn't put up power numbers in the minor leagues—*unless* he has consistently batted over .300.
6. The player is projected as an outfielder and has no speed, regardless of his other numbers.
7. The player is a second baseman or shortstop and does not hit for average or power in the minors, regardless of defensive ability.
8. The player is a second baseman or shortstop and has no speed.

Apply these rules to this year's rookie cards and see how many cards you're left with. If you whittle your choice down to five or six cards, don't get nervous—odds are that you've picked the five or six hitters with the most long-term potential. Sure, you might miss a flash in the pan or two, but you can always give in and waste your money on their cards later if you're feeling paranoid. Just remember, rarely do more than three or four great players emerge from a single season, so there's no point in blowing your budget on thirty different cards if the odds say you should concentrate on five or six.

If you need any more convincing, apply these rules to some recent sets and see what you come up with. The 1985 Donruss set was a pretty good one for hitters, according to the price guides. How did it fare under these rookie rules?

Here are the twelve cards you would have purchased using this set of criteria: Danny Tartabull, Daryl Boston, Steve Kiefer, Shawon Dunston, Billy Hatcher, Jim Traber, Alvin Davis, Jim Presley, Eric Davis, Kirby Puckett, Sid Bream, and Jeff Stone. The total cost for these cards in 1985 was $7. Obviously, the Puckett card is the winner, with Davis and Tartabull having some value, as well. Dunston, Hatcher, and Davis all have a little value, too. The selling price for these cards today is around $60, so if you budgeted $35 for rookie hitters in 1985, your investment would be worth around $300. And with the Puckett card being a good bet to top $50 and stay there, you could sell a whole lot to a dealer today for about $175. In short, you would have made back five times what you spent.

How many cards would you *not* have bought? Twenty, including such blowouts as Steve Lyons, Larry Sheets, Scott Bradley, Alex Sanchez, R. J. Reynolds, Franklin Stubbs, Barbaro Garbey, Rex Hudler, Mike Pagliarulo, Dan Gladden, Phil Bradley, Dan Pasqua, and Tim Hulett. With eight years' hindsight, it's easy to look at these players and say, "Who would have bought their cards anyway?" But in 1985, buyers *were* zeroing in on their cards. Gladden, Pasqua, Stubbs, Sheets, Garbey, Sanchez, and both Bradleys were all hailed as future stars, and each of their cards commanded a premium. The total cost for these twenty cards in 1985, in fact, was $6, but the payoff today is less than $3. Had you played it safe and allocated your $35 for *all* of the rookie hitters in 1985, your investment would be worth only $180 and would fetch only $90 from a dealer. In other words, not being selective in 1985 would have cost you $85 in 1993, or more than two and a half times your original investment.

## PITCHERS

If you didn't buy the system for predicting the long-term potential of hitters, you might as well skip this entire section. Picking future pitching stars with any kind of accuracy is extremely difficult; picking hurlers with *staying power* is virtually impossible. Why? Mostly it has to do with the nature of pitching. There are several things that conspire to keep talented pitchers from consistently putting up big numbers over the course of, say, a ten-year period.

Because a pitching staff normally consists of ten pitchers, only four or five can be starters, and only one can be a closer. Those roles rarely go to rookies, unless a team is so bad that it's willing to let a youngster learn how to pitch on the major-league level. Quite often, that team's offense is weak and its defense is shoddy, which means that a rookie starter is going to be putting up lousy numbers until he and the team begin to mature. So just because a rookie is handed a starting job in spring training—or was a solid starter in the minors—it doesn't guarantee that he'll be effective over the course of an entire season. Furthermore, a young pitcher saddled with a poor supporting cast often stops trying to win and starts trying *not* to lose, which means he stops doing the things that got him to the majors and lands himself in the bullpen or back in the minors.

Zane Smith, a marvelous twenty-four-year-old minor-league pitcher who came up with a miserable Atlanta team in 1984, fell prey to this problem and didn't show how good he really was until he went to the Pirates in 1990. Before his arrival in Pittsburgh he was a nibbler, afraid to throw the ball over the plate because one or two runs might mean the ball game. That made for a lot of 3–1 fastballs, which hitters battered mercilessly in tiny Fulton County Stadium. Still, Smith's ERA with the Braves was around 4.00, which was pretty good considering how bad his defense was. When he got to Pittsburgh, he finally was confident enough to fire the ball over the plate and let his defense do its job. His ERA dropped by a run a game, and his strikeout-to-walk ration went from 7:5 to 4:1. Unfortunately, he was thirty by then—too old to be of interest to card buyers. Had he come up with a good team, he probably would have had a shot at 200+ wins for his career, which would have been far more interesting.

Another problem in judging the potential of pitchers is how they are used. Zane Smith was ready to pitch in the majors when the Braves inserted him into their starting rotation in 1985, but things had gotten so bad in Atlanta that they might have done so even if he had still been a year or two away. In fact, they did this with three other young hurlers in 1988: John Smoltz (twenty-one), Tom Glavine (twenty-two), and Pete Smith (twenty-two). Of the three, Pete Smith was the one projected to have the most success. When Smoltz self-destructed after a mid-season call-up and Glavine led the league in losses, they didn't take a lot of heat. Smith, on the other hand, bore the brunt of the fans' disenchantment, even though (at 7–15, 3.69) he had by far the best season of the three. The following year, Smoltz went 12–11 and lowered his ERA by over 2 runs a game, while Glavine turned in a solid 14–8 season. Poor Pete, who was still considered the class of the staff going into 1989, came out of the season as the low man on the totem pole with a 5–14 record, his confidence completely shot. All three of these players had rookie cards in 1988—Glavine and Smith in regular issues, and Smoltz in the Fleer update set. In the spring of '88, Smith's Fleer rookie was selling briskly at 25 to 50 cents. Glavine's didn't sell at all, and Smoltz's, which was released in August, couldn't draw flies, much less buyer interest. How things have changed. In 1993, the Smoltz update card is holding the line somewhere around $3, and Glavine's Fleer rookie does brisk business above $6. Smith's rookie cards? Commons, even after a strong September.

What this says about young pitchers is that a lot of intangibles come into play that affect long-term potential. And card buyers *hate* intangibles. They can range from a talented young pitcher getting "stuck" behind reliable veterans on a winning team, to poor coaching, to out-and-out misuse of a pitcher's abilities. The intangibles in the case of the three Braves centered around how getting called up a year or two too early—and getting pummeled—would affect the respective psyches of these three pitchers. Smoltz and Glavine dealt with it well, Smith did not. From a card buyer's standpoint, that's very frustrating, because there's nothing in the stats that suggests how a young hurler will deal with adversity. The only relevant stats available in this case were from the season before, when all three pitchers were in the minor leagues. Yet, had you looked at the minor-league records of Smoltz, Glavine, and Smith in 1987, you would have drawn the same conclusions the Braves did: Smoltz was a disaster and Glavine wasn't much better, but Smith looked like he had the makings of an effective major-league starter.

If all the scouting, coaching, and administrative talent of a major-league organization can't decide whether a young pitcher "has it" or not, how can you? You can't. The mental aspects of baseball have a huge bearing on the career paths of young pitchers, and minor-league stats don't always tell the whole story. Indeed, when a minor-league pitcher puts up big numbers, it can mean several things.

For instance, a young pitcher with a lot of wins and a low ERA might have just enough control to upset the timing of inexperienced hitters, but not enough zip on his fastball or bite on his curve to get past major leaguers. What do you look for in his minor-league stats that would suggest this flaw? Then again, how do you know he won't survive this initial battering and develop into the kind of pitcher who can get major-league hitters out? But then what if he isn't strong enough to go seven innings and ends up a career middle reliever? It can drive you nuts! The same dilemmas can arise when analyzing the minor-league stats of a young fireballer. How do you know that beefy strikeout-to-walk ratio wasn't the result of free-swinging twenty-one-year-olds being unselective at the plate? How do you know that major-league hitters won't wait your fireballer out until he gets behind in the count and has to lay one over the plate? Then again, what if he finds his control and becomes Roger Clemens or Mike Mussina? But then what if he blows out his arm?

That, by the way, is the most infuriating thing about buying the cards of rookie pitchers. You can do everything right—you can pick a pitcher with great major-league stats, a strong psyche, an unimpeded opportunity, and a great supporting cast—only to watch him grab his elbow or shoulder on the news one night and realize that he'll never be the same again. The injury factor takes an unbelievably heavy toll on pitchers and has destroyed the values of some extremely promising rookie cards. In the last ten years alone, more than forty pitchers who appeared to be on the fast track to potential Hall of Fame careers have been derailed by injuries. If you purchased any of the following players' rookie cards, you probably thought you were sitting pretty: Storm Davis, Alejandro Pena, Kevin Gross, Ron Darling, Mark Gubicza, Jimmy Key, Danny Jackson, Kirk McCaskill, Mike Dunne, Orel Hershiser, Teddy Higuera, Neal Heaton, Floyd Youmans, Todd Worrell, Bobby Witt, Jose Guzman, Chris Hammond, Ed Correa, Joe Magrane, Jeff Robinson, Al Leiter, Mike Campbell, John Farrell, Jack Armstrong, and Mike Harkey. It says a lot for their talent that most of these guys are still pitching. It says a lot about what an injury can do to a pitcher's chances for immortality that each one of these pitchers was red hot with card buyers at some point in his career—and rightly so—but now all their rookie cards are ice cold.

Given the risks and uncertainties, why even bother buying up rookie cards of pitchers? Because you hate to miss out on a Roger Clemens or a David Cone! The odds say stay away, but everyone thinks they can beat the odds. Besides, if you unload your cards when the players are hot, you can clean up on pitchers. So if you've made up your mind to take a shot at some pitchers, it might be a good idea to look at that "universe" of hurlers from the 1980s and see what lessons you can learn.

The pitchers were Abbott, Avery, Benes, Clemens, Cone, Glavine, Gooden, Hershiser, Maddux, Martinez, McDowell, Reardon, Saberhagen, Smith, Smoltz, Valenzuela, and Viola. And their vital stats break down as follows:

| Age When Rookie Card Was Issued | Number of Pitchers |
|---|---|
| Age 19 | 1 |
| Age 20 | 3 |
| Age 21 | 5 |
| Age 22 | 4 |
| Age 23 | 0 |
| Age 24 | 2 |
| Age 25 | 1 |
| Age 26 | 1 |

| Age at Major-League Debut | Number of Pitchers |
|---|---|
| Age 19 | 2 |
| Age 20 | 4 |
| Age 21 | 7 |
| Age 22 | 1 |
| Age 23 | 2 |
| Age 24 | 1 |

| Age When Skills Were Established | Number of Pitchers |
|---|---|
| Age 19 | 1 |
| Age 20 | 2 |
| Age 21 | 4 |
| Age 22 | 2 |
| Age 23 | 3 |
| Age 24 | 3 |
| Age 25 | 2 |

Any surprises? Well, each of these pitchers had established himself before the age of twenty-six, but that shouldn't come as much of a shock, unless you've been loading up on cards of twenty-six-, twenty-seven-, and twenty-eight-year-old rookies. The problem with these numbers is that the "universe" is too small to be very meaningful. But that's the problem with pitchers! You could expand this group by adding more names, but those names would be Dave Stieb, Bruce Hurst, Gregg Olson, Sid Fernandez, etc.—all fine pitchers, but none with the staying power that you look for in a rookie card. As it is, this group of seventeen pitchers may only contain four or five Hall of Famers, so there's no advantage to diluting it even further.

The fact is pitchers are a huge gamble. You're much better off waiting until pitchers hit their thirties in good health and *then* buying the rookie cards of the guys you believe will keep going. No one paid much attention to Don Sutton, Bert Blyleven, Phil Niekro, Jack Morris, Lee Smith, or Jeff Reardon until they were in their thirties, yet they all have a shot at the Hall of Fame. If you've zeroed in on a veteran pitcher, but his rookie card is too expensive, just be patient—he'll have an off year or an injury and you'll be able to scoop up his cards at half price. That's the nature of the beast!

In terms of this group of seventeen pitchers, though, there are some other conclusions you can draw. If a pitcher hits the majors early and establishes his skills before the age of twenty-two, he's probably worth a gamble. The two firemen on this list—Smith and Reardon—didn't become solid closers until they were twenty-four, so you can wait a few more years for relievers to mature.

That brings up another point, however. If you're playing the odds, you may want to avoid relievers altogether. They tend to experience an injury or a slight drop in effectiveness within six or seven years, and teams are generally unwilling to put up with that. Smith and Reardon were no exceptions, and their teams traded them away, but they bounced back strong. Be aware, however, that most closers are turned into setup men when they falter and that few ever reemerge from that role to rack up big save numbers again.

One interesting aspect of this group of pitchers is that when they arrived at the major-league level, each was considered a hard thrower. Even Glavine, Hershiser, and Valenzuela—the "weaklings" of the group—had big-time fastballs with plenty of movement as rookies. Therefore, it's probably safe to avoid pitchers who can't get the ball up around ninety miles per hour.

What about a second pitch? Well, of the fifteen starters in this group, only six had a second pitch they could control. Cone, Hershiser, and Saberhagen could all throw hard sliders for strikes, Gooden and Viola had command of their off-speed pitches, and Valenzuela had that great screwball. The others were still working on second pitches when they arrived, and some have yet to develop them. They'll have to, but for now they can get by fine with pure heat and whatever else happens to be working.

Does control make a difference? It does, in the sense that a pitcher has to be able to get the ball over the plate. But minor-league control numbers, for reasons already stated, aren't always much help. Control generally develops within three to four years at the major-league level, which doesn't help much if you want to buy a pitcher's rookie card. Needless to say, if a starter can't shake his control problems by mid-career, his chances to rack up Hall of Fame numbers are virtually nil.

And that's about it. As undefined as these guidelines are, there's nothing else that can be said. So here are the rookie rules for buying pitchers, such as they are:

Don't buy a pitcher's rookie card if . . .

1. The player is projected to be a closer.
2. The player has not established himself in the starting rotation before the age of twenty-six.
3. The player does not have a good, live fastball.

Obviously, these guidelines greatly broaden the number of rookie cards you'd have to buy in order to cover yourself completely. How effective are they? Take another look at the 1985 Donruss issue, which is perhaps the best set ever where rookie pitchers are concerned. Had you applied these criteria, you would have grabbed the following twelve: Calvin Schiraldi, Mark Gubicza, Dwight Gooden, Bret Saberhagen, Roger Clemens, Curt Kepshire, Ron Romanick, Jose Rijo, Mark Langston, Orel Hershiser, Al Nipper, and Tom Browning. Not a bad haul!

You also would have avoided costly errors like Mike Bielecki, Al Pulido, Ricky Horton, Joe Hesketh, Jeff Robinson, Clay Christianson, Jaime Cocanower, Curt Kauffman, Jeff Dedmon, Tom Wadell, and Ken Howell. Two pretty good cards *would* have slipped through your fingers—John Franco and Jimmy Key, both of whom pitched exclusively in relief—but the upside of this method obviously would have paid off.

Granted, 1985 was a spectacular year for rookie pitchers, and those who were buying cards back then would be quick to point out that *everyone* was on to Saberhagen, Gooden, Rijo, and Hershiser. But what they forget is that *no one* was on to Roger Clemens. Given what's happened to that card during the last few years, this relatively simple set of rules looks like an unqualified triumph. It's also worth noting that the Gooden card was selling for $4 right out of the gate that year, and that the Saberhagen card moved past $1.50 within a couple of months. You don't have to run all the numbers to realize that had you invested $35 in rookie pitchers *without* tapping into the Clemens, your position would not be terribly strong today.

Picking a winner this season may be a little trickier given the National League's two new teams, the Rockies and the Marlins. Expansion tends to throw baseball out of whack for a few years, especially from a statistical standpoint, as well as clearing a path to the majors for dozens of players who just aren't ready. But if you stick to a systematic evaluation of this year's rookie cards, you shouldn't get hurt.

Who fits the profile? Of the players taken in No-

vember's draft whose first cards are debuting in 1993, David Nied, Doug Bochtler, Marcus Moore, Jose Martinez, Kip Yaughn, John Johnstone, Andres Berumen, Robert Person, and Scott Baker—all pitchers—make the minimum age cut, as do hitters Roberto Mejia, Pedro Castellano, Nigel Wilson, Ramon Martinez, Darrell Whitmore, Jesus Tavares, and Kerwin Moore. Not surprisingly, the standouts are the first two players who were chosen, Nied (24) and Wilson (23). Beyond that, it's pretty dicey. Most interesting is Jose Martinez, a crafty pitcher from the Mets' system who, at 22, still has time to develop major-league speed.

Actually, you'l be better off paying close attention to some other players, including Hawblitzell and Carl Everett, whose first cards were issued in 1992 and 1991, respectively. The two fit the profile, although Everett's lack of baseball experience makes him the classic all-or-nothing prospect. Besides Wilson, Nied, and perhaps Bret Barberie, these might be your two best long-term bets. The guys to avoid—especially considering how much media attention they're likely to get—are Steve Decker (a catcher), Brad Ausmus (a catcher), Eric Young (too old), Jeff Conine (too old), Mo Sanford (too old), Trevor Hoffman (a reliever), and Eric Wedge (injury prone). You want a trio of real dark horses? Try Chuck Carr, Braulio Castillo, and Butch Henry on for size. Needless to say, the best plan of action for dealing with Rockies and Marlins is to proceed with caution.

# THE INSIDER'S PRICE GUIDE

As you might have guessed by now, the price guide in this book is quite unlike anything you've ever encountered. You may, in fact, find it a little unsettling. This price guide looks at things from a slightly different perspective from the one taken by the monthly guides and the annuals. You might say it looks at the business from the dealer's point of view.

What's different about that? Well, every other price guide out there bases its evaluations on what dealers have already sold their cards for. Therefore, the only information you're getting is what other buyers have believed a card was worth. If you think about it, those guides shed absolutely no light on how dealers view the cards they currently offer for sale, because the cards priced in the guides have already been sold.

To get at the missing information—indeed, to truly appreciate it—try the following experiment:

Ask a buyer what he thinks the card he just bought is worth. (For the sake of argument, say it's a 1986 Harold Reynolds rookie.) You'll get one of three answers. He'll either give you the price he paid, the price he thinks it's worth, or what he thinks it will sell for one day. Then go to a dealer and ask the same question. You know what? You'll get one of those three answers again. If you hooked

that dealer up to a polygraph, however, he'd have to give you a very different answer in order to prevent the needle from flying off the page. As a dealer, he views that Reynolds card a lot differently from the way his customers do. To him, it is not a 50- or 75-cent card. Granted, he'll price it at that level—and be very pleased when someone strolls in and takes it off his hands at that price—but the truth is that, in his mind, it is about a 15- to 20-cent card.

What does this mean? It means that when a dealer purchases a card, he rarely does so based upon what he *thinks* he can sell it for—he purchases based upon what he *knows* he can sell it for. In the case of the Reynolds card, a dealer might think he can get 50 or 75 cents for it, but under no condition will he pay 25 or 35 cents to obtain it. Instead, he draws on his knowledge of the card, the player, the market, his customers, and his own past experience to arrive at a price he knows he can sell it for. That way, even if he gets stuck with the card, he stands a good chance of unloading it while still making a profit. So, from a dealer's standpoint, the value of the Reynolds card is probably around 15 or 20 cents, which means that he won't pay more than a dime for it.

This is how all bright, experienced dealers think about their cards—the ones who don't, don't stay

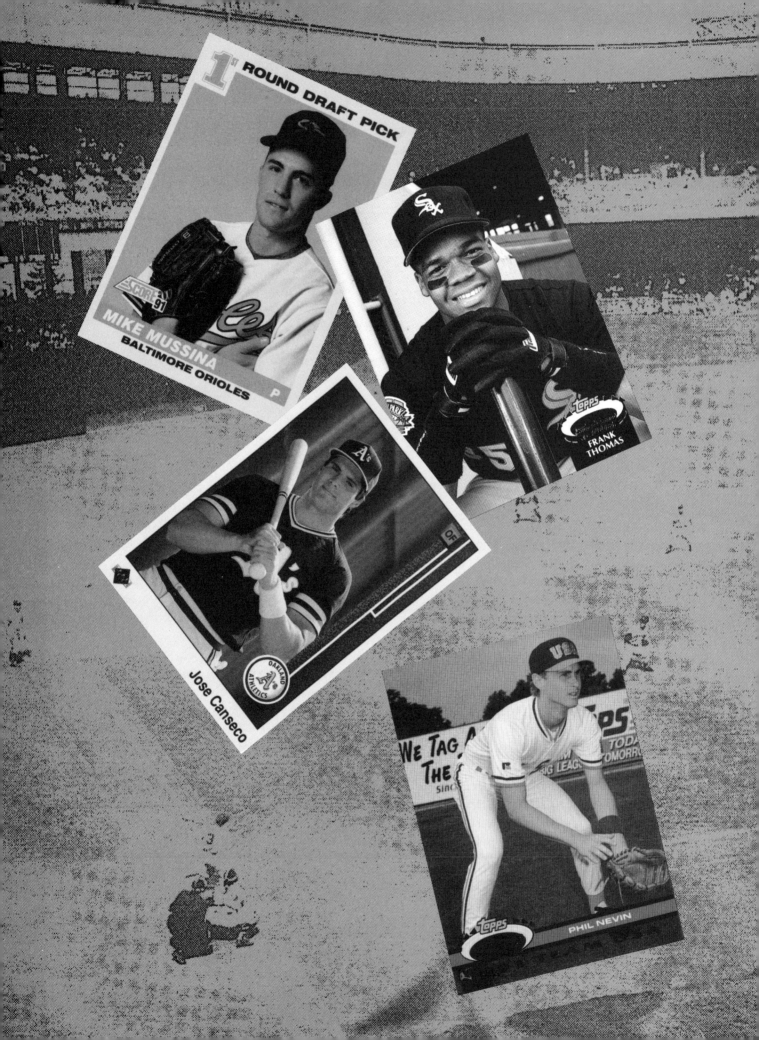

in business very long. There is, in fact, an "inside" price like this for virtually every card on the market (as discussed in the chapter on price guides). And these are the prices you'll find listed in this guide.

What makes these prices different? First, they take into consideration the prices at which cards *haven't* sold. Second, they are prices for the cards you'll be buying—not prices for cards that other buyers have already purchased. This information, about what a typical dealer thinks his cards are worth, has never been available in any form to retail buyers . . . until now.

What value does this information have to you, the card buyer? It can save you a lot of money. For instance, say you want to buy a 1977 Jack Clark rookie. If you look in the monthly price guides, you'll see it listed for around $10. So you walk into a card shop and see the card priced at $8. A pretty good deal, right? Not necessarily. For the last six or eight years, dealers have been having a difficult time collecting a significant premium for this card and, in turn, have stopped paying a significant premium for it. The consensus seems to be that to actually sell this card, its price must go down to $4 or $5. There's a very good chance that the dealer whose shop you've entered has no more than $2 or $3 tied up in his Clark rookie. That $8 price tag may look like a good deal to you; to the dealer it's a dream. If you buy that card at that price, guess what? You've made his dream come true! If, however, you had a feel for the dealer's bottom-line price, you might be able to buy it for half. If that's not value, then what is?

Are the prices in this guide for real? Does this concept of "inside" pricing really exist? You'd better believe it. If you don't, there are three very good tests to prove it to yourself.

The first involves a little game you've no doubt played before. Offer to sell a dealer two cards that according to the monthly guides are worth about the same. Ask for separate offers on each. More likely than not, one card will bring a much lower offer than the other, despite the apparent equality in value. Ask the dealer why he's offering less for the one card. If his answer is something like "I don't need this card as much," an alarm should go off. Why would he "need" one card any less than the other, assuming he planned to go by the book and put identical price stickers on each? That's absurd. It's also a lie. If he's in the business of selling cards for a profit and the selling price of each card is the same, why would he "need" one card less than the other? What the dealer is essentially telling you is that despite what his price stickers and the monthly guides say, the actual selling prices of these cards are not the same.

The second way of determining whether inside pricing exists is to show a dealer this book. Open it up to the price guide section for him and then just watch his body language—notice the look of concern that comes across his face, the dilating of his pupils. Watch his lips twitch and his brow furrow. Then listen politely while he hands this book back to you and tells you that these prices don't exist, that they're way too low, and that you'd never be able to buy any of these cards at these prices. Then, if you're still not convinced that these prices exist, try the final experiment.

This is the litmus test. Pick five or six cards and jot down the prices listed for them in this guide. (These must be cards you want to buy, of course, and you must be prepared to buy them). Next, go to a local card show and determine which dealers have most or all of the cards you want—there should at least be two or three. Once you've made your rounds, approach each again. The ensuing conversation should go something like this:

DEALER: "Is there something you're looking for, something I can help you with?"
YOU: "Sure. I know what I want, but everyone seems to have it. What I'm looking for is a fair price."
DEALER: "Well, tell me what you want and maybe we can work something out."
YOU: "Okay, but first maybe you can answer a question for me. There's something I don't understand."
DEALER: "What's that?"
YOU: "Everyone's showcases are full of the same stuff—piles of it! And everyone's got the same

prices, like no one can think for himself, like the price guide is some sort of bible. Meanwhile, I see a lot of people milling around not spending any money. Look, I've sold cards to dealers before, so I know that there's a pretty big profit margin in this business. My question is why can't a smart dealer come in here, price his cards a little lower than everyone else, and walk out a big winner? I mean, isn't that why you blow a perfectly good weekend to set up at a show?"

DEALER: "Hey, sometimes I wonder the same thing. But listen, that's why I'm here. Let's make a deal. I'll work with you. Just tell me what you want."

YOU: "The cards you have that interest me are the ——, ——, ——, and ——. I've been looking around, and it seems to me that a fair price—if I'm buying them all from the same dealer—would be $——. I don't know, maybe you paid too much for those cards. But I can't believe everyone's got that kind of money tied up in them. My feeling is that unless a card is *really* in high demand, you can't just blindly spend more and more for it if they're still easy to find. And from the dealers I've spoken to at the show today, it seems like you all feel that way, too. For instance, I'd find it hard to believe that you have more than half what I offered you invested in those cards. And even if you did, what's wrong with making a 50 percent profit? This is the only business I've ever heard of where people won't sell something if they're 'only' making a 50 percent profit. It seems like a good racket, if you can actually pull it off."

Apologies if this sounds like a scene from a "Dragnet" rerun, but in order to get at a dealer's inside prices, you sometimes have to get inside a dealer. The exact words aren't important in this situation, but the strategy is.

Notice what you've established *before* any specific purchase is even discussed: (1) there are a number of other dealers in the same room offering the cards you came to buy, (2) they are offering them at the same prices, (3) a lot of buyers have walked by this dealer's table and chosen not to spend their money there, (4) you know that this

dealer is working on very large margins, (5) you're wondering if he's the smartest guy in the room, and (6) the only way he can prove he *is* is to give you a significant—but fair—discount on an as yet undetermined quantity of cards. Everything you've communicated to the dealer thus far has prepared him to think in terms of his "inside" prices.

Notice, too, the groundwork you continue to lay *after* you've told him which cards you want and how much money is involved: (1) as the smartest guy in the room, he can be assured that you will do *all* of your business with him, (2) as the smartest guy in the room, he surely couldn't have paid more than half of what you're offering him, (3) as the smartest guy in the room, he should know that the cards you want are *not* in high demand, and (4) if he disagrees with anything you've said, he's probably not the smartest guy in the room, which means the money you'll be spending that day will be spent on the same cards he has—but with someone else, someone smarter.

The idea, of course, is to let a dealer know that you know what's going on—that the prices in this book *have* to exist—without coming right out and saying it. Obviously, you don't shove this book in a dealer's face and demand he sell you the cards you want at these prices—indeed, it's probably a good idea to keep this book out of sight! Dealers are not going to be pleased by the information contained herein and should have a particular distaste for the prices in the price guide. Suddenly, buyers have access to information that dealers never imagined would be made public, and the dealers will do almost anything to keep this information from spreading.

In fact, you can take this on faith: the same dealer who sells you cards at inside prices after a short conversation and a little bargaining will not give you the same deal if he sees you walking around with this book. The scariest thing for dealers is the prospect of buyers who not only hold their ground, but also know what ground to hold. Why? Because, a buyer who wants to purchase a card at a price that although it's below "book" still leaves room for a decent profit, can take his business somewhere else, and put that profit in the pocket of a competitor.

A lot of dealers see this as a catch-22. If they do sell cards at inside prices, they make a profit, but if all dealers sold at these prices, then the prices in the guides would come down, which means that they'd have to charge even less and make no profit at all. On the other hand, if they don't sell cards at inside prices, their customers will go to dealers who do, which means no profit at all, and the prices in the guides will still go down, which means they end up in the same boat without ever having sold any cards. That's a lot of uncertainty to be caused by a pretty simple idea.

Will the price guide in this book save you money? Yes, if you use it correctly. Will it cost dealers money? On a per-card basis it might, but if buyers spend the same amount of money on cards, the profit margin will still be there and a lot of dead inventory can be moved. The bottom line is that the information in this book poses no threat whatsoever to the card business. If buyers choose to approach the market intelligently for a change, and exercise demand with a greater regard for supply, then the business as a whole becomes healthier and everyone gets to be the smartest guy in the room!

## USING THIS GUIDE

There are several things you should keep in mind when looking through this guide:

1. The prices in this guide reflect the values for cards in *near mint* condition. Premiums for *mint* cards are a matter of personal choice and have already been discussed in the chapter on condition and grading.

2. Each card listed carries a "category designation," which refers to the potential of the card. These designations were made based on performances through the 1992 season. During the 1993 season, a few cards will move from one category to another, which will affect their long-term potential. Make sure you know what the categories mean, and be sure to note when a player jumps from one category to another.

3. Several stars and rookies may appear to be "missing" from this guide. *They are not missing—they have been purposely excluded.* If you can't find a card listed, it either sells for less than a quarter or the player depicted on that card has little chance of making the Hall of Fame. Because a card's long-term potential almost always comes down to whether or not the player is elected to Cooperstown, it's best to avoid these cards, from an investment standpoint.

4. All-Star, League Leader, World Series, and other "special" cards that have yet to establish steady demand have been omitted from this guide. If you want a 1968 Hank Aaron, *buy* a 1968 Hank Aaron. Don't waste $10 on his low-demand All-Star card. If you must buy one of these unlisted cards, throw away the monthly guides and make your best deal—as a rule, there are more of these cards out there than there are collectors interested in buying them.

5. You will not always be able to purchase the cards you want at these prices. The dollar amounts herein reflect what experienced dealers *know* they can get for their cards, but dealers price their cards at what they *hope* to get for them. They are, however, usually willing to negotiate down. Your job is to negotiate them down to the prices in this book, relatively secure in the knowledge that they can afford to let cards go at these prices. Sometimes, however, their prices reflect what they *have* to get for them—in other words, sometimes dealers pay too much for a card. If this is the case, all the negotiation in the world won't make them budge, so you'll just have to move on. Rest assured, though, that most dealers work off these inside prices—and that they won't be losing money—so if one dealer won't budge, eventually you'll find another who will. Be patient and be prepared to shop around.

6. Because dealers are far more likely to negotiate down if they can sell a quantity of cards, be

prepared to buy the cards you want in groups of three or more. If you approach a dealer on a single card and ask for a significant discount, he may ask you what else you want. This is his way of saying, "Sure, I'm willing to bargain, but you're going to have to buy a couple of other cards at the same time."

7. The more competition a dealer has, the more likely he'll be to meet the prices in this guide. Initially, you'll find it easier to work with show dealers than shop dealers. Not only is the competition for show dealers just a few feet away, but they know that if they don't deal with you right then and there, they might never see you again. In reality, the competition is no less intense for shop dealers. The ones who recognize this will eventually agree to meet a great many of these inside prices, although you may have to spend a little time cultivating relationships. The ones who think they have no competition won't meet these prices. You know the type. However, you can take some satisfaction in the knowledge that they'll eventually run their businesses into the ground.

8. Be civil. Don't demand things. Just be firm, explain your thinking, and be prepared to hold your ground. If the inside price for a card is $10 and a dealer offers it to you at $12, don't buy it unless you are sure that *recent* demand has upped the ante a couple of bucks. Remember, the dealer is probably working off a $10 price in the first place, so he's just playing a little game of "chicken." If you flinch first, you lose.

9. This guide is not meant to replace the monthly price guides. It should augment them. Obviously, these prices were compiled prior to the start of the 1993 season, so if demand soars for a young player having a breakthrough year, it won't be reflected here. However, players who are on the cusp of stardom going into this year *are* highlighted in this guide, with special attention paid to age and long-term potential. These players fall into the Volatile Card or VC category—if one of them becomes an estab-

lished star and demand begins to snowball, that's where the monthly guides come into play. They are fairly reliable indicators of who's hot and who's not. So if a player takes off—and he's listed as a Volatile Card—you'll have to use what you've learned about the market to determine a new price for his cards. Update these prices up *and* down as often as possible.

10. In the listings for recent sets, you'll notice that cards selling for less than 25 cents have been omitted, including those of some stars and promising rookies. This does not mean you should avoid these cards—it simply means that demand has not yet caught up with supply at any kind of set price. Generally speaking, cards that sell for less than a quarter can sell for anywhere between a couple of pennies to a couple of dimes. There is no hard and fast rule. The monthly price guides, which list values like ".04" and ".12," aren't much help, either. How do they make the distinction between a 10-cent and 12-cent card? The bottom line with these cheap cards is to identify which players you feel have significant potential and then buy in quantity to save money and avoid wasting time. You should pay no more than a nickel or a dime apiece for these cards in quantity. As for the rookies, review the methods for hedging your bets outlined in Chapter 8, do your homework, and buy the players who you think will beat the odds and become superstars.

11. In the sets of the 1950s, 1960s, 1970s, and of course the 1980s and 1990s, there are several non–Hall of Famers listed. These are the players who seem to have the best shot of making it to Cooperstown. If they make the Hall, will their cards experience a huge upsurge in demand? Possibly. But possibly not. Before George Kell made the Hall of Fame, no one was particularly interested in his cards. After he made it, demand barely picked up at all. There's always that risk. Some players—like Rizzuto, Maris, and Hodges—are already

priced like Hall of Famers. Others—like Fox, Doby, Rice, Boone, Sutton, and John—might make it, or they might not. At the moment, their prices reflect this uncertainty and will surely rise if they do indeed gain enshrinement. The players who are not included but who still could conceivably make it to Cooperstown—like Colavito, Groat, Oliva, Lyle, and Darrell Evans—are discussed in the set descriptions. Look for them in the "Tough Call" section of the year their rookie cards appeared. They're all tough calls, of course, so you're always taking a chance when you buy them. Be careful.

12. Pay close attention to the market and keep an eye on rising stars and players having breakthrough years. This means reading the paper, watching the sports reports on television, talking to other people in the business, and watching the little arrows in the monthly price guides. These are all good resources for determining potential shifts in the market, but only if you use all of them. If a card catches fire, *update its price in this guide.* Don't be afraid to write on the pages of this price guide! This is your primary card-buying tool! Don't save this book for posterity—within a year, many of these prices may be meaningless!

13. Pay attention to the category designations accompanying each card and understand what they mean:

   PC: A Premium Card, which is attractive to buyers outside the hobby and has the potential for tremendous appreciation.

   VC: A Volatile Card, which is very likely to rise well above (or drop well below) the price in this guide.

   BC: A Blue Chip Card of a Hall of Famer or (in the case of active players) a certain Hall of Famer, which should hold its value, with the *potential* for significant increases in value.

   OTF: An On-the-Fence Card, or a card of a player who has a reasonable chance at making the Hall of Fame. Cards of current players in this category will rise and fall depending on

how they do in 1993. Cards of older players are more likely to rise and fall on the whims of buyers—and whether they do indeed make it to Cooperstown.

14. Finally, don't panic about these prices in terms of the value of the cards you already own. That's the kind of mentality this book is trying to eliminate! Your cards are *not* worth less—they're worth the same as they always were. Put simply, before you bought this book, your cards were worth what a dealer would be willing to pay for them. That hasn't changed, has it? No. What *has* changed, however, is that you now know what dealers believe *their* cards are worth, which means that for the first time you can negotiate on an equal footing.

**1948 BOWMAN.** A sturdy little set that has aged very well. There are quite a few *mint* cards out there and there always have been. The entire set was selling for $300 in the mid-1970s, and a lot of people had it. Who knows where those sets are today? *Warning:* A dozen cards were short-printed, but the only one of consequence is Phil Rizzuto's. The others sell for a 50 to 75 percent premium over the regular common price. Don't pay more than a 20 percent premium for a *mint* card, and make sure the cards you buy are well centered.

   *Avoid:* Elliott, Blackwell, Reiser, Sain, Page, Sauer, Thomson, and Koslo.

   *Tough Call:* Allie Reynolds and Tommy Henrich. Had Reynolds established himself in the majors a little sooner (the war was a factor here) or gotten to the Yankees right away, things might have been different. He was, in his prime, a big-game pitcher of the highest degree. Unfortunately, he was out of baseball by the mid-1950s. Henrich also lost time to the war. He was regarded as an exceptional clutch player, but never a truly great one.

*Set: $2,700.00*
*Commons (1–36): $15.00*
*Commons (37–48): $22.00*
*Short Prints: $26.00–$33.00*

| 3 | KINER | 130.00 | BC |
|----|-------------|--------|-----|
| 4 | MIZE | 60.00 | BC |
| 5 | FELLER | 185.00 | BC |
| 6 | BERRA | 400.00 | BC |
| 8 | RIZZUTO | 150.00 | OTF |
| 17 | SLAUGHTER | 55.00 | BC |
| 18 | SPAHN | 195.00 | BC |
| 36 | MUSIAL | 600.00 | BC |
| 38 | SCHOENDIENST | 90.00 | BC |
| 40 | MARION | 40.00 | OTF |

**1949 BOWMAN.** Some stories were circulating twenty years ago about someone who had hit a mother lode of *mint* 1949 Bowmans—tens of thousands, in fact—somewhere in rural Pennsylvania. And for a while there an unusual number of complete sets were on the market. If you didn't buy them, you're out of luck, for this set is one of the toughest to put together.

*Warning:* There are several variations in the first three series, in which cards were issued with and without a player's name on the front. Cards with the name on the front command a 75 percent premium over the regular price and are identified with an asterisk. In the fourth series, cards existed with a player's name written in script or printed on the back. Cards with printed names command a 75 percent premium as well.

*Avoid:* Bickford, Simmons, Brown, Yost, Raschi, Dark, Cox, Stanky, Roe, Branca, Coleman, and Lopat.

*Tough Call:* Mickey Vernon, Carl Furillo, Dom DiMaggio, Charlie Keller, and Joe Gordon. Vernon put up some pretty interesting numbers over a very long career but was never thought of as a superstar. His two batting titles were major aberrations from the norm, as he was a moderately successful slash hitter the rest of his career. As for Furillo, he has never garnered any serious consideration for enshrinement, but he epitomized the working stiff

appeal of the Dodgers during their final years in Brooklyn. There will always be demand for his cards, but not the kind that sends a rookie skyrocketing. DiMaggio was not "better than his brother, Joe," as the Beantown faithful used to sing. He was a solid all-around player who didn't have enough pop to take advantage of the friendliest ballpark in which a right-handed hitter could have possibly played. Keller was a meteoric slugger who lost time to the war and flamed out a little early, while Gordon was considered one of the two best second basemen in the league when he played. Both of these ex-Yankees could get a second look from the Veterans Committee, but they are the very longest of long shots until more players from the 1940s are voted in.

*Set: $12,500*
*Commons (1–144): $13.50*
*Commons (145–240): $65.00*

| 11 | BOUDREAU | 35.00 | BC |
|-----|-------------|--------|-----|
| 23 | DOERR | 35.00 | BC |
| 24 | MUSIAL | 400.00 | BC |
| 26 | KELL | 30.00 | BC |
| 27 | FELLER | 120.00 | BC |
| 29 | KINER | 70.00 | BC |
| 33 | SPAHN | 120.00 | BC |
| 36 | REESE | 170.00 | BC |
| 46 | ROBERTS | 200.00 | BC |
| 50 | ROBINSON | 675.00 | BC |
| 60 | BERRA | 225.00 | BC |
| 65 | SLAUGHTER | 55.00 | BC |
| 84 | CAMPANELLA | 575.00 | BC |
| 85 | MIZE* | 55.00 | BC |
| 98 | RIZZUTO* | 85.00 | OTF |
| 100 | HODGES | 170.00 | OTF |
| 110 | WYNN | 75.00 | BC |
| 111 | SCHOENDIENST | 50.00 | BC |
| 175 | APPLING | 95.00 | BC |
| 214 | ASHBURN | 300.00 | OTF |
| 224 | PAIGE | 900.00 | BC |
| 226 | SNIDER | 950.00 | BC |
| 233 | DOBY | 100.00 | OTF |
| 238 | LEMON | 150.00 | BC |

**1950 BOWMAN.** Bowman's first color set and its one and only year as the country's sole card manufacturer. This set is attractive but limited by its size. Portraits abound, and the few full-body images issued were so small that they could be anybody. The Williams card in this set, for instance, would probably be worth over $1,000 had Bowman gone with a portrait instead of a miniature swinging Ted.

*Warning:* There are a lot of these cards available in *near mint* condition, so don't pay full price for a card you feel is a shade below this grade.

*Avoid:* Parnell, Zernial, Sievers, Newcombe, Crandall, Mueller, Konstanty, Rosen, and Demars.

*Tough Call:* Leo Durocher. He makes it as a manager, maybe, which doesn't promise much in the way of dramatic appreciation. His cards are already far too expensive.

*Set: $8,000.00*
*Commons (1–72): $37.50*
*Commons (73–252): $13.50*

| | | | |
|-----|-------------|--------|-----|
| 6 | FELLER | 140.00 | BC |
| 8 | KELL | 55.00 | BC |
| 11 | RIZZUTO | 145.00 | OTF |
| 19 | SPAHN | 130.00 | BC |
| 21 | REESE | 170.00 | BC |
| 22 | ROBINSON | 575.00 | BC |
| 32 | ROBERTS | 80.00 | BC |
| 33 | KINER | 90.00 | BC |
| 35 | SLAUGHTER | 80.00 | BC |
| 37 | APPLING | 65.00 | BC |
| 39 | DOBY | 65.00 | OTF |
| 43 | DOERR | 70.00 | BC |
| 46 | BERRA | 300.00 | BC |
| 71 | SCHOENDIENST | 70.00 | BC |
| 75 | CAMPANELLA | 240.00 | BC |
| 77 | SNIDER | 230.00 | BC |
| 84 | ASHBURN | 65.00 | OTF |
| 94 | BOUDREAU | 30.00 | BC |
| 98 | WILLIAMS | 650.00 | BC |
| 112 | HODGES | 75.00 | OTF |
| 139 | MIZE | 50.00 | BC |
| 148 | WYNN | 35.00 | BC |
| 217 | STENGEL | 100.00 | BC |
| 229 | FRISCH | 25.00 | BC |

**1951 TOPPS.** Have you ever met anyone who actually collects these cards? A lot of buyers don't even consider them a regular issue. Yet the price guides continue to publish their dramatic increases and decreases as if dealers were actually selling them. They are, of course, but not in sufficient quantities to warrant a monthly report.

*Warning:* There are actually two sets—one with red backs, the other with blue backs—each consisting of fifty-two cards, with the blue backs much harder to find than the red backs. Tommy Holmes is listed as either playing for Hartford or Boston, with the Boston card being worth about 50 percent more. Gus Zernial is listed as either playing for Philadelphia or Chicago, with the Chicago card worth about 50 percent more.

*Avoid:* Billy Pierce.

## BLUE BACKS

*Set: $1,350.00*
*Commons: $20.00*

| | | | |
|----|--------------|--------|-----|
| 3 | ASHBURN | 95.00 | OTF |
| 6 | SCHOENDIENST | 70.00 | BC |
| 30 | SLAUGHTER | 80.00 | BC |
| 37 | DOERR | 70.00 | BC |
| 50 | MIZE | 100.00 | BC |

## RED BACKS

*Set: $550.00*
*Commons: $5.00*

| | | | |
|----|---------|-------|-----|
| 1 | BERRA | 90.00 | BC |
| 5 | RIZZUTO | 27.50 | OTF |
| 8 | WYNN | 12.50 | BC |
| 15 | KINER | 22.50 | BC |
| 22 | FELLER | 30.00 | BC |
| 30 | SPAHN | 30.00 | BC |
| 31 | HODGES | 25.00 | OTF |
| 38 | SNIDER | 65.00 | BC |
| 50 | IRVIN | 27.50 | BC |

**1951 BOWMAN.** The switch to a larger format was a major improvement, as the paintings, though still a bit flat, gave a better feel of what the players were really like. The Mays and Mantle rookies account for more than half the set's value.

*Warning:* Check the card backs carefully for slight stains. Also, Whitey Ford's card drops to around $275 in *excellent* condition.

*Avoid:* Garagiola, Maglie, Pierce, Law, Woodling, Jensen, Erskine, Burgess, Adcock, and Pramesa.

*Tough Call:* Luke Easter, Jimmy Piersall, and Gene Mauch. Easter was already past his prime when he played with the Indians, but before that he was a major force in the Negro Leagues. There has been some talk recently of electing more players who starred in the hinterlands before blacks were accepted by the majors, and Easter may well turn out to be one of them. Piersall was a very good but not great outfielder who, for a number of reasons, has no hope of entering the Hall of Fame. That card buyers continue to invest in his card—and yes, they are investing—is a complete mystery. Mauch, of course, could get into Cooperstown on his managerial achievements. Which are? You got it: he's never won a thing. Being a good field general for a losing team only counts if you're Erwin Rommel.

*Set: $17,500*
*Commons (1–72): $14.00*
*Commons (73–252): $10.00*
*Commons (253–324): $37.50*

| 1 | FORD | 900.00 | BC |
|---|------|--------|----|
| 2 | BERRA | 380.00 | BC |
| 3 | ROBERTS | 50.00 | BC |
| 7 | HODGES | 65.00 | OTF |
| 10 | SCHOENDIENST | 50.00 | BC |
| 26 | RIZZUTO | 95.00 | OTF |
| 30 | FELLER | 95.00 | BC |
| 31 | CAMPANELLA | 225.00 | BC |
| 32 | SNIDER | 225.00 | BC |
| 46 | KELL | 30.00 | BC |
| 50 | MIZE | 42.50 | BC |
| 53 | LEMON | 35.00 | BC |

| 58 | SLAUGHTER | 40.00 | BC |
|----|-----------|-------|----|
| 62 | BOUDREAU | 30.00 | BC |
| 78 | WYNN | 30.00 | BC |
| 80 | REESE | 120.00 | BC |
| 134 | SPAHN | 95.00 | BC |
| 151 | DOBY | 25.00 | OTF |
| 165 | WILLIAMS | 580.00 | BC |
| 181 | STENGEL | 70.00 | BC |
| 187 | ASHBURN | 35.00 | OTF |
| 198 | IRVIN | 70.00 | BC |
| 232 | FOX | 85.00 | OTF |
| 253 | MANTLE | 8,000.00 | PC |
| 282 | FRISCH | 60.00 | BC |
| 290 | DICKEY | 120.00 | BC |
| 295 | LOPEZ | 57.50 | BC |
| 305 | MAYS | 2,900.00 | PC |

**1952 TOPPS.** There is a distinction that must be made between the cards in this set and the set as a whole. The individual cards are bought and sold by buyers and dealers just like any others. The complete set, however, has become a commodity that is traded outside the hobby by lawyers, doctors, movie stars, and other wealthy people. The Mantle card has become a commodity, too. The price listed below frankly isn't worth the paper on which it is printed, for a '52 Mantle (though not his rookie) is worth whatever someone's willing to pay for it. This may be true of other cards someday—like the 1968 Nolan Ryan—but for now the '52 Mantle is the only one. That said, the only thing you need to know about this set is that it was unique when it was first issued and remains so today. It was the first set of "big" cards, and even forty-one years ago kids knew it. They coddled and protected this set as best they knew how, which accounts for the overall good condition of these cards today.

*Warning:* Do not give these cards the benefit of the doubt if they are in between grades. There are too many 1952 cards around in *excellent* condition to try forcing a *very-good-to-excellent* card into your portfolio. The Johnny Sain and Joe Page cards exist with each others' backs and sell for around $250, but that shouldn't interest you unless you're into errors. As for the Andy Pafko card, it does indeed sell for over $1,000 with razor-sharp edges and perfect corners. Below that condition, however, its price plummets to around $150, which is just too much. The Mathews card, at the other end of the set, is a little easier to find in *near mint* condition, but it, too, drops down—to around $500—in *excellent*. The Billy Loes card may have been short-printed, and carries a 75 percent premium. Meanwhile, three cards in the rare last series had to be double-printed to fill out sheets. It's no coincidence that Mantle, Jackie Robinson, and Bobby Thomson—the most popular player on each of the New York teams— were chosen for this "honor."

*Avoid:* Loes, Woodling, Jensen, Houk, Patko, Garagiola, Black, McDougald, Nuxhall, and Davey and Dick Williams.

*Tough Call:* Billy Martin, Dick Groat, and Minnie Minoso. It's a shame Martin's gone, but he wasn't headed for enshrinement anyway. Some say what he was headed for was exactly what happened to him. At any rate, the buyer demand that boosted his card prices over the last decade has already started to subside; it's just that the dealers haven't bothered to inform the people who publish the price guides. If you've got Martin cards, keep them for old times' sake. But for goodness' sake, don't buy any more at their current levels. As for Groat, he was never, ever considered the best shortstop in the league when he played, despite his MVP award in 1960. His career numbers don't quite entitle him to a bronze plaque, so it would be a major miracle if the Hall of Fame ever opens its doors to him. Minoso was not considered a superstar, either. In fact, until Bill Veeck started trotting him out once a decade, no one considered his cards anything other than commons. A comparable player from today would be someone like Willie McGee or Bip Roberts, and the only way those guys are going to Cooperstown is on the bus with everyone else.

Set: $70,000.00
Commons (81–250): $17.50
Commons (311–407): $120.00
All Others: $35.00

| 11 | RIZZUTO | 160.00 | OTF |
|---|---|---|---|
| 26 | IRVIN | 85.00 | BC |
| 33 | SPAHN | 190.00 | BC |
| 36 | HODGES | 160.00 | OTF |
| 37 | SNIDER | 250.00 | BC |
| 59 | ROBERTS | 100.00 | BC |
| 65 | SLAUGHTER | 100.00 | BC |
| 88 | FELLER | 120.00 | BC |
| 91 | SCHOENDIENST | 60.00 | BC |
| 129 | MIZE | 70.00 | BC |
| 191 | BERRA | 365.00 | BC |
| 216 | ASHBURN | 75.00 | OTF |
| 246 | KELL | 60.00 | BC |
| 261 | MAYS | 1,950.00 | PC |
| 268 | LEMON | 120.00 | BC |
| 277 | WYNN | 120.00 | BC |
| 311 | MANTLE | 27,500.00 | PC |
| 312 | ROBINSON | 975.00 | BC |
| 314 | CAMPANELLA | 1,600.00 | BC |
| 333 | REESE | 975.00 | BC |
| 392 | WILHELM | 500.00 | BC |
| 394 | HERMAN | 200.00 | BC |
| 400 | DICKEY | 525.00 | BC |
| 407 | MATHEWS | 1,900.00 | BC |

**1952 BOWMAN.** This set was, in a sense, the beginning of the end for Bowman. Topps blew kids away with its larger format, real photos, statistics, and 155 more cards—and Bowman suddenly found itself playing catch-up. It wasn't that these cards weren't attractive. Indeed, Bowman improved the sharpness of its illustrations and came up with the novel idea of putting facsimile signatures on the fronts of its cards. Unfortunately, Topps used the autograph idea, too, but did it bigger and better. How did kids react? Well, throughout the 1960s you could still find unopened boxes of 1952 Bowmans, and wax packs were still floating around at shows in the early 1970s. Apparently, a lot of candy store owners didn't unload all their Bowmans in 1952.

*Warning:* Keep an eye out for printing imperfections—double images, streaks, lines, etc.—and check the backs for slight stains.

*Avoid:* Friend, McMillan, Crosetti, Loes, and Burdette.

*Tough Call:* Same players as in the Topps set.

*Set: $7,500.00*
*Commons (1–72): $13.50*
*Commons (73–216): $10.00*
*Commons (217–252): $20.00*

| 1 | BERRA | 400.00 | BC |
|---|---|---|---|
| 4 | ROBERTS | 47.50 | BC |
| 8 | REESE | 87.50 | BC |
| 11 | KINER | 50.00 | BC |
| 21 | FOX | 30.00 | OTF |
| 23 | LEMON | 42.50 | BC |
| 30 | SCHOENDIENST | 42.50 | BC |
| 43 | FELLER | 95.00 | BC |
| 44 | CAMPANELLA | 165.00 | BC |
| 52 | RIZZUTO | 75.00 | OTF |
| 53 | ASHBURN | 37.50 | OTF |
| 75 | KELL | 27.50 | BC |
| 80 | HODGES | 60.00 | OTF |
| 101 | MANTLE | 2,200.00 | PC |
| 116 | SNIDER | 150.00 | BC |
| 142 | WYNN | 37.50 | BC |
| 145 | MIZE | 45.00 | BC |
| 156 | SPAHN | 80.00 | BC |
| 162 | IRVIN | 32.50 | BC |
| 196 | MUSIAL | 400.00 | BC |
| 217 | STENGEL | 120.00 | BC |
| 218 | MAYS | 950.00 | BC |
| 232 | SLAUGHTER | 70.00 | BC |

**1953 TOPPS.** In many respects this set is much more attractive than the fabled 1952 set. The paintings are bold and beautiful and capture the players' personalities far better than the two-dimensional renderings produced by Bowman from 1950 to 1952. Notice the innocent looks of the young players and the relaxed confidence of the veterans. It's no wonder that Topps chose this set as the basis for its 1991 Archives issue. Unfortunately, these cards didn't hold up very well. You'll be hard-pressed to find *near mint* examples, much less *mint* ones. Part of the reason for this may be that kids mixed them in with the slightly slimmer Bowman cards issued

that year, causing the side damage that seems to be so prevalent. This would certainly explain why the 1953 Bowmans exist in much better overall condition.

*Warning:* There are a lot of double prints in this set, most notably the Robinson, Campanella, Mathews, Feller, Irvin, Mize, Reynolds, Woodling, and Dom DiMaggio cards. There were also some short prints, including the Early Wynn card.

*Avoid:* Carey, Cerv, Gilliam, Haddix, and Milt Bolling.

*Tough Call:* Roy Face. He was the original. The late-inning guy with the trick pitch. And for a decade he was the best. Once the Reardons, Eckersleys, Gossages, and Smiths are all in Cooperstown, the Veterans Committee may take a look at Elroy and give him his due. If you are a true believer, then this is the card you want—but not for more than $60.

*Set: $14,000.00*
*Commons (1–220): $16.50*
*Double Prints (1–220): $10.00*
*Commons (221–280): $55.00*
*Double Prints (221–280): $25.00*

| 1 | ROBINSON | 475.00 | BC |
|---|---|---|---|
| 27 | CAMPANELLA | 150.00 | BC |
| 37 | MATHEWS | 65.50 | BC |
| 41 | SLAUGHTER | 65.00 | BC |
| 54 | FELLER | 65.00 | BC |
| 61 | WYNN | 70.00 | BC |
| 62 | IRVIN | 25.00 | BC |
| 76 | REESE | 140.00 | BC |
| 77 | MIZE | 35.00 | BC |
| 78 | SCHOENDIENST | 42.50 | BC |
| 82 | MANTLE | 2,900.00 | PC |
| 104 | BERRA | 235.00 | BC |
| 114 | RIZZUTO | 95.00 | OTF |
| 138 | KELL | 37.50 | BC |
| 147 | SPAHN | 95.00 | BC |
| 151 | WILHELM | 45.00 | BC |
| 191 | KINER | 47.50 | BC |
| 207 | FORD | 120.00 | BC |
| 220 | PAIGE | 375.00 | BC |

| 228 | NEWHOUSER | 85.00 | BC |
| 244 | MAYS | 2,100.00 | PC |

## 1953 BOWMAN COLOR.

From desperation came the most beautiful card set of the postwar era. Bowman switched to a larger format and spent a bundle on photography and printing to come up with these stunning color cards. A popular theory is that a hundred years from now these cards will be a major information resource for baseball scholars. Of course, you'll be dead in a hundred years, so whatever these scholars will be willing to pay for '53 Bowmans won't do you a lick of good. The only flaw in this set is that Bowman couldn't afford to sign some superstars, many of whom inked exclusive deals with Topps.

*Warning:* If you stare at these cards too long, you won't get any work done.

*Avoid:* The usual. Rosen, Erskine, Jensen, Raschi, Minoso, etc. There are no tempting rookies in this set.

*Tough Call:* Same as 1953 Topps.

*Set: $9,500.00*
*Commons (1–112): $25.00*
*Commons (113–160): $37.50*

| 9 | RIZZUTO | 95.00 | OTF |
| 10 | ASHBURN | 65.00 | OTF |
| 18 | FOX | 47.50 | OTF |
| 32 | MUSIAL | 450.00 | BC |
| 33 | REESE | 375.00 | BC |
| 44 | MANTLE, BERRA, & BAUER | 400.00 | PC |
| 46 | CAMPANELLA | 220.00 | BC |
| 51 | IRVIN | 40.00 | BC |
| 57 | BOUDREAU | 30.00 | BC |
| 59 | MANTLE | 2,300.00 | PC |
| 61 | KELL | 40.00 | BC |
| 65 | ROBERTS | 65.00 | BC |
| 80 | KINER | 67.50 | BC |
| 81 | SLAUGHTER | 55.00 | BC |
| 92 | HODGES | 95.00 | OTF |
| 93 | RIZZUTO & MARTIN | 180.00 | OTF |

| 97 | MATHEWS | 140.00 | BC |
| 99 | SPAHN | 135.00 | BC |
| 101 | SCHOENDIENST | 67.50 | BC |
| 114 | FELLER | 285.00 | BC |
| 117 | SNIDER | 500.00 | BC |
| 121 | BERRA | 450.00 | BC |
| 143 | LOPEZ | 45.00 | BC |
| 146 | WYNN | 85.00 | BC |
| 153 | FORD | 375.00 | BC |

## 1953 BOWMAN B&W.

This 64-card black-and-white set was Bowman's last gasp to catch up with Topps's 274-card issue. The cards are intriguing, as well as scarce, but outside of the obvious players, buyer interest has always been lukewarm.

*Warning:* Don't start buying commons unless you plan on finishing the set. They are very pricey.

*Avoid:* Vinegar Bend Mizell and Stu Miller, as if you didn't know.

*Tough Call:* Same as the 1953 Topps.

*Set: $1,800.00*
*Commons: $20.00*

| 15 | MIZE | 95.00 | BC |
| 27 | LEMON | 90.00 | BC |
| 28 | WILHELM | 95.00 | BC |
| 39 | STENGEL | 265.00 | BC |

## 1954 TOPPS.

If you like head shots, look no further. This set is lousy with them. The card backs are actually more interesting than the fronts! Still, two Ted Williams cards and the Banks, Kaline, and Aaron rookies make a pretty good poker hand.

*Warning:* These cards tend to scuff easily, so check carefully for even the most minute amount of surface wear. Also, watch the centering, especially from top to bottom.

*Avoid:* Kuenn, Turley, and Skowron.

*Tough Call:* Tommy LaSorda. It is entirely conceivable that he'll be voted into the Hall of Fame and, like it or not, this is the man's only major-issue baseball card. It has risen from the status of common to its current $130 price tag based solely on his run with the Dodgers. Where he goes after that—and how much card buyers see of him—may determine the future direction of this card. Keep two things in mind: Walt Alston's rookie card can be had for $30, and diet commercials don't count as continued exposure.

Set: $7,200.00
Commons (51–75): $18.50
All Others: $8.50

| 1 | WILLIAMS | 475.00 | BC |
|---|---|---|---|
| 3 | IRVIN | 20.00 | BC |
| 10 | ROBINSON | 240.00 | BC |
| 17 | RIZZUTO | 60.00 | OTF |
| 20 | SPAHN | 80.00 | BC |
| 30 | MATHEWS | 70.00 | BC |
| 32 | SNIDER | 115.00 | BC |
| 36 | WILHELM | 27.50 | BC |
| 37 | FORD | 90.00 | BC |
| 45 | ASHBURN | 25.00 | OTF |
| 50 | BERRA | 190.00 | BC |
| 86 | HERMAN | 15.00 | BC |
| 90 | MAYS | 425.00 | BC |
| 94 | BANKS | 625.00 | BC |
| 102 | HODGES | 70.00 | OTF |
| 128 | AARON | 1,700.00 | PC |
| 183 | COMBS | 15.00 | BC |
| 187 | MANUSH | 15.00 | BC |
| 201 | KALINE | 700.00 | BC |
| 250 | WILLIAMS | 500.00 | BC |

**1954 BOWMAN.** Whoever came up with the idea for the 1953 set must have been fired and replaced by someone's nephew, who worked all night to come up with the concept for these cards. A strong contender for the lackluster set of all time, the 1954 Bowmans were trounced that year by a Topps set that wasn't much better. The cards feature players in various unnatural poses, with facsimile autographs in little boxes identifying who they are. Apparently, Bowman couldn't even round up all the signatures it needed, for several players are identified by plain block lettering. You'd think that some enterprising young artist would have scrawled out these names on a piece of paper and tried to fudge it. Worst of all, the inks chosen to

reproduce the colors for players' faces made them look like they'd been embalmed! This set was so unpopular at the time that, as with the 1952 set, there were plenty of unopened boxes lying around well into the 1960s.

*Warning:* Because kids never laid their hands on these cards, a lot of them are still in perfect condition. Think twice before paying *any* premium for *mint* cards. As for variations, a minor one exists on Dave Philley's card, but no buyer has had this on his hit list for years. Also, the Ted Williams card had to be pulled early in the print run and was replaced with a Jimmy Piersall card. The scarce Williams, which is not considered part of the issue, is actually worth as much as the entire set!

*Avoid:* Don Larsen.
*Tough Call:* Same as the 1954 Topps set.

Set: $3,250.00
Commons: $7.50

| 1 | RIZZUTO | 85.00 | OTF |
|---|---|---|---|
| 15 | ASHBURN | 25.00 | OTF |
| 45 | KINER | 30.00 | BC |
| 50 | KELL | 17.50 | BC |
| 57 | WILHELM | 20.00 | BC |
| 58 | REESE | 60.00 | BC |
| 62 | SLAUGHTER | 27.50 | BC |
| 64 | MATHEWS | 50.00 | BC |
| 65 | MANTLE | 750.00 | BC |
| 66 | WILLIAMS | 3,800.00 | PC |
| 89 | MAYS | 300.00 | BC |
| 90 | CAMPANELLA | 95.00 | BC |
| 95 | ROBERTS | 25.00 | BC |
| 110 | SCHOENDIENST | 22.50 | BC |
| 132 | FELLER | 67.50 | BC |
| 138 | HODGES | 52.50 | OTF |
| 161 | BERRA | 140.00 | BC |
| 164 | WYNN | 32.50 | BC |
| 170 | SNIDER | 120.00 | BC |
| 177 | FORD | 85.00 | BC |
| 196 | LEMON | 32.50 | BC |

**1955 TOPPS.** A tiny and expensive set, in some ways it is Topps's most beautiful. The cards had wonderful sheen when they came out of the packs—and many cards have survived to this day with that original gloss still intact. The border war with Bowman hit its peak by 1955, with Topps having superstars Ted Williams, Jackie Robinson, Warren Spahn, and Duke Snider in its arsenal, to counter its rival's stronger stable of Roy Campanella, Pee Wee Reese, Early Wynn, Whitey Ford, Enos Slaughter, Richie Ashburn, Bob Feller, Robin Roberts, Ralph Kiner, and Mickey Mantle. It's no wonder Bowman was going broke. Imagine the chaos that would ensue today if Fleer had exclusive deals with Barry Bonds and Ken Griffey, Donruss had exclusive deals with Juan Gonzales and Roger Clemens, and so on.

*Warning:* If a card does not have the aforementioned gloss, it cannot grade better than *near mint.* Also, don't look for cards 175, 186, 203, and 209. They were pulled by Topps and "replaced" by double-printed cards of Jim Pearce, Frank Baumholtz, Harry Perkowski, and Charlie Silvera.

*Avoid:* Amoros, Mossi, Spooner, Zimmer, Tanner, and Harry Agganis.

*Tough Call:* Ken Boyer. His relatively short life as a productive hitter is the only thing that's kept him out of Cooperstown. Once Kell was voted in, a lot of buyers began investing in this card, but so far Boyer's been shut out. At $50, his rookie card may not be worth the risk.

*Set: $6,300.00*
*Commons (1–150): $5.50*
*Commons (151–210): $17.50*

| | | | |
|---|---|---|---|
| 2 | WILLIAMS | 380.00 | BC |
| 4 | KALINE | 195.00 | BC |
| 24 | NEWHOUSER | 12.50 | BC |
| 28 | BANKS | 180.00 | BC |
| 31 | SPAHN | 60.00 | BC |
| 47 | AARON | 325.00 | BC |
| 50 | ROBINSON | 220.00 | BC |
| 100 | IRVIN | 17.50 | BC |
| 123 | KOUFAX | 1,200.00 | PC |
| 124 | KILLEBREW | 240.00 | BC |
| 155 | MATHEWS | 87.50 | BC |

| | | | |
|---|---|---|---|
| 164 | CLEMENTE | 1,200.00 | BC |
| 187 | HODGES | 120.00 | OTF |
| 189 | RIZZUTO | 115.00 | BC |
| 194 | MAYS | 475.00 | BC |
| 198 | BERRA | 200.00 | BC |
| 210 | SNIDER | 400.00 | BC |

**1955 BOWMAN.** Bowman's swan-song set has turned out to be a winner. In its final push to outdo Topps, the company resorted to the appliance of the future—color TV. The ploy worked. Kids responded. And a war wagon of superstars kept the company afloat for a good part of the summer. By the last series, however, Bowman had run out of ideas and started to print cards of umpires, platoon players, and unknown rookies. Yet nearly four decades later, the set still has legs. People outside the business love the funky color TV motif, and the same kids who threw away the umpires in 1955 are now buying them back for up to $75 apiece. It's too bad Topps decided to reintroduce the Bowman name in 1989. Beating this dead horse saddened a lot of longtime collectors.

*Warning:* Check carefully for good centering, and steer clear of fuzzy, out-of-register images. Look for corner wear—it's not always obvious upon quick inspection. There are five misspelled names in this set, including Harvey Kuenn's, that were corrected very late. The corrected versions of cards 48, 101, 157, and 204—not the errors—are worth double the price of common cards. Erv Palica's card with a traded line is also worth double the price of a common card.

*Avoid:* Temple, Zimmer, Narleski, Lary, Skowron, Neal, Virdon, Malzone, and George Susce.

*Tough Call:* Ironically, the umpires. They are novelty cards, as proved by the abject failure of a recently produced umpires set. Still, some of these guys are Hall of Famers. Ultimately, it comes down to a matter of personal choice. As for players, Elston Howard is a tough one. Casey Stengel never found a regular position for Ellie, a devastating young talent who was far too good to be platooned. Some claim that race was at issue. Who knows? Howard was a marvelous player for the Yankees into his mid-thirties and surprised everyone with his MVP season in 1963. Four years later, he inspired a team of no-names to Boston's first pennant in over twenty years. But Howard's final numbers simply did not impress the Hall of Fame voters, and it's unlikely they ever will.

*Set: $4,800.00*
*Commons (1–224): $5.00*
*Commons (225–320): $12.50*

| | | | |
|---|---|---|---|
| 1 | WILHELM | 55.00 | BC |
| 10 | RIZZUTO | 40.00 | OTF |
| 22 | CAMPANELLA | 85.00 | BC |
| 23 | KALINE | 110.00 | BC |
| 29 | SCHOENDIENST | 17.50 | BC |
| 37 | REESE | 57.50 | BC |
| 38 | WYNN | 17.50 | BC |
| 59 | FORD | 55.00 | BC |
| 60 | SLAUGHTER | 17.50 | BC |
| 89 | BOUDREAU | 12.50 | BC |
| 103 | MATHEWS | 42.50 | BC |
| 130 | ASHBURN | 15.00 | OTF |
| 134 | FELLER | 50.00 | BC |
| 158 | HODGES | 32.50 | OTF |
| 171 | ROBERTS | 17.50 | BC |
| 179 | AARON | 190.00 | BC |
| 184 | MAYS | 190.00 | BC |
| 191 | LEMON | 17.50 | BC |
| 197 | KINER | 20.00 | BC |
| 202 | MANTLE | 475.00 | BC |
| 213 | KELL | 12.50 | BC |
| 242 | BANKS | 290.00 | BC |
| 308 | LOPEZ | 30.00 | BC |

**1956 TOPPS.** A beautiful set that's easy—albeit expensive—to put together. The purchase of competitor Bowman meant that Topps owned the card contracts to virtually ever player and for the first time could issue a set that included all of the day's major stars.

*Warning:* There are a lot of fuzzy-cut borders in this set. Even if a card is otherwise perfect, pay no more than the *near mint* price—lower, if the cut is really bad. There are two unnumbered checklists

in this set, each of which sells for around $150. Cards from the first two series come with white or gray backs, with no premium for either (although the white backs are preferable from the standpoint of aesthetics). The cards of Ken Boyer, Ernie Banks, and Jackie Robinson were double-printed, so be choosy about condition. Finally, the team cards of the Braves, Orioles, Cubs, Phillies, Indians, and Reds exist with a 1955 date, and these sell for around $45.

*Avoid:* Craig, Score, Howard, Larsen, and Charlie Neal.

*Tough Call:* Walter Alston. Sure, he's in the Hall of Fame, but where's his card going? If you have a thing for older men, then grab Walt's "rookie" card—it's the only one of him in a Brooklyn uniform.

*Set: $6,900.00*
*Commons (1–100): $5.00*
*Commons (101–340): $9.00*

| | | | |
|---|---|---|---|
| 5 | WILLIAMS | 270.00 | BC |
| 10 | SPAHN | 65.00 | BC |
| 15 | BANKS | 75.00 | BC |
| 20 | KALINE | 90.00 | BC |
| 30 | ROBINSON | 120.00 | BC |
| 31 | AARON | 220.00 | BC |
| 33 | CLEMENTE | 320.00 | BC |
| 79 | KOUFAX | 320.00 | BC |
| 101 | CAMPANELLA | 100.00 | BC |
| 107 | MATHEWS | 50.00 | BC |
| 109 | SLAUGHTER | 22.50 | BC |
| 110 | BERRA | 110.00 | BC |
| 113 | RIZZUTO | 47.50 | OTF |
| 120 | ASHBURN | 25.00 | OTF |
| 130 | MAYS | 300.00 | BC |
| 135 | MANTLE | 950.00 | PC |
| 145 | HODGES | 40.00 | OTF |
| 150 | SNIDER | 110.00 | BC |
| 164 | KILLEBREW | 110.00 | B C |
| 165 | SCHOENDIENST | 22.50 | BC |
| 166 | DODGERS TEAM | 145.00 | BC |
| 180 | ROBERTS | 25.00 | BC |
| 187 | WYNN | 25.00 | BC |

| 194 | IRVIN | 22.50 | BC |
| 195 | KELL | 20.00 | BC |
| 200 | FELLER | 110.00 | BC |
| 240 | FORD | 120.00 | BC |
| 251 | YANKEES | 165.00 | BC |
| 255 | LEMON | 22.50 | BC |
| 260 | REESE | 120.00 | BC |
| 292 | APARICIO | 110.00 | BC |
| 307 | WILHELM | 25.00 | BC |
| | CHECKLISTS | 150.00 | BC |

**1957 TOPPS.** Topps had the market to itself by 1957 and decided it was safe to reduce costs by reducing the size of its cards to what is now considered the standard 2½″ x 3½″ size. Did kids feel cheated? A little. But Topps treated them to sixty-seven more cards, a lot of colorful, full-body poses, and a contest where they could win television sets and other prizes. Now, of course, this set is regarded as a masterpiece. It doesn't compare with the 1953 Bowman set—many of the images are grainy and dark—but it's still quite nice. This was also the last set to feature the Brooklyn Dodgers and the New York Giants.

*Warning:* Several cards in the scarce fourth series were double-printed, including Podres, Koufax, and Kubek. Gene Baker's error card is extremely rare and sells for between $150 and $250. There are five known contest cards for which you should not pay more than $10. There are also four expensive cards for checklist collectors, which are listed below. Finally, don't get too excited if you come across a Hank Aaron card that has him batting left-handed—they're all that way.

*Avoid:* Herzog, McDaniel, Terry, Kubek, and Clete Boyer.

*Tough Call:* Rocky Colavito and Bobby Richardson. Had either or both been elected to the Hall of Fame already, no one would be screaming. They were both terrific players. Colavito had immense power and a rocket throwing arm, but flamed out in the mid-1960s. Richardson was probably the best second baseman of his era—Nellie Fox was getting old by then—but his era only lasted about eight years, due to injuries. If the Veterans Com-

mittee is feeling generous, Colavito could get in. For now, pass on his rookie card unless you come across it for $75 or less.

*Set: $6,750.00*
*Commons (265–352): $13.50*
*Double Prints (265–352): $7.50*
*All Others: $3.75*

| 1 | WILLIAMS | 350.00 | BC |
| 2 | BERRA | 120.00 | BC |
| 7 | APARICIO | 25.00 | BC |
| 10 | MAYS | 190.00 | BC |
| 15 | ROBERTS | 15.00 | BC |
| 18 | DRYSDALE | 200.00 | BC |
| 20 | AARON | 200.00 | BC |
| 24 | MAZEROSKI | 45.00 | OTF |
| 25 | FORD | 50.00 | BC |
| 30 | REESE | 52.50 | BC |
| 35 | F. ROBINSON | 220.00 | BC |
| 38 | FOX | 15.00 | OTF |
| 40 | WYNN | 15.00 | BC |
| 55 | BANKS | 85.00 | BC |
| 70 | ASHBURN | 15.00 | OTF |
| 76 | CLEMENTE | 190.00 | BC |
| 80 | HODGES | 40.00 | OTF |
| 90 | SPAHN | 55.00 | BC |
| 95 | MANTLE | 825.00 | BC |
| 120 | LEMON | 15.00 | BC |
| 125 | KALINE | 75.00 | BC |
| 154 | SCHOENDIENST | 15.00 | BC |
| 170 | SNIDER | 87.50 | BC |
| 203 | WILHELM | 15.00 | BC |
| 210 | CAMPANELLA | 80.00 | BC |
| 215 | SLAUGHTER | 17.50 | BC |
| 230 | KELL | 12.50 | BC |
| 250 | MATHEWS | 30.00 | BC |
| 302 | KOUFAX | 300.00 | BC |
| 324 | DODGERS TEAM | 80.00 | BC |
| 328 | B. ROBINSON | 335.00 | PC |
| 338 | BUNNING | 120.00 | OTF |
| 400 | DODGERS SLUGGERS | 185.00 | BC |
| 407 | YANKS POWER HITTERS | 325.00 | BC |

| CHECKLIST ½ | 150.00 | BC |
|---|---|---|
| CHECKLIST ⅔ | 225.00 | BC |
| CHECKLIST ¾ | 450.00 | BC |
| CHECKLIST ⅘ | 550.00 | BC |

**1958 TOPPS.** Bowwow. Considering how lovely Topps's 1957 set was, this effort can only be considered atrocious. It had to be a cost-cutting measure, because the same person who approved the previous year's design could not have looked at the 1958 set and honestly thought it was a fitting follow-up. Worse, the company produced dozens of hard-to-find variations in this set, none of which anyone has much interest in collecting.

*Warning:* Dealers generally don't pay more than $5 to $10 for the various yellow name and yellow team variations, and they almost always have a hard time selling them. If you're going to spend money on these variations, stick to the Blue Chip cards and don't pay more than a 30 percent premium. Cards with these variations are identified below with an asterisk. The team cards in this set exist with variations, too, most notably the Braves, Tigers, Orioles, and Reds (or "Redlegs," as they were known during the Cold War). Each of these four team cards normally has an alphabetical checklist on the back and sells for under $10; a numerical checklist, however, boosts its price to $50. A very hard-to-price variation exists on Pancho Herrera's card. The card with his name spelled "Herrer" was pulled and corrected almost immediately, and it sells for anywhere between $175 and $600. Finally, just as in the 1957 set, steer clear of the contest cards unless you can find them for $10 or less. Finally, be aware that the All-Star cards (Topps's first ever) are not considered high numbers, even though they fall at the end of the set. They were issued all year long, and there seem to be three or four Mantle and Musial cards for every other All-Star.

*Avoid:* McCormick, Roseboro, Siebern, Throneberry, Duren, Lau, and Flood.

*Tough Call:* Orlando Cepeda and Vada Pinson. Both players produced well into the 1970s and did everything that Hall of Fame voters like. The problem is that neither did quite enough. Pinson wound things up as a part-timer for a rising Royals team and fell just short of 3,000 hits. Cepeda's knees betrayed him just as he started to take aim at the Green Monster in Fenway. The knock on Pinson is that he was never considered a superstar; the case against Cepeda has more to do with a drug conviction than anything else. If you're looking for a couple of dark horses, these could be the guys—but keep your total investment for their two rookie cards under $60.

*Set: $4,500.00*
*Commons (1–110): $4.75*
*Commons (111–495): $2.25*

| 1 | WILLIAMS | 250.00 | BC |
|---|---|---|---|
| 2 | LEMON* | 12.50 | BC |
| 5 | MAYS | 150.00 | BC |
| 25 | DRYSDALE | 60.00 | BC |
| 30 | AARON* | 160.00 | BC |
| 40 | KELL | 7.50 | BC |
| 47 | MARIS | 350.00 | PC |
| 52 | CLEMENTE* | 140.00 | BC |
| 70 | KALINE | 60.00 | BC |
| 85 | APARICIO* | 17.50 | BC |
| 88 | SNIDER | 60.00 | BC |
| 90 | ROBERTS | 12.50 | BC |
| 100 | WYNN* | 12.50 | BC |
| 115 | BUNNING | 12.50 | OTF |
| 142 | SLAUGHTER | 15.00 | BC |
| 150 | MANTLE | 485.00 | BC |
| 162 | HODGES | 17.50 | OTF |
| 187 | KOUFAX | 160.00 | BC |
| 190 | SCHOENDIENST | 12.50 | BC |
| 230 | ASHBURN | 10.00 | OTF |
| 238 | MAZEROSKI | 10.00 | OTF |
| 270 | SPAHN | 37.50 | BC |
| 285 | F. ROBINSON | 67.50 | BC |
| 288 | KILLEBREW | 60.00 | BC |
| 307 | B. ROBINSON | 85.00 | BC |
| 310 | BANKS | 70.00 | BC |
| 314 | BOSS & POWER | 15.00 | BC |
| 320 | FORD | 32.50 | BC |
| 321 | SLUGGERS SUPREME | 25.00 | BC |

| 324 | WILHELM | 12.50 | BC |
|---|---|---|---|
| 351 | BRAVES FENCE BUSTERS | 15.00 | BC |
| 370 | BERRA | 80.00 | BC |
| 375 | REESE | 42.50 | BC |
| 400 | FOX | 10.00 | OTF |
| 418 | BATTING FOES | 130.00 | BC |
| 424 | DOBY | 5.00 | OTF |
| 436 | FENCE BUSTERS | 47.50 | BC |
| 440 | MATHEWS | 27.50 | BC |
| 476 | MUSIAL ALL-STAR | 20.00 | BC |
| 485 | WILLIAMS ALL-STAR | 55.00 | BC |
| 486 | MAYS ALL-STAR | 37.50 | BC |
| 487 | MANTLE ALL-STAR | 70.00 | BC |
| 488 | AARON ALL-STAR | 40.00 | BC |

**1959 TOPPS.** Some love the "ace in the hole" design of this set; others hate it. It is, for lack of a more descriptive phrase, "very fifties." The cards in this set have held up well over the years, including the last series, which offers only three players of consequence outside of the All-Star subset. There is a grainy highlight subset (which has never really caught on with buyers) and a number of intriguingly titled cards featuring multiple players (which have).

*Warning:* For anyone dying to throw away $75, the cards of Ralph Lumenti, Bob Giallombardo, Harry Hanebrink, Billy Loes, Willard Nixon, and Dolan Nichols are available without "option" or "traded."

*Avoid:* Osteen, Wagner, Stuart, Cuellar, Allison, Blanchard, Callison, Fairly, Deron Johnson, Bill White, and Felipe Alou.

*Tough Call:* Sparky Anderson and Norm Cash. Anderson will probably make the Hall of Fame on his managing record, but Hall of Fame managers are rarely in demand. The movement on Sparky's rookie card thus far has been in anticipation of his enshrinement, but where does the card go after that? Try "down." If you must own a Sparky rookie, try not to cough up more than $20. As for Cash, he probably deserves to be in the Hall of Fame. He was arguably the most consistent first sacker in the league while he played, and he put up some pretty good numbers. Ironically, his breakthrough 1961 season may have submarined his chances at Cooperstown, because everyone expected him to hit .361 again. Don't hold your breath, but don't totally give up hope. In the meantime, steer clear of his 1959 rookie unless you can steal it away for less than $40.

*Set: $4,200.00*
*Commons (1–110): $4.00*
*Commons (111–506): $2.00*
*Commons (507–572): $9.00*

| 10 | MANTLE | 375.00 | BC |
|---|---|---|---|
| 20 | SNIDER | 47.50 | BC |
| 30 | FOX | 7.50 | OTF |
| 40 | SPAHN | 40.00 | BC |
| 50 | MAYS | 125.00 | BC |
| 149 | BUNNING | 7.50 | OTF |
| 150 | MUSIAL | 125.00 | BC |
| 155 | SLAUGHTER | 12.50 | BC |
| 163 | KOUFAX | 130.00 | BC |
| 180 | BERRA | 70.00 | BC |
| 202 | MARIS | 120.00 | OTF |
| 212 | FENCE BUSTERS | 30.00 | BC |
| 260 | WYNN | 10.00 | BC |
| 270 | HODGES | 12.50 | OTF |
| 300 | ASHBURN | 7.50 | OTF |
| 310 | APARICIO | 12.50 | BC |
| 317 | HITTING KINGS | 15.00 | OTF |
| 349 | WILHELM | 12.50 | BC |
| 350 | BANKS | 55.00 | BC |
| 352 | ROBERTS | 12.50 | BC |
| 360 | KALINE | 47.50 | BC |
| 380 | AARON | 95.00 | BC |
| 387 | DRYSDALE | 27.50 | BC |
| 408 | KEYSTONE COMBO | 5.00 | OTF |
| 415 | MAZEROSKI | 5.00 | OTF |
| 430 | FORD | 30.00 | BC |
| 435 | F. ROBINSON | 37.50 | BC |
| 439 | B. ROBINSON | 42.50 | BC |
| 450 | MATHEWS | 22.50 | BC |
| 461 | HILITE: MANTLE | 30.00 | BC |
| 478 | CLEMENTE | 87.50 | BC |

| | | | |
|---|---|---|---|
| 480 | SCHOENDIENST | 10.00 | BC |
| 514 | GIBSON | 325.00 | BC |
| 515 | KILLEBREW | 100.00 | BC |
| 543 | CORSAIR TRIO | 45.00 | BC |
| 550 | CAMPANELLA | 100.00 | BC |
| 552 | STENGEL ALL-STAR | 22.50 | BC |
| 555 | MAZEROSKI ALL-STAR | 15.00 | OTF |
| 556 | FOX ALL-STAR | 15.00 | OTF |
| 559 | BANKS ALL-STAR | 37.50 | BC |
| 560 | APARICIO ALL-STAR | 20.00 | BC |
| 561 | AARON ALL-STAR | 90.00 | BC |
| 562 | KALINE ALL-STAR | 37.50 | BC |
| 563 | MAYS ALL-STAR | 90.00 | BC |
| 564 | MANTLE ALL-STAR | 240.00 | BC |
| 571 | SPAHN ALL-STAR | 25.00 | BC |

**1960 TOPPS.** Topps returned to the horizontal format for a year, and then never again issued a major set with this orientation. McCovey, Yastrzemski, and of course, Mantle carry this set, which isn't all that easy to find in collectible condition.

*Warning:* Because of the horizontal format, many cards incurred slight damage as a result of kids turning them sideways right out of the packs. Check for hairlines on even the best-looking cards.

*Avoid:* Tommy Davis, Dallas Green, and Jim Gentile.

*Tough Call:* Frank Howard and Jim Kaat. Howard's home run totals were definitely held back by the rules changes that favored pitchers in the 1960s. Unfortunately, home runs are what the Hall of Fame voters look for when evaluating a slugger like Frank. Kaat's chances will improve if people like Tommy John, Don Sutton, and Bert Blyleven are voted in. Like them, he pitched forever and racked up a lot of wins. Unlike them, however, he was a truly dominant pitcher for a couple of years. If you want to play a hunch, don't play it with his $25 1960 card—his 1964 and 1972 cards cost a third as much and are just as hard to find.

*Set: $3,300.00*
*Commons (1–506): $2.25*
*Commons (507–572): $7.50*

| | | | |
|---|---|---|---|
| 1 | WYNN | 22.50 | BC |
| 10 | BANKS | 37.50 | BC |
| 28 | B. ROBINSON | 42.50 | BC |
| 35 | FORD | 32.50 | BC |
| 50 | KALINE | 37.50 | BC |
| 55 | MAZEROSKI | 3.75 | OTF |
| 73 | GIBSON | 50.00 | BC |
| 100 | FOX | 6.00 | OTF |
| 148 | YASTRZEMSKI | 275.00 | BC |
| 160 | RIVAL ALL-STARS | 32.50 | BC |
| 200 | MAYS | 95.00 | BC |
| 210 | KILLEBREW | 20.00 | BC |
| 227 | STENGEL | 12.50 | BC |
| 240 | APARICIO | 10.00 | BC |
| 250 | MUSIAL | 80.00 | BC |
| 264 | ROBERTS | 10.00 | BC |
| 295 | HODGES | 12.50 | OTF |
| 300 | AARON | 100.00 | BC |
| 305 | ASHBURN | 5.00 | OTF |
| 316 | MCCOVEY | 175.00 | BC |
| 326 | CLEMENTE | 100.00 | BC |
| 335 | SCHOENDIENST | 7.50 | BC |
| 343 | KOUFAX | 110.00 | BC |
| 350 | MANTLE | 345.00 | BC |
| 377 | MARIS | 85.00 | OTF |
| 395 | WILHELM | 7.50 | BC |
| 420 | MATHEWS | 22.50 | BC |
| 445 | SPAHN | 37.50 | BC |
| 475 | DRYSDALE | 35.00 | BC |
| 480 | BERRA | 65.00 | BC |
| 490 | F. ROBINSON | 42.50 | BC |
| 493 | SNIDER | 50.00 | BC |
| 502 | BUNNING | 7.50 | OTF |
| 554 | MCCOVEY ALL-STAR | 50.00 | BC |
| 555 | FOX ALL-STAR | 12.50 | OTF |
| 558 | MATHEWS ALL-STAR | 22.50 | BC |
| 559 | APARICIO ALL-STAR | 15.00 | BC |
| 560 | BANKS ALL-STAR | 40.00 | BC |
| 561 | KALINE ALL-STAR | 40.00 | BC |
| 563 | MANTLE ALL-STAR | 240.00 | BC |
| 564 | MAYS ALL-STAR | 80.00 | BC |
| 565 | MARIS ALL-STAR | 85.00 | OTF |
| 566 | AARON ALL-STAR | 80.00 | BC |
| 570 | DRYSDALE ALL-STAR | 25.00 | BC |

**1961 TOPPS.** A yawner from a visual standpoint, this set is nonetheless expensive. Topps ended the last series with an All-Star subset for the fourth time, but in 1961 a late release and limited distribution made it more of an adventure than ever to complete. Three decades later, it hasn't gotten any easier—especially if you want perfectly centered cards. The MVP, World Series, and Thrills cards are much less taxing, while league leaders appear for the first time. An ironic footnote to this set is that in 1961 the card that generated the most interest was #75, entitled "Lindy Shows Larry." Shows him what? If you're in your early forties, this should bring back a few memories.

*Warning:* A lot of otherwise *mint* cards look dirty due to printing imperfections. Grade them slightly better than *excellent.* Berra's MVP card was short printed, as was Mazeroski's regular card. Maz looks like a good bet to make the Hall of Fame soon, at which point this card may challenge his 1957 rookie for "best" card honors. The cards of Charlie Neal, Ray Barker, and Bill Skowron were also short-printed and sell for around $5, $5, and $25, respectively, if you even care.

*Avoid:* Versailles, Howser, Maloney, Willie Davis, and Matty Alou. Also steer clear of All-Stars that are not listed below, unless you can find them in *near mint* or better for under $20.

*Tough Call:* No one. Ron Santo has too good a chance of making the Hall of Fame someday to ignore—especially if you can still buy his cards cheaply.

Set: $4,900.00
Commons (1–522): $2.25
Commons (523–589): $18.50

| | | | |
|---|---|---:|---|
| 2 | MARIS | 155.00 | PC |
| 10 | B. ROBINSON | 25.00 | BC |
| 20 | ROBERTS | 7.50 | BC |
| 30 | FOX | 5.00 | OTF |
| 35 | SANTO | 32.50 | OTF |
| 44 | LEADERS: MANTLE | 20.00 | BC |
| 80 | KILLEBREW | 15.00 | BC |
| 88 | ASHBURN | 5.00 | OTF |
| 120 | MATHEWS | 17.50 | BC |
| 141 | WILLIAMS | 85.00 | BC |
| 150 | MAYS | 80.00 | BC |
| 160 | FORD | 25.00 | BC |
| 200 | SPAHN | 22.50 | BC |
| 207 | DODGER SOUTHPAWS | 12.50 | BC |
| 211 | GIBSON | 27.50 | BC |
| 260 | DRYSDALE | 17.50 | BC |
| 287 | YASTRZEMSKI | 115.00 | BC |
| 290 | MUSIAL | 80.00 | BC |
| 300 | MANTLE | 345.00 | BC |
| 307 | SERIES: MANTLE | 22.50 | BC |
| 312 | SERIES: MAZEROSKI | 7.50 | OTF |
| 344 | KOUFAX | 85.00 | BC |
| 350 | BANKS | 25.00 | BC |
| 360 | F. ROBINSON | 30.00 | BC |
| 388 | CLEMENTE | 80.00 | BC |
| 401 | THRILL: RUTH | 20.00 | BC |
| 406 | THRILL: MANTLE | 30.00 | BC |
| 415 | AARON | 100.00 | BC |
| 417 | MARICHAL | 110.00 | BC |
| 425 | BERRA | 57.50 | BC |
| 429 | KALINE | 30.00 | BC |
| 430 | MAZEROSKI | 27.50 | OTF |
| 440 | APARICIO | 10.00 | BC |
| 443 | SNIDER | 32.50 | BC |
| 455 | WYNN | 7.50 | BC |
| 460 | HODGES | 10.00 | OTF |
| 471 | MVP: RIZZUTO | 10.00 | OTF |
| 472 | MVP: BERRA | 42.50 | BC |
| 475 | MVP: MANTLE | 90.00 | BC |
| 478 | MVP: MARIS | 32.50 | BC |
| 480 | MVP: CAMPANELLA | 22.50 | BC |
| 482 | MVP: MAYS | 30.00 | BC |
| 484 | MVP: AARON | 32.50 | BC |
| 485 | MVP: BANKS | 17.50 | BC |
| 490 | BUNNING | 7.00 | OTF |
| 505 | SCHOENDIENST | 10.00 | BC |
| 517 | MCCOVEY | 47.50 | BC |
| 545 | WILHELM | 45.00 | BC |
| 570 | FOX ALL-STAR | 30.00 | OTF |

| 571 | MAZEROSKI ALL-STAR | 30.00 | OTF |
|-----|------|-------|-----|
| 572 | B. ROBINSON ALL-STAR | 80.00 | BC |
| 574 | APARICIO ALL-STAR | 35.00 | BC |
| 575 | BANKS ALL STAR | 75.00 | BC |
| 576 | MARIS ALL-STAR | 120.00 | OTF |
| 577 | AARON ALL-STAR | 120.00 | BC |
| 578 | MANTLE ALL-STAR | 350.00 | BC |
| 579 | MAYS ALL-STAR | 120.00 | BC |
| 580 | KALINE ALL-STAR | 75.00 | BC |
| 581 | F. ROBINSON ALL-STAR | 80.00 | BC |
| 586 | FORD ALL-STAR | 80.00 | BC |
| 589 | SPAHN ALL-STAR | 110.00 | BC |

**1962 TOPPS.** If you collect every card in this set, you deserve a medal. Most of the high numbers are impossible to find in *near mint* condition, there are variations ranging from different tints to completely different photos, and—worst of all—about 25 percent of the cards in the set often carry some sort of premium. Everyone likes this set. It has a lot of little surprises, like a Babe Ruth subset, an In Action subset, World Series cards, special cards with hokey titles, and a Rookie Parade subset with five decapitated players per card.

*Warning:* There are a lot of cards around that appear, at first glance, to be in *mint* condition. Take a second glance before you spot a dealer a 25 percent premium. Pay particular attention to centering and corner wear. As for variations, Lee Walls, Billy Hoeft, Bill Kunkel, Hal Reniff, Carlton Willey, Eddie Yost, and Wally Moon come in the $1.50 flavor and the $15 flavor. Bob Buhl and Willie Tasby with airbrushed hats will set you back a cool $50. Do yourself a favor and pass on all of these guys.

*Avoid:* Tresh, Fregosi, Rodgers, Tartabull, Hubbs, McCauliffe, McDowell, Bouton, Pepitone, and Hickman. Also, if you're into the Mets, don't pay a premium for their cards—there are plenty available outside the Big Apple.

*Tough Call:* Boog Powell, Joe Torre, Tim Mc-Carver, and Bob Uecker. Powell was a feared slugger for over a decade, and probably lost the extra 50 homers that would have put him in the Hall of Fame to the rules changes of the mid-1960s. Don't count on seeing him at Cooperstown, unless he's doing a beer commercial. Torre may make it. In fact, of all the players that the Hall has passed over, Torre looks like he's closest to having enough to get in on the second go-round. He was a terrific hitter for a catcher, a terrific hitter for a third baseman, and a terrific hitter for a first baseman. Had he played in the American League, he would have been a terrific DH. He might be worth a few discretionary dollars, but only if you can snag his rookie card in *mint* for less than $15. McCarver and Uecker are a buyer's nightmare. Because they are media stars, their card prices have climbed steadily, and a lot of people are kicking themselves for not getting in on the ground floor. The question is, who's buying them and why? This may be a case of buyers (or dealers) investing in cards purely on the assumption that someone, somewhere, will be willing to pay them more. That's worked so far, but where will it stop? No one knows. The safe bet at this point, however, is to keep your distance. Uecker was never much of a player and found a way to make a fortune off that fact. McCarver was very good, but not great. Bob Boone, Freehan, and a few others will make it before he does.

*Set: $4,500.00*
*Commons (1–370): $1.50*
*Commons (371–522): $3.75*
*Commons (523–598): $10.00*

| 1 | MARIS | 170.00 | PC |
|-----|------|-------|-----|
| 5 | KOUFAX | 95.00 | BC |
| 10 | CLEMENTE | 85.00 | BC |
| 18 | MANAGER'S DREAM | 90.00 | BC |
| 25 | BANKS | 30.00 | BC |
| 29 | STENGEL | 12.50 | BC |
| 30 | MATHEWS | 12.50 | BC |
| 45 | B. ROBINSON | 27.50 | BC |
| 50 | MUSIAL | 85.00 | BC |
| 53 | LEADERS: MARIS | 25.00 | BC |

| | | | |
|---|---|---|---|
| 70 | KILLEBREW | 12.50 | BC |
| 73 | FOX | 5.00 | OTF |
| 85 | HODGES | 10.00 | OTF |
| 100 | SPAHN | 22.50 | BC |
| 150 | KALINE | 25.00 | BC |
| 170 | SANTO | 7.50 | OTF |
| 199 | PERRY | 135.00 | BC |
| 200 | MANTLE | 400.00 | BC |
| 243 | ROBERTS | 7.50 | BC |
| 288 | WILLIAMS | 27.50 | BC |
| 300 | MAYS | 115.00 | BC |
| 310 | FORD | 27.50 | BC |
| 318 | MANTLE IN ACTION | 42.50 | BC |
| 320 | AARON | 115.00 | BC |
| 325 | APARICIO | 10.00 | BC |
| 340 | DRYSDALE | 27.50 | BC |
| 350 | F. ROBINSON | 37.50 | BC |
| 360 | BERRA | 65.00 | BC |
| 385 | WYNN | 10.00 | BC |
| 387 | BROCK | 155.00 | BC |
| 394 | AARON ALL-STAR | 25.00 | BC |
| 395 | MAYS ALL-STAR | 25.00 | BC |
| 401 | HOMER KINGS | 25.00 | BC |
| 425 | YASTRZEMSKI | 190.00 | BC |
| 460 | BUNNING | 7.50 | OTF |
| 471 | MANTLE ALL-STAR | 110.00 | BC |
| 500 | SNIDER | 40.00 | BC |
| 505 | MARICHAL | 27.50 | BC |
| 530 | GIBSON | 150.00 | BC |
| 544 | MCCOVEY | 145.00 | BC |
| 545 | WILHELM | 37.50 | BC |
| 575 | SCHOENDIENST | 35.00 | BC |

**1963 TOPPS.** This set survived the Pete Rose debacle to take on its own special personality. Interesting and well designed, it features hard-to-find cards of Clemente, Snider, Ford, Brock, McCovey, Killebrew, and Nellie Fox. The group shots on the special cards are especially good, but the layout of the rookie cards and league leaders leaves something to be desired.

*Warning:* You may encounter some bad printing in this set, so look for thin lines, spots, and streaking, then grade accordingly. Cards in the sixth series are a little harder to find than those in the

seventh. The Freehan, Tresh, Thomas, Killebrew, and Long cards appear to have been short-printed, and year variations exist on the Culp and Debusschere rookie cards, which shouldn't interest you anyway. Also, the $90 price tag you'll see on the Mets team card reflects a heavy East Coast influence, so don't pay more than $50 for it if you live in, say, Arkansas.

*Avoid:* Debusschere, Hunt, Mota, Harper, and McNally. Also avoid the league leader cards in this set—demand is far lower than dealers would have you think. If you must buy, card #3 has the most potential.

*Tough Call:* Tony Oliva, Bill Freehan, and Rusty Staub. Anyone who saw the young Tony O will tell you that he was better than Boggs, Gwynn, and Carew. Don't doubt them for a moment. Oliva played most of his career during a time when pitchers had a big edge, yet he still managed to top .300 on an annual basis. When his knees started to go, it was thought that the DH rule would give him a chance to put in those last few seasons to make the Hall of Fame, but he was just in too much pain. Still, he probably should be in. Oliva's a very tough call, but the voters don't seem to cotton to this lifelong Twin, so hold off on his cards until things start looking a little brighter. Freehan should be in, too. He was a very good hitter during this era of low batting averages, and easily the best catcher in the American League. If you see Oliva make it, it might mean that the voters are beginning to recognize the artificially low batting stats of the time, so start thinking about grabbing some Freehan cards. Staub was another guy whose numbers were hurt during the 1960s, although he ended up putting in a Methuselahan career. Never in the same class as Oliva and Freehan, he's a serious longshot.

*Set: $4,600.00*
*Commons (1–446): $1.75*
*Commons (447–576): $7.50*

| | | | |
|---|---|---|---|
| 25 | KALINE | 22.50 | BC |
| 108 | WILHELM | 7.50 | BC |
| 115 | YASTRZEMSKI | 57.50 | BC |

| 120 | MARIS | 50.00 | OTF |
|---|---|---|---|
| 125 | ROBERTS | 7.50 | BC |
| 135 | ASHBURN | 7.50 | OTF |
| 138 | PRIDE OF N.L. | 27.50 | BC |
| 169 | PERRY | 22.50 | BC |
| 173 | BOMBERS BEST | 50.00 | BC |
| 200 | MANTLE | 385.00 | BC |
| 205 | APARICIO | 10.00 | BC |
| 210 | KOUFAX | 135.00 | BC |
| 233 | STENGEL | 12.50 | BC |
| 242 | POWER PLUS | 22.50 | BC |
| 245 | HODGES | 12.50 | OTF |
| 250 | MUSIAL | 95.00 | BC |
| 252 | SANTO | 5.00 | OTF |
| 275 | MATHEWS | 15.00 | BC |
| 300 | MAYS | 120.00 | BC |
| 320 | SPAHN | 27.50 | BC |
| 323 | MAZEROSKI | 3.50 | OTF |
| 340 | BERRA | 57.50 | BC |
| 345 | B. ROBINSON | 37.50 | BC |
| 353 | WILLIAMS | 17.50 | BC |
| 360 | DRYSDALE | 27.50 | BC |
| 365 | BUNNING | 5.00 | OTF |
| 380 | BANKS | 47.50 | BC |
| 390 | AARON | 120.00 | BC |
| 400 | F. ROBINSON | 37.50 | BC |
| 412 | BIG THREE | 25.00 | BC |
| 415 | GIBSON | 35.00 | BC |
| 440 | MARICHAL | 20.00 | BC |
| 446 | FORD | 30.00 | BC |
| 472 | BROCK | 115.00 | BC |
| 490 | MCCOVEY | 110.00 | BC |
| 500 | KILLEBREW | 85.00 | BC |
| 537 | ROSE | 575.00 | OTF |
| 540 | CLEMENTE | 175.00 | BC |
| 550 | SNIDER | 67.50 | BC |
| 553 | STARGELL | 220.00 | BC |

**1964 TOPPS.** No one much likes this set. The card fronts feature a dull design and uninspired photography. The card backs feature hard-to-read statistics and—worst of all—a rub-off game that wreaked havoc with condition. There are, however, a lot of good cards in this set, so if you subscribe to the theory that buyers go for "bargain"

Hall of Famers, there might be room to work here. Note the demand for the still-inexpensive leader cards—the first to use the full-photo format as opposed to the old floating heads.

*Warning:* If you see a card that has been "scratched off," check very carefully for hairlines, dents, and light creases. As a rule, don't pay a *mint* premium for a card that has been "scratched off." Also, don't get suckered into buying rookie cards of future managers. For checklist hounds, card #517 comes in two flavors—$5 and $10, with the latter featuring out-of-sequence numbering.

*Avoid:* Grote, LaRussa, Shannon, Wood, Torborg, Parker, Horton, Wise, Woodward, and Ken Harrelson.

*Tough Call:* Mickey Lolich, Lou Piniella, Tony Conigliaro, and Dick Allen. Lolich pitched well for a lot of years, but all he's got to show for it is a great World Series, a phenomenal 1972 season, and a doughnut shop. A bronze plaque is not in his future. Piniella shouldn't even be on this list, yet buyers continue to shell out $20 and more for his 1964 card. Had it not taken him six years to stick in the majors, his career numbers might be of Cooperstown quality. But it did, and they're not. Conigliaro shouldn't be on this list, either, but again, some buyers insist on paying $20 for his 1964 card. They must be the same people who are buying up all the Alvin Davis and Pete Incaviglia cards. Allen, however, is a different story. On the days he brought his head to the ballpark, he was by far and away the most destructive hitter in baseball. When he didn't, he was still very good. There are guys in the Hall of Fame right now who couldn't carry his jockstrap, yet Dick (or Rich or Richie) apparently made too many enemies in the baseball world ever to join them.

*Set:* $2,500.00
*Commons (1–370):* $1.25
*Commons (371–522):* $3.00
*Commons (523–587):* $5.75

| 3 | LEADERS: KOUFAX | 10.00 | BC |
|---|---|---|---|
| 13 | WILHELM | 5.00 | BC |

| 21 | BERRA | 30.00 | BC |
|---|---|---|---|
| 29 | BROCK | 27.50 | BC |
| 35 | MATHEWS | 12.50 | BC |
| 50 | MANTLE | 195.00 | BC |
| 55 | BANKS | 17.50 | BC |
| 120 | DRYSDALE | 12.50 | BC |
| 125 | ROSE | 110.00 | OTF |
| 136 | SERIES: KOUFAX | 7.50 | BC |
| 146 | JOHN | 50.00 | OTF |
| 150 | MAYS | 95.00 | BC |
| 155 | SNIDER | 25.00 | BC |
| 175 | WILLIAMS | 12.50 | BC |
| 177 | KILLEBREW | 12.50 | BC |
| 200 | KOUFAX | 85.00 | BC |
| 205 | FOX | 3.50 | OTF |
| 210 | YASTRZEMSKI | 60.00 | BC |
| 225 | MARIS | 55.00 | OTF |
| 230 | B. ROBINSON | 25.00 | BC |
| 250 | KALINE | 22.50 | BC |
| 260 | F. ROBINSON | 20.00 | BC |
| 265 | BUNNING | 3.50 | OTF |
| 280 | MARICHAL | 7.50 | BC |
| 285 | ROBERTS | 5.00 | BC |
| 300 | AARON | 95.00 | BC |
| 324 | STENGEL | 12.50 | BC |
| 331 | A.L. BOMBERS | 75.00 | BC |
| 342 | STARGELL | 32.50 | BC |
| 350 | MCCOVEY | 17.50 | BC |
| 375 | SANTO | 3.50 | OTF |
| 380 | FORD | 22.50 | BC |
| 400 | SPAHN | 25.00 | BC |
| 423 | TOPS IN N.L. | 75.00 | BC |
| 440 | CLEMENTE | 100.00 | BC |
| 460 | GIBSON | 27.50 | BC |
| 468 | PERRY | 32.50 | BC |
| 540 | APARICIO | 12.50 | BC |
| 541 | NIEKRO | 150.00 | OTF |
| 570 | MAZEROSKI | 7.50 | OTF |

**1965 TOPPS.** A very straightforward set with few twists and turns. Notable only for the rookie cards of Hunter, Carlton, Morgan, and Perez.

*Warning:* There are a lot of cheap, mildly tempting rookies in this set, so make sure you understand what you're buying. Also several cards were short-printed in the final series—which, by the way, was issued in relative abundance—including those of Perez and Hunter. This is important in the case of Perez, because when he makes the Hall of Fame, buyers will be flocking to his "best" card. Is it his short-printed (albeit cluttered) rookie card? Do a little digging in the 1967 set before making up your mind.

*Avoid:* Petrocelli, Alomar, Lanier, Agee, Tovar, Blass, Northrup, Cardenal, Dierker, Briles, Beckert, Lonborg, Cleon Jones, and Davey Johnson.

*Tough Call:* Mel Stottlemyre, Denny McLain, Luis Tiant, Tug McGraw, and Bert Campaneris. Nothing tough here, really, although you may need to be reminded why you shouldn't expect much from these players. Stottlemyre was very good, but not great—and certainly never a dominant pitcher. Denny McLain is an interesting story, but not to anyone up in Cooperstown. Tiant lost time to injury in the prime of his career, which kept him from racking up superstar numbers. McGraw may make it if they throw the doors wide open to relievers, but he's at least tenth in line. And a reasonable case could be made for Campaneris, but there are plenty of other non–Hall of Fame infielders who are more deserving.

*Set:* $3,300.00
*Commons (1–196):* $.75
*Commons (97–370):* $1.50
*Commons (371–598):* $3.25
*Short Prints:* $7.50

| 3 | LEADERS: MANTLE | 8.00 | BC |
|---|---|---|---|
| 5 | LEADERS: MANTLE | 8.00 | BC |
| 8 | LEADERS: KOUFAX | 10.00 | BC |
| 15 | ROBERTS | 5.00 | BC |
| 16 | MORGAN | 125.00 | BC |
| 20 | BUNNING | 2.50 | OTF |
| 50 | MARICHAL | 7.00 | BC |
| 95 | MAZEROSKI | 2.00 | OTF |
| 110 | SANTO | 2.50 | OTF |
| 120 | F. ROBINSON | 20.00 | BC |
| 130 | KALINE | 20.00 | BC |
| 134 | SERIES: MANTLE | 25.00 | BC |

| 150 | B. ROBINSON | 20.00 | BC |
|---|---|---|---|
| 155 | MARIS | 45.00 | OTF |
| 160 | CLEMENTE | 60.00 | BC |
| 170 | AARON | 80.00 | BC |
| 176 | MCCOVEY | 12.50 | BC |
| 187 | STENGEL | 10.00 | BC |
| 193 | PERRY | 12.50 | BC |
| 205 | SPAHN | 15.00 | BC |
| 207 | ROSE | 100.00 | OTF |
| 208 | JOHN | 7.50 | OTF |
| 220 | WILLIAMS | 7.50 | BC |
| 250 | MAYS | 85.00 | BC |
| 260 | DRYSDALE | 15.00 | BC |
| 276 | WILHELM | 5.00 | BC |
| 300 | KOUFAX | 100.00 | BC |
| 320 | GIBSON | 22.50 | BC |
| 330 | FORD | 20.00 | BC |
| 350 | MANTLE | 400.00 | BC |
| 377 | STARGELL | 17.50 | BC |
| 385 | YASTRZEMSKI | 77.50 | BC |
| 400 | KILLEBREW | 27.50 | BC |
| 410 | APARICIO | 7.50 | BC |
| 461 | NIEKRO | 37.50 | OTF |
| 470 | BERRA | 42.50 | BC |
| 477 | CARLTON | 450.00 | BC |
| 485 | FOX | 7.50 | OTF |
| 500 | MATHEWS | 27.50 | BC |
| 510 | BANKS | 60.00 | BC |
| 526 | HUNTER | 110.00 | BC |
| 540 | BROCK | 37.50 | BC |
| 581 | PEREZ | 140.00 | BC |

**1966 TOPPS.** No one has been able to offer a satisfactory explanation for it, but there do seem to be a lot of cards from this set in very collectible condition. This is true even of the last two series, which are very scarce. Therefore, don't be too anxious to pay more than a 20 percent premium for *mint* cards. And by all means don't accept off-center cards, which were a problem throughout the issue. This set was poo-pooed for years because the Rose and Mantle cards were double-printed, but with rookie cards of Palmer, Jenkins, and Sutton, it's bounced back with a vengeance. For fans of black humor, there's another bonus: Dick Ells-

worth's card actually depicts Ken Hubbs, who had died a few years earlier in a plane crash.

*Warning:* Several cards in the last series were short-printed, including those of McCovey, Perry, and Billy Williams. Short-printed commons from this series sell for $20 in *near mint*, but drop down below $10 in *excellent*. There is some missing type on the cards of Merritt Ranew, Alex Johnson, Dick Groat, and Bob Uecker. These error cards all sell for around $20, although dealers will always try to get twice as much for Uecker. Let the dealers keep him at that price. Some second-series checklists list card #115 as Warren Spahn and command a 50 percent premium from checklist fanatics.

*Avoid:* Lee May, George Scott, Grant Jackson, and the Twins and Tigers team cards.

*Tough Call:* Bobby Murcer. Sorry, New Yorkers, there just isn't a chance. A very good player and a decent guy, but do you really think his plaque belongs with those of Willie Mays, Duke Snider, and Mickey Mantle?

*Set: $3,750.00*
*Commons (1–283): $1.00*
*Commons (284–446): $2.00*
*Commons (447–522): $4.00*
*Commons (523–598): $10.00*
*Short Prints: $20.00*

| 1 | MAYS | 100.00 | BC |
|---|---|---|---|
| 28 | NIEKRO | 10.00 | OTF |
| 30 | ROSE | 25.00 | OTF |
| 36 | HUNTER | 20.00 | BC |
| 50 | MANTLE | 135.00 | BC |
| 70 | YASTRZEMSKI | 30.00 | BC |
| 72 | PEREZ | 22.50 | BC |
| 90 | APARICIO | 5.00 | BC |
| 100 | KOUFAX | 85.00 | BC |
| 110 | BANKS | 17.50 | BC |
| 120 | KILLEBREW | 12.50 | BC |
| 125 | BROCK | 15.00 | BC |
| 126 | PALMER | 175.00 | BC |
| 160 | FORD | 17.50 | BC |
| 195 | MORGAN | 30.00 | BC |
| 200 | MATHEWS | 7.50 | BC |

| 215 | LEADERS: MAYS | 15.00 | BC |
| 254 | JENKINS | 100.00 | BC |
| 255 | STARGELL | 12.50 | BC |
| 288 | SUTTON | 110.00 | OTF |
| 300 | CLEMENTE | 75.00 | BC |
| 310 | F. ROBINSON | 27.50 | BC |
| 320 | GIBSON | 17.50 | BC |
| 365 | MARIS | 42.50 | OTF |
| 390 | B. ROBINSON | 20.00 | BC |
| 410 | KALINE | 20.00 | BC |
| 420 | MARICHAL | 7.50 | BC |
| 430 | DRYSDALE | 15.00 | BC |
| 435 | BUNNING | 5.00 | OTF |
| 486 | JOHN | 7.50 | OTF |
| 500 | AARON | 80.00 | BC |
| 510 | WILHELM | 7.50 | BC |
| 530 | ROBERTS | 27.50 | BC |
| 550 | MCCOVEY | 100.00 | BC |
| 580 | WILLIAMS | 70.00 | BC |
| 598 | PERRY | 220.00 | BC |

**1967 TOPPS.** Considered by many to be the Cadillac of 1960s card sets. The overall condition of available cards is pretty good, so grade conservatively.

*Warning:* Several cards in the high number series were double-printed, including Carew. Double-printed commons sell for around $5. There is a missing line of type on some of the cards of Mike McCormick, Bob Bruce, and Bob Priddy. The error cards sell for around $10 to $15. The first card in the set, which depicts Hank Bauer and the two Robinsons, seems to have been double-printed, as were the cards of Kaline and Frank Robinson, so be picky about condition. The toughest card to find in perfect shape may be the Tony Perez card, which appears to have been short-printed.

*Avoid:* Bando, Holtzman, Johnstone, Harrelson, Rader, Monday, Joe Niekro, Reggie Smith, and the Red Sox team card.

*Tough Call:* Mark Belanger and Maury Wills. Wills was the more productive of the two, but Belanger probably has a better shot at the Hall of Fame because of his stellar defense. The inevitable election of Ozzie Smith to the Hall has gotten voters rethinking the old position on glove men, which might clear the way for players like Belanger. If that happens, however, he won't be the first in line. Wills, on the other hand, could make it on his offensive skills. He is credited with returning the stolen base to major-league arsenals (although it was really Aparicio who did this), and as more speedsters enter Cooperstown, Wills might get enough "pioneer" votes to squeak through the Veterans Committee. He didn't make a lot of friends when he played, however, so it's unlikely he'll have any friends among the voters.

*Set: $4,900.00*
*Commons (1–196): $.75*
*Commons (197–370): $1.50*
*Commons (371–457): $2.25*
*Commons (458–533): $4.75*
*Commons (534–609): $11.00*

| 5 | FORD | 12.50 | BC |
| 30 | KALINE | 10.00 | BC |
| 45 | MARIS | 32.50 | OTF |
| 55 | DRYSDALE | 10.00 | BC |
| 60 | APARICIO | 5.00 | BC |
| 70 | SANTO | 2.50 | OTF |
| 100 | F. ROBINSON | 10.00 | BC |
| 140 | STARGELL | 12.50 | BC |
| 146 | CARLTON | 100.00 | BC |
| 150 | MANTLE | 215.00 | BC |
| 166 | MATHEWS | 7.50 | BC |
| 200 | MAYS | 75.00 | BC |
| 210 | GIBSON | 15.00 | BC |
| 215 | BANKS | 15.00 | BC |
| 236 | LEADERS: KOUFAX | 10.00 | BC |
| 250 | AARON | 75.00 | BC |
| 285 | BROCK | 15.00 | BC |
| 315 | WILLIAMS | 7.50 | BC |
| 320 | PERRY | 10.00 | BC |
| 333 | JENKINS | 22.50 | BC |
| 337 | MORGAN | 20.00 | BC |
| 355 | YASTRZEMSKI | 65.00 | BC |
| 369 | HUNTER | 12.50 | BC |
| 400 | CLEMENTE | 57.50 | BC |
| 422 | WILHELM | 5.00 | BC |

| | | | |
|---|---|---|---|
| 423 | FENCE BUSTERS | 12.50 | BC |
| 430 | ROSE | 47.50 | OTF |
| 445 | SUTTON | 22.50 | OTF |
| 456 | NIEKRO | 10.00 | OTF |
| 460 | KILLEBREW | 37.50 | BC |
| 475 | PALMER | 85.00 | BC |
| 476 | PEREZ | 85.00 | BC |
| 480 | MCCOVEY | 27.50 | BC |
| 500 | MARICHAL | 17.50 | BC |
| 560 | BUNNING | 37.50 | OTF |
| 569 | CAREW | 485.00 | BC |
| 581 | SEAVER | 1,250.00 | PC |
| 600 | B. ROBINSON | 185.00 | BC |
| 609 | JOHN | 75.00 | OTF |

**1968 TOPPS.** A few years ago buyers were calling this set bland—stiff photography, lousy statistics, and a border that looked like wallpaper in a cheap motel. Boy, have they changed their tune. Thanks to Nolan Ryan, whose rookie card accounts for more than half the value of the set, this ugly duckling has turned into a swan!

*Warning:* Someone, somewhere, is trying to figure a way to counterfeit the Ryan card, so stay on your toes. Variations exist on the cards of Ed Brinkman, Mike McCormick, and Casey Cox—the ones with the team name in yellow are the good ones, and sell for $20, $50, and $45, respectively. Also, this set has always been hard to find in *mint* condition—it just seems more "fragile" than the four previous sets.

*Avoid:* Sanguillen, McRae, and Mike Marshall.

*Tough Call:* There are no other significant rookies in this set except for Johnny Bench (which is what the old complaint used to be), so you needn't make any serious judgment calls.

Set: $3,200.00
Commons (1–457): $.50
Commons (458–598): $2.75

| | | | |
|---|---|---|---|
| 20 | B. ROBINSON | 15.00 | BC |
| 37 | WILLIAMS | 7.50 | BC |
| 45 | SEAVER | 225.00 | BC |
| 50 | MAYS | 47.50 | BC |

| | | | |
|---|---|---|---|
| 58 | MATHEWS | 7.50 | BC |
| 72 | JOHN | 3.00 | OTF |
| 80 | CAREW | 135.00 | BC |
| 85 | PERRY | 7.50 | BC |
| 86 | STARGELL | 7.50 | BC |
| 100 | GIBSON | 17.50 | BC |
| 103 | SUTTON | 7.50 | OTF |
| 110 | AARON | 55.00 | BC |
| 130 | PEREZ | 15.00 | BC |
| 144 | MORGAN | 10.00 | BC |
| 145 | DRYSDALE | 7.50 | BC |
| 150 | CLEMENTE | 40.00 | BC |
| 177 | RYAN | 1,500.00 | PC |
| 205 | MARICHAL | 5.00 | BC |
| 215 | BUNNING | 2.50 | OTF |
| 220 | KILLEBREW | 10.00 | BC |
| 230 | ROSE | 25.00 | OTF |
| 240 | KALINE | 12.50 | BC |
| 247 | BENCH | 250.00 | BC |
| 250 | YASTRZEMSKI | 30.00 | BC |
| 257 | NIEKRO | 5.00 | OTF |
| 280 | MANTLE | 160.00 | BC |
| 290 | MCCOVEY | 7.50 | BC |
| 310 | APARICIO | 3.50 | BC |
| 330 | MARIS | 27.50 | OTF |
| 350 | WILHELM | 3.50 | BC |
| 355 | BANKS | 15.00 | BC |
| 385 | HUNTER | 7.50 | BC |
| 390 | MAZEROSKI | 2.00 | OTF |
| 408 | CARLTON | 45.00 | BC |
| 410 | JENKINS | 12.50 | BC |
| 490 | SUPERSTARS | 87.50 | BC |
| 500 | F. ROBINSON | 17.50 | BC |
| 520 | BROCK | 17.50 | BC |
| 575 | PALMER | 50.00 | BC |

**1969 TOPPS.** Topps did a commendable job with this set, considering the many obstacles it faced. For starters, the four new expansion teams created problems in that a lot of old head shots had to be dug out of the files to make up cards for the Padres, Expos, Royals, and Pilots in the early series. Topps then hustled down to spring training in time to snap pictures to be used in the later series. Between the expansion players who were immediately traded and those who didn't make their respective teams, it must have been total chaos over at Topps. That the company produced a clean, colorful set is remarkable. That a number of errors, variations, and double-printed cards were produced in mid-summer is understandable, as is the decision not to print team cards. Less understandable—but far more amusing—is that in all the craziness, Topps mistakenly printed the picture of a fuzzy-faced batboy instead of Aurelio Rodriguez, who looks like Don Johnson's boss on "Miami Vice."

*Warning:* Several cards in the fourth series exist with white lettering, including those of McCovey, Perry, and Mantle. Some white-letter cards, as well as All-Star cards, were double-printed, while some were not. In other words, if you see a $20 price tag on a Mel Stottlemyre card, don't have a coronary. Also, Graig Nettles's card exists with a loop around the team name, which commands a 50 percent premium. Other errors occurred on the cards of immortals such as Paul Popovich, Ellie Rodriguez, Clay Dalyrimple, and Donn Clendenon. These cards are hard to find, but no one's really looking for them, either. They sell for between $7 and $10 each. Finally, the cards of Billy Williams, Tommy John, and Tom Seaver were double-printed, so be choosy about condition.

*Avoid:* Otis, Patek, Cox, Fosse, Hendricks, Messersmith, Watson, Gaston, and Rudi.

*Tough Call:* Al Oliver, Earl Weaver, Sparky Lyle, and Bobby Bonds. Oliver was a wonderful hitter who terrorized pitchers in both leagues for nearly two decades. He approached the kind of batting totals one normally associates with Hall of Famers, but never quite got over the hump in any one category. He may make it one day, but don't bet more than a couple of bucks on it. Weaver definitely *will* be in the Hall of Fame. But he's a manager who never played in the majors, and thus the only Weaver cards that exist are manager cards. And manager cards are almost never in demand. If you must buy a Weaver card, this is the one to buy. Keep in mind, however, that you'll be paying the same price you would for Ted Williams. Then ask

yourself whose card you'd rather have twenty years from now. Lyle was one of the best in the business in the early and mid-1970s, but he seemingly lost his stuff overnight. He put in ten good years as a closer, though, which might one day be recognized by the voters. If you must gamble on the guy, pass on his 1969 rookie and consider his 1971 card—it's next to impossible to find in *mint* condition. As for Bonds, let's all remember that he's not in the Hall of Fame and that he never will be. His son, however, has a very good shot, which accounts for the renewed interest in his cards. If you disagree, there are better ways to voice your opinion than by blowing $25 on his rookie card.

*Set: $2,300.00*
*Commons: $1.00*

| | | | |
|---|---|---|---|
| 20 | BANKS | 15.00 | BC |
| 35 | MORGAN | 7.50 | BC |
| 50 | CLEMENTE | 35.00 | BC |
| 75 | APARICIO | 2.50 | BC |
| 85 | BROCK | 12.50 | BC |
| 95 | BENCH | 140.00 | BC |
| 99 | NETTLES | 10.00 | OTF |
| 100 | AARON | 40.00 | BC |
| 120 | ROSE | 22.50 | OTF |
| 130 | YASTRZEMSKI | 20.00 | BC |
| 175 | BUNNING | 2.00 | OTF |
| 190 | MAYS | 52.50 | BC |
| 200 | GIBSON | 10.00 | BC |
| 216 | SUTTON | 5.00 | OTF |
| 235 | HUNTER | 10.00 | BC |
| 250 | F. ROBINSON | 17.50 | BC |
| 255 | CARLTON | 42.50 | BC |
| 260 | JACKSON | 585.00 | PC! |
| 295 | PEREZ | 12.50 | BC |
| 335 | MAZEROSKI | 2.00 | OTF |
| 355 | NIEKRO | 3.50 | OTF |
| 370 | MARICHAL | 5.00 | BC |
| 375 | KILLEBREW | 12.50 | BC |
| 400 | DRYSDALE | 7.50 | BC |
| 410 | KALINE | 12.50 | BC |
| 440 | MCCOVEY | 10.00 | BC |
| 450 | B. WILLIAMS | 5.00 | BC |

| 465 | JOHN | 2.00 | OTF |
|---|---|---|---|
| 480 | SEAVER | 125.00 | BC |
| 485 | PERRY | 7.50 | BC |
| 500 | MANTLE | 200.00 | BC |
| 510 | CAREW | 62.50 | BC |
| 533 | RYAN | 475.00 | PC |
| 545 | STARGELL | 10.00 | BC |
| 550 | B. ROBINSON | 15.00 | BC |
| 565 | WILHELM | 5.00 | BC |
| 570 | SANTO | 3.50 | OTF |
| 572 | GIANTS HEROES | 7.50 | BC |
| 573 | PALMER | 32.50 | BC |
| 597 | FINGERS | 120.00 | BC |
| 640 | JENKINS | 12.50 | BC |
| 650 | T. WILLIAMS | 7.50 | BC |

**1970 TOPPS.** This set is notable in that for kids it was easily the most confusing one ever issued. First of all, Topps ignored the fact that the Pilots had become the Brewers the previous winter and continued to issue cards of players in Seattle uniforms well into September. That was a minor affront. The major one was that the company hiked its pack price from a nickel to a dime. It didn't matter that you got twice as many cards—you got half the gum you were supposed to, half the number of comic books and scratch-off inserts you were supposed to, and worst of all, you had to scrape up a whopping $2.40 for a box of twenty-four packs! Besides this major trauma, the only significant thing about this set—outside of the fact that Topps tinkered with some other packaging ideas that summer—is the attractive All-Star subset it issued in the fourth and fifth series. These cards are similar to the 1961 All-Stars and have begun to attract attention from serious buyers. For now, the only card that has much life to it is the Reggie Jackson.

*Warning:* The gray borders of these cards can mask minor wear, so check all *mint* and *near mint* cards carefully.

*Avoid:* Blue, Reuss, Garr, Russell, Gamble, and McNamara.

*Tough Call:* Bill Buckner, Darrell Evans, and Larry Bowa. Buckner put up some big numbers in Fenway when everyone figured he was washed up,

and for a while there, buyers entertained the idea of his surpassing 3,000 hits. But he didn't—and he was never considered anything other than a solid hitter—so Cooperstown doesn't appear to be in his future. Evans is not only a tough call, he's something of a test case. Do 400 home runs guarantee enshrinement? The voters will have to start thinking about that. And while they're at it, they'll have to discuss what it means when a pitcher racks up 300 wins over twenty years. Chances are that Evans—who was never once considered the best at his position—won't make it. As for Bowa, a little more stick would have helped. If he makes it, look for Mark Belanger, Bert Campaneris, and a million other guys to get in.

*Set: $2,000.00*
*Commons (1–459): $.50*
*Commons (460–633): $1.25*
*Commons (634–720): $4.00*

| 10 | YASTRZEMSKI | 22.50 | BC |
|---|---|---|---|
| 17 | WILHELM | 2.00 | BC |
| 140 | JACKSON | 130.00 | BC |
| 150 | KILLEBREW | 5.00 | BC |
| 160 | NIEKRO | 3.00 | OTF |
| 170 | B. WILLIAMS | 4.00 | BC |
| 180 | JOHN | 1.00 | OTF |
| 189 | MUNSON | 75.00 | OTF |
| 197 | NLCS: RYAN | 10.00 | BC |
| 210 | MARICHAL | 4.00 | BC |
| 211 | T. WILLIAMS | 7.00 | BC |
| 220 | CARLTON | 30.00 | BC |
| 230 | B. ROBINSON | 9.00 | BC |
| 240 | JENKINS | 7.00 | BC |
| 250 | MCCOVEY | 7.00 | BC |
| 290 | CAREW | 35.00 | BC |
| 300 | SEAVER | 95.00 | BC |
| 315 | APARICIO | 2.00 | BC |
| 330 | BROCK | 7.00 | BC |
| 350 | CLEMENTE | 35.00 | BC |
| 380 | PEREZ | 7.00 | BC |
| 403 | BUNNING | 1.00 | OTF |
| 440 | MAZEROSKI | 1.00 | OTF |
| 449 | PALMER | 15.00 | BC |

| 470 | STARGELL | 7.00 | BC |
|---|---|---|---|
| 491 | NETTLES | 3.00 | OTF |
| 500 | AARON | 42.50 | BC |
| 502 | FINGERS | 27.50 | BC |
| 530 | GIBSON | 10.00 | BC |
| 537 | MORGAN | 9.00 | BC |
| 560 | PERRY | 9.00 | BC |
| 565 | HUNTER | 9.00 | BC |
| 580 | ROSE | 45.00 | OTF |
| 600 | MAYS | 67.50 | BC |
| 622 | SUTTON | 9.00 | OTF |
| 630 | BANKS | 27.50 | BC |
| 660 | BENCH | 140.00 | BC |
| 670 | SANTO | 5.00 | OTF |
| 700 | F. ROBINSON | 32.50 | BC |
| 712 | RYAN | 465.00 | PC |

**1971 TOPPS.** It takes a deal with the devil to complete this set in *mint* condition. The black borders not only reveal slight flaws, but also don't hold up very well. The last series was done rather unscientifically, resulting in several common cards being short-printed. The Playoff and World Series cards were not terribly interesting, making 1971 the first year Topps didn't deliver on its popular postseason subset. There is one exception: card #335 depicts Brooks Robinson down and dirty after one of his many memorable plays during the series. It is the only card from the subset that has experienced constant demand.

*Warning:* Some cards were short-printed in the last series, including Aparicio's. Remember, do not consider the overall poor condition of most 1971 cards when grading. *Excellent* is *excellent*. *Very good* is *very good*. You should, however, be prepared to pay a premium of up to 30 percent for a true *mint* card. Also, check closely for nicks, chips, and layering that has been filled in with a black felt-tip pen.

*Avoid:* Singleton, Gullett, Grieve, Valentine, Grich, Cedeno, Luzinski, Hrabosky, and Matlack.

*Tough Call:* Don Baylor and George Foster. Baylor was a winner who distinguished himself during every stop of his career. But outside of his monster 1979 season, he was never considered one of the league's dominant players. Enshrinement could be in the cards, but don't bet $25 on it. As for Foster, there was a time when you would have thought that he'd be standing on the podium at Cooperstown this summer. Then it all came apart. Turns out he benefited more from hitting behind Rose, Morgan, Griffey, et al., than anyone had imagined. Never a favorite of the fans—although not a bad guy—he just doesn't figure to make the Hall.

*Set: $1,900.00*
*Commons (1–393): $.50*
*Commons (394–523): $.75*
*Commons (524–643): $2.00*
*Commons (644–752): $3.50*
*Short Prints: $4.50*

| 5 | MUNSON | 30.00 | OTF |
|---|---|---|---|
| 14 | CONCEPCION | 15.00 | OTF |
| 20 | JACKSON | 95.00 | BC |
| 26 | BLYLEVEN | 35.00 | OTF |
| 30 | NIEKRO | 2.50 | OTF |
| 45 | HUNTER | 5.00 | BC |
| 50 | MCCOVEY | 7.50 | BC |
| 55 | CARLTON | 22.50 | BC |
| 100 | ROSE | 27.50 | OTF |
| 110 | MAZEROSKI | 1.00 | OTF |
| 117 | SIMMONS | 12.50 | OTF |
| 140 | PERRY | 6.00 | BC |
| 160 | SEAVER | 52.50 | BC |
| 180 | KALINE | 12.50 | BC |
| 210 | CAREW | 37.50 | BC |
| 220 | SANTO | 1.50 | OTF |
| 230 | STARGELL | 7.50 | BC |
| 248 | WILHELM | 2.50 | BC |
| 250 | BENCH | 45.00 | BC |
| 264 | MORGAN | 7.50 | BC |
| 280 | JENKINS | 7.50 | BC |
| 300 | B. ROBINSON | 12.50 | BC |
| 324 | NETTLES | 2.00 | OTF |
| 325 | MARICHAL | 4.00 | BC |
| 331 | SERIES: B. ROBINSON | 3.00 | BC |
| 341 | GARVEY | 67.50 | OTF |
| 350 | B. WILLIAMS | 4.00 | BC |
| 361 | SUTTON | 5.00 | OTF |

| 380 | T. WILLIAMS | 5.00 | BC |
|---|---|---|---|
| 384 | FINGERS | 10.00 | BC |
| 400 | AARON | 37.50 | BC |
| 450 | GIBSON | 10.00 | BC |
| 513 | RYAN | 230.00 | BC |
| 520 | JOHN | 3.00 | OTF |
| 525 | BANKS | 27.50 | BC |
| 530 | YAZ | 30.00 | BC |
| 550 | KILLEBREW | 15.00 | BC |
| 570 | PALMER | 27.50 | BC |
| 574 | BUNNING | 3.00 | OTF |
| 580 | PEREZ | 10.00 | BC |
| 600 | MAYS | 72.50 | BC |
| 625 | BROCK | 22.50 | BC |
| 630 | CLEMENTE | 52.50 | BC |
| 640 | F. ROBINSON | 30.00 | BC |
| 740 | APARICIO | 12.50 | BC |

**1972 TOPPS.** From a photographic standpoint, this may have been Topps's best effort ever. Sharp, clear, and well-composed action and posed images featured uncharacteristically vivid colors. The border design, however, is a matter of personal taste. Known as the "stained glass" or "mod" set, there hasn't been anything quite like it since. An In Action subset featured interesting shots of many stars and a few scrubs, with each card following a player's regular card. Players with In Action cards—which are valued at roughly 40 percent of regular cards—are identified with an asterisk. Other innovations include a Kid's Picture subset, which was never really popular, and Topps's first Traded subset, which was immensely popular right out of the gate. This was the largest set the company manufactured in its first thirty years, and the final series wasn't easy to find before Labor Day that year.

*Warning:* For some reason, top-to-bottom centering was a particular problem with this set. That's easy to spot. But another problem—uneven inking on the backs of cards—is not. This snafu appears as "faded" printing and is usually found near the center of a card's back. For this reason, you must be extra careful when grading 1972 cards—the Ryan card is especially prone to this problem. Also, there are a lot more high-number

cards around than dealers would have you believe.

*Avoid:* A lot of needlessly overpriced rookies: Richard, Harrah, Cruz, Chambliss, Porter, Speier, Hough, Burroughs, Rivers, Stone, Zisk, Hendrick, Milner, and Dempsey.

*Tough Call:* Ron Cey and Dave Kingman. There's no denying that Cey was a winner, as well as a productive and high-profile star. A case could even be made that behind Schmidt, he was the best at his position while he played. But "The Penguin" has little hope of enshrinement. Kingman is tougher. Had he not tortured the press—many of whom are now Hall of Fame voters—his gaudy power stats might have enabled him to squeak in. Who knows, fifty years from now someone on the Veteran's Committee may dig up some old film clips and convince a lot of guys who aren't even born yet to vote him in. Stranger things have happened in upstate New York.

Set: $1,700.00
Commons (1–132): $.25
Commons (133–525): $.50
Commons (526–656): $1.50
Commons (657–787): $3.50

| 37 | YASTRZEMSKI* | 10.00 | BC |
|---|---|---|---|
| 49 | MAYS* | 20.00 | BC |
| 51 | KILLEBREW* | 3.00 | BC |
| 79 | FISK | 110.00 | BC |
| 80 | PEREZ | 3.00 | BC |
| 100 | F. ROBINSON | 4.00 | BC |
| 130 | GIBSON | 4.00 | BC |
| 132 | MORGAN | 3.50 | BC |
| 154 | SIMMONS | 1.50 | OTF |
| 200 | BROCK | 4.00 | BC |
| 241 | FINGERS | 5.00 | BC |
| 264 | JOHN | 1.00 | OTF |
| 267 | CONCEPCION | 1.00 | OTF |
| 270 | PALMER | 10.00 | BC |
| 280 | MCCOVEY | 4.00 | BC |
| 285 | PERRY | 5.00 | BC |
| 299 | AARON* | 25.00 | BC |
| 309 | CLEMENTE* | 27.50 | BC |
| 313 | APARICIO* | 1.50 | BC |

| 330 | HUNTER | 3.00 | BC |
|---|---|---|---|
| 410 | JENKINS | 5.00 | BC |
| 420 | CARLTON | 17.50 | BC |
| 433 | BENCH* | 32.50 | BC |
| 435 | JACKSON* | 40.00 | BC |
| 439 | B. WILLIAMS* | 3.00 | BC |
| 441 | MUNSON* | 15.00 | OTF |
| 445 | SEAVER* | 35.00 | BC |
| 447 | STARGELL* | 3.50 | BC |
| 510 | T. WILLIAMS | 5.00 | BC |
| 515 | BLYLEVEN | 7.00 | OTF |
| 530 | SUTTON | 3.50 | OTF |
| 550 | B. ROBINSON | 17.50 | BC |
| 555 | SANTO* | 2.50 | OTF |
| 559 | ROSE* | 27.50 | OTF |
| 567 | MARICHAL* | 5.00 | BC |
| 590 | NETTLES | 2.50 | OTF |
| 595 | RYAN | 195.00 | BC |
| 600 | KALINE | 15.00 | BC |
| 620 | NIEKRO | 4.00 | OTF |
| 686 | GARVEY | 62.50 | OTF |
| 695 | CAREW* | 90.00 | BC |
| 751 | TRADED: CARLTON | 42.50 | BC |
| 752 | TRADED: MORGAN | 35.00 | BC |
| 754 | TRADED: ROBINSON | 25.00 | BC |
| 760 | MAZEROSKI | 5.00 | OTF |
| 777 | WILHELM | 10.00 | BC |

**1973 TOPPS.** This was the final set Topps issued by series. The fifth and last series is the toughest. A somewhat bizarre subset of All-Time Leaders was included, which included two cards of Ty Cobb and Walter Johnson and only one of Babe Ruth. To make matters worse, it's not entirely clear which team's uniform Ruth is wearing. Hank Aaron is also featured in this subset, wearing his hideous 1972 Braves softball uniform. Needless to say, these cards have never been all that popular. Also, for the second year in a row, a Kid's Picture subset was issued. No one liked it the first year, and no one liked it in 1973, either. The last series contains only one great card: the Mike Schmidt rookie. But for daredevils, the pricey Boone and Evans rookies are there, too.

*Warning:* As with most thick, white-border sets, there is a problem. In this case, layering is more prevalent than chipping, and bubbles seem to be a problem, too. Meanwhile, many cards have surfaced with wrong backs. Are they, as many dealers would have you think, worth five times what a regular card goes for? Consider the source. Attention, checklist collectors: there's a $15 baby in the last series.

*Avoid:* Reuschel, Bell, Maddox, Lacy, Vukovich, Lopes, and Gary Matthews.

*Tough Call:* No one, unless you think Buddy Bell is headed for the Hall.

*Set: $950.00*
*Commons (1–397): $.25*
*Commons (398–528): $.50*
*Commons (529–660): $1.25*

| 1 | HR LEADERS | 17.50 | BC |
|---|---|---|---|
| 10 | SUTTON | 2.00 | OTF |
| 50 | CLEMENTE | 25.00 | BC |
| 67 | LEADERS: RYAN | 7.00 | BC |
| 84 | FINGERS | 4.50 | BC |
| 85 | SIMMONS | 1.00 | OTF |
| 90 | B. ROBINSON | 4.50 | BC |
| 100 | AARON | 20.00 | BC |
| 115 | SANTO | .50 | OTF |
| 130 | ROSE | 12.50 | OTF |
| 142 | MUNSON | 8.50 | OTF |
| 160 | PALMER | 7.50 | BC |
| 165 | APARICIO | 1.50 | BC |
| 170 | KILLEBREW | 3.00 | BC |
| 174 | GOSSAGE | 12.50 | OTF |
| 175 | F. ROBINSON | 3.50 | BC |
| 180 | JENKINS | 2.50 | BC |
| 190 | GIBSON | 4.00 | BC |
| 193 | FISK | 37.50 | BC |
| 199 | BLYLEVEN | 2.00 | OTF |
| 200 | WILLIAMS | 2.00 | BC |
| 213 | GARVEY | 9.00 | OTF |
| 220 | RYAN | 72.50 | BC |
| 230 | MORGAN | 3.00 | BC |
| 235 | HUNTER | 2.50 | BC |
| 245 | YASTRZEMSKI | 10.00 | BC |

| | | | |
|---|---|---|---|
| 255 | JACKSON | 30.00 | BC |
| 275 | PEREZ | 3.50 | BC |
| 280 | KALINE | 3.50 | BC |
| 300 | CARLTON | 10.00 | BC |
| 305 | MAYS | 25.00 | BC |
| 320 | BROCK | 3.50 | BC |
| 330 | CAREW | 12.50 | BC |
| 350 | SEAVER | 25.00 | BC |
| 370 | STARGELL | 3.00 | BC |
| 380 | BENCH | 17.50 | BC |
| 400 | PERRY | 2.50 | BC |
| 410 | MCCOVEY | 3.50 | BC |
| 474 | RUTH | 5.00 | BC |
| 480 | MARICHAL | 2.50 | BC |
| 498 | NETTLES | 1.50 | OTF |
| 503 | NIEKRO | 2.00 | OTF |
| 554 | CONCEPCION | 2.50 | OTF |
| 613 | BOONE | 30.00 | OTF |
| 614 | EVANS | 60.00 | OTF |
| 614 | SCHMIDT | 425.00 | PC |

**1974 TOPPS.** The first set that Topps released all at once (instead of in series) obviously benefited from this mode of distribution. There are a great number of cards available in very collectible condition—and a noticeable absence of rubber band marks and other signs of wear normally associated with sets issued in small series. The set is noticeably lacking in great rookie cards—Winfield and Parker are about it—but there are plenty of Hall of Famers.

*Warning:* The first cases shipped by Topps contained cards of players identified as playing for Washington. That winter it looked like the Padres would be moving to D.C., and Topps was trying to hedge its bets. The error was quickly corrected. The Washington cards, though hard to find, have never been very popular and are probably worth less than half of what most dealers try to get for them. Had the Winfield rookie been produced with this variation, it would probably sell for $500. But it wasn't, so quit dreaming. Another error occurred when Topps left the position off of Jesus Alou's card. This was corrected at the same time as the Washington cards, but has never gen-

erated much buyer interest. Also, the "sideways" or horizontally oriented cards in this set are a little harder to find in perfect shape. Why? Perhaps damage was incurred as a result of kids turning the cards carelessly as they came out of the packs. The same problem exists in the 1973 set, but it's not as bad. Buyers of Fisk, Frank Robinson, Santo, Seaver, and Garvey shouldn't blink at a 25 percent premium for true *mint* cards.

*Avoid:* Thomas, Dent, Madlock, Tanana, Downing, and Frank White.

*Tough Call:* Ken Griffey. He was very good, but not great. Had he learned to pull the ball when he arrived at Yankee Stadium things might have been different. But that was not the kind of hitter Griffey was. Unless the Hall of Fame voters want a father-son parlay or decide to give out plaques for good genes, Griffey will probably fall short. Thanks to his son, Ken's rookie card is three times what it should be.

*Set: $525.00*
*Commons: $.20*

| | | | |
|---|---|---|---|
| 1 | AARON | 22.50 | BC |
| 7 | HUNTER | 2.50 | BC |
| 10 | BENCH | 10.00 | BC |
| 20 | RYAN | 50.00 | BC |
| 29 | NIEKRO | 1.50 | OTF |
| 35 | PERRY | 2.00 | BC |
| 40 | PALMER | 7.00 | BC |
| 50 | CAREW | 10.00 | BC |
| 55 | F. ROBINSON | 3.00 | BC |
| 60 | BROCK | 3.00 | BC |
| 61 | APARICIO | 1.00 | BC |
| 80 | SEAVER | 17.50 | BC |
| 85 | MORGAN | 3.00 | BC |
| 87 | JENKINS | 2.50 | BC |
| 95 | CARLTON | 7.50 | BC |
| 98 | BLYLEVEN | 1.50 | OTF |
| 100 | STARGELL | 2.00 | BC |
| 105 | FISK | 22.50 | BC |
| 110 | WILLIAMS | 2.00 | BC |
| 130 | JACKSON | 22.50 | BC |
| 131 | BOONE | 2.00 | OTF |

| 160 | B. ROBINSON | 4.00 | BC |
|-----|-------------|------|-----|
| 207 | LEADERS: RYAN | 7.50 | BC |
| 212 | FINGERS | 5.00 | BC |
| 215 | KALINE | 3.00 | BC |
| 220 | SUTTON | 2.00 | OTF |
| 230 | PEREZ | 3.00 | BC |
| 250 | MCCOVEY | 3.00 | BC |
| 250 | MCCOVEY (WAS.) | 20.00 | BC |
| 251 | NETTLES | 1.00 | OTF |
| 252 | PARKER | 25.00 | OTF |
| 260 | SIMMONS | 1.00 | OTF |
| 270 | SANTO | .50 | OTF |
| 280 | YASTRZEMSKI | 9.00 | BC |
| 283 | SCHMIDT | 70.00 | BC |
| 300 | ROSE | 7.50 | OTF |
| 330 | MARICHAL | 2.00 | BC |
| 340 | MUNSON | 7.50 | OTF |
| 350 | GIBSON | 3.00 | BC |
| 351 | EVANS | 10.00 | OTF |
| 400 | KILLEBREW | 2.50 | BC |
| 435 | CONCEPCION | 1.00 | OTF |
| 451 | JOHN | 1.00 | OTF |
| 456 | WINFIELD | 85.00 | BC |
| 542 | GOSSAGE | 3.00 | OTF |
| 575 | GARVEY | 7.00 | OTF |

**1975 TOPPS.** A high-powered set that's increasingly difficult to find in collectible condition. The bright two-tone border design makes even the slightest wear very obvious. A nice innovation was the MVP subset, a spin on Topps's 1961 effort. Also, a set of mini cards was issued that same year, and although it was snapped up immediately, it has never really taken off. Cards from the mini set sell for little more than 50 percent above the prices for cards from the regular set.

*Warning:* Centering was a big problem in this set, so pay attention—don't let the flashy colors dull your senses while grading.

*Avoid:* Decinces, Rhoden, Lynn, and Claudell Washington.

*Tough Call:* Nothing tough, except the MVP cards, which should be regarded as little more than novelties.

*Set: $750.00*
*Commons: $.15*

| 1 | HILITE: AARON | 17.50 | BC |
|-----|---------------|-------|-----|
| 5 | HILITE: RYAN | 10.00 | BC |
| 17 | CONCEPCION | 1.00 | OTF |
| 20 | MUNSON | 7.50 | OTF |
| 21 | FINGERS | 3.50 | BC |
| 29 | PARKER | 8.00 | OTF |
| 30 | BLYLEVEN | 1.50 | OTF |
| 35 | SANTO | .50 | OTF |
| 47 | JOHN | 1.00 | OTF |
| 50 | B. ROBINSON | 4.00 | BC |
| 60 | JENKINS | 2.50 | BC |
| 61 | WINFIELD | 25.00 | BC |
| 70 | SCHMIDT | 55.00 | BC |
| 75 | SIMMONS | 1.00 | OTF |
| 80 | FISK | 17.50 | BC |
| 100 | STARGELL | 2.00 | BC |
| 130 | NIEKRO | 2.50 | OTF |
| 140 | GARVEY | 5.00 | OTF |
| 150 | GIBSON | 3.50 | BC |
| 160 | NETTLES | 1.00 | OTF |
| 180 | MORGAN | 4.50 | BC |
| 185 | CARLTON | 7.50 | BC |
| 195 | MVP: MANTLE/AARON | 7.50 | BC |
| 220 | SUTTON | 2.00 | OTF |
| 223 | YOUNT | 200.00 | BC |
| 228 | BRETT | 200.00 | BC |
| 230 | HUNTER | 2.00 | BC |
| 255 | EVANS | 4.50 | OTF |
| 260 | BENCH | 10.00 | BC |
| 280 | YASTRZEMSKI | 7.50 | BC |
| 300 | JACKSON | 20.00 | BC |
| 312 | LEADERS: RYAN | 7.50 | BC |
| 320 | ROSE | 10.00 | OTF |
| 335 | PALMER | 6.50 | BC |
| 351 | BOONE | .50 | OTF |
| 370 | SEAVER | 17.50 | BC |
| 450 | MCCOVEY | 3.00 | BC |
| 500 | RYAN | 55.00 | BC |
| 530 | PERRY | 2.50 | BC |
| 540 | BROCK | 3.00 | BC |
| 545 | WILLIAMS | 2.00 | BC |
| 554 | GOSSAGE | 1.50 | OTF |

| | | | |
|---|---|---|---|
| 560 | PEREZ | 2.50 | BC |
| 580 | F. ROBINSON | 3.00 | BC |
| 600 | CAREW | 8.50 | BC |
| 616 | RICE | 15.00 | OTF |
| 620 | CARTER | 35.00 | BC |
| 623 | HERNANDEZ | 15.00 | OTF |
| 640 | KILLEBREW | 3.00 | BC |
| 660 | AARON | 17.50 | BC |

**1976 TOPPS.** By some accounts an overrated set. There is only one rookie card of consequence—Eckersley's—and because of his odd-though-successful career, he is by no means a shoo-in for Cooperstown. Also, there seem to be far more 1976 cards available in collectible condition than there are 1975 and 1977 cards, which no one has ever been able to fully explain.

*Warning:* The All-Time Greats subset is notoriously difficult to sell, despite the presence of Ruth, Gehrig, Williams, and Cobb.

*Avoid:* Tekulve, Candaleria, Flanagan, and Randolph.

*Tough Call:* Ron Guidry. As terrific as he was, he was only terrific for a few years. Then again, Hal Newhouser made the Hall of Fame.

Set: $345.00
Commons: $ .10

| | | | |
|---|---|---|---|
| 1 | RECORD: AARON | 10.00 | BC |
| 19 | BRETT | 47.50 | BC |
| 48 | CONCEPCION | .50 | OTF |
| 55 | PERRY | 2.00 | BC |
| 95 | ROBINSON | 3.00 | BC |
| 98 | ECKERSLEY | 42.50 | VC |
| 100 | HUNTER | 2.00 | BC |
| 150 | GARVEY | 3.50 | OTF |
| 160 | WINFIELD | 15.00 | BC |
| 169 | NETTLES | .75 | OTF |
| 180 | GOSSAGE | 1.50 | OTF |
| 185 | PARKER | 3.50 | OTF |
| 230 | YASTRZEMSKI | 6.50 | BC |
| 235 | BLYLEVEN | 1.50 | OTF |

| | | | |
|---|---|---|---|
| 240 | ROSE | 7.50 | OTF |
| 250 | JENKINS | 2.00 | BC |
| 270 | STARGELL | 2.00 | BC |
| 290 | SIMMONS | .50 | OTF |
| 300 | BENCH | 8.00 | BC |
| 316 | YOUNT | 47.50 | BC |
| 318 | BOONE | .50 | OTF |
| 325 | PEREZ | 2.00 | BC |
| 330 | RYAN | 47.50 | BC |
| 340 | RICE | 4.50 | OTF |
| 341 | GEHRIG | 4.00 | BC |
| 345 | RUTH | 6.00 | BC |
| 346 | COBB | 3.50 | BC |
| 347 | T. WILLIAMS | 4.00 | BC |
| 355 | CARLTON | 5.50 | BC |
| 365 | FISK | 9.50 | BC |
| 400 | CAREW | 6.50 | BC |
| 405 | FINGERS | 3.00 | BC |
| 416 | JOHN | .50 | OTF |
| 420 | MORGAN | 3.50 | BC |
| 435 | NIEKRO | 1.50 | OTF |
| 441 | CARTER | 7.50 | BC |
| 450 | PALMER | 5.00 | BC |
| 480 | SCHMIDT | 32.50 | BC |
| 500 | JACKSON | 17.50 | BC |
| 520 | MCCOVEY | 2.50 | BC |
| 525 | B. WILLIAMS | 1.50 | BC |
| 530 | SUTTON | 2.00 | OTF |
| 542 | HERNANDEZ | 2.50 | OTF |
| 550 | AARON | 17.50 | BC |
| 575 | EVANS | 1.50 | OTF |
| 600 | SEAVER | 12.50 | BC |
| 650 | MUNSON | 6.00 | OTF |

**1977 TOPPS.** Bright white borders make the cards in this set very hard to find in *mint* condition. That means you shouldn't shy away from a 20 percent premium for perfect cards—it will definitely pay off down the road, especially for players like Eckersley, Nettles, Boone, Fisk, Gossage, Simmons, Niekro, etc., who have emerged relatively recently as serious Hall of Fame candidates. This was an interesting set for another reason: 1977 saw a big surge in card prices, as the national media finally picked up on the fact that people were spending serious money on cards. A lot of new buyers joined the fray and bought this set, which might account for the poor condition of so many key cards.

*Warning:* There were some boo-boos during the printing process, and many cards feature "smudges" or "faded" areas. Steer clear of these cards.

*Avoid:* Templeton, Fidrych, Clark, and Gantner.

*Tough Call:* Bruce Sutter and Dennis Martinez. Sutter barely qualifies for Cooperstown, although some claim that he revolutionized relief pitching. He could make it, but other closers will make it before him. As for Martinez, he's one of the game's best pitchers and most inspiring stories, but he's been pitching in bad luck for too many years. A couple of 20-win seasons would change the picture dramatically.

*Set: $385.00*
*Commons: $ .08*

| | | | |
|---|---|---|---|
| 6 | LEADERS: RYAN | 6.00 | BC |
| 10 | JACKSON | 12.50 | BC |
| 20 | NETTLES | .50 | OTF |
| 25 | EVANS | 1.50 | OTF |
| 60 | RICE | 2.00 | OTF |
| 70 | BENCH | 7.50 | BC |
| 95 | HERNANDEZ | 1.50 | OTF |
| 100 | MORGAN | 2.50 | BC |
| 110 | CARLTON | 5.50 | BC |
| 120 | CAREW | 5.50 | BC |
| 128 | JOHN | .50 | OTF |
| 140 | SCHMIDT | 20.00 | BC |
| 150 | SEAVER | 9.00 | BC |
| 152 | PERRY | 1.00 | BC |
| 170 | MUNSON | 4.50 | OTF |
| 234 | RECORD: RYAN | 8.00 | BC |
| 270 | PARKER | 2.50 | OTF |
| 280 | HUNTER | 1.50 | BC |
| 285 | ROBINSON | 3.00 | BC |
| 295 | CARTER | 4.00 | BC |
| 319 | GOSSAGE | .75 | OTF |
| 355 | BROCK | 2.50 | BC |

| | | | |
|---|---|---|---|
| 390 | WINFIELD | 9.00 | BC |
| 400 | GARVEY | 2.00 | OTF |
| 430 | JENKINS | 1.50 | BC |
| 450 | ROSE | 6.00 | OTF |
| 460 | STARGELL | 1.50 | BC |
| 470 | SIMMONS | .25 | OTF |
| 473 | DAWSON | 55.00 | BC |
| 476 | MURPHY | 30.00 | BC |
| 480 | YASTRZEMSKI | 5.00 | BC |
| 523 | FINGERS | 2.50 | BC |
| 525 | ECKERSLEY | 10.00 | VC |
| 545 | BOONE | .25 | OTF |
| 547 | MCCOVEY | 2.00 | BC |
| 560 | CONCEPCION | .25 | OTF |
| 580 | BRETT | 32.50 | BC |
| 600 | PALMER | 4.00 | BC |
| 615 | NIEKRO | 1.00 | OTF |
| 620 | SUTTON | 1.00 | OTF |
| 630 | BLYLEVEN | .50 | OTF |
| 635 | YOUNT | 32.50 | BC |
| 640 | FISK | 6.50 | BC |
| 650 | RYAN | 32.50 | BC |
| 655 | PEREZ | 1.50 | BC |

**1978 TOPPS.** If you believe in Paul Molitor and Alan Trammel, this is your set. The two share a rookie card that could conceivably be the first to depict two Hall of Famers. Otherwise, a sloppy effort by Topps, with airbrushed action shots as well as spotty color and contrast.

*Warning:* A lot of off-center cards in this set. The Murray rookie in particular—a certain $100 card—is hard to find perfectly centered. Also, many cards feature rough or fuzzy cuts, so check all four borders carefully. Four key cards were double-printed: Perez, Rose, Nettles, and Morris. Be choosy about condition on these cards. Double-printed commons sell for a penny or two.

*Avoid:* Ray Knight. Also, don't pay a premium for Lance Parrish's rookie card—you're only buying Dale Murphy.

*Tough Call:* Everyone's pretty clear-cut here.

*Set: $300.00*
*Commons: $ .06*

| 6 | RECORD: RYAN | 5.00 | BC |
|---|---|---|---|
| 10 | NIEKRO | 1.00 | OTF |
| 15 | PEREZ | .50 | BC |
| 20 | ROSE | 2.00 | OTF |
| 34 | MCCOVEY | 1.50 | BC |
| 36 | MURRAY | 65.00 | BC |
| 40 | YASTRZEMSKI | 3.00 | BC |
| 60 | MUNSON | 3.50 | OTF |
| 70 | GOSSAGE | .50 | OTF |
| 72 | DAWSON | 12.50 | BC |
| 100 | BRETT | 15.00 | BC |
| 120 | CARTER | 2.00 | BC |
| 122 | ECKERSLEY | 5.50 | VC |
| 131 | BLYLEVEN | .25 | OTF |
| 140 | FINGERS | 2.50 | BC |
| 143 | HERNANDEZ | 1.00 | OTF |
| 160 | PALMER | 3.00 | BC |
| 161 | BOONE | .25 | OTF |
| 170 | BROCK | 2.00 | BC |
| 173 | YOUNT | 15.00 | BC |
| 180 | CONCEPCION | .25 | OTF |
| 200 | JACKSON | 8.00 | BC |
| 250 | NETTLES | .25 | OTF |
| 270 | FISK | 4.50 | BC |
| 300 | MORGAN | 2.00 | BC |
| 310 | SUTTON | 1.00 | OTF |
| 350 | GARVEY | 2.00 | OTF |
| 360 | SCHMIDT | 12.50 | BC |
| 375 | JOHN | .50 | OTF |
| 380 | SIMMONS | .25 | OTF |
| 400 | RYAN | 25.00 | BC |
| 450 | SEAVER | 6.00 | BC |
| 460 | HUNTER | 1.50 | BC |
| 510 | STARGELL | 1.50 | BC |
| 530 | WINFIELD | 6.00 | BC |
| 540 | CARLTON | 3.00 | BC |
| 560 | PARKER | 2.00 | OTF |
| 580 | CAREW | 3.50 | BC |
| 670 | RICE | 1.50 | OTF |
| 686 | PERRY | 1.00 | BC |
| 695 | EVANS | 1.00 | OTF |
| 700 | BENCH | 3.50 | BC |
| 703 | MORRIS | 10.00 | VC |
| 704 | WHITAKER | 12.50 | OTF |
| 707 | MOLITOR/ TRAMMEL | 40.00 | VC |
| 708 | MURPHY | 12.50 | BC |
| 720 | JENKINS | 1.50 | BC |

**1979 TOPPS.** Many of the rookie cards in this set have taken a nosedive of late, diminishing buyer demand, which was never all that high, due to the fact that Topps decided to double-print a number of Hall of Famers. But there are plenty of good cards here, and it's as straightforward an issue as you'll find.

*Warning:* The Seaver, Morgan, Garvey, Bench, Hunter, and Jackson cards were double-printed, so be picky about condition. Double-printed commons sell for a penny or two. Also, the Bump Wills card depicts him on either the Blue Jays or the Rangers—don't nibble at any price.

*Avoid:* Whitson, Lansford, Welch, Wilson, Parrish, Clark, Horner, Baylor, Bass, Guerrero, Sanderson, and Lonnie Smith.

*Tough Call:* No borderline players appear in this set—either they've got a decent shot at the Hall of Fame or no chance at all.

*Set: $215.00*
*Commons: $ .04*

| 20 | MORGAN | .75 | BC |
|---|---|---|---|
| 24 | MOLITOR | 6.00 | VC |
| 25 | CARLTON | 2.75 | BC |
| 30 | WINFIELD | 5.00 | BC |
| 39 | MURPHY | 5.00 | BC |
| 40 | ECKERSLEY | 4.00 | OTF |
| 50 | GARVEY | .75 | OTF |
| 55 | STARGELL | 1.00 | BC |
| 90 | BOONE | .25 | OTF |
| 95 | YOUNT | 10.00 | BC |
| 100 | SEAVER | 2.00 | BC |
| 115 | RYAN | 22.50 | BC |
| 116 | SMITH | 55.00 | BC |
| 123 | WHITAKER | 4.00 | VC |
| 155 | EVANS | .75 | OTF |
| 170 | SUTTON | .75 | OTF |
| 200 | BENCH | 2.00 | BC |

| 215 | MCCOVEY | 1.00 | BC |
|---|---|---|---|
| 225 | GOSSAGE | .75 | OTF |
| 251 | MORRIS | 5.00 | VC |
| 255 | JOHN | .50 | OTF |
| 300 | CAREW | 2.75 | BC |
| 308 | BLYLEVEN | .25 | OTF |
| 310 | MUNSON | 2.75 | OTF |
| 320 | YASTRZEMSKI | 2.75 | BC |
| 321 | PERRY | 1.25 | BC |
| 330 | BRETT | 10.00 | BC |
| 340 | PALMER | 2.00 | BC |
| 348 | DAWSON | 8.50 | BC |
| 358 | TRAMMELL | 7.50 | VC |
| 390 | FINGERS | 1.00 | BC |
| 400 | RICE | .75 | OTF |
| 430 | PARKER | 1.00 | OTF |
| 450 | CONCEPCION | .25 | OTF |
| 460 | NETTLES | .25 | OTF |
| 495 | PEREZ | .75 | BC |
| 520 | CARTER | 2.00 | BC |
| 544 | JENKINS | .75 | BC |
| 595 | NIEKRO | .75 | OTF |
| 610 | SCHMIDT | 8.50 | BC |
| 640 | MURRAY | 17.50 | BC |
| 650 | ROSE | 2.75 | OTF |
| 665 | BROCK | 1.50 | BC |
| 670 | HUNTER | .50 | BC |
| 680 | FISK | 4.00 | BC |
| 695 | HERNANDEZ | 1.00 | OTF |
| 700 | JACKSON | 2.75 | BC |

**1980 TOPPS.** The last year Topps had the market to itself. Because none of these cards is difficult to find in collectible condition, only the Henderson and Ryan cards should be purchased in less than *excellent* condition.

*Warning:* The Schmidt, Carew, and Yastrzemski cards were double-printed, so be extremely choosy if you decide to buy them. Double-printed commons sell for a penny or two. Also, look closely for chipped borders.

*Avoid:* Steib, Scott, Welch, Sutcliffe, and Mike Morgan.

*Tough Call:* Quisenberry. He was the best when he played, but did he play long enough to crack into Cooperstown? If you're a gambler, go for it—but don't blow more than half a buck.

*Set: $235.00*
*Commons: $ .04*

| 40 | FISK | 4.00 | BC |
|---|---|---|---|
| 70 | CARTER | 1.75 | BC |
| 100 | BENCH | 2.50 | BC |
| 125 | PEREZ | .75 | BC |
| 140 | GOSSAGE | .50 | OTF |
| 160 | MURRAY | 9.00 | BC |
| 200 | RICE | .35 | OTF |
| 210 | CARLTON | 2.75 | BC |
| 230 | WINFIELD | 3.50 | BC |
| 232 | TRAMMELL | 3.00 | VC |
| 235 | DAWSON | 6.50 | BC |
| 245 | NIEKRO | .75 | OTF |
| 265 | YOUNT | 9.00 | BC |
| 270 | SCHMIDT | 2.50 | BC |
| 274 | MURPHY | 2.50 | BC |
| 280 | PERRY | .75 | BC |
| 290 | GARVEY | 1.00 | OTF |
| 310 | PARKER | 1.00 | OTF |
| 320 | ECKERSLEY | 1.50 | OTF |
| 321 | HERNANDEZ | .75 | OTF |
| 335 | MCCOVEY | 1.00 | BC |
| 358 | WHITAKER | 2.00 | VC |
| 371 | MORRIS | 3.00 | VC |
| 390 | JENKINS | .75 | BC |
| 393 | SMITH | 10.00 | BC |
| 405 | EVANS | .75 | OTF |
| 406 | MOLITOR | 2.75 | VC |
| 440 | SUTTON | .75 | OTF |
| 450 | BRETT | 9.00 | BC |
| 457 | BLYLEVEN | .25 | OTF |
| 470 | BOONE | .25 | OTF |
| 482 | HENDERSON | 110.00 | BC |
| 500 | SEAVER | 3.00 | BC |
| 540 | ROSE | 2.75 | OTF |
| 580 | RYAN | 15.00 | BC |
| 590 | PALMER | 2.25 | BC |
| 600 | JACKSON | 4.75 | BC |
| 610 | STARGELL | 1.00 | BC |
| 650 | MORGAN | 1.00 | BC |

| | | | |
|---|---|---|---|
| 651 | FINGERS | .75 | BC |
| 690 | JOHN | .25 | OTF |
| 700 | CAREW | 1.00 | BC |
| 720 | YASTRZEMSKI | 1.00 | BC |

**1981 TOPPS.** Of the three 1981 sets, this has clearly been the buyers' choice for a decade. But there's not much to buy other than the Reardon card. It spent a lot of years banging around in commons boxes and can be hard to find in true *mint* condition. Overall, these cards have held up well, so be choosy.

*Warning:* The Schmidt and Trammell cards were double-printed, so only buy them if they're perfect. Double-printed commons sell for a penny or two. Also, keep an eye on centering—it looks like someone was asleep at the controls of the Topps cutting machine in '81!

*Avoid:* A ton of overpriced rookies: Tudor, Leibrandt, Brooks, Baines, Gibson, Boddicker, Pena, Gullickson, and Hurst.

*Tough Call:* Sadly, Fernando. He qualifies for the Hall under only the most liberal criteria and his rookie card looks doomed to become little more than a novelty item.

*Set: $75.00*
*Commons: $ .03*

| | | | |
|---|---|---|---|
| 100 | CAREW | 1.75 | BC |
| 110 | YASTRZEMSKI | 1.75 | BC |
| 125 | DAWSON | 2.25 | BC |
| 158 | JENKINS | .25 | BC |
| 180 | ROSE | 2.00 | OTF |
| 210 | PALMER | 1.75 | BC |
| 220 | SEAVER | 1.50 | BC |
| 229 | FINGERS | 1.25 | BC |
| 234 | WHITAKER | .50 | OTF |
| 240 | RYAN | 8.50 | BC |
| 254 | SMITH | 3.75 | BC |
| 261 | HENDERSON | 15.00 | BC |
| 275 | EVANS | .25 | OTF |
| 300 | MOLITOR | 1.00 | OTF |
| 370 | WINFIELD | 1.50 | BC |
| 380 | STARGELL | .75 | BC |

| | | | |
|---|---|---|---|
| 387 | NIEKRO | .35 | OTF |
| 400 | JACKSON | 2.75 | BC |
| 420 | HERNANDEZ | .30 | OTF |
| 456 | REARDON | 8.00 | BC |
| 479 | RAINES | 5.00 | VC |
| 480 | FISK | 2.50 | BC |
| 490 | MURRAY | 3.25 | BC |
| 500 | RICE | .25 | OTF |
| 504 | MURPHY | .75 | BC |
| 515 | YOUNT | 3.75 | BC |
| 530 | GARVEY | .40 | OTF |
| 540 | SCHMIDT | 1.50 | BC |
| 560 | MORGAN | .60 | BC |
| 572 | MORRIS | 1.75 | OTF |
| 575 | PEREZ | .40 | BC |
| 582 | PERRY | .30 | BC |
| 600 | BENCH | 1.75 | BC |
| 605 | SUTTON | .30 | OTF |
| 620 | ECKERSLEY | 1.25 | OTF |
| 630 | CARLTON | 1.50 | BC |
| 640 | PARKER | .40 | OTF |
| 660 | CARTER | .75 | BC |
| 700 | BRETT | 3.75 | BC |
| 709 | TRAMMELL | .50 | OTF |

## 1981 TOPPS TRADED
*Set: $40.00*

| | | | |
|---|---|---|---|
| 738 | BLYLEVEN | .50 | OTF |
| 761 | FINGERS | 2.50 | BC |
| 762 | FISK | 6.00 | BC |
| 807 | MORGAN | 1.50 | BC |
| 812 | PERRY | 1.00 | BC |
| 816 | RAINES | 7.75 | VC |
| 819 | REARDON | 12.50 | BC |
| 839 | SUTTON | 1.50 | OTF |
| 855 | WINFIELD | 6.75 | BC |

**1981 DONRUSS.** A potentially interesting set that was ruined by inconsistent printing, worthless errors, flimsy stock, and vile-tasting gum. Until Henderson's card took off three years ago, this set could still be purchased at its 1981 price.

*Warning:* A lot of errors that don't make one lick of difference, even on the premium cards. Also, if you must buy any cards in this set, at least try to pick ones that are centered and have colors that approximate human flesh tones—don't laugh, it's harder than you think!

   *Avoid:* See 1981 Topps.
   *Tough Call:* See 1981 Topps.

*Set: $45.00*
*Commons: $ .01*

| | | | |
|---|---|---|---|
| 1 | SMITH | 1.75 | BC |
| 2 | FINGERS | .50 | BC |
| 5 | TRAMMELL | .35 | OTF |
| 11 | SCHMIDT | 1.25 | BC |
| 12 | STARGELL | .35 | BC |
| 18 | MORGAN | .25 | BC |
| 33 | CARLTON | 1.00 | BC |
| 49 | CAREW | .75 | BC |
| 56 | GARVEY | .35 | OTF |
| 62 | BENCH | .75 | BC |
| 90 | CARTER | .50 | BC |
| 94 | YASTRZEMSKI | 1.00 | BC |
| 96 | ECKERSLEY | .75 | OTF |
| 100 | BRETT | 2.00 | BC |
| 112 | MURRAY | 1.50 | BC |
| 119 | HENDERSON | 8.50 | BC |
| 127 | MORRIS | .75 | OTF |
| 131 | ROSE | .75 | OTF |
| 132 | STARGELL | .25 | BC |
| 156 | REARDON | 5.00 | BC |
| 169 | CAREW | .75 | BC |
| 176 | GARVEY | .35 | OTF |
| 182 | BENCH | 1.00 | BC |
| 203 | MOLITOR | .75 | OTF |
| 212 | DAWSON | .75 | BC |
| 214 | YASTRZEMSKI | 1.00 | BC |
| 228 | JACKSON | 1.75 | BC |
| 251 | ROSE | .75 | OTF |
| 260 | RYAN | 6.00 | BC |
| 323 | YOUNT | 2.00 | BC |
| 328 | NIEKRO | .30 | OTF |
| 324 | PEREZ | .25 | BC |
| 335 | FISK | 1.00 | BC |
| 348 | JACKSON | 1.75 | BC |
| 353 | PALMER | .75 | BC |
| 364 | WINFIELD | 1.25 | BC |
| 365 | WHITAKER | .30 | OTF |
| 371 | ROSE | .75 | OTF |
| 422 | SEAVER | 1.00 | BC |
| 425 | SEAVER | 1.00 | BC |
| 437 | MURPHY | .35 | BC |
| 468 | JACKSON | 1.75 | BC |
| 471 | PERRY | .25 | BC |
| 473 | PALMER | .75 | BC |
| 538 | RAINES | 2.50 | VC |

**1981 FLEER.** Once buyers got over the hype about the Nettles error, they realized that this wasn't a bad first effort. It was certainly better than the Donruss set and didn't look bad next to Topps.

   *Warning:* Steer clear of errors and variations.
   *Avoid:* See 1981 Topps.
   *Tough Call:* See 1981 Topps.

*Set: $47.50*
*Commons: $ .02*

| | | | |
|---|---|---|---|
| 1 | ROSE | 1.00 | BC |
| 5 | SCHMIDT | 1.25 | BC |
| 6 | CARLTON | 1.00 | BC |
| 28 | BRETT | 2.00 | BC |
| 57 | RYAN | 6.75 | BC |
| 78 | MORGAN | .30 | BC |
| 79 | JACKSON | 1.75 | BC |
| 87 | NETTLES ERROR | 7.50 | OTF |
| 91 | PERRY | .25 | BC |
| 110 | GARVEY | .30 | OTF |
| 142 | CARTER | .50 | BC |
| 145 | DAWSON | .75 | BC |
| 169 | PALMER | .75 | BC |
| 184 | MURRAY | 1.75 | BC |
| 196 | BENCH | 1.00 | BC |
| 200 | SEAVER | 1.00 | BC |
| 221 | YASTRZEMSKI | 1.00 | BC |
| 226 | ECKERSLEY | .75 | OTF |
| 241 | PEREZ | .20 | BC |
| 242 | NIEKRO | .30 | OTF |
| 243 | MURPHY | .35 | BC |
| 268 | CAREW | .75 | BC |
| 335 | REARDON | 6.00 | BC |
| 351 | HENDERSON | 7.50 | BC |

| | | | |
|---|---|---|---|
| 360 | PARKER | .25 | OTF |
| 363 | STARGELL | .35 | BC |
| 434 | MCCOVEY | .35 | BC |
| 461 | TRAMMELL | .35 | OTF |
| 463 | WHITAKER | .30 | OTF |
| 475 | MORRIS | .75 | OTF |
| 484 | WINFIELD | 1.25 | BC |
| 485 | FINGERS | .50 | BC |
| 488 | SMITH | 1.50 | BC |
| 511 | YOUNT | 2.00 | BC |
| 515 | MOLITOR | .75 | OTF |
| 574 | HENDERSON | 8.50 | BC |
| 606 | GARVEY | .35 | OTF |
| 638 | YASTRZEMSKI | 1.00 | BC |
| 640 | SCHMIDT | 1.25 | BC |
| 650 | JACKSON | 1.75 | BC |
| 655 | BRETT | 2.00 | BC |
| 660 | CARLTON | 1.00 | BC |

**1982 TOPPS.** An intriguing set that was available in great quantities for $40 before Cal Ripken answered his 1991 wake-up call. A lot of "maybes" in the rookie card category and an Action subset with possible long-term potential give this issue a life of its own. The question is, will it flourish or die? In this set, a player's In Action card follows his regular card and is worth about a third of the price listed below. Noteworthy players with In Action cards are marked with an asterisk.

*Warning:* Keep an eye out for printing imperfections in this set. Some Pascual Perez cards were released without his position listed. As few as there are, however, there are even fewer buyers for them. Slight variations in the All-Star cards of Seaver and George Foster are available, but no one really cares. There are plenty of Ripkens around in collectible collection, so don't jump at an off-condition example. Also, Dave Henderson's rookie card priced at anything more than a quarter is an outrage.

*Avoid:* Ainge, Hayes, Stewart, Wallach, Barfield, Ojeda, Righetti, Brunansky, and Chili Davis.

*Tough Call:* George Bell and Brett Butler. Two great players who enjoyed great years, but Bell's knees have betrayed him, and Butler had seen the

better side of twenty-five before he became a competent major leaguer.

*Set: $125.00*
*Commons: $ .02*

| | | | |
|---|---|---|---|
| 21 | RIPKEN | 70.00 | VC |
| 30 | SEAVER* | 1.75 | BC |
| 39 | WHITAKER | .25 | OTF |
| 40 | PARKER* | .25 | OTF |
| 70 | RAINES | .75 | VC |
| 80 | PALMER* | 1.00 | BC |
| 90 | RYAN | 8.00 | BC |
| 95 | O. SMITH | 1.75 | BC |
| 100 | SCHMIDT* | 2.75 | BC |
| 110 | FISK* | 1.50 | BC |
| 115 | PERRY | .25 | BC |
| 179 | GARVEY* | .35 | OTF |
| 185 | NIEKRO | .25 | OTF |
| 195 | MOLITOR | .75 | OTF |
| 200 | BRETT* | 2.50 | BC |
| 255 | PEREZ* | .35 | BC |
| 300 | JACKSON* | 2.00 | BC |
| 305 | SUTTON* | .25 | OTF |
| 390 | MURRAY | 2.00 | BC |
| 400 | BENCH* | 1.50 | BC |
| 435 | YOUNT | 2.50 | BC |
| 450 | MORRIS | 1.00 | OTF |
| 452 | L. SMITH | 7.75 | VC |
| 475 | TRAMMELL | .75 | OTF |
| 480 | CARLTON* | 1.25 | BC |
| 490 | ECKERSLEY | 1.00 | OTF |
| 500 | CAREW* | 1.00 | BC |
| 540 | DAWSON | 1.25 | BC |
| 585 | FINGERS* | .50 | BC |
| 600 | WINFIELD | 1.50 | BC |
| 610 | HENDERSON | 6.50 | BC |
| 624 | JENKINS | .25 | BC |
| 650 | YASTRZEMSKI* | 1.25 | BC |
| 667 | REARDON | 2.50 | BC |
| 668 | MURPHY | .75 | BC |
| 681 | SAX | 4.00 | VC |
| 715 | STARGELL | .50 | BC |
| 730 | CARTER | .50 | BC |
| 754 | MORGAN | .35 | BC |

| 766 | HRBEK | 1.50 | VC |
|-----|-------|------|-----|
| 780 | ROSE* | 1.25 | OTF |

## 1982 TOPPS TRADED
*Set: $260.00*

| 44 | HRBEK | 2.50 | VC |
|-----|----------|--------|-----|
| 47 | JACKSON | 7.50 | BC |
| 49 | JENKINS | 1.25 | BC |
| 88 | PERRY | 1.25 | BC |
| 98 | RIPKEN | 250.00 | VC |
| 103 | SAX | 6.00 | VC |
| 109 | O. SMITH | 12.75 | BC |

## 1982 DONRUSS.
A big improvement on the 1981 set, but still no great shakes. Oddly enough, buyers preferred the Fleer set at the time, and lots of Donruss wax boxes were around for under $25 more than five years later. Noteworthy in that it was the first time buyers could get a set straight from the factory.

*Warning:* Errors were made on both Trammell cards, and they sell for about twice as much as the corrected versions.

*Avoid:* The Chicken.

*Tough Call:* See 1982 Topps.

*Set: $85.00*
*Factory Set: $90.00*
*Commons: $ .01*

| 28 | FINGERS | .30 | BC |
|-----|-------------|-------|-----|
| 30 | ECKERSLEY | .50 | OTF |
| 31 | WINFIELD | 1.00 | BC |
| 34 | BRETT | 1.75 | BC |
| 42 | CARLTON | .75 | BC |
| 74 | YASTRZEMSKI | .75 | BC |
| 76 | TRAMMELL | .35 | OTF |
| 78 | MOLITOR | .50 | OTF |
| 84 | GARVEY | .30 | OTF |
| 88 | DAWSON | .75 | BC |
| 94 | O. SMITH | 1.00 | BC |
| 95 | PARKER | .25 | OTF |
| 107 | MORRIS | .75 | OTF |
| 113 | HENDERSON | 2.25 | BC |
| 114 | CARTER | .35 | BC |

| 148 | SEAVER | 1.00 | BC |
|-----|-----------|-------|-----|
| 168 | ROSE | .75 | OTF |
| 214 | RAINES | .35 | VC |
| 216 | CAREW | .50 | BC |
| 231 | PALMER | .75 | BC |
| 252 | L. SMITH | 5.75 | VC |
| 294 | SCHMIDT | 1.25 | BC |
| 299 | MURPHY | .35 | BC |
| 312 | MORGAN | .25 | BC |
| 405 | RIPKEN | 50.00 | VC |
| 419 | RYAN | 5.75 | BC |
| 454 | WHITAKER | .25 | OTF |
| 483 | MURRAY | 1.25 | BC |
| 495 | FISK | 1.00 | BC |
| 510 | YOUNT | 1.75 | BC |
| 535 | JACKSON | 1.50 | BC |
| 547 | REARDON | 1.50 | BC |
| 557 | HRBEK | 1.25 | VC |
| 624 | SAX | 2.00 | VC |
| 639 | STARGELL | .35 | BC |

## 1982 FLEER.
An absolute abomination. There are kids at ball games with $10 cameras who could have taken better shots than the ones featured in this set. If you buy this set, keep a tongue depressor handy—it's been known to cause seizures.

*Warning:* A real humdinger for error collectors in this set is the immortal John Littlefield's card. If you want a picture of him fielding a ball left-handed, it'll set you back $150. If you can get it autographed, it'll be worth $151!

*Avoid:* The other errors, including the Hrabosky card. Plain old "Al" Hrabosky will only cost you 50 cents. However, if you want "All" Hrabosky (and who wouldn't?) there's an extra charge of $10.

*Tough Call:* See 1982 Topps.

*Set: $80.00*
*Commons: $ .01*

| 5 | GARVEY | .25 | OTF |
|----|----------|------|-----|
| 21 | SAX | 1.75 | VC |
| 39 | JACKSON | 1.25 | BC |
| 56 | WINFIELD | .75 | BC |
| 57 | BENCH | .50 | BC |

| | | | |
|---|---|---|---|
| 82 | SEAVER | .75 | BC |
| 92 | HENDERSON | 2.00 | BC |
| 141 | FINGERS | .25 | BC |
| 148 | MOLITOR | .50 | OTF |
| 155 | YOUNT | 1.50 | BC |
| 174 | MURRAY | 1.00 | BC |
| 175 | PALMER | .75 | BC |
| 176 | RIPKEN | 42.50 | VC |
| 185 | CARTER | .30 | BC |
| 187 | DAWSON | .75 | BC |
| 202 | RAINES | .75 | VC |
| 204 | REARDON | 1.00 | BC |
| 229 | RYAN | 5.50 | BC |
| 243 | CARLTON | .50 | BC |
| 256 | ROSE | .50 | OTF |
| 258 | SCHMIDT | 1.25 | BC |
| 274 | MORRIS | .75 | OTF |
| 283 | TRAMMELL | .30 | OTF |
| 292 | ECKERSLEY | .50 | OTF |
| 312 | YASTRZEMSKI | .50 | BC |
| 343 | FISK | 1.00 | BC |
| 397 | MORGAN | .25 | BC |
| 405 | BRETT | 1.50 | BC |
| 443 | MURPHY | .35 | BC |
| 499 | STARGELL | .30 | BC |
| 455 | CAREW | .50 | BC |
| 582 | O. SMITH | 1.00 | BC |
| 603 | L. SMITH | 5.50 | VC |

**1983 TOPPS.** Four cards—Sandberg, Gwynn, Boggs, and Ripken—anchor this interestingly designed set. There's not much else to say. A subset of Super Veterans has never really caught on with buyers, but that could change—no fewer than eighteen of the players depicted on these cards could end up as Hall of Famers. As in the 1982 set, a player's Super Veteran card follows his regular card—those players are marked with an asterisk—and is valued at about a third.

*Warning:* This set is laced with rookie pitchers who could still put up big numbers—don't get suckered into buying them.

*Avoid:* McGee, Moore, Black, Dravecky, and Gaetti.

*Tough Call:* Frankie Viola. He could have done it

with the Mets, but he choked, virtually erasing any chance at immortality. A nice pitcher and a nice guy, but he's starting to look like a black hole for buyers.

*Set: $160.00*
*Commons: $ .02*

| | | | |
|---|---|---|---|
| 20 | FISK | 1.50 | BC |
| 35 | FINGERS* | .50 | BC |
| 60 | BENCH* | 1.25 | BC |
| 65 | MORRIS | .75 | OTF |
| 70 | CARLTON* | 1.00 | BC |
| 83 | SANDBERG | 47.50 | BC |
| 95 | TRAMMELL | .50 | OTF |
| 100 | ROSE* | 1.00 | OTF |
| 163 | RIPKEN | 22.50 | VC |
| 180 | HENDERSON | 4.50 | BC |
| 200 | CAREW* | 1.00 | BC |
| 205 | PARKER | .30 | OTF |
| 245 | SAX | .50 | VC |
| 270 | ECKERSLEY | .75 | OTF |
| 290 | REARDON | 1.75 | BC |
| 300 | SCHMIDT* | 2.25 | BC |
| 350 | YOUNT | 2.00 | BC |
| 360 | RYAN* | 7.00 | BC |
| 370 | CARTER | .40 | BC |
| 482 | GWYNN | 32.50 | BC |
| 490 | PALMER* | .75 | BC |
| 498 | BOGGS | 27.50 | BC |
| 500 | JACKSON* | 1.75 | BC |
| 509 | WHITAKER | .25 | OTF |
| 530 | MURRAY | 1.75 | BC |
| 540 | O. SMITH | 1.25 | BC |
| 550 | YASTRZEMSKI* | 1.75 | BC |
| 580 | SEAVER* | 1.25 | BC |
| 595 | RAINES | .40 | VC |
| 600 | BRETT | 2.00 | BC |
| 603 | MORGAN * | .30 | BC |
| 610 | GARVEY | .30 | OTF |
| 630 | MOLITOR | .50 | OTF |
| 680 | DAWSON | 1.25 | BC |
| 690 | HRBEK | .25 | VC |
| 699 | L. SMITH | 1.75 | VC |
| 715 | PEREZ* | .25 | BC |

| | | | |
|---|---|---|---|
| 760 | MURPHY | .50 | BC |
| 770 | WINFIELD | 1.25 | BC |

## 1983 TOPPS TRADED

*Set: $90.00*

| | | | |
|---|---|---|---|
| 34 | FRANCO | 9.00 | VC |
| 37 | GARVEY | .75 | OTF |
| 43 | HERNANDEZ | .35 | OTF |
| 77 | MORGAN | 1.25 | BC |
| 85 | PEREZ | 1.00 | BC |
| 101 | SEAVER | 6.75 | BC |
| 108 | STRAWBERRY | 70.00 | VC |

**1983 DONRUSS.** A clone of the 1982 set, but with a little more punch.

*Warning:* There's a Ron Jackson error that runs about $10. If you care—or if your last name is Jackson—demand a discount.

*Avoid:* Slaught and Maldonado.

*Tough Call:* See 1983 Topps.

*Set: $110.00*
*Factory Set: $120.00*
*Commons: $ .01*

| | | | |
|---|---|---|---|
| 35 | HENDERSON | 3.00 | BC |
| 42 | ROSE | .75 | OTF |
| 47 | MURPHY | .25 | BC |
| 77 | PALMER | .50 | BC |
| 78 | FINGERS | .35 | BC |
| 90 | CAREW | .75 | BC |
| 104 | FISK | .75 | BC |
| 107 | MORRIS | .50 | OTF |
| 115 | JACKSON | 1.00 | BC |
| 118 | RYAN | 5.00 | BC |
| 120 | O. SMITH | 1.00 | BC |
| 122 | SEAVER | 1.00 | BC |
| 168 | SCHMIDT | 1.25 | BC |
| 194 | REARDON | .75 | BC |
| 207 | TRAMMELL | .35 | OTF |
| 219 | CARLTON | .75 | BC |
| 258 | YOUNT | 1.50 | BC |
| 277 | SANDBERG | 32.50 | BC |
| 279 | RIPKEN | 15.00 | VC |
| 326 | YASTRZEMSKI | .75 | BC |

| | | | |
|---|---|---|---|
| 328 | JOHNSON | 5.50 | VC |
| 336 | SAX | .25 | VC |
| 338 | BRETT | 1.50 | BC |
| 340 | CARTER | .25 | BC |
| 403 | L. SMITH | 1.00 | VC |
| 405 | MURRAY | 1.25 | BC |
| 409 | WINFIELD | 1.00 | BC |
| 487 | ECKERSLEY | .50 | OTF |
| 500 | BENCH | .75 | BC |
| 518 | DAWSON | 1.00 | BC |
| 525 | FRANCO | 5.00 | VC |
| 586 | BOGGS | 18.50 | BC |
| 598 | GWYNN | 20.00 | BC |
| 610 | STARGELL | .25 | BC |

**1983 FLEER.** Good photography, a clean, though heavy-handed, design, and just a touch of whimsy make this set very collectible. In fact, a lot of dealers feel that this set is going to take off down the road. Of course, the ones who say this always seem to have about a dozen for sale.

*Warning:* Look for stains on these cards—apparently, some came right out of the packs that way.

*Avoid:* Kittle

*Tough Call:* See 1983 Topps.

*Set: $110.00*
*Commons: $ .01*

| | | | |
|---|---|---|---|
| 22 | O. SMITH | 1.00 | BC |
| 33 | FINGERS | .35 | BC |
| 51 | YOUNT | 1.50 | BC |
| 67 | MURRAY | 1.25 | BC |
| 69 | PALMER | .50 | BC |
| 70 | RIPKEN | 16.00 | VC |
| 81 | CAREW | .75 | BC |
| 93 | JACKSON | 1.00 | BC |
| 108 | BRETT | 1.50 | BC |
| 142 | MURPHY | .25 | BC |
| 155 | CARLTON | .75 | BC |
| 171 | ROSE | .75 | OTF |
| 179 | BOGGS | 19.50 | BC |
| 182 | ECKERSLEY | .50 | OTF |
| 200 | YASTRZEMSKI | .75 | BC |
| 220 | SAX | .25 | VC |

| 235 | FISK | 1.00 | BC |
|---|---|---|---|
| 278 | CARTER | .25 | BC |
| 280 | DAWSON | 1.00 | BC |
| 293 | REARDON | .75 | BC |
| 324 | STARGELL | .24 | BC |
| 332 | JOHNSON | 5.00 | VC |
| 336 | MORRIS | .50 | OTF |
| 260 | GWYNN | 21.00 | BC |
| 398 | WINFIELD | 1.00 | BC |
| 463 | RYAN | 5.00 | BC |
| 507 | SANDBERG | 35.00 | BC |
| 508 | L. SMITH | 1.00 | VC |
| 519 | HENDERSON | 1.00 | BC |
| 584 | BENCH | .75 | BC |
| 601 | SEAVER | 1.00 | BC |
| 616 | HRBEK | .25 | VC |

**1984 TOPPS.** Definitely not a set for the faint-hearted. The two big cards—Mattingly and Strawberry—have been overpriced for seven or eight years, as has the set itself, for which some people have foolishly shelled out over $100. Should Darryl and Don fall short of Cooperstown, this set could be the deadliest of the decade.

*Warning:* Inspect these cards carefully, as their edges tend to chip.

*Avoid:* Virtually every rookie in this set besides Mattingly, Strawberry, and Julio Franco.

*Tough Call:* Slick Van Slyke. If the guy had learned how to hit lefties a little earlier, he'd be on his way to Cooperstown, because he sure can do everything else. A bad back will probably prevent him from playing well into his thirties.

*Set: $70.00*
*Commons: $ .01*

| 8 | MATTINGLY | 9.50 | VC |
|---|---|---|---|
| 10 | YOUNT | 1.25 | BC |
| 30 | BOGGS | 3.25 | BC |
| 48 | FRANCO | 1.00 | VC |
| 100 | JACKSON | .75 | BC |
| 130 | O. SMITH | .50 | BC |
| 150 | MURPHY | .30 | BC |
| 176 | L. SMITH | .35 | VC |

| 182 | STRAWBERRY | 10.00 | VC |
|---|---|---|---|
| 195 | MORRIS | .40 | OTF |
| 200 | DAWSON | .50 | BC |
| 230 | HENDERSON | 3.00 | BC |
| 240 | MURRAY | .75 | BC |
| 251 | GWYNN | 3.75 | BC |
| 300 | ROSE | .50 | OTF |
| 450 | CARTER | .25 | BC |
| 460 | WINFIELD | .50 | BC |
| 470 | RYAN | 5.50 | BC |
| 490 | RIPKEN | 8.00 | VC |
| 495 | FINGERS | .25 | BC |
| 500 | BRETT | 1.25 | BC |
| 510 | TRAMMELL | .30 | OTF |
| 560 | FISK | .75 | BC |
| 595 | REARDON | .40 | BC |
| 596 | SANDBERG | 8.00 | BC |
| 600 | CAREW | .40 | BC |
| 700 | SCHMIDT | 1.50 | BC |
| 740 | SEAVER | 1.00 | BC |
| 745 | ECKERSLEY | .50 | OTF |
| 750 | PALMER | .50 | BC |
| 780 | CARLTON | .50 | BC |

## 1984 TOPPS TRADED
*Set: $65.00*

| 34 | ECKERSLEY | 6.00 | OTF |
|---|---|---|---|
| 42 | GOODEN | 22.50 | VC |
| 43 | GOSSAGE | .25 | OTF |
| 82 | MORGAN | 1.00 | BC |
| 84 | NIEKRO | 1.00 | OTF |
| 90 | PARKER | 1.00 | OTF |
| 91 | PEREZ | 1.25 | BC |
| 103 | ROSE | 5.00 | OTF |
| 104 | SABERHAGEN | 12.50 | VC |
| 108 | SEAVER | 5.50 | BC |

**1984 DONRUSS.** Unable to strong-arm dealers into placing big preorders, Donruss cut its production dramatically. Buyers picked up on the fact that this set was hard to find, but didn't realize *how* hard until the late 1980s. The card design is quite nice, but the photography on some cards leaves a bit to be desired. The set has survived the free-falling Mattingly rookie to gain the distinction of being the most expensive regular issue of the decade.

*Warning:* Mattingly knockoffs are all over the place—look for diagonal shadows on the phonies. Also, numbers were omitted from the Darling and Stenhouse cards. The ones *with* numbers are the good ones, "good" being a relative term here.

*Avoid:* Gagne, Darling, Schoefield, Teufel, Henke, Harper, Pena, Phillips, Owen, Candiotti, Jacoby, Russell, Doran, Danny Jackson, Sid Fernandez, and the ubiquitous Chicken.

*Tough Call:* Kevin McReynolds. No, not really.

*Set: $325.00*
*Factory Set: $365.00*
*Commons: $ .09*

| | | | |
|---|---|---|---|
| 32 | FERNANDEZ | 4.50 | VC |
| 41 | J. CARTER | 32.00 | VC |
| 47 | MURRAY | 4.00 | BC |
| 48 | YOUNT | 5.75 | BC |
| 51 | WINFIELD | 3.75 | BC |
| 53 | BRETT | 5.75 | BC |
| 54 | HENDERSON | 10.00 | BC |
| 55 | G. CARTER | .75 | BC |
| 57 | JACKSON | 4.00 | BC |
| 59 | O. SMITH | 3.75 | BC |
| 60 | RYAN | 20.00 | BC |
| 61 | ROSE | 3.25 | OTF |
| 63 | GARVEY | .75 | OTF |
| 66 | MURPHY | 1.25 | BC |
| 68 | STRAWBERRY | 35.00 | VC |
| 70 | HRBEK | .50 | VC |
| 97 | DAWSON | 3.50 | BC |
| 104 | SAX | .50 | VC |
| 106 | RIPKEN | 25.00 | VC |
| 107 | MOLITOR | 1.25 | OTF |
| 111 | CARLTON | 3.50 | BC |
| 116 | SEAVER | 5.50 | BC |
| 129 | BLYLEVEN | .50 | OTF |
| 151 | BOGGS | 12.00 | BC |
| 183 | SCHMIDT | 12.00 | BC |
| 188 | NIEKRO | .75 | OTF |
| 189 | JENKINS | .75 | BC |
| 216 | FRANCO | 2.75 | VC |

| | | | |
|---|---|---|---|
| 227 | WHITAKER | .50 | OTF |
| 238 | HERNANDEZ | .25 | OTF |
| 248 | MATTINGLY | 35.00 | VC |
| 279 | REARDON | 1.25 | BC |
| 288 | PARKER | .75 | OTF |
| 289 | L. SMITH | 1.25 | VC |
| 293 | TRAMMELL | 2.25 | OTF |
| 299 | RAINES | .50 | OTF |
| 302 | FISK | 3.75 | BC |
| 311 | SANDBERG | 23.50 | BC |
| 324 | GWYNN | 14.00 | BC |
| 352 | CAREW | 3.50 | BC |
| 355 | MORGAN | .75 | BC |
| 395 | EVANS | .35 | OTF |
| 415 | MORRIS | 2.00 | OTF |
| 503 | PEREZ | .75 | BC |
| 576 | PALMER | 2.75 | BC |
| 639 | ECKERSLEY | 3.00 | OTF |
| A | LIVING LEGENDS | 4.50 | BC |
| B | LIVING LEGENDS | 6.50 | BC |

**1984 FLEER.** Buying this set instead of the Donruss is like kissing your cousin—it's nice, but it ain't the real thing.

*Warning:* Save your money until you can afford the real thing.

*Avoid:* Hawkins, Krueger, and Kevin Gross.

*Tough Call:* See 1984 Topps and Donruss.

*Set: $170.00*
*Commons: $ .05*

| | | | |
|---|---|---|---|
| 14 | MURRAY | 2.75 | BC |
| 16 | PALMER | 1.50 | BC |
| 17 | RIPKEN | 17.50 | VC |
| 25 | CARLTON | 1.50 | BC |
| 43 | MORGAN | .50 | BC |
| 44 | PEREZ | .35 | BC |
| 46 | ROSE | 1.25 | OTF |
| 48 | SCHMIDT | 6.75 | BC |
| 58 | FISK | 1.50 | BC |
| 87 | MORRIS | 1.00 | OTF |
| 91 | TRAMMELL | .75 | OTF |
| 92 | WHITAKER | .35 | OTF |
| 112 | SAX | .25 | VC |

| 131 | MATTINGLY | 20.00 | VC |
|---|---|---|---|
| 143 | WINFIELD | 2.00 | BC |
| 152 | FERNANDEZ | 2.75 | VC |
| 186 | MURPHY | .75 | BC |
| 187 | NIEKRO | .35 | OTF |
| 199 | FINGERS | .50 | BC |
| 207 | MOLITOR | .50 | OTF |
| 215 | SUTTON | .35 | OTF |
| 219 | YOUNT | 3.25 | BC |
| 230 | RYAN | 13.00 | BC |
| 258 | PARKER | .35 | OTF |
| 271 | CARTER | .50 | BC |
| 273 | DAWSON | 2.00 | BC |
| 281 | RAINES | .35 | OTF |
| 283 | REARDON | 1.00 | BC |
| 300 | GARVEY | .35 | OTF |
| 301 | GWYNN | 9.50 | BC |
| 336 | O. SMITH | 2.00 | BC |
| 344 | BRETT | 3.25 | BC |
| 352 | PERRY | .35 | BC |
| 392 | BOGGS | 7.00 | BC |
| 396 | ECKERSLEY | 1.50 | OTF |
| 412 | YASTRZEMSKI | 1.25 | BC |
| 447 | HENDERSON | 6.50 | BC |
| 462 | BENCH | 1.25 | BC |
| 494 | JENKINS | .35 | BC |
| 504 | SANDBERG | 16.75 | BC |
| 505 | L. SMITH | 1.00 | VC |
| 511 | CAREW | 1.25 | BC |
| 520 | JACKSON | 2.25 | BC |
| 542 | FRANCO | 2.25 | VC |
| 567 | HRBEK | .25 | VC |
| 595 | SEAVER | 4.00 | BC |
| 599 | STRAWBERRY | 25.00 | VC |

## 1984 FLEER UPDATE
*Set: $850.00*

| 27 | CLEMENS | 375.00 | VC |
|---|---|---|---|
| 34 | ECKERSLEY | 11.50 | OTF |
| 39 | JO. FRANCO | 6.50 | VC |
| 43 | GOODEN | 75.00 | VC |
| 44 | GOSSAGE | .50 | OTF |
| 80 | MORGAN | 5.00 | BC |
| 83 | NIEKRO | 3.75 | OTF |

| 89 | PARKER | 3.00 | OTF |
|---|---|---|---|
| 91 | PEREZ | 4.50 | OTF |
| 93 | PUCKETT | 320.00 | VC |
| 102 | ROSE | 12.50 | OTF |
| 103 | SABERHAGEN | 27.50 | VC |
| 106 | SEAVER | 20.00 | BC |

**1985 TOPPS.** Much ballyhooed over the years, this set has more or less met all expectations. Granted, a lot of "sure things" fizzled, but look who's left: Clemens, Puckett, McGwire, Gooden, and Saberhagen. Then there's Hershiser, Pendelton, Rijo, Hojo, John Franco, and Eric Davis—one or two of whom could still make the Hall of Fame. An interesting footnote to this set is that, thanks to the mercurial performance of Gooden that year, it was the first to draw significant interest from people who did not collect cards. Perhaps this explains why there appear to be far fewer *mint* 1985 Topps cards around than there should be—people who don't normally collect cards tend not to store them too well.

*Warning:* Check these cards closely—especially for hairlines and bubbles.

*Avoid:* Gubicza, Key, Swift, Mack, Snyder, and Alvin Davis, as tempting as they may be.

*Tough Call:* Samuel, Dunston, Langston, and Belcher. Major-league history is strewn with talented players who never quite lived up to early billing. In the cases of Belcher and Dunston, injuries have taken their toll. In the case of Langston, he's been touted as a savior every time he's switched teams, and he's fallen short each time. As for Samuel, there's no logical explanation for his dogging it during what should have been the prime of his career. All four of these guys could turn it around—until that happens, however, your money is best spent elsewhere.

*Set: $85.00*
*Commons: $ .01*

| 23 | SABERHAGEN | 1.50 | VC |
|---|---|---|---|
| 30 | RIPKEN | 3.50 | VC |
| 48 | FERNANDEZ | .35 | VC |

| | | | |
|---|---|---|---|
| 100 | BRETT | .65 | BC |
| 115 | HENDERSON | 1.25 | BC |
| 163 | ECKERSLEY | .30 | OTF |
| 180 | WINFIELD | .40 | BC |
| 181 | CLEMENS | 22.50 | VC |
| 192 | JOHNSON | 1.25 | VC |
| 200 | JACKSON | .45 | BC |
| 237 | JU. FRANCO | .30 | VC |
| 278 | #1: STRAWBERRY | 1.00 | VC |
| 238 | RIJO | 1.00 | VC |
| 300 | CAREW | .25 | BC |
| 340 | YOUNT | .65 | BC |
| 346 | PENDELTON | 1.50 | VC |
| 350 | BOGGS | 1.25 | BC |
| 360 | CARLTON | .35 | BC |
| 375 | REARDON | .25 | BC |
| 401 | MCGWIRE | 24.00 | VC |
| 417 | JO. FRANCO | .40 | VC |
| 420 | DAWSON | .35 | BC |
| 460 | SANDBERG | 2.50 | BC |
| 493 | HERSHISER | .75 | VC |
| 500 | SCHMIDT | 1.00 | BC |
| 536 | PUCKETT | 17.50 | VC |
| 570 | STRAWBERRY | 2.75 | VC |
| 600 | ROSE | .35 | OTF |
| 605 | O. SMITH | .30 | BC |
| 610 | MORRIS | .25 | OTF |
| 620 | GOODEN | 3.00 | VC |
| 627 | DAVIS | 3.00 | VC |
| 660 | GWYNN | 1.75 | BC |
| 665 | MATTINGLY | 2.00 | VC |
| 670 | SEAVER | .40 | BC |
| 694 | J. CARTER | 3.50 | VC |
| 700 | MURRAY | .40 | BC |
| 760 | RYAN | 3.25 | BC |
| 770 | FISK | .45 | BC |

## 1985 TOPPS TRADED
*SET: $25.00*

| | | | |
|---|---|---|---|
| 17 | G. CARTER | .50 | BC |
| 49 | HENDERSON | 3.25 | BC |
| 64 | JOHNSON | 1.50 | VC |

**1985 DONRUSS.** Another good set, although Topps and Fleer included all the right players, too.

The Clemens and Puckett cards should take this set into the $250 range.

*Warning:* The Tom Seaver card depicting Ron Reed is *not* the good one—the corrected card is the keeper. The "Two for the Title" card of Winfield and Mattingly sells for a 300 percent premium with white lettering. Also, Terry Pendelton's rookie card incorrectly identifies him as "Jeff." The corrected card is the one you've seen bringing $15.

*Avoid:* Hatcher, Hudler, and Pasqua.
*Tough Call:* See 1985 Topps.

*Set: $185.00*
*Factory Set: $220.00*
*Commons: $ .02*

| | | | |
|---|---|---|---|
| 27 | TARTABULL | 7.00 | VC |
| 47 | MURRAY | 1.25 | BC |
| 48 | YOUNT | 2.25 | BC |
| 51 | WINFIELD | 1.25 | BC |
| 53 | BRETT | 2.25 | BC |
| 55 | G. CARTER | .25 | BC |
| 57 | JACKSON | 1.25 | BC |
| 59 | O. SMITH | 1.00 | BC |
| 60 | RYAN | 8.25 | BC |
| 61 | SCHMIDT | 4.00 | BC |
| 63 | GWYNN | 5.50 | BC |
| 66 | MURPHY | .35 | BC |
| 67 | SANDBERG | 7.75 | BC |
| 85 | CAREW | 1.00 | BC |
| 94 | JU. FRANCO | .75 | BC |
| 164 | JO. FRANCO | .75 | BC |
| 169 | RIPKEN | 8.50 | VC |
| 171 | TRAMMELL | .35 | OTF |
| 172 | BOGGS | 3.25 | BC |
| 176 | HENDERSON | 3.25 | BC |
| 190 | GOODEN | 6.75 | VC |
| 208 | FISK | 1.00 | BC |
| 222 | SABERHAGEN | 3.50 | VC |
| 247 | JOHNSON | 1.50 | VC |
| 254 | ROSE | 1.00 | OTF |
| 273 | CLEMENS | 55.00 | VC |
| 295 | MATTINGLY | 6.00 | VC |
| 305 | CARLTON | .75 | BC |
| 311 | L. SMITH | .50 | OTF |

| | | | |
|---|---|---|---|
| 312 | STRAWBERRY | 7.50 | VC |
| 325 | DAVIS | 7.50 | VC |
| 331 | REARDON | .50 | BC |
| 415 | MORRIS | .50 | OTF |
| 421 | DAWSON | 1.00 | BC |
| 424 | SEAVER ERROR | 1.00 | BC |
| 424 | SEAVER CORRECT | 23.00 | BC |
| 438 | PUCKETT | 47.50 | VC |
| 442 | ECKERSLEY | .50 | OTF |
| 534 | PENDELTON J. | 5.00 | VC |
| 534 | PENDELTON T. | 14.50 | VC |
| 581 | HERSHISER | 2.00 | VC |
| 616 | J. CARTER | 5.75 | VC |
| 641 | ROSE | 1.00 | BC |
| 651 | TWO FOR TITLE | 2.50 | OTF |

**1985 FLEER.** A little easier to find in *mint* condition than the Donruss, so demand *mint* cards. Otherwise, it's the same guys with different borders.

*Warning:* The jury's still out on the specials and the In Action subset, but buyers seem to be moving toward acceptance.

*Avoid:* Deer, Bielecki, Zane Smith, and Glenn Davis.

*Tough Call:* Kelly Gruber. He has never been able to bust out and dominate the way the Jays thought he would. Injuries have been a problem, but perhaps the monster talent's just not there. He may be Doug Decinces's evil twin.

*Set:* $180.00
*Commons:* $ .02

| | | | |
|---|---|---|---|
| 12 | JOHNSON | 1.50 | VC |
| 18 | MORRIS | .50 | OTF |
| 23 | TRAMMELL | .35 | OTF |
| 34 | GWYNN | 5.50 | BC |
| 57 | ECKERSLEY | .50 | OTF |
| 65 | SANDBERG | 7.50 | BC |
| 67 | L. SMITH | .50 | OTF |
| 82 | GOODEN | 6.50 | VC |
| 93 | STRAWBERRY | 7.25 | VC |
| 133 | MATTINGLY | 5.75 | VC |
| 146 | WINFIELD | 1.00 | BC |

| | | | |
|---|---|---|---|
| 151 | BOGGS | 3.25 | BC |
| 155 | CLEMENS | 52.50 | VC |
| 184 | MURRAY | 1.25 | BC |
| 187 | RIPKEN | 8.25 | VC |
| 199 | BRETT | 2.25 | BC |
| 212 | SABERHAGEN | 3.25 | VC |
| 236 | PENDELTON | 5.00 | VC |
| 240 | O. SMITH | 1.00 | BC |
| 246 | CARLTON | .75 | BC |
| 265 | SCHMIDT | 4.00 | BC |
| 286 | PUCKETT | 45.00 | VC |
| 297 | CAREW | .50 | BC |
| 303 | JACKSON | 1.00 | BC |
| 335 | MURPHY | .35 | BC |
| 359 | RYAN | 8.00 | BC |
| 371 | HERSHISER | 2.00 | VC |
| 393 | G. CARTER | .25 | BC |
| 394 | DAWSON | 1.00 | BC |
| 407 | REARDON | .50 | BC |
| 425 | HENDERSON | 3.25 | BC |
| 443 | J. CARTER | 5.50 | VC |
| 448 | JU. FRANCO | .75 | VC |
| 513 | FISK | 1.00 | BC |
| 526 | SEAVER | 1.00 | BC |
| 533 | DAVIS | 7.25 | VC |
| 536 | JO. FRANCO | .75 | VC |
| 550 | ROSE | 1.00 | OTF |
| 601 | YOUNT | 2.25 | BC |
| 647 | TARTABULL | 6.00 | VC |

## 1985 FLEER UPDATE
*Set:* $23.50

| | | | |
|---|---|---|---|
| 21 | G. CARTER | .50 | BC |
| 51 | HENDERSON | 3.00 | BC |
| 62 | JOHNSON | 1.50 | VC |

**1986 TOPPS.** Thank God for Cecil Fielder. Otherwise, these unattractive, overproduced cards would still be sitting around in unopened, unwanted wax packs. All the usual suspects are here, but nothing in the way of high-demand cards. Proceed with caution.

*Warning:* The borders of these cards are half black and half white, which means that even the slightest mishandling will show up somewhere.

Buy them *mint* and try your best to keep them that way.

*Avoid:* Calderon, Tettleton, Aguilera, Reynolds, and Glenn Davis.

*Tough Call:* Dykstra, Guillen, Daulton, and Coleman. Again, injuries are the red flags here. Dykstra looked as if he were on the fast track when he escaped from New York, but has been banged up two years in a row. Guillen may recover fully from his 1992 injury, but how quick will he be five years from now? Coleman had Cooperstown written all over him until he arrived at Shea, at which point his hamstrings gave out. Daulton's monster year may not be a fluke, but remember, he's a catcher. Of the four, Coleman is the most attractive in terms of long-term potential. If he starts running again, he can get back on the fast track. But even Coleman admits he'll never steal 100 again, and stolen bases are the only thing that gets him into the Hall of Fame. Look up "caveat emptor" before you open your wallet.

*Set: $25.00*
*Factory Set: 30.00*
*Commons: $ .005*

| 1 | ROSE | .40 | OTF |
|---|---|---|---|
| 10 | GWYNN | .75 | BC |
| 28 | DAVIS | .25 | VC |
| 30 | MURRAY | .30 | BC |
| 35 | REARDON | .25 | BC |
| 70 | WINFIELD | .25 | BC |
| 80 | STRAWBERRY | .75 | VC |
| 100 | RYAN | 2.25 | BC |
| 180 | MATTINGLY | .65 | VC |
| 200 | SCHMIDT | .50 | BC |
| 250 | GOODEN | .40 | VC |
| 290 | FISK | .25 | BC |
| 300 | BRETT | .35 | BC |
| 329 | PUCKETT | 2.50 | VC |
| 340 | RIPKEN | 2.00 | BC |
| 377 | J. CARTER | .50 | VC |
| 386 | FIELDER | 5.00 | VC |
| 390 | SEAVER | .30 | BC |
| 500 | HENDERSON | .65 | BC |

| 510 | BOGGS | .65 | BC |
|---|---|---|---|
| 661 | CLEMENS | 3.25 | VC |
| 690 | SANDBERG | 1.00 | BC |
| 700 | JACKSON | .30 | BC |
| 730 | O. SMITH | .25 | BC |
| 780 | YOUNT | .35 | BC |

## 1986 TOPPS TRADED
*Set: $20.00*

| 11 | BONDS | 3.75 | VC |
|---|---|---|---|
| 12 | BONILLA | 1.50 | VC |
| 20 | CANSECO | 5.00 | VC |
| 24 | CLARK | 5.00 | VC |
| 101 | SEAVER | .30 | BC |
| 108 | TARTABULL | .50 | VC |

**1986 DONRUSS.** Another winner for Donruss right out of the gate. When the set hit the stores, Canseco was selling for $5 out of the packs, Cory Snyder was selling for $3, and Gooden was selling for $2. Lost in the shuffle were two Toronto rookies who ended up in the commons bin. Mr. Fielder, I'd like you to meet Mr. McGriff—you'll be battling for the same spot this spring.

*Warning:* Jose Canseco fakes are starting to surface—and they're much better than the 1984 Mattinglys. Also, Donruss screwed up Seaver's card again. The one with yellow lettering carries a 100 percent premium.

*Avoid:* Daniels, Guzman, Galarraga, and Worrell.

*Tough Call:* Paul O'Neill. A blue chip player, but not a Blue Chip card. His inability to handle most lefties has kept him from becoming the 40-homer guy the Reds had wanted to back up Larkin, Davis, and Daniels. Nothing he did last year shows he's matured at the plate, and meanwhile he's getting awful mature. Resist this brand new Yankee.

*Set: $130.00*
*Factory Set: $140.00*
*Commons: $ .01*

| 28 | MCGRIFF | 23.00 | VC |
|---|---|---|---|
| 39 | CANSECO | 50.00 | VC |

| 38 | TARTABULL | 1.00 | VC |
|---|---|---|---|
| 48 | YOUNT | 1.25 | BC |
| 51 | HENDERSON | 1.50 | BC |
| 53 | BRETT | 1.25 | BC |
| 59 | O. SMITH | .50 | BC |
| 61 | SCHMIDT | 1.75 | BC |
| 62 | ROSE | .50 | OTF |
| 67 | SANDBERG | 3.00 | BC |
| 72 | PUCKETT | 7.50 | VC |
| 75 | GOODEN | .75 | VC |
| 87 | DAWSON | .50 | BC |
| 88 | MURRAY | .50 | BC |
| 100 | SABERHAGEN | .35 | VC |
| 105 | MORRIS | .30 | OTF |
| 112 | GWYNN | 2.00 | BC |
| 144 | L. SMITH | .35 | OTF |
| 164 | DAVIS | 1.00 | VC |
| 171 | TRAMMELL | .25 | OTF |
| 172 | CLEMENS | 10.00 | VC |
| 173 | MATTINGLY | 2.00 | VC |
| 183 | CARLTON | .50 | BC |
| 197 | STRAWBERRY | 2.00 | VC |
| 205 | PENDELTON | .75 | VC |
| 209 | REARDON | .35 | BC |
| 210 | RIPKEN | 4.00 | BC |
| 216 | JU. FRANCO | .25 | OTF |
| 224 | J. CARTER | 1.25 | OTF |
| 239 | ECKERSLEY | .35 | OTF |
| 248 | WINFIELD | .50 | BC |
| 258 | RYAN | 4.75 | BC |
| 280 | CAREW | .35 | BC |
| 312 | JOHNSON | .35 | OTF |
| 366 | FISK | .75 | BC |
| 371 | BOGGS | 1.25 | BC |
| 377 | JACKSON | .75 | BC |
| 512 | FIELDER | 20.00 | VC |
| 609 | SEAVER | .75 | BC |

## 1986 DONRUSS ROOKIES
*Set: $44.00*

| 11 | BONDS | 9.50 | VC |
|---|---|---|---|
| 22 | CANSECO | 7.75 | VC |
| 30 | BONILLA | 4.00 | VC |
| 32 | CLARK | 9.50 | VC |

| 45 | TARTABULL | 1.00 | VC |
|---|---|---|---|
| 52 | SIERRA | 9.00 | VC |

**1986 FLEER.** A slight relapse in the photography department, but nothing like 1982.

*Warning:* This set has held up much better over seven years than either the Topps or the Donruss, so be choosy about condition.

*Avoid:* See 1986 Topps and Donruss.

*Tough Call:* See 1986 Topps and Donruss.

*Set: $90.00*
*Factory Set: $95.00*
*Commons: $ .01*

| 5 | BRETT | 1.25 | BC |
|---|---|---|---|
| 19 | SABERHAGEN | .35 | VC |
| 44 | PENDELTON | .25 | VC |
| 46 | O. SMITH | .50 | BC |
| 81 | GOODEN | .75 | VC |
| 85 | JOHNSON | .35 | OTF |
| 96 | STRAWBERRY | 2.00 | VC |
| 108 | HENDERSON | 1.50 | BC |
| 109 | MATTINGLY | 2.00 | VC |
| 121 | WINFIELD | .50 | BC |
| 151 | CAREW | .35 | BC |
| 175 | DAVIS | 1.00 | VC |
| 191 | ROSE | .50 | OTF |
| 204 | FISK | .75 | BC |
| 216 | SEAVER | .75 | BC |
| 232 | MORRIS | .30 | OTF |
| 241 | TRAMMELL | .25 | OTF |
| 246 | DAWSON | .50 | BC |
| 257 | REARDON | .35 | BC |
| 282 | MURRAY | .50 | BC |
| 284 | RIPKEN | 3.75 | BC |
| 310 | RYAN | 4.50 | BC |
| 323 | GWYNN | 2.00 | BC |
| 341 | BOGGS | 1.25 | BC |
| 345 | CLEMENS | 9.50 | VC |
| 368 | ECKERSLEY | .35 | OTF |
| 378 | SANDBERG | 3.00 | BC |
| 380 | L. SMITH | .35 | OTF |

| 401 | PUCKETT | 7.50 | VC |
|-----|---------|------|-----|
| 435 | CARLTON | .50 | BC |
| 450 | SCHMIDT | 1.75 | BC |
| 476 | TARTABULL | 1.00 | VC |
| 506 | YOUNT | 1.25 | BC |
| 583 | J. CARTER | 1.25 | OTF |
| 586 | JU. FRANCO | .25 | OTF |
| 644 | SANTIAGO | 1.75 | VC |
| 649 | CANSECO | 29.00 | VC |
| 653 | FIELDER | 15.50 | VC |

## 1986 FLEER UPDATE
Set: $25.00

| 14 | BONDS | 7.75 | VC |
|-----|---------|------|-----|
| 15 | BONILLA | 3.00 | VC |
| 20 | CANSECO | 5.75 | VC |
| 25 | CLARK | 8.00 | VC |
| 105 | SIERRA | 5.75 | VC |

**1987 TOPPS.** Now we're talking! As with the 1985 set, some initially hot players have crashed and burned, but all in all not a bad effort. There may not be any "best" cards in this set, but there are some darn good ones.

*Warning:* Errors were made and then quickly corrected on the All-Star cards of Mattingly and Gooden—in ten years few will remember these variations and even fewer will care. Also, there are a lot of unopened wax boxes still lying around, so don't believe it when you hear that these cards are scarce.

*Avoid:* Some very tempting rookies, namely Joyner, Kruk, White, Magadan, Mulholland, Incaviglia, Roberts, Jackson, Myers, Greenwell, Witt, and Mitch Williams.

*Tough Call:* Drabek, Finley, Thigpen, and Mitchell. Both starting pitchers have reached thirty without two great back-to-back seasons and would have to become truly dominant starters over the next five years to be considered among the all-time greats. Thigpen's great year in 1990 may have done him in in terms of longevity. Baseball people say he's never been quite the same. Mitchell's knees are disintegrating, which is too bad—five more healthy years could conceivably put him within range of 400 homers.

Set: $22.50
*Factory Set: $27.50*
*Commons: $ .005*

| 150 | BOGGS | .25 | BC |
|-----|-----------|------|-----|
| 178 | FIELDER | .50 | VC |
| 184 | BONILLA | .70 | VC |
| 261 | SIERRA | 1.50 | VC |
| 300 | JACKSON | .25 | BC |
| 319 | SWINDELL | .25 | VC |
| 320 | BONDS | 1.50 | VC |
| 340 | CLEMENS | 1.00 | VC |
| 366 | MCGWIRE | 1.75 | VC |
| 420 | CLARK | 1.75 | VC |
| 430 | SCHMIDT | .30 | BC |
| 450 | PUCKETT | .65 | VC |
| 460 | STRAWBERRY | .25 | OTF |
| 530 | GWYNN | .30 | BC |
| 620 | CANSECO | 1.75 | VC |
| 634 | PALMEIRO | 1.00 | VC |
| 648 | LARKIN | .75 | VC |
| 680 | SANDBERG | .40 | BC |
| 735 | HENDERSON | .25 | BC |
| 757 | RYAN | .75 | BC |
| 784 | RIPKEN | .75 | BC |

## 1987 TOPPS TRADED
Set: $6.50

| 24 | CONE | 1.00 | VC |
|-----|---------|------|-----|
| 52 | JACKSON | .30 | BC |
| 70 | MADDUX | 1.50 | VC |
| 74 | MCGRIFF | 1.75 | VC |
| 114 | SMILEY | .45 | VC |
| 129 | WILLIAMS | 1.25 | VC |

**1987 DONRUSS.** Everyone thought this was the set to get. Oops. The upside, of course, is that a lot of the big names will run you three for a buck.

*Warning:* Errors on the Walker, Davis, and McReynolds Diamond Kings cards were hot when those players were hot, but now no one cares. Also, the packing machines at Donruss must have short-circuited for a while, because a lot of cards came out of the packs cut in half, scraped, scratched, and otherwise destroyed. Worse, some packs contained two of those annoying puzzle cards and not enough regular cards. Think twice before plunking down $70 for a wax box.

*Avoid:* Steinbach, Ward, and Glenallen Hill.
*Tough Call:* See 1987 Topps.

*Set: $45.00*
*Factory Set: $50*
*Commons: $ .01*

| 31 | SANTIAGO | .25 | VC |
|---|---|---|---|
| 32 | SWINDELL | .35 | VC |
| 36 | MADDUX | 2.75 | VC |
| 43 | PALMEIRO | 3.75 | VC |
| 46 | MCGWIRE | 6.75 | VC |
| 52 | MATTINGLY | .35 | OTF |
| 54 | BRETT | .35 | BC |
| 64 | GWYNN | .35 | BC |
| 66 | CLARK | 8.00 | VC |
| 77 | SANDBERG | 1.25 | BC |
| 89 | RIPKEN | 1.50 | BC |
| 97 | CANSECO | 5.00 | VC |
| 118 | STRAWBERRY | .35 | OTF |
| 126 | YOUNT | .35 | BC |
| 138 | RYAN | 2.25 | BC |
| 139 | SCHMIDT | .50 | BC |
| 149 | PUCKETT | 1.50 | VC |
| 156 | J. CARTER | .35 | OTF |
| 210 | JACKSON | .35 | BC |
| 228 | HENDERSON | .35 | BC |
| 247 | FISK | .35 | BC |
| 252 | BOGGS | .25 | BC |
| 276 | CLEMENS | 2.50 | VC |
| 346 | SIERRA | 6.75 | VC |
| 361 | BONDS | 6.50 | VC |
| 492 | LARKIN | 2.25 | VC |
| 502 | CONE | 2.25 | VC |
| 558 | BONILLA | 3.75 | VC |
| 621 | MCGRIFF | 2.75 | VC |
| 627 | BROWN | 1.25 | VC |

## 1987 DONRUSS ROOKIES.

*Set: $16.00*

| 1 | MCGWIRE | 3.50 | VC |
|---|---|---|---|
| 31 | MCGRIFF | 2.75 | VC |

| 35 | CONE | 1.00 | VC |
|---|---|---|---|
| 39 | SMILEY | .50 | VC |
| 44 | SANTIAGO | .25 | VC |
| 45 | WILLIAMS | 2.50 | VC |
| 47 | PALMEIRO | 2.00 | VC |
| 52 | MADDUX | 1.50 | VC |

**1987 FLEER.** In retrospect, there was absolutely no question that these cards were harder to find than the Donruss. Two interesting innovations in this set were the use of nontraditional statistics on the card backs and a "breaking the plane" design on the card fronts. Kevin Seitzer carried the set until his knees couldn't stand it anymore, but since then Will the Thrill, Sierra, and Bobby Bonds's boy have pushed it to new heights.

*Warning:* Some dealers have mentioned that spending more than an hour or two sorting the bright blue cards in this set has bothered their eyes. These may be the same people who can't listen to Mary Hart's voice.

*Avoid:* Seitzer.
*Tough Call:* See 1987 Topps.

*Set: $75.00*
*Factory Set: $80*
*Commons: $ .02*

| 9 | GOODEN | .35 | OTF |
|---|---|---|---|
| 13 | JOHNSON | .25 | OTF |
| 23 | STRAWBERRY | 1.25 | OTF |
| 29 | BOGGS | .75 | BC |
| 32 | CLEMENS | 3.75 | VC |
| 45 | SEAVER | .35 | BC |
| 67 | RYAN | 3.25 | BC |
| 84 | JACKSON | .50 | BC |
| 101 | HENDERSON | .75 | BC |
| 104 | MATTINGLY | .75 | OTF |
| 120 | WINFIELD | .50 | BC |
| 138 | SIERRA | 12.00 | VC |
| 158 | MORRIS | .25 | OTF |
| 167 | TRAMMELL | .25 | OTF |
| 187 | SCHMIDT | 1.00 | BC |
| 198 | DAVIS | .35 | VC |
| 204 | LARKIN | 4.75 | VC |
| 213 | ROSE | .25 | OTF |

| 249 | J. CARTER | .75 | OTF |
|-----|-----------|-----|-----|
| 269 | CLARK | 23.00 | VC |
| 308 | O. SMITH | .50 | BC |
| 361 | YOUNT | 1.00 | BC |
| 366 | BRETT | 1.00 | BC |
| 389 | CANSECO | 7.00 | VC |
| 416 | GWYNN | .75 | BC |
| 478 | RIPKEN | 2.75 | BC |
| 490 | CARLTON | .25 | BC |
| 496 | FISK | .75 | BC |
| 549 | PUCKETT | 3.25 | VC |
| 572 | SANDBERG | 2.25 | BC |
| 598 | TARTABULL | 1.00 | VC |
| 604 | BONDS | 13.00 | VC |
| 605 | BONILLA | 6.50 | VC |
| 644 | SWINDELL | .75 | VC |

## 1987 FLEER UPDATE

*Set: $11.50*

| 31 | FIELDER | 1.25 | VC |
|-----|-----------|------|-----|
| 49 | JACKSON | .35 | BC |
| 68 | MADDUX | 1.50 | VC |
| 75 | MCGRIFF | 2.75 | VC |
| 76 | MCGWIRE | 3.50 | VC |
| 110 | SMILEY | .50 | VC |
| 129 | WILLIAMS | 2.00 | VC |

**1988 TOPPS.** An uninspired set, to say the least. So bad, in fact, that the traded set issued that summer sells for almost twice as much!

*Warning:* An error on Keith Comstock's rookie card was corrected early, but no one cares.

*Avoid:* Reed, Caminiti, Polonia, Montgomery, and Nokes.

*Tough Call:* Burks. He enjoyed four tremendous seasons at the beginning of his career, but as he entered his prime, his numbers flat-lined. Who knows why? Fenway Park was the perfect stage for his talents, yet that .320–25–100 season never materialized. If you stick with Ellis for a couple more years (he's only twenty-eight), no one could blame you, but these mystery men have a way of remaining mysteries until they hang up their spikes. Keep

what you've bought so far, but hold off buying more until you see something positive.

*Set: $10.00*
*Factory Set: $12.50*
*Commons: $ .005*

| 70 | CLEMENS | .25 | BC |
|-----|-----------|------|-----|
| 250 | RYAN | .30 | BC |
| 350 | CLARK | .35 | VC |
| 370 | CANSECO | .30 | VC |
| 372 | WILLIAMS | .50 | VC |
| 423 | SMILEY | .25 | VC |
| 450 | BONDS | .25 | VC |
| 463 | MCGRIFF | .30 | VC |
| 650 | RIPKEN | .25 | BC |
| 779 | GLAVINE | 1.75 | VC |

## 1988 TOPPS TRADED

*Set: $30.00*

| 1 | ABBOTT | 5.50 | VC |
|-----|-----------|------|-----|
| 4 | ALOMAR | 6.50 | VC |
| 14 | BENES | 2.75 | VC |
| 39 | GANT | 3.25 | VC |
| 42 | GRACE | 1.75 | VC |
| 57 | KELLY | .75 | VC |
| 68 | MCDOWELL | 1.25 | VC |
| 74 | NAGY | 1.75 | VC |
| 109 | SLUSARSKI | .25 | VC |
| 124 | VENTURA | 9.50 | VC |

**1988 DONRUSS.** In order to "meet demand," Donruss kept the presses going day and night. The question is, why? Very possibly the worst set of the last five years, although some heady buyers made a few bucks selling short on the Grace and Jefferies rookies.

*Warning:* There are twenty-six "short-printed" cards in this set, which means that there are only *half* a zillion of them available. Wanna buy a wax box?

*Avoid:* Devereaux, Polonia, and Melido Perez.

*Tough Call:* Todd Stottlemyre. Like his dad, he's got plenty of stuff, but just not enough.

Set: $11.00
Factory Set: $12.00
Commons: $ .005

| 34 | ALOMAR | 3.50 | VC |
|---|---|---|---|
| 40 | GRACE | .75 | VC |
| 47 | MCDOWELL | .75 | VC |
| 51 | CLEMENS | .25 | BC |
| 61 | RYAN | .25 | BC |
| 171 | RIPKEN | .25 | BC |
| 204 | CLARK | .40 | VC |
| 256 | MCGWIRE | .25 | VC |
| 302 | CANSECO | .35 | VC |
| 326 | BONDS | .25 | VC |
| 368 | PUCKETT | .25 | VC |
| 449 | SMILEY | .25 | VC |
| 628 | WILLIAMS | .75 | VC |
| 635 | KELLY | 1.00 | VC |
| 644 | GLAVINE | 1.75 | VC |
| 654 | GANT | 3.25 | VC |
| 657 | JEFFERIES | .50 | VC |

## 1988 DONRUSS ROOKIES

Set: $12.50

| 1 | GRACE | 1.50 |
|---|---|---|
| 16 | KELLY | .75 |
| 35 | ALOMAR | 6.75 |
| 40 | MCDOWELL | 1.25 |
| 47 | GANT | 3.50 |

**1988 FLEER.** A tenacious set. Every time a hot player cools off, another one steps right up to carry the load. Not as scarce as was originally thought, but Topps, Donruss, and Score printed a whole lot more. Put one of these babies away for five years, and you might be looking at a $100 item.

*Warning:* Keith Moreland is disguised as Jody Davis on card #425. Better yet, on card #462 Jerry Browne is made up to look like Bobby Brower! What would their mothers say? Each will cost you a buck.

*Avoid:* Burkett, Weiss, and Jay Bell.

*Tough Call:* Edgar Martinez, despite his big year. Now that Nintendo owns the Mariners, maybe they'll put Edgar in a video game. He could certainly use the exposure—and about 2,000 more hits over the next dozen years.

Set: $33.00
Factory Set: $34.00
Commons: $ .005

| 19 | PUCKETT | .75 | VC |
|---|---|---|---|
| 78 | CLARK | 2.00 | VC |
| 101 | WILLIAMS | 2.00 | VC |
| 110 | FIELDER | .35 | VC |
| 118 | MCGRIFF | 1.25 | VC |
| 131 | CONE | .35 | VC |
| 137 | JEFFERIES | 1.00 | VC |
| 151 | STRAWBERRY | .25 | OTF |
| 178 | YOUNT | .35 | BC |
| 209 | HENDERSON | .25 | BC |
| 212 | KELLY | 2.00 | VC |
| 214 | MATTINGLY | .25 | OTF |
| 239 | LARKIN | .25 | VC |
| 254 | BRETT | .35 | BC |
| 276 | CANSECO | 1.25 | VC |
| 283 | JACKSON | .25 | BC |
| 286 | MCGWIRE | 2.00 | VC |
| 315 | SCHMIDT | .35 | BC |
| 322 | BONDS | .75 | VC |
| 323 | BONILLA | .35 | VC |
| 340 | SMILEY | .35 | VC |
| 345 | BOGGS | .25 | BC |
| 349 | CLEMENS | 1.00 | BC |
| 397 | FISK | .30 | BC |
| 407 | MCDOWELL | 2.50 | VC |
| 423 | MADDUX | .50 | BC |
| 429 | PALMEIRO | .50 | VC |
| 431 | SANDBERG | .50 | BC |
| 455 | RYAN | 1.00 | BC |
| 479 | SIERRA | .75 | VC |
| 538 | GANT | 5.75 | VC |
| 539 | GLAVINE | 6.75 | VC |
| 570 | RIPKEN | 1.00 | BC |
| 585 | GWYNN | .35 | BC |
| 605 | J. CARTER | .25 | OTF |
| 641 | GRACE | 2.75 | VC |

## 1988 FLEER UPDATE

*Set: $11.50*

| 74 | SMOLTZ | 2.75 | VC |
|----|--------|------|-----|
| 77 | GRACE | 1.50 | VC |
| 83 | DIBBLE | .35 | VC |
| 122 | ALOMAR | 7.50 | VC |

**1988 SCORE.** Based largely on the positive feedback it received from dealers late in 1987, Score decided to let the presses run a little longer on its debut set. The result is that there are still countless unopened cases and factory sets hanging around.

*Warning:* There's a hard-to-find Greg Walker error card that no one's trying to find.

*Avoid:* Paying hard currency for this set. If you have to have one, trade instead.

*Tough Call:* See 1988 Topps.

*Set: $10.00*
*Factory Set: $11.00*
*Commons: $ .005*

| 5 | MCGWIRE | .25 | VC |
|-----|-----------|------|-----|
| 45 | CANSECO | .25 | VC |
| 78 | CLARK | .30 | VC |
| 107 | MCGRIFF | .30 | VC |
| 110 | CLEMENS | .30 | BC |
| 118 | WILLIAMS | .75 | VC |
| 265 | BONDS | .25 | VC |
| 550 | RIPKEN | .30 | BC |
| 575 | RYAN | .30 | BC |
| 634 | KELLY | .60 | VC |
| 638 | GLAVINE | 1.75 | VC |
| 645 | JEFFERIES | .50 | VC |
| 647 | GANT | 1.50 | VC |

## 1988 SCORE TRADED
*Set: $75.00*

| 20 | L. SMITH | .50 |
|----|----------|------|
| 27 | RIJO | .25 |
| 50 | PARKER | .25 |
| 80 | GRACE | 11.00 |
| 85 | MCDOWELL | 12.00 |

| 86 | DIBBLE | 1.25 |
|-----|--------|-------|
| 105 | ALOMAR | 47.50 |

**1989 TOPPS.** An ambitious Draft Pick subset may one day make up for the absence of a Ken Griffey, Jr., card, but for now buyers are pretty cool on this set. Visually, it's not too bad—the photos in particular are crisp and colorful—but nothing compared with the Upper Deck issue that premiered that same year. Is this set a sleeper? Maybe. However, if Ventura, Benes, Avery, Olson, Lewis, Dibble, Sheffield, Smoltz, Abbott, and the Alomars aren't knocking on Cooperstown's door in ten years, this set could turn comatose.

*Warning:* An error on Bob Welch's card was quickly corrected, but no one paid much attention after he came back down to earth from his 27-win season. Otherwise, nothing tricky here—what you see is what you get.

*Avoid:* Ricky Jordan, but then you probably knew that already. Also, steer clear of the once highly touted Ty Griffin.

*Tough Call:* Brady Anderson, Chris Sabo, Craig Biggio, Randy Johnson, Bryan Harvey, and Monty Farriss. Anderson and Sabo are both good ballplayers, but the odds say "too little too late" where immortality is concerned. Biggio's move to the infield will make him a little more ordinary in the eyes of Hall of Fame voters, unless he transforms himself into a stellar defender. He's young enough, though, and certainly has a good bat. Randy Johnson is a huge question mark, too. Literally. What are the chances of a six-foot-ten flamethrower with control problems becoming a consistently dominant pitcher? No one knows, because he's the first one. If he finds his way up to Cooperstown, it may be as a closer. Reliever Bryan Harvey may not have long-term potential, either. Of the draft picks who have yet to establish themselves, Monty Farriss looks like the next name you'll be hearing about. He's not fast and he strikes out a lot, but he's knocked in a lot of runs for a minor-league infielder. However, if you know Alan Trammell, you know he's no Alan Trammell.

*Set: $10.00*
*Factory Set: $12.50*
*Commons: $ .005*

| | | | |
|---|---|---|---|
| 157 | GLAVINE | .35 | VC |
| 206 | R. ALOMAR | .45 | VC |
| 222 | LEWIS | .25 | VC |
| 225 | MARTINEZ | .40 | VC |
| 250 | RIPKEN | .25 | BC |
| 296 | GANT | .35 | VC |
| 343 | SHEFFIELD | 1.25 | VC |
| 382 | SMOLTZ | .35 | VC |
| 437 | BENES | .35 | VC |
| 486 | MCDOWELL | .25 | VC |
| 530 | RYAN | .35 | BC |
| 573 | ABBOTT | .60 | VC |
| 764 | VENTURA | 1.00 | VC |
| 784 | AVERY | .75 | VC |

### 1989 TOPPS TRADED

*Set: $5.50*

| | | | |
|---|---|---|---|
| 2 | ABBOTT | .60 | VC |
| 41 | GRIFFEY | 4.00 | VC |
| 106 | RYAN | 1.00 | BC |
| 110 | SANDERS | .75 | VC |

**1989 DONRUSS.** Buyers were watching Donruss like hawks after its 1988 debacle. Welcome to the 1989 debacle. Not even Ken Griffey's card could save this set.

*Warning:* A lot of double prints in this set.

*Avoid:* Tom Gordon.

*Tough Call:* Hal Morris. The bottom line is that he started a little too late to put up the kind of career numbers he'll need to be considered one of the greats. However, the kid can hit! If he learns to turn on the ball and starts whacking homers, you might want to reconsider him.

*Set: $10.00*
*Factory Set: $11.50*
*Commons: $ .005*

| | | | |
|---|---|---|---|
| 31 | SHEFFIELD | 1.25 | VC |
| 33 | GRIFFEY | 4.00 | VC |
| 38 | JOSE | .50 | VC |
| 50 | GANT | .30 | VC |
| 51 | RIPKEN | .25 | BC |
| 154 | RYAN | .30 | BC |
| 246 | ALOMAR | .45 | VC |
| 381 | GLAVINE | .35 | VC |
| 464 | MARTINEZ | .40 | VC |
| 642 | SMOLTZ | .35 | VC |

### 1989 DONRUSS ROOKIES

*Set: $10.00*

| | | | |
|---|---|---|---|
| 1 | SHEFFIELD | 2.00 | VC |
| 3 | GRIFFEY | 5.75 | VC |
| 6 | SANDERS | .65 | VC |
| 16 | ABBOTT | 1.00 | VC |
| 45 | MARTINEZ | .50 | VC |

**1989 FLEER.** This set is notable in that it was the first ever to offer buyers an actual written obscenity on a baseball card. The Billy Ripken error—and its subsequent corrections—drew enough attention away from Upper Deck's new set that spring that the new premium cards could still be had for less than a dollar a pack in some cases. Speaking of cases, there are still quite a few 1989 Fleer "error" cases around.

*Warning:* There's a good, non-hyped error on Jeff Treadway's card, if you're into that kind of thing. It'll run you about $4.

*Avoid:* Billy Ripken, no matter what's on the knob of his bat.

*Tough Call:* Kevin Reimer. You may be seeing him up with the league leaders for a couple of years, but he's strictly a John Kruk type of player. If that.

*Set: $13.00*
*Factory Set: $14.00*
*Commons: $ .005*

| | | | |
|---|---|---|---|
| 15 | JOSE | .50 | VC |
| 67 | MARTINEZ | .50 | VC |
| 196 | SHEFFIELD | 1.50 | VC |
| 299 | ALOMAR | .65 | VC |
| 368 | RYAN | .35 | BC |

| 548 | GRIFFEY | 5.50 | VC |
|-----|---------|------|-----|
| 590 | GANT | .35 | VC |
| 602 | SMOLTZ | .40 | VC |
| 617 | RIPKEN | .30 | BC |
| 641 | BROWN | .35 | VC |

## 1989 FLEER UPDATE
*Set: $6.50*

| 11 | ABBOTT | .80 | VC |
|-----|---------|------|-----|
| 23 | VENTURA | 2.25 | VC |
| 25 | BELLE | 1.50 | VC |
| 41 | VAUGHN | .65 | VC |
| 53 | SANDERS | .65 | VC |
| 67 | RYAN | 1.00 | BC |
| 122 | ZEILE | .65 | VC |
| 131 | SCHMIDT | .30 | BC |

## 1989 SCORE.
The only interesting thing about this set was that it contained Dwight Smith's rookie. And Smith was only interesting for about eight weeks.

*Warning:* An error on the Clemens card may be worth looking into. It was corrected very early in the run.

*Avoid:* See 1989 Topps.

*Tough Call:* See 1989 Topps.

*Set: $11.00*
*Factory Set: $12.00*
*Commons: $ .005*

| 15 | RIPKEN | .25 | BC |
|-----|---------|------|-----|
| 232 | ALOMAR | .45 | VC |
| 300 | RYAN | .30 | BC |
| 372 | GANT | .30 | VC |
| 616 | SMOLTZ | .35 | VC |
| 625 | SHEFFIELD | 1.25 | VC |
| 629 | JOSE | .50 | VC |
| 635 | MARTINEZ | .40 | VC |

## 1989 SCORE TRADED
*Set: $6.50*

| 2 | RYAN | 1.00 | BC |
|-----|---------|------|-----|
| 88 | ABBOTT | 1.00 | VC |
| 89 | BROWN | .25 | VC |

| 100 | GRIFFEY | 4.00 | VC |
|-----|---------|------|-----|
| 106 | BELLE | 1.50 | VC |

## 1989 UPPER DECK.
You surely know all about this set. It changed the business forever, forcing the other manufacturers to improve the quality of their sets and establishing once and for all that buyers would be willing to pay a per-pack premium of 100 percent and more to obtain high-quality cards. The print run was kept low, as promised.

*Warning:* A reversed negative card of Dale Murphy is probably the most unstable card of the last four years. It has sold for anywhere between $15 and $100. Steer clear of it unless you know something everyone else doesn't.

*Avoid:* Overpaying for low-potential rookies, just because the set is good.

*Tough Call:* See 1989 Topps.

*Set: $130.00*
*Factory Set (includes extended series): $175.00*
*Commons: $ .02*

| 1 | GRIFFEY | 50.00 | VC |
|-----|-----------|-------|-----|
| 5 | S. ALOMAR | .65 | VC |
| 9 | JEFFERIES | .50 | VC |
| 13 | SHEFFIELD | 11.00 | VC |
| 17 | SMOLTZ | 2.75 | VC |
| 18 | MARTINEZ | 3.00 | VC |
| 22 | JOSE | 3.25 | VC |
| 120 | SANDBERG | 1.50 | BC |
| 140 | GRACE | 1.00 | VC |
| 145 | RYAN | 3.25 | BC |
| 155 | CLARK | 1.50 | OTF |
| 190 | J. CARTER | .35 | OTF |
| 195 | CLEMENS | 1.75 | BC |
| 200 | MATTINGLY | .75 | OTF |
| 205 | DAWSON | .35 | BC |
| 210 | HENDERSON | 1.00 | BC |
| 215 | BRETT | .65 | BC |
| 235 | PALMEIRO | .35 | VC |
| 247 | WILLIAMS | .50 | VC |
| 260 | STRAWBERRY | .75 | OTF |
| 265 | O. SMITH | .35 | BC |
| 270 | LARKIN | .35 | VC |

| 275 | MURRAY | .35 | BC |
|---|---|---|---|
| 285 | YOUNT | .65 | BC |
| 300 | MCGWIRE | 1.25 | OTF |
| 349 | WINFIELD | .40 | BC |
| 360 | GLAVINE | 2.25 | VC |
| 364 | FIELDER | .75 | OTF |
| 371 | CANSECO | 1.25 | OTF |
| 375 | DIBBLE | .25 | VC |
| 376 | PUCKETT | 1.25 | BC |
| 378 | GANT | 1.75 | VC |
| 384 | GWYNN | 1.00 | BC |
| 389 | BOGGS | .75 | BC |
| 406 | SCHMIDT | 1.25 | BC |
| 410 | DAVIS | .30 | OTF |
| 416 | SIERRA | 1.00 | VC |
| 440 | BONDS | 1.25 | VC |
| 467 | RIPKEN | 2.25 | BC |
| 471 | ALOMAR | 3.50 | VC |
| 530 | MCDOWELL | 1.25 | VC |
| 565 | GOODEN | .30 | OTF |
| 572 | MCGRIFF | .75 | OTF |
| 578 | BONILLA | .50 | VC |
| 590 | KELLY | .50 | VC |
| 609 | FISK | .35 | BC |

## 1989 UPPER DECK EXTENDED

*Factory Set: $12.00*

| 723 | OLSON | .75 | VC |
|---|---|---|---|
| 744 | HARNISCH | .50 | VC |
| 752 | BROWN | .35 | VC |
| 754 | ZEILE | 1.25 | VC |
| 755 | ABBOTT | 3.50 | VC |
| 763 | MURRAY | .30 | BC |
| 772 | PALMEIRO | .40 | VC |
| 774 | RYAN | 3.50 | BC |

**1990 TOPPS.** Apparently reeling from intense competition, Topps issued a blindingly ugly set of cards with only two notable players: Frank Thomas and Juan Gonzales. Another "Draft Pick" subset was issued, featuring some embarrassingly bad picks, which in fairness was not Topps's fault.

*Warning:* Look up "caveat emptor" again.

*Avoid:* Speculating in any card not listed below.

*Tough Call:* John Wetteland, Stan Belinda, Bernie Williams, and Kevin Appier. Wetteland is still a project. Belinda is pitching for a team that has been traditionally unwilling to hand the closer's role to one man. Meanwhile, Williams has been a prospect for four years and hasn't been dominant in the minors, either. A lot of people consider him a suspect right now. As for Appier, he's got the talent, but may not have the intellect. Consider this story, which circulated a couple of years ago: Appier (a righty) was going over the hitters with his catcher before the game when the discussion turned to how they would pitch to a particular switch-hitter. Appier asked his catcher whether he thought the guy would bat right-handed or left-handed against him.

*Set: $12.50*
*Factory Set: $17.50*
*Commons: $ .005*

| 1 | RYAN | .35 | BC |
|---|---|---|---|
| 44 | SALKELD | .30 | VC |
| 61 | SANDERS | .25 | VC |
| 121 | VENTURA | .60 | VC |
| 224 | DESHIELDS | .30 | VC |
| 283 | BELLE | .30 | VC |
| 331 | GONZALES | 1.25 | VC |
| 336 | GRIFFEY | .75 | VC |
| 414 | THOMAS | 3.25 | VC |
| 714 | GRISSOM | .30 | VC |
| 718 | SHEFFIELD | .25 | VC |
| 757 | WALKER | .30 | VC |
| 774 | MCDONALD | .40 | VC |

## 1990 TOPPS TRADED
*Set: $5.00*

| 4 | AVERY | .65 | VC |
|---|---|---|---|
| 6 | BAERGA | .50 | VC |
| 29 | ERICKSON | .50 | VC |
| 33 | FRYMAN | 1.00 | VC |
| 41 | HOLLINS | .35 | VC |
| 48 | JUSTICE | .75 | VC |
| 70 | MCDONALD | .40 | VC |
| 83 | OLERUD | .25 | VC |

**1990 DONRUSS.** An attractive set, but as was

the case in the previous two years, Donruss simply made too many. All the talk was about the Ryan and Baines errors—each sold for over $10 at one time—even though the real winner turned out to be the Juan Gonzales error in the Rated Rookies subset.

*Warning:* There are more inconsequential errors in this set than in any other Donruss issue. The Baines and Ryan errors are all over the place for $2 or less. The Gonzales card that pictures him swinging left-handed sells at a 100 percent premium.

*Avoid:* Mercker, Lee Stevens, and Mark Gardner.

*Tough Call:* Eric Anthony. It's probably too early to draw any definitive conclusions on the guy, but he's got an awful lot of growing up to do at the plate. Will he do it? Not with Houston—at least, that's not the organization's strong suit. Every time he gets going well—shortening his swing, waiting on the curve, working the count—he inevitably reverts back to his old form, if that's what you'd call it. Don't give up on him yet, but don't expect miracles, either.

*Set: $11.00*
*Factory Set: $12.00*
*Commons: $ .005*

| 28 | VENTURA | .50 | VC |
|---|---|---|---|
| 32 | MCDONALD | .40 | VC |
| 33 | GONZALES | 1.25 | VC |
| 36 | GRISSOM | .30 | VC |
| 39 | AVERY | .50 | VC |
| 41 | BENES | .25 | VC |
| 42 | DESHIELDS | .30 | VC |
| 166 | RYAN | .30 | BC |
| 365 | GRIFFEY | .75 | VC |
| 390 | BELLE | .30 | VC |
| 427 | SANDERS | .25 | VC |
| 501 | SHEFFIELD | .25 | VC |
| 529 | PALMER | .75 | VC |
| 578 | WALKER | .30 | VC |
| 659 | RYAN 5,000 K | .25 | BC |
| 665 | RYAN KING | .25 | BC |
| 704 | JUSTICE | .75 | VC |
| 711 | OLERUD | .25 | VC |

## 1990 DONRUSS ROOKIES

*Set: $5.00*

| 2 | OLERUD | .25 | VC |
|---|---|---|---|
| 14 | JUSTICE | .75 | VC |
| 15 | VENTURA | .50 | VC |
| 19 | BAERGA | .50 | VC |
| 30 | MCDONALD | .40 | VC |
| 42 | AVERY | .50 | VC |
| 45 | GRISSOM | .25 | VC |

**1990 LEAF.** When this set hit $75 within a few months of its debut, some buyers shied away from purchasing the set and instead started buying singles. That drove the set price up even more, especially when Frank Thomas, Robin Ventura, and Steve Avery blossomed the following summer. So far, it's running neck and neck with the 1991 Stadiums for "Set of the Decade" honors.

*Warning:* There are some pretty good Thomas fakes around.

*Avoid:* Huson, Sojo, Coolbaugh, Villanueva, Boskie, and Hibbard.

*Tough Call:* Commons. They've been selling for as much as 20 cents each. Normally, you'd stay away from common cards this new. But so many people have been buying the stars from this set that they may one day want to finish the set off. If you don't mind commons, buy 'em. Otherwise, steer clear.

*Set: $265.00*
*Commons: $ .09*

| 7 | OLSON | .40 | VC |
|---|---|---|---|
| 10 | FISK | .65 | BC |
| 12 | CLEMENS | 3.50 | BC |
| 13 | GLAVINE | 7.50 | VC |
| 17 | KELLY | .65 | VC |
| 18 | LARKIN | .65 | OTF |
| 21 | RYAN | 6.75 | BC |
| 29 | ECKERSLEY | .65 | OTF |
| 31 | ABBOTT | 2.75 | VC |
| 39 | HARNISCH | .50 | VC |
| 51 | BOGGS | 1.50 | BC |

| 56 | BENES | 3.25 | VC |
|----|-------|------|-----|
| 59 | SMOLTZ | 3.00 | VC |
| 62 | MCGWIRE | 2.75 | OTF |
| 69 | MATTINGLY | 1.50 | OTF |
| 71 | YOUNT | 1.00 | BC |
| 72 | SABERHAGEN | .25 | OTF |
| 75 | R. ALOMAR | 4.75 | VC |
| 85 | NAVARRO | 1.50 | VC |
| 91 | BONDS | 2.25 | OTF |
| 94 | WILLIAMS | .50 | VC |
| 98 | SANDBERG | 3.00 | BC |
| 100 | PALMEIRO | .50 | OTF |
| 107 | GRISSOM | 3.75 | VC |
| 108 | CANSECO | 3.00 | OTF |
| 111 | VAUGHN | 2.00 | VC |
| 123 | PUCKETT | 2.75 | BC |
| 132 | MCGRIFF | 1.50 | OTF |
| 137 | GRACE | .50 | VC |
| 139 | GOODEN | .40 | OTF |
| 142 | O. SMITH | .65 | BC |
| 147 | R. MARTINEZ | 2.00 | VC |
| 154 | GWYNN | 2.00 | BC |
| 157 | SHEFFIELD | 15.00 | VC |
| 160 | HENDERSON | 2.00 | BC |
| 165 | FIELDER | 1.75 | OTF |
| 167 | VENTURA | 12.00 | VC |
| 172 | CLARK | 3.00 | OTF |
| 177 | DAWSON | .50 | BC |
| 178 | BRETT | 1.00 | BC |
| 180 | BELLE | 7.50 | VC |
| 181 | MURRAY | .65 | BC |
| 189 | DAVIS | .50 | OTF |
| 193 | DESHIELDS | 3.75 | VC |
| 196 | BONILLA | 1.00 | OTF |
| 197 | RIPKEN | 5.00 | BC |
| 205 | JU. FRANCO | .25 | OTF |
| 218 | TRAMMELL | .25 | OTF |
| 220 | SOSA | .50 | VC |
| 221 | ZEILE | 1.00 | VC |
| 232 | S. ALOMAR | .30 | VC |
| 237 | OLERUD | 3.25 | VC |
| 242 | MOLITOR | .35 | OTF |
| 243 | MURPHY | .25 | BC |
| 245 | GRIFFEY | 20.00 | VC |

| 249 | MCDONALD | 4.00 | VC |
|-----|----------|------|-----|
| 250 | STRAWBERRY | 1.50 | OTF |
| 257 | SIERRA | 2.00 | OTF |
| 260 | PENDELTON | .30 | OTF |
| 265 | RYAN KING | 5.00 | BC |
| 269 | TAPANI | 2.00 | VC |
| 272 | JOHNSON | .25 | OTF |
| 276 | REARDON | .30 | BC |
| 297 | JUSTICE | 20.00 | VC |
| 300 | THOMAS | 55.00 | VC |
| 325 | WALKER | 3.75 | VC |
| 353 | GILKEY | .75 | VC |
| 359 | D. SANDERS | 4.75 | VC |
| 376 | GANT | 2.50 | VC |
| 379 | J. CARTER | 1.00 | OTF |
| 385 | JOSE | 2.25 | VC |
| 246 | WINFIELD | .65 | BC |
| 443 | BAERGA | 5.00 | VC |
| 464 | OFFERMAN | .65 | VC |
| 481 | AVERY | 12.50 | VC |
| 482 | MORRIS | .30 | OTF |

**1990 FLEER.** With apologies to the late William Gaines. . . . Eccch!

*Warning:* Some marginally correctible errors on the Players of the Decade subset caused a stir—especially the misspelled Ripkin card, which goes for around $2.

*Avoid:* See 1990 Topps.

*Tough Call:* Moises Alou. You've probably heard how he led Montreal's big youth movement last year. Well, he was twenty-six at season's end, which is not youthful enough to start a career that adds up to Cooperstown. At best, he'll come as close as his dad, Felipe, who actually came pretty close. Alou had excellent minor-league credentials—all the things you look for, in fact. But he had injury problems and was stuck behind all those outfielders in Pittsburgh. Had he received the chance to be a Cecil Espy or Lloyd McClendon for a year, his star might have risen back in 1991. By the way, Derrick May—*his* dad was traded for Hank Aaron—is the guy you want out of the rookie subset.

Set: $11.00
Factory Set: $12.00
Commons: $ .005

| 151 | BENES | .25 | VC |
|-----|-------|-----|-----|
| 180 | MCDONALD | .35 | VC |
| 297 | GONZALES | 1.25 | VC |
| 313 | RYAN | .25 | BC |
| 336 | SHEFFIELD | .25 | VC |
| 347 | GRISSOM | .30 | VC |
| 363 | WALKER | .30 | VC |
| 454 | SANDERS | .25 | VC |
| 485 | BELLE | .30 | VC |
| 513 | GRIFFEY | 1.00 | VC |
| 586 | JUSTICE | .75 | VC |

## 1990 FLEER UPDATE
Set: $6.50

| 1 | AVERY | .50 | VC |
|-----|-------|-----|-----|
|   | DESHIELDS | .25 | VC |
| 43 | HOLLINS | .35 | VC |
| 84 | A. FERNANDEZ | .25 | VC |
| 87 | THOMAS | 3.25 | VC |
| 90 | BAERGA | .50 | VC |
| 96 | FRYMAN | 1.00 | VC |
| 128 | OLERUD | .25 | VC |
| 131 | RYAN | .35 | BC |

**1990 SCORE.** From a distribution standpoint, this set was an unmitigated disaster for card buyers. Originally thought to be scarce, cards in this set sold at a small premium for much of the spring and summer. When more and more started to appear, however, prices began to inch down. Finally, in the fall, Score sent a whole slew of factory sets (sets that no one knew it still had) to toy stores, dropping prices back down to where they should have been all along. Buyers never forgave Score for this and took it out on their next two sets.

*Warning:* There are two factory sets. The one you want has ten extra cards, including short-printed Ventura and Grissom cards. Also, there are a few uninteresting errors in this set, including one on Milt Cuyler's card. The only good one, however, is the Sandberg "highlight" listing his position as "3B" on the front. It sells for about $6.

*Avoid:* Eddie Zosky, Bart Giamatti, and Bo's football card.

*Tough Call:* Kevin Maas and Mo Vaughn. Sorry, New Yorkers. Kevin was twenty-four when he learned how to hit, and it took him another year to make it to the bigs. He's built for Yankee Stadium, however, so he could come back and have some nice years. But long-term there's not much there. As for Vaughn, when he's not battling his weight, he's been battling people like Carlos Quintana and Scott Cooper for the first-base job. Enough said.

Set: $11.00
Factory Set (704 cards): $12.00
Factory Set (714 cards): $23.00
Commons: $ .005

| 97 | SHEFFIELD | .25 | VC |
|-----|-------|-----|-----|
| 250 | RYAN | .25 | BC |
| 508 | BELLE | .30 | VC |
| 560 | GRIFFEY | 1.00 | VC |
| 578 | BENES | .25 | VC |
| 586 | SANDERS | .25 | VC |
| 589 | OLERUD | .25 | VC |
| 591 | GRISSOM | .30 | VC |
| 594 | PALMER | .60 | VC |
| 595 | VENTURA | .50 | VC |
| 611 | NAGY | .30 | VC |
| 631 | WALKER | .30 | VC |
| 637 | GONZALES | 1.25 | VC |
| 645 | DESHIELDS | .30 | VC |
| 650 | JUSTICE | .75 | VC |
| 663 | THOMAS | 4.75 | VC |
| 666 | HOSEY | .25 | VC |
| 669 | ELDRED | .50 | VC |
| 672 | KNOBLAUCH | 1.25 | VC |
| 674 | SALKELD | .35 | VC |
| 680 | MCDONALD | .35 | VC |
| −3 | ZEILE | .35 | VC |
| −6 | VENTURA | 6.50 | VC |
| −8 | VAUGHN | 1.25 | VC |
| −9 | GRISSOM | 3.00 | VC |

## 1990 SCORE TRADED
*Set: $12.00*

| | | | |
|---|---|---|---|
| 74 | BAERGA | .50 | VC |
| 75 | HOLLINS | .35 | VC |
| 81 | D. BELL | .50 | VC |
| 84 | LANKFORD | .50 | VC |
| 86 | THOMAS | 5.75 | VC |
| 100 | LINDROS | 5.00 | VC |
| 106 | GILKEY | .25 | VC |
| 109 | AVERY | 1.25 | VC |

**1990 UPPER DECK.** Some feel this set is better looking than Upper Deck's first. Most feel it would look a lot better with a Griffey-caliber rookie leading it off. Keep your eye on those two kids in Texas.

*Warning:* The Ben McDonald error has settled in at around $20, but that could move if he keeps pitching as he did in 1992. The Nolan Ryan 6th No-Hitter card in the extended series is available with or without mention of his 300th win. *With* will cost you 75 cents. *Without* costs almost ten times as much. Also, a Reggie Jackson Heroes subset was inserted in high-number packs. These cards sell for between $2 and $3, with the header going for triple that price. These cards are not included in the boxed extended series.

*Avoid:* Hamelin, Greene, Hammond, and Bobby Rose.

*Tough Call:* Tino Martinez. What does a guy have to do to make the Mariners? He hit for average and power at AAA for two years and still got stuck behind bums like Alvin Davis and Pete O'Brien! Poor Tino. If he were a little faster, they could have stuck him in the outfield instead of Greg Briley or Dave Cochrane or Henry Cotto. But nooooo. The Mariners didn't want to rush him. Now he's got a lot of catching up to do. No one doubts he'll put in a fine career, but is it too late to set his sights on Cooperstown? He'll be twenty-six after this season ends, and history says he can't do it. Buy only if you're playing the short-term—and buy his 1988 Topps Traded card, not this one.

*Set: $32.00*
*Factory Set (includes extended series): $42.00*
*Commons: $.01*

| | | | |
|---|---|---|---|
| 9 | GRISSOM | 1.00 | VC |
| 13 | D. SANDERS | 1.00 | VC |
| 17 | SOSA | .25 | VC |
| 21 | VENTURA | 2.00 | VC |
| 25 | VAUGHN | .35 | VC |
| 34 | RYAN SPECIAL | .50 | BC |
| 54 | MCDONALD | 1.25 | VC |
| 55 | BENES | .65 | VC |
| 56 | OLERUD | 1.00 | VC |
| 65 | AVERY | 2.00 | VC |
| 66 | CANSECO | .30 | OTF |
| 72 | JU. GONZALES | 6.50 | VC |
| 74 | PALMER | 2.00 | VC |
| 87 | TAPANI | .50 | VC |
| 156 | GRIFFEY | 4.00 | VC |
| 157 | SHEFFIELD | .75 | VC |
| 171 | MCGWIRE | .30 | OTF |
| 227 | BONDS | .30 | VC |
| 228 | JOSE | .25 | VC |
| 232 | GANT | .45 | VC |
| 236 | PUCKETT | .35 | BC |
| 266 | RIPKEN | .75 | BC |
| 323 | CLEMENS | .40 | BC |
| 324 | SANDBERG | .40 | BC |
| 346 | R. ALOMAR | .75 | VC |
| 355 | SIERRA | .25 | OTF |
| 446 | BELL | 1.50 | VC |
| 466 | WALKER | 1.25 | VC |
| 544 | RYAN | 1.00 | BC |
| 545 | ZEILE | .25 | VC |
| 556 | CLARK | .35 | OTF |
| 571 | GLAVINE | .45 | VC |
| 646 | NAVARRO | .25 | VC |

## 1990 UPPER DECK EXTENDED

*Set: $9.00*

| | | | |
|---|---|---|---|
| 702 | ROOKIE THREATS | .30 | VC |
| 711 | JUSTICE | 4.25 | VC |
| 734 | RYAN 6TH | 6.00 | BC |
| 734 | RYAN 6TH/300TH | .75 | BC |
| 736 | MAY | .35 | VC |

| 737 | BAERGA | 1.50 | VC |
|---|---|---|---|
| 746 | DESHIELDS | 1.00 | VC |
| 755 | LANKFORD | 1.50 | VC |
| 765 | ALVAREZ | .25 | VC |
| 785 | HOLLINS | 1.00 | VC |
| 786 | FIELDER | .25 | OTF |

## 1991 TOPPS.

An attractive set featuring Topps's fortieth anniversary logo and loaded with interesting rookies. A Draft Pick set was included again.

*Warning:* Errors exist on a number of cards, including those of Randy Tomlin, Wes Chamberlain, Don Mattingly, Moises Alou, and Wilson Alvarez. The long-term impact of these errors is as yet unclear.

*Avoid:* Any rookies not listed below, especially those who, like Mark Whiten and Geronimo Pena, have passed age twenty-five without establishing themselves as stars.

*Tough Call:* Wes Chamberlain. Okay, so you've already blown a lot of money on him. Just hang on and hope for the best. If you're thinking about plowing more dough into Wes, you should know one thing. No one's sure which is worse—Chamberlain's attitude or his mechanics. He's still young, however, so he could straighten himself out. Just don't get seduced by one of his patented 5-homer weeks.

*Set: $12.50*
*Factory Set: $17.50*
*commons: $ .005*

| 1 | RYAN | .25 | BC |
|---|---|---|---|
| 79 | THOMAS | 1.00 | VC |
| 128 | FRYMAN | .30 | VC |
| 224 | GONZALES | .25 | VC |
| 474 | PL ANTIER | .35 | VC |
| 529 | NEWFIELD | .35 | VC |
| 682 | LANKFORD | .25 | VC |
| 790 | GRIFFEY | .35 | VC |

## 1991 TOPPS TRADED

*Set: $6.50*

| 4 | BAGWELL | .75 | VC |
|---|---|---|---|
| 51 | HAMMONDS | .75 | VC |

| 61 | C. JOHNSON | .75 | VC |
|---|---|---|---|
| 69 | KNOBLAUCH | .75 | VC |
| 83 | NEVIN | .75 | VC |
| 101 | I. RODRIGUEZ | .75 | VC |

## 1991 TOPPS STADIUM CLUB.

This was the first true super-premium set, and it caught everyone by surprise. There was so much prepublicity about the $1.25 pack price that buyers were trying to figure *if* they'd pay that much. What they should have been thinking about was *how much* they'd be willing to pay.

*Warning:* Two things could work against the price of cards set: the super-premium sets issued this year and last and the fact that there are still quite a few cases that haven't been opened yet.

*Avoid:* Buying packs. At $4 to $7 each, the odds just aren't in your favor.

*Tough Call:* Whether demand will continue to be strong enough for the top cards in this set to hold their prices.

*Set: $240.00*
*Commons: $ .07*

| 5 | CLARK | 3.00 | OTF |
|---|---|---|---|
| 8 | GRISSOM | 1.00 | VC |
| 21 | MATTINGLY | 1.25 | OTF |
| 26 | JUSTICE | 8.25 | VC |
| 37 | DAVIS | .35 | OTF |
| 44 | DICKSON | .25 | VC |
| 48 | AVERY | 4.25 | VC |
| 51 | BENES | 1.00 | VC |
| 56 | BROWN | .30 | VC |
| 57 | THOMAS | 27.50 | VC |
| 86 | JOHNSON | .25 | OTF |
| 87 | MCDOWELL | .75 | VC |
| 92 | LARKIN | .65 | OTF |
| 93 | WALKER | 1.00 | VC |
| 95 | SHEFFIELD | 4.00 | VC |
| 100 | GOODEN | .30 | OTF |
| 110 | PUCKETT | 2.50 | BC |
| 115 | BAERGA | 1.50 | VC |
| 120 | HENDERSON | 1.50 | BC |
| 123 | SIERRA | 1.50 | OTF |
| 124 | ABBOTT | .75 | VC |

| | | | |
|---|---|---|---|
| 126 | MADDUX | .25 | VC |
| 135 | VAUGHN | .50 | VC |
| 139 | BONILLA | .75 | OTF |
| 147 | A. FERNANDEZ | .50 | VC |
| 154 | O. SMITH | .65 | BC |
| 155 | CANSECO | 2.75 | OTF |
| 159 | BRETT | .75 | BC |
| 161 | TAPANI | .50 | VC |
| 170 | BOGGS | 1.25 | BC |
| 173 | JU. FRANCO | .25 | OTF |
| 177 | MURRAY | .50 | BC |
| 178 | TOMLIN | 1.00 | VC |
| 180 | FISK | .50 | BC |
| 186 | FIELDER | 1.50 | OTF |
| 194 | DESHIELDS | 1.00 | VC |
| 200 | RYAN | 12.00 | BC |
| 215 | COLBRUNN | .25 | VC |
| 220 | BONDS | 2.50 | OTF |
| 230 | SANDBERG | 3.00 | BC |
| 237 | GONZALES | 13.00 | VC |
| 243 | MURPHY | .25 | BC |
| 255 | ZEILE | .35 | VC |
| 263 | WINFIELD | .50 | BC |
| 264 | MCDONALD | 1.00 | VC |
| 270 | GRIFFEY | 13.00 | VC |
| 272 | TARTABULL | .25 | OTF |
| 274 | VENTURA | 3.25 | VC |
| 290 | GRACE | .50 | OTF |
| 295 | WILLIAMS | .25 | OTF |
| 301 | STRAWBERRY | 1.00 | OTF |
| 304 | R. ALOMAR | 3.25 | VC |
| 308 | GWYNN | 1.50 | BC |
| 309 | CLEMENS | 3.50 | BC |
| 310 | DAWSON | .50 | BC |
| 318 | MUNOZ | 2.00 | VC |
| 319 | KELLY | .50 | OTF |
| 327 | PENDELTON | .25 | OTF |
| 332 | ECKERSLEY | .30 | OTF |
| 355 | FRYMAN | 8.75 | VC |
| 357 | MCGRIFF | 1.00 | OTF |
| 362 | D. LEWIS | .50 | VC |
| 365 | SMOLTZ | .75 | VC |
| 366 | CONE | .30 | VC |
| 367 | JOSE | .75 | VC |
| 388 | BAGWELL | 8.00 | VC |
| 399 | MCGWIRE | 2.00 | OTF |
| 402 | GILKEY | .50 | VC |
| 430 | RIPKEN | 4.50 | BC |
| 436 | NAVARRO | .40 | VC |
| 442 | D. SANDERS | 1.50 | VC |
| 447 | MORRIS | .35 | OTF |
| 454 | GANT | 2.00 | VC |
| 459 | PLANTIER | 6.50 | VC |
| 465 | BELLE | 2.00 | VC |
| 470 | CUYLER | .50 | VC |
| 472 | NAGY | 1.50 | VC |
| 476 | CEDENO | 1.00 | VC |
| 478 | MCRAE | 1.25 | VC |
| 482 | OLERUD | .75 | VC |
| 492 | M. LEWIS | .75 | VC |
| 502 | PALMEIRO | .35 | OTF |
| 509 | YOUNT | .75 | BC |
| 513 | J. CARTER | .50 | OTF |
| 516 | MARTINEZ | .35 | VC |
| 537 | LANKFORD | 2.50 | VC |
| 548 | KNOBLAUCH | 5.00 | VC |
| 558 | GLAVINE | 2.00 | VC |
| 560 | ERICKSON | 1.50 | VC |
| 576 | GONZALES | .75 | VC |
| 587 | D. WILSON | .40 | VC |
| 596 | SCOTT | .25 | VC |

**1991 DONRUSS.** The first set Donruss ever issued in two series. Unfortunately for the company, when buyers got a load of the first series, they had no interest in buying the second. Faced with the prospect of getting stuck with a huge number of cards, Donruss scrambled to repackage its factory sets with promo cards of the 1991 Leaf and 1991 Studio sets.

*Warning:* The value of the promo cards, and thus the factory sets, is very iffy. There are still a lot of these factory sets sitting around in job-lot warehouses, so if you see an $8 price tag on the Justice studio promo card, take it with a grain of salt.

*Avoid:* The factory set with *no* promo cards in it. Whatever the other sets are worth, this one's definitely worth *less*.

*Tough Call:* See 1991 Topps.

Set: $8.50
Factory Set: $9.50
Factory Set (Leaf): $20.00
Factory Set (Studio): $15.00
Commons: $ .005

| 41 | PLANTIER | .35 | VC |
|---|---|---|---|
| 43 | LANKFORD | .25 | VC |
| 77 | GRIFFEY | .35 | VC |
| 89 | RYAN | .25 | BC |
| 371 | GONZALES | .25 | VC |
| 421 | KNOBLAUCH | .25 | VC |
| 477 | THOMAS | 1.00 | VC |
| 768 | FRYMAN | .30 | VC |

## 1991 DONRUSS ROOKIES

Set: $4.00

| 7 | VAN POPPEL | .50 | VC |
|---|---|---|---|
| 8 | LANKFORD | .25 | VC |
| 9 | HUNTER | .25 | VC |
| 30 | BAGWELL | .75 | VC |
| 33 | I. RODRIGUEZ | .75 | VC |
| 39 | KNOBLAUCH | .25 | VC |

**1991 LEAF.** Doesn't have nearly the *oomph* of the 1990 Leaf set, although not a bad-looking issue. Gold bonus cards were randomly inserted into packs and can be very hard to find.

*Warning:* Buyer demand was split between this set and the Fleer Ultras before everyone realized that Stadiums were the place to be, so it's unclear how many of these cards are really available. There do seem to be a lot of foil packs for sale, so be careful.

*Avoid:* DeLucia, Marak, Howard, and Decker.
*Tough Call:* See 1991 Topps.

Set: $40.00
Commons: $ .01

| 22 | GRISSOM | .30 | VC |
|---|---|---|---|
| 35 | L. GOMEZ | .65 | VC |
| 77 | JUSTICE | 1.75 | VC |
| 97 | SIERRA | .30 | OTF |
| 101 | HENDERSON | .25 | BC |

| 106 | FIELDER | .25 | OTF |
|---|---|---|---|
| 116 | YOUNT | .25 | BC |
| 117 | MCDONALD | .25 | VC |
| 119 | JU. GONZALES | 3.75 | VC |
| 129 | GANT | .25 | OTF |
| 139 | DESHIELDS | .30 | VC |
| 149 | FRYMAN | 3.25 | VC |
| 172 | GLAVINE | .30 | VC |
| 173 | SHEFFIELD | .75 | VC |
| 182 | CANSECO | .65 | OTF |
| 186 | P. MUNOZ | 1.00 | VC |
| 203 | TOMLIN | .60 | VC |
| 207 | SANDBERG | .65 | BC |
| 208 | PUCKETT | .60 | BC |
| 225 | BAERGA | .35 | VC |
| 235 | MCRAE | .45 | VC |
| 238 | CLARK | .65 | OTF |
| 239 | BELLE | .40 | VC |
| 241 | WALKER | .30 | VC |
| 261 | BONDS | .40 | OTF |
| 267 | R. ALOMAR | .75 | VC |
| 271 | VENTURA | .75 | VC |
| 273 | BOGGS | .25 | BC |
| 275 | BENES | .25 | OTF |
| 281 | THOMAS | 6.00 | VC |
| 289 | M. LEWIS | .35 | VC |
| 290 | GWYNN | .25 | BC |
| 296 | A. FERNANDEZ | .25 | VC |
| 335 | BRETT | .25 | BC |
| 340 | MCDOWELL | .25 | OTF |
| 372 | GRIFFEY | 2.25 | VC |
| 377 | STRAWBERRY | .25 | OTF |
| 384 | FISK | .25 | BC |
| 396 | KNOBLAUCH | 1.75 | VC |
| 423 | RYAN | 2.25 | BC |
| 425 | MATTINGLY | .25 | OTF |
| 430 | RIPKEN | 1.00 | BC |
| 436 | D. SANDERS | .35 | VC |
| 466 | NEAGLE | .30 | VC |
| 487 | MCGWIRE | .50 | OTF |
| 488 | CLEMENS | .75 | BC |
| 510 | AVERY | 1.00 | VC |
| 523 | LANKFORD | 1.25 | VC |
| 527 | ERICKSON | .75 | VC |

## 1991 LEAF BONUS CARDS

| 2 | L. GONZALES | 2.00 | VC |
|---|---|---|---|
| 3 | CORDERO | 3.00 | VC |
| 4 | SCOTT | 1.00 | VC |
| 5 | BANKS | 2.25 | VC |
| 6 | RHODES | 3.50 | VC |
| 9 | VAN POPPEL | 5.00 | VC |
| 10 | R. SANDERS | 9.50 | VC |
| 12 | MUSSINA | 11.50 | VC |
| 14 | BAGWELL | 10.00 | VC |
| 15 | SCHOUREK | 1.00 | VC |
| 19 | SALKELD | 4.00 | VC |
| 20 | CEDENO | 1.75 | VC |
| 21 | KLESKO | 7.00 | VC |
| 25 | RYAN | 3.50 | BC |
| 26 | HENDERSON | 1.75 | BC |

**1991 O-PEE-CHEE.** An unattractive set from Donruss that buyers have all but given up on. The best thing about this set is that all the players are in alphabetical order.

*Warning:* Distributed in far greater quantities than buyers were led to (or led themselves to) believe, all the cards in this set should be considered Volatile in a *downward* direction.

*Avoid:* All but the hottest cards.

*Tough Call:* Whether to ever trust O-Pee-Chees again.

*Set: $15.00*
*Factory Set: $22.50*

| 1 | ALOMAR | .50 | VC |
|---|---|---|---|
| 8 | BELLE | .35 | |
| 12 | BONDS | .25 | |
| 18 | CANSECO | .25 | OTF |
| 22 | CLARK | .25 | OTF |
| 23 | CLEMENS | .50 | BC |
| 52 | L. GOMEZ | .25 | VC |
| 54 | JU. GONZALES | 4.00 | VC |
| 56 | GRIFFEY | 2.25 | VC |
| 70 | JUSTICE | 1.50 | VC |
| 72 | LANKFORD | .50 | VC |
| 96 | PUCKETT | .25 | BC |
| 100 | RIPKEN | .75 | BC |

| 103 | SANDBERG | .25 | BC |
|---|---|---|---|
| 121 | THOMAS | 5.50 | VC |

**1991 FLEER.** The following story may not be true, but it's too good to pass up. A card buyer in therapy is engaged in word association with his psychoanalyst. The psychoanalyst says, "Yellow." The card buyer says, "'91 Fleer."

*Warning:* This set may also be dangerous to your financial health.

*Avoid:* See 1991 Topps.

*Tough Call:* Ditto.

*Set: $11.00*
*Factory Set: $13.50*
*Commons: $.005*

| 107 | PLANTIER | .35 | VC |
|---|---|---|---|
| 138 | THOMAS | 1.00 | VC |
| 286 | GONZALES | .25 | VC |
| 302 | RYAN | .25 | BC |
| 336 | FRYMAN | .30 | VC |
| 450 | GRIFFEY | .35 | VC |
| 637 | LANKFORD | .25 | VC |

## 1991 FLEER UPDATE

*Set: $6.50*

| 37 | KNOBLAUCH | .25 | VC |
|---|---|---|---|
| 62 | I. RODRIGUEZ | .75 | VC |
| 87 | BAGWELL | .75 | VC |

**1991 FLEER ULTRA.** More plentiful than first thought, this set is almost always priced lower in the showcases than in the monthly guides. Some dealers bought in at $30 a box. Others have scooped up overstocks at $15. These are the guys you should be buying from.

*Warning:* Wax boxes are coming out of the woodwork, as this premium set has turned out to be anything but premium.

*Avoid:* The gold All-Star cards that were randomly inserted into packs. Buyer interest is pretty random.

*Tough Call:* Whether or not to hold off on this

set until it drops totally out of sight. If you buy now, you'll still be paying premium prices.

*Set: $24.00*
*Commons: $ .01*

| | | | |
|---|---|---|---|
| 1 | AVERY | .75 | VC |
| 7 | JUSTICE | 1.25 | VC |
| 16 | L. GOMEZ | .25 | VC |
| 24 | RIPKEN | .40 | BC |
| 31 | CLEMENS | .25 | BC |
| 38 | PLANTIER | 1.50 | VC |
| 66 | SANDBERG | .25 | BC |
| 85 | THOMAS | 4.00 | VC |
| 86 | VENTURA | .40 | VC |
| 106 | BAERGA | .30 | VC |
| 122 | FRYMAN | 2.00 | VC |
| 135 | CEDENO | .25 | VC |
| 152 | MCRAE | .25 | VC |
| 180 | SHEFFIELD | .50 | VC |
| 192 | P. MUNOZ | .65 | VC |
| 195 | PUCKETT | .25 | BC |
| 244 | CANSECO | .25 | OTF |
| 251 | MCGWIRE | .25 | OTF |
| 275 | BONDS | .25 | OTF |
| 290 | LANKFORD | .50 | VC |
| 323 | D. LEWIS | .25 | VC |
| 336 | GRIFFEY | 2.00 | VC |
| 355 | RYAN | .75 | BC |
| 358 | R. ALOMAR | .35 | VC |
| 380 | KARROS | 2.00 | VC |
| 382 | KNOBLAUCH | 1.00 | VC |
| 383 | NEAGLE | .25 | VC |

## 1991 FLEER ULTRA UPDATE

*Set: $23.00*

| | | | |
|---|---|---|---|
| 4 | MUSSINA | 5.75 | VC |
| 13 | W. ALVAREZ | .25 | VC |
| 14 | A. FERNANDEZ | .25 | VC |
| 20 | NAGY | .75 | VC |
| 36 | ERICKSON | .75 | VC |
| 37 | KNOBLAUCH | 2.00 | VC |
| 55 | JU. GONZALES | 5.00 | VC |
| 56 | PALMER | 2.00 | VC |
| 58 | I. RODRIGUEZ | 3.00 | VC |
| 60 | GUZMAN | 7.50 | VC |
| 67 | HUNTER | .50 | VC |
| 79 | BAGWELL | 3.50 | VC |
| 82 | L. GONZALES | .35 | VC |
| 93 | WALKER | .40 | VC |
| 103 | TOMLIN | .75 | VC |

**1991 SCORE.** An immense set. Also the first with which it *definitely* doesn't pay to make up a set. The payoff for the three or so hours it takes to put all 893 cards in order is less than $13.00. In case your math's no good, that comes out to minimum wage. Not to mention a $25 investment in wax packs!

*Warning:* The sexy Dream Team subset, which debuted here, caused a ripple throughout the industry. For about seven seconds. Exactly who was Score trying to entice into card collecting?

*Avoid:* This set. Like the plague. You'd flip if you knew just how many wax boxes are still lying around. If you must buy, go for the factory set. It has seven Cooperstown cards to ease the pain.

*Tough Call:* The Franchise subset. You can't quibble with the players Score chose, and the black-and-white cards aren't bad looking. But just to be on the safe side, give them a pass.

*Set: $13.50*
*Factory Set: $18.00*
*Commons: $ .005*

| | | | |
|---|---|---|---|
| 2 | GRIFFEY | .35 | VC |
| 4 | RYAN | .25 | BC |
| 348 | PLANTIER | .35 | VC |
| 380 | BURNITZ | .25 | VC |
| 383 | MUSSINA | .75 | VC |
| 389 | VAN POPPEL | .40 | VC |
| 391 | NEWFIELD | .35 | VC |
| 570 | FRYMAN | .30 | VC |
| 677 | OSBORNE | .30 | VC |
| 731 | LANKFORD | .25 | VC |
| 805 | GONZALES | .25 | VC |
| 840 | THOMAS | 1.00 | VC |
| 874 | THOMAS | .40 | VC |
| 892 | GRIFFEY | .50 | VC |

| | | | |
|---|---|---|---|
| C-1 | BOGGS | .50 | VC |
| C-2 | LARKIN | .50 | VC |
| C-3 | GRIFFEY | 2.50 | VC |
| C-4 | HENDERSON | .75 | VC |
| C-5 | BRETT | .75 | VC |
| C-6 | CLARK | 1.00 | VC |
| C-7 | RYAN | 2.50 | VC |

## 1991 SCORE TRADED

*Set: $4.50*

| | | | |
|---|---|---|---|
| 82 | I. RODRIGUEZ | .75 | VC |
| 93 | KNOBLAUCH | .25 | VC |
| 96 | BAGWELL | .75 | VC |

**1991 UPPER DECK.** Very similar to the 1990 design, but a bit more plentiful. Take note of the fact that a lot of the cards that sell for between 5 and 20 cents in other sets have established prices in this one.

*Warning:* No one's really sure what the short-printed Michael Jordan card is worth, so watch it very carefully. Also, the high-number packs included a short-printed card featuring Ryan and Henderson, as well as a Hank Aaron hologram. They sell for $4.50 and $2.50 respectively and are not included in the boxed extended series.

*Avoid:* Mike Gardiner, Henry Rodriguez, and Jeff Conine.

*Tough Call:* The Hall of Fame cards (Killebrew, Perry, and Jenkins) that were randomly inserted into packs. They started off big last year, then dropped like rocks. Oddly enough, the cheap one—the header card—may turn out to be the most valuable. Each sells for anywhere between $7.50 and $12.50. Stay tuned.

*Set: $27.00*
*Factory Set (includes extended series): $32.00*
*Commons: $ .01*

| | | | |
|---|---|---|---|
| 2 | PLANTIER | 1.25 | VC |
| 6 | L. GOMEZ | .25 | VC |
| 17 | M. LEWIS | .25 | VC |
| 19 | NAGY | .60 | VC |

| | | | |
|---|---|---|---|
| 23 | CEDENO | .25 | VC |
| 24 | KARROS | 2.00 | VC |
| 40 | KNOBLAUCH | 1.00 | VC |
| 53 | VAN POPPEL | 1.00 | VC |
| 60 | CORDERO | .35 | VC |
| 61 | CLAYTON | .65 | VC |
| 63 | SALKELD | .50 | VC |
| 65 | MUSSINA | 2.25 | VC |
| 71 | R. SANDERS | 1.75 | VC |
| 225 | FRYMAN | 1.75 | VC |
| 246 | THOMAS | 3.50 | VC |
| 263 | VENTURA | .25 | VC |
| 266 | SHEFFIELD | .25 | VC |
| 345 | RYAN | .50 | BC |
| 346 | LANKFORD | .30 | VC |
| 347 | RIPKEN | .35 | BC |
| 363 | JUSTICE | .30 | VC |
| 365 | AVERY | .25 | VC |
| 432 | MUNOZ | .45 | VC |
| 522 | ERICKSON | .60 | VC |
| 543 | MCRAE | .25 | VC |
| 555 | GRIFFEY | .75 | VC |
| 564 | D. LEWIS | .25 | VC |
| 567 | L. GONZALES | .25 | VC |
| 646 | JU. GONZALES | .60 | VC |
| 655 | CLEMENS | .25 | BC |
| SP2 | JORDAN | 6.00 | VC |

## 1991 UPPER DECK EXTENDED

*Set: $6.50*

| | | | |
|---|---|---|---|
| 755 | BAGWELL | 1.50 | VC |
| 763 | R. ALOMAR | .25 | VC |

**1992 TOPPS.** No more bubble gum stains! Topps finally bowed to pressure from older card buyers and removed the pink stuff from packs for good. At the same time, the company improved the backs of its cards. Yet another Draft Pick subset was issued, and Topps returned to its multiplayer rookie-card format. But the real news was the gold card frenzy. The company inserted one gold card in each wax box, as well as selling entire sets of gold cards. This was a good move—it generated a renewed interest in the product and added a little drama to the drudgery of opening packs. The bad move was to insert into each pack a game card with which buyers could win gold cards. The game cards were designed so that a buyer had to scratch off three matching statistics at random. Unfortunately, there was nothing random about the game cards in the first shipment—you could see right through the little gray circles that covered the correct answers and win every time! Rather than refusing to honor the avalanche of winning game cards, Topps stamped "Winner" on the gold cards it sent back, decreasing their value in relation to the gold cards that were pulled out of packs.

*Warning:* The prices for gold cards are still fluctuating wildly as more and more continue to surface. Generally, they are valued at twenty times the selling price of regular cards, with some—like Ryan, Ripken, Griffey, Clemens, Puckett, and Thomas—selling for fifty- to seventy-five times the price of regular cards. Until the gold dust settles, consider all of these cards highly Volatile and watch the market carefully.

*Avoid:* Gold cards stamped "Winner." Since Topps bypassed dealers on these cards, no one except Topps knows how many are really out there. And Topps ain't talking.

*Tough Call:* Too soon to tell on any of the young players.

*Set: $12.50*
*Factory Set: $22.50*
*Commons: $ .005*

| | | | |
|---|---|---|---|
| 1 | RYAN | .25 | BC |
| 6 | TAYLOR | 2.00 | VC |
| 50 | GRIFFEY | .30 | OTF |
| 78 | RODRIGUEZ | .35 | VC |
| 126 | ROOKIES | .40 | VC |
| 156 | RAMIREZ | .25 | VC |
| 192 | FLEMING | .50 | VC |
| 194 | KARROS | .25 | VC |
| 242 | MUSSINA | .35 | VC |
| 520 | BAGWELL | .25 | VC |
| 555 | THOMAS | .50 | VC |

| | | | |
|---|---|---|---|
| 662 | GUZMAN | .50 | VC |
| 676 | ROOKIES | .40 | VC |

## 1992 TOPPS TRADED

*Set: $9.50*

| | | |
|---|---|---|
| 45 | HAMMONDS | .40 |
| 56 | JOHNSON | .35 |
| 65 | LISTACH | 1.00 |
| 78 | MURRAY | .30 |
| 82 | NEVIN | .60 |
| 119 | TUCKER | .35 |
| 126 | WALLACE | .50 |

## 1992 TOPPS STADIUM CLUB.

Topps seems to have printed around two to three times as many of these super-premium cards as it did the year before. This time, however, the company got a serious run for its money from Fleer and Score.

*Warning:* Some snafus in the packing process caused the middle cards in many packs to become seriously damaged. If you get a box like this, bring it back to your dealer. Also, you can see through the wrappers, so avoid buying these from other buyers or from dealers whom you don't know or don't entirely trust.

*Avoid:* Paying big premiums for untried rookies.

*Tough Call:* Too early to tell which super-premium card will end up as the 1992 winner.

*Set: $95.00*
*Commons: $ .04*

| | | | |
|---|---|---|---|
| 1 | RIPKEN | 3.00 | VC |
| 8 | LANKFORD | .50 | VC |
| 15 | D. SANDERS | .35 | VC |
| 50 | SANDBERG | 1.00 | VC |
| 59 | FRYMAN | 1.50 | VC |
| 60 | AVERY | .75 | OTF |
| 70 | VENTURA | .75 | OTF |
| 80 | CLEMENS | 1.00 | VC |
| 110 | ERICKSON | .25 | VC |
| 120 | GRISSOM | .25 | VC |
| 129 | VAN POPPEL | 1.00 | VC |
| 143 | BAERGA | .30 | VC |

| | | | | | | | | |
|---|---|---|---|---|---|---|---|---|
| 150 | BRETT | .40 | VC | | 599 | FIELDER | .30 | OTF |
| 159 | ALOMAR | .75 | OTF | | 600 | SANDBERG | 1.00 | BC |
| 182 | JUSTICE | 1.25 | VC | | 601 | KNOBLAUCH | .75 | VC |
| 211 | PALMER | 1.00 | VC | | 603 | GRIFFEY | 3.00 | VC |
| 220 | BELLE | .50 | VC | | 604 | BONDS | .75 | OTF |
| 225 | MUSSINA | 3.25 | VC | | 605 | RYAN | 2.25 | BC |
| 236 | KARROS | 2.25 | VC | | 606 | BAGWELL | 1.25 | VC |
| 240 | J. GONZALES | 2.25 | VC | | 607 | YOUNT | .40 | BC |
| 250 | FIELDER | .50 | OTF | | 608 | BONILLA | .25 | OTF |
| 256 | WALKER | .25 | VC | | 609 | BRETT | .40 | BC |
| 301 | THOMAS | 5.00 | VC | | 620 | BONDS | .75 | OTF |
| 309 | SHEFFIELD | 1.00 | VC | | 630 | CLAYTON | .60 | VC |
| 327 | ELDRED | .30 | VC | | 641 | RHODES | .45 | VC |
| 330 | BAGWELL | 1.50 | VC | | 695 | LOFTON | 1.00 | VC |
| 360 | THOME | .40 | VC | | 730 | GANT | .25 | OTF |
| 370 | CANSECO | 1.00 | OTF | | 750 | HENDERSON | .60 | BC |
| 387 | SIERRA | .65 | OTF | | 757 | LISTACH | 1.50 | VC |
| 389 | NAGY | .25 | VC | | 760 | PLANTIER | .75 | VC |
| 395 | GLAVINE | .40 | OTF | | 766 | SHEFFIELD | 1.00 | VC |
| 400 | GRIFFEY | 3.00 | OTF | | 770 | RYAN | 2.25 | BC |
| 402 | GUZMAN | 3.75 | VC | | 802 | CIANFRACCO | .25 | VC |
| 415 | RODRIGUEZ | 1.75 | VC | | 825 | GWYNN | .60 | BC |
| 420 | MATTINGLY | .40 | OTF | | 630 | KNOBLAUCH | .75 | VC |
| 432 | HUNTER | .25 | VC | | 865 | SANDERS | 1.75 | VC |
| 450 | YOUNT | .40 | BC | | 878 | HANSEN | .25 | VC |
| 460 | CLARK | 1.00 | OTF | | D-1 | JONES | 5.00 | VC |
| 475 | MCGWIRE | .75 | OTF | | D-2 | TAYLOR | 12.50 | VC |
| 480 | FISK | .25 | BC | | D-3 | NEVIN | 8.00 | VC |
| 490 | MCDONALD | .25 | VC | | | | | |
| 500 | PUCKETT | .75 | BC | | | | | |
| 505 | DESHIELDS | .25 | VC | | | | | |
| 520 | BOGGS | .50 | BC | | | | | |
| 541 | MUNOZ | .30 | VC | | | | | |
| 555 | D. BELL | .30 | VC | | | | | |
| 560 | STRAWBERRY | .25 | OTF | | | | | |
| 577 | MCNEELY | .35 | VC | | | | | |
| 580 | MCGRIFF | .25 | OTF | | | | | |
| 591 | THOMAS | 5.00 | VC | | | | | |
| 592 | JUSTICE | 1.25 | VC | | | | | |
| 593 | CLEMENS | 1.00 | BC | | | | | |
| 594 | AVERY | .75 | OTF | | | | | |
| 595 | RIPKEN | 1.25 | BC | | | | | |
| 597 | CANSECO | 1.00 | OTF | | | | | |
| 598 | CLARK | .75 | OTF | | | | | |

**1992 DONRUSS.** A nice effort, but unfortunately this set was overshadowed by its own limited series of Diamond Kings.

*Warning:* If it's true that you can't teach an old dog new tricks, then there may be a lot of these cards lying around a warehouse somewhere. Also, the factory set does *not* include the Diamond Kings.

*Avoid:* The Diamond Kings that are not listed below.

*Tough Call:* You may not want to stop buying the Diamond Kings, but at the very least consider them extremely Volatile. The first series, which contains all the good ones, seems to have been largely absorbed by buyers, whereas the second series was still kicking around last winter.

*Set: $14.50*
*Factory Set: $29.00*
*Commons: $ .005*

| 13 | KLESKO | .35 | VC |
|----|--------|-----|-----|
| 16 | KARROS | .25 | VC |
| 165 | GRIFFEY | .35 | OTF |
| 289 | RODRIGUEZ | .35 | VC |
| 358 | BAGWELL | .30 | VC |
| 393 | GONZALES | .25 | VC |
| 403 | MAHOMES | .25 | VC |
| 404 | FLEMING | .60 | VC |
| 415 | R. SANDERS | .25 | VC |
| 534 | GUZMAN | .60 | VC |
| 592 | THOMAS | .60 | VC |
| 632 | MUSSINA | .35 | VC |
| 707 | RYAN | .25 | BC |

## 1992 DONRUSS DIAMOND KINGS

*Set: $50.00*

| 2 | CLARK | 3.50 | OTF |
|----|-------|------|-----|
| 3 | J. CARTER | 1.50 | OTF |
| 4 | JU. FRANCO | 1.00 | OTF |
| 5 | RIPKEN | 6.00 | BC |
| 6 | JUSTICE | 3.75 | VC |
| 8 | THOMAS | 11.50 | VC |
| 9 | BOGGS | 1.75 | BC |
| 11 | BAGWELL | 4.00 | VC |
| 13 | JOSE | 1.00 | OTF |
| 15 | GOODEN | 1.00 | OTF |
| 16 | MCRAE | 1.00 | VC |
| 21 | ERICKSON | 1.00 | VC |
| 26 | MCGRIFF | 2.00 | OTF |

## 1992 DONRUSS ROOKIES

*Set: $7.50*

| 5 | ASHLEY | .25 |
|----|--------|-----|
| 6 | ASTACIO | .30 |
| 86 | NIED | 1.00 |
| 98 | RAMIREZ | .30 |
| 121 | WAKEFIELD | 1.50 |

**1992 LEAF.** Spotty photography and overproduction make this set a major yawn, so don't be surprised if singles from this set are still hanging around at bargain prices come the year 2000.

*Warning:* The *Black Gold* cards, which came one to a pack, sell for about three times the price of regular cards. This might actually be a set worth completing . . . just wait until later this year, when dealers start dumping them on the market.

*Avoid:* Paying more than $1.25 a pack.

*Tough Call:* Whether or not these are worth the time and trouble.

*Set: $37.50*
*Commons: .01*

| 13 | MUSSINA | 1.75 | VC |
|----|---------|------|-----|
| 16 | MCGWIRE | .25 | OTF |
| 17 | VENTURA | .25 | OTF |
| 19 | CLEMENS | .40 | BC |
| 28 | BAGWELL | .60 | VC |
| 35 | GUZMAN | 1.50 | VC |
| 41 | RYAN | 1.00 | BC |
| 50 | PLANTIER | .35 | VC |
| 52 | RIPKEN | .60 | BC |
| 59 | AVERY | .35 | VC |
| 62 | GONZALES | 1.00 | VC |
| 98 | PUCKETT | .35 | BC |
| 116 | HENDERSON | .25 | BC |
| 153 | FIELDER | .25 | OTF |
| 194 | RODRIGUEZ | .75 | VC |
| 206 | GWYNN | .25 | BC |
| 225 | PALMER | .35 | VC |
| 230 | KNOBLAUCH | .30 | VC |
| 233 | ALOMAR | .35 | OTF |
| 241 | CLARK | .35 | OTF |
| 248 | VAN POPPEL | .40 | VC |
| 267 | CANSECO | .35 | OTF |
| 272 | CLAYTON | .25 | VC |
| 275 | BONDS | .35 | OTF |
| 293 | KARROS | 1.00 | VC |
| 304 | FRYMAN | .75 | VC |
| 317 | SANDBERG | .35 | BC |
| 337 | JORDAN | .40 | VC |
| 349 | THOMAS | 2.50 | VC |

| 360 | SANDERS | .75 | VC |
| 370 | LISTACH | .75 | VC |
| 383 | SIERRA | .25 | OTF |
| 392 | GRIFFEY | 1.50 | OTF |
| 404 | JUSTICE | .30 | OTF |
| 446 | SHEFFIELD | .40 | VC |
| 493 | CIANFRACCO | .25 | VC |
| 494 | FLEMING | 1.50 | VC |

## 1992 GOLD LEAF ROOKIES

*Set: $50.00*

| 1 | CURTIS | 3.00 | VC |
| 2 | GATES | 2.00 | VC |
| 3 | MARTINEZ | 4.75 | VC |
| 4 | LOFTON | 4.00 | VC |
| 5 | WENDELL | 1.25 | VC |
| 6 | HUTTON | 2.25 | VC |
| 8 | STAIRS | 2.25 | VC |
| 9 | TAUBENSEE | 1.25 | VC |
| 10 | NIED | 3.00 | VC |
| 11 | TORRES | 3.00 | VC |
| 12 | BOONE | 3.00 | VC |
| 13 | RUFFIN | 1.50 | VC |
| 14 | MARTEL | 1.50 | VC |
| 15 | TRLICEK | 1.50 | VC |
| 16 | MONDESI | 2.50 | VC |
| 17 | MAHOMES | 3.25 | VC |
| 18 | WILSON | 2.25 | VC |
| 19 | OSBORNE | 3.25 | VC |
| 22 | NEAGLE | 1.00 | VC |
| 23 | HOSEY | 2.25 | VC |
| 24 | DOHERTY | 1.50 | VC |

**1992 FLEER.** Fleer also upped the quality of its cards in 1992 and included two special, limited-run glossy subsets. The first is of Roger Clemens's career, and the second depicts All-Stars. The Donruss Diamond Kings stole the initial thunder from these two series, and just when buyers were starting to take notice, the super-premium sets arrived.

*Warning:* The factory set does *not* include these subsets. It does, however, come with a special subset of Lumber Company cards, which may experience some movement down the road. Also, an error was made on the Rob Maurer card, which sells for about 50 cents.

*Avoid:* The Pro-Vision cards. They're interesting, but a waste of money in the long run.

*Tough Call:* How many Fleer cards are out there. There are, however, a lot more than people originally thought.

*Set: $25.00*
*Factory Set: $30.00*
*Commons: $ .005*

| 20 | MUSSINA | .35 | VC |
| 100 | THOMAS | .60 | VC |
| 279 | GRIFFEY | .35 | OTF |
| 316 | RODRIGUEZ | .35 | VC |
| 320 | RYAN | .25 | BC |
| 330 | GUZMAN | .60 | VC |
| 421 | R. SANDERS | .25 | VC |
| 425 | BAGWELL | .30 | VC |

## FLEER ALL STARS

*Set: $30.00*

| 1 | JOSE | .75 | VC |
| 2 | GWYNN | 1.25 | VC |
| 3 | BONDS | 1.75 | VC |
| 4 | BONILLA | .75 | VC |
| 6 | GLAVINE | 1.75 | VC |
| 10 | ERICKSON | .60 | VC |
| 11 | THOMAS | 9.50 | VC |
| 13 | CLARK | 2.25 | VC |
| 14 | SANDBERG | 2.25 | VC |
| 15 | PENDELTON | .75 | VC |
| 16 | LARKIN | .75 | VC |
| 19 | VENTURA | 1.75 | VC |
| 20 | RIPKEN | 4.00 | VC |
| 21 | CARTER | .75 | VC |
| 22 | PUCKETT | 1.75 | VC |
| 23 | GRIFFEY | 5.00 | VC |
| 24 | CANSECO | 1.75 | VC |

## ROOKIE SENSATIONS

*Set: $125.00*

| 1 | THOMAS | 37.50 | VC |
|---|---|---|---|
| 2 | VAN POPPEL | 7.50 | VC |
| 4 | BAGWELL | 15.00 | VC |
| 6 | LEWIS | 3.50 | VC |
| 7 | CUYLER | 3.50 | VC |
| 9 | MCRAE | 3.50 | VC |
| 10 | KNOBLAUCH | 10.00 | VC |
| 12 | RODRIGUEZ | 15.00 | VC |
| 13 | GUZMAN | 15.00 | VC |
| 15 | WOHLERS | 3.50 | VC |
| 17 | LANKFORD | 8.50 | VC |
| 19 | PLANTIER | 12.50 | VC |

## TEAM LEADERS

*Set: $20.00*

| 1 | MATTINGLY | 1.25 | VC |
|---|---|---|---|
| 4 | FISK | .75 | VC |
| 5 | PUCKETT | 2.00 | VC |
| 6 | FIELDER | 1.25 | VC |
| 7 | GWYNN | 1.50 | VC |
| 8 | CLARK | 2.00 | VC |
| 9 | BONILLA | .75 | VC |
| 11 | GLAVINE | 1.50 | VC |
| 13 | BOGGS | 1.25 | VC |
| 15 | GRIFFEY | 5.00 | VC |
| 16 | STRAWBERRY | 1.00 | VC |
| 17 | RIPKEN | 4.00 | VC |
| 19 | CANSECO | 2.00 | VC |
| 20 | DAWSON | 1.00 | VC |

## 1992 FLEER UPDATE

*Set: $50.00 (including Headliners)*

| 10 | SALMON | 1.25 |
|---|---|---|
| 36 | LISTACH | 2.25 |
| 55 | FLEMING | .75 |
| 68 | NIED | 4.50 |
| 117 | WAKEFIELD | 5.00 |
| HEADLINER: | GRIFFEY | 10.00 |
| HEADLINER: | YOUNT | 3.00 |
| HEADLINER: | FIELDER | 2.00 |

## 1992 FLEER ULTRA.

A big television ad campaign helped move these cards as soon as they hit the shelves, so it's not entirely clear whether they were produced in greater quantity than the Stadium Clubs. They differ from the Stadiums in that they rely almost entirely on action shots. A Tony Gwynn subset was issued, as were subsets of Award Winners, Rookies, and All-Stars. The Gwynn set sells for around $30.

*Warning:* There were some problems getting the diagonal gold lines at the bottom of the cards to hit the mark every time. Does this make them out of register? Who knows? Play it safe, and only buy cards that have well-struck diagonal gold lines.

*Avoid:* Subset singles that are not listed below.

*Tough Call:* How many second-series cards were issued in relation to the fast-moving first series.

*Set: $62.50*
*Commons: $ .03*

| 9 | MUSSINA | 3.25 | VC |
|---|---|---|---|
| 11 | RIPKEN | 1.75 | BC |
| 15 | CLEMENS | 1.00 | BC |
| 33 | FISK | .25 | BC |
| 44 | THOMAS | 5.00 | VC |
| 46 | BAERGA | .30 | VC |
| 47 | BELLE | .50 | VC |
| 54 | THOME | .40 | VC |
| 59 | FIELDER | .50 | OTF |
| 60 | FRYMAN | 1.50 | VC |
| 68 | BRETT | .40 | BC |
| 83 | SHEFFIELD | 1.00 | VC |
| 87 | YOUNT | .40 | BC |
| 90 | ERICKSON | .25 | VC |
| 97 | PUCKETT | .75 | BC |
| 105 | MATTINGLY | .40 | OTF |
| 110 | CANSECO | 1.00 | OTF |
| 114 | HENDERSON | .60 | BC |
| 115 | MCGWIRE | .75 | OTF |
| 118 | VAN POPPEL | 1.00 | VC |
| 123 | GRIFFEY | 3.00 | OTF |
| 132 | J. GONZALES | 2.25 | VC |
| 137 | PALMER | 1.00 | VC |
| 139 | RODRIGUEZ | 1.75 | VC |

| | | | |
|---|---|---|---|
| 141 | RYAN | 2.25 | BC |
| 142 | SIERRA | .65 | OTF |
| 143 | ALOMAR | .75 | OTF |
| 157 | AVERY | .75 | OTF |
| 161 | GANT | .25 | OTF |
| 162 | GLAVINE | .40 | OTF |
| 163 | HUNTER | .25 | VC |
| 164 | JUSTICE | 1.25 | VC |
| 181 | SANDBERG | 1.00 | BC |
| 198 | BAGWELL | 1.50 | VC |
| 219 | STRAWBERRY | .25 | OTF |
| 220 | DESHIELDS | .25 | VC |
| 251 | BONDS | .75 | OTF |
| 265 | LANKFORD | .50 | VC |
| 277 | GWYNN | .60 | BC |
| 282 | MCGRIFF | .25 | OTF |
| 303 | MCDONALD | .25 | OTF |
| 311 | BOGGS | .50 | BC |
| 318 | PLANTIER | .75 | VC |
| 323 | CURTIS | .65 | VC |
| 343 | VENTURA | .75 | OTF |
| 350 | LOFTON | 1.00 | VC |
| 351 | NAGY | .25 | VC |
| 385 | LISTACH | 1.50 | VC |
| 398 | MAHOMES | .40 | VC |
| 399 | MUNOZ | .30 | VC |
| 448 | BELL | .30 | VC |
| 449 | GUZMAN | 3.75 | VC |
| 464 | D. SANDERS | .35 | OTF |
| 486 | R. SANDERS | 1.75 | VC |
| 498 | WILLIAMS | .60 | VC |
| 508 | KARROS | 2.25 | VC |
| 515 | CIANFRACCO | .25 | VC |
| 518 | GRISSOM | .25 | OTF |
| 525 | WALKER | .25 | OTF |
| 570 | OSBORNE | .50 | VC |
| 582 | SHEFFIELD | 1.00 | VC |

## ULTRA AWARD WINNERS

*Set: $125.00*

| | | | |
|---|---|---|---|
| 2 | KNOBLAUCH | 5.50 | VC |
| 3 | BASWELL | 7.00 | VC |
| 4 | PENDELTON | 3.75 | VC |

| | | | |
|---|---|---|---|
| 5 | RIPKEN | 9.50 | VC |
| 6 | CLEMENS | 8.00 | VC |
| 7 | GLAVINE | 7.00 | VC |
| 9 | SMITH | 3.75 | VC |
| 11 | BONDS | 6.75 | VC |
| 12 | GWYNN | 5.50 | VC |
| 14 | CLARK | 7.50 | VC |
| 15 | VENTURA | 7.50 | VC |
| 19 | MATTINGLY | 5.50 | VC |
| 20 | ALOMAR | 8.50 | VC |
| 21 | RIPKEN | 11.00 | VC |
| 22 | GRIFFEY | 12.00 | VC |
| 23 | PUCKETT | 7.00 | VC |
| 25 | SANDBERG | 7.50 | VC |

## ULTRA ALL-ROOKIE TEAM

*Set: $37.50*

| | | | |
|---|---|---|---|
| 1 | KARROS | 8.75 | VC |
| 4 | CIANFRACCO | 3.00 | VC |
| 6 | CURTIS | 4.75 | VC |
| 7 | LOFTON | 6.00 | VC |
| 8 | SANDERS | 7.00 | VC |
| 9 | MAHOMES | 5.50 | VC |
| 10 | OSBORNE | 5.50 | VC |

## ULTRA ALL STARS

*Set: $100.00*

| | | | |
|---|---|---|---|
| 1 | MCGWIRE | 7.00 | VC |
| 2 | ALOMAR | 8.50 | VC |
| 3 | RIPKEN | 9.50 | VC |
| 4 | BOGGS | 5.00 | VC |
| 6 | GRIFFEY | 12.00 | VC |
| 7 | KELLY | 3.25 | VC |
| 8 | PUCKETT | 7.00 | VC |
| 9 | THOMAS | 16.00 | VC |
| 10 | MCDOWELL | 4.50 | VC |
| 11 | CLARK | 7.50 | VC |
| 12 | SANDBERG | 7.50 | VC |
| 13 | LARKIN | 3.50 | VC |
| 14 | SHEFFIELD | 7.50 | VC |
| 16 | BONDS | 6.75 | VC |
| 17 | SANDERS | 5.50 | VC |

| 18 | STRAWBERRY | 5.00 | VC |
| 19 | CONE | 3.25 | VC |
| 20 | GLAVINE | 7.00 | VC |

**1992 SCORE.** Because Score was the only company that did not upgrade the quality of its cards in 1992, this set looks like the year's big loser. Limited-run inserts of Musial, Mantle, Yastrzemski, and DiMaggio were issued with this set.

*Warning:* Rumor has it that there were more of these inserts sent to the East Coast than the West Coast. The Mantle sells for about $30, the DiMaggio for about $70, and the other two cards go for $15 or $20 apiece. A card depicting Mantle, Musial, and Yaz sells for around $20, too.

*Avoid:* The insert cards. There are literally thousands of unopened Score cases lying around, so it's possible that these cards will be coming out of the woodwork for the next few years. Also, skip the Dream Team cards, except for Thomas. They're interesting, but not *that* interesting.

*Tough Call:* Whether all the cards in this set will *ever* be absorbed into the market.

Set: $13.00
Factory Set: $20.00
Commons: $ .005

| 1 | GRIFFEY | .25 | OTF |
| 424 | GUZMAN | .60 | VC |
| 505 | THOMAS | .50 | VC |
| 576 | BAGWELL | .25 | VC |
| 700 | RODRIGUEZ | .25 | VC |
| 755 | MUSSINA | .25 | VC |
| 800 | RAMIREZ | .40 | VC |
| 827 | KARROS | .25 | VC |
| 893 | DREAM TEAM: THOMAS | .60 | VC |

**1992 SCORE PINNACLE.** Buyers are pretty well divided on this issue. Those who jumped on Pinnacle football jumped on these cards as well, although the football design was clearly superior. Others, distrustful of Score's distribution history

have shied away. There's clearly room in the business for more than one super premium set, but is there room for three? If there isn't, Pinnacle's a good bet to be the odd one out. As for random inserts, this set offers *Team Pinnacle* and *Rookie Idols* cards in the regular packs and *Team 2000* cards in the surprisingly plentiful jumbo packs.

*Warning:* Black borders! What a great idea!

*Tough Call:* How many are really out there. At the end of the season, packs were showing up on urban newsstands and in other conspicuously *non-premium* outlets.

Set: $50.00
Commons: .02

| 1 | THOMAS | 2.25 | VC |
| 10 | SANDBERG | .40 | BC |
| 14 | SIERRA | .25 | OTF |
| 20 | PUCKETT | .30 | BC |
| 45 | ALOMAR | .40 | OTF |
| 50 | RYAN | 1.00 | BC |
| 51 | PLANTIER | .35 | VC |
| 70 | BAGWELL | .50 | VC |
| 75 | GLAVINE | .25 | OTF |
| 95 | CLEMENS | .45 | BC |
| 100 | JUSTICE | .50 | OTF |
| 110 | FRYMAN | .50 | OTF |
| 119 | KNOBLAUCH | .25 | VC |
| 121 | VENTURA | .30 | OTF |
| 122 | CLARK | .40 | OTF |
| 127 | GONZALEZ | 1.00 | VC |
| 130 | CANSECO | .45 | OTF |
| 156 | RODRIGUEZ | .75 | VC |
| 183 | GUZMAN | 1.75 | VC |
| 200 | RIPKEN | .75 | BC |
| 204 | MUSSINA | 1.75 | VC |
| 217 | MCGWIRE | .30 | OTF |
| 231 | AVERY | .30 | VC |
| 235 | SHEFFIELD | .40 | VC |
| 251 | RHODES | .25 | VC |
| 256 | KARROS | 1.00 | VC |
| 268 | CLAYTON | .30 | VC |
| 275 | FLEMING | 1.50 | VC |
| 295 | RAMIREZ | .75 | VC |

| 296 | FLOYD | .40 | VC |
|-----|-------|-----|-----|
| 297 | SHIRLEY | .40 | VC |
| 301 | HILL | .40 | VC |
| 302 | GIL | .25 | VC |
| 303 | GREEN | .65 | VC |
| 401 | HENDERSON | .30 | VC |
| 440 | SANDERS | 1.00 | VC |
| 472 | MAHOMES | .30 | VC |
| 500 | BONDS | .35 | OTF |
| 510 | CIANFROCCO | .25 | VC |
| 523 | CURTIS | .30 | VC |
| 540 | WILLIAMS | .35 | VC |
| 541 | OSBORNE | .35 | VC |
| 548 | JONES | .30 | VC |
| 549 | GRIFFEY | 1.50 | OTF |
| 555 | JORDAN | .35 | VC |
| 562 | LISTACH | .75 | VC |
| 574 | VAN POPPEL | .45 | VC |
| 582 | LOFTON | .45 | VC |
| 583 | STAIRS | .25 | VC |
| 618 | RYAN | .30 | BC |

## TEAM PINNACLE

*Set: $320.00*

| 1 | CLEMENS/ MARTINEZ | 30.00 | VC |
|-----|-------|-----|-----|
| 2 | ABBOTT/AVERY | 25.00 | VC |
| 3 | RODRIGUEZ/ SANTIAGO | 25.00 | VC |
| 4 | THOMAS/CLARK | 60.00 | VC |
| 5 | ALOMAR/ SANDBERG | 45.00 | VC |
| 6 | VENTURA/ WILLIAMS | 25.00 | VC |
| 7 | RIPKEN/LARKIN | 45.00 | VC |
| 8 | TARTABULL/BONDS | 32.50 | VC |
| 9 | GRIFFEY/BUTLER | 45.00 | VC |
| 10 | SIERRA/JUSTICE | 37.50 | VC |
| 11 | ECKERSLEY/ DIBBLE | 20.00 | VC |
| 12 | RADINSKY/ FRANCO | 10.00 | VC |

## ROOKIE IDOLS

*Set: $200.00*

| 1 | SANDERS | 17.50 | VC |
|-----|-------|-----|-----|
| 2 | FAJARDO | 10.00 | VC |
| 3 | COOPER | 10.00 | VC |
| 4 | WOHLERS | 20.00 | VC |
| 5 | MERCEDES | 10.00 | VC |
| 6 | BANKS | 10.00 | VC |
| 7 | LOFTON | 20.00 | VC |
| 8 | MITCHELL | 10.00 | VC |
| 9 | BAPTISTE | 10.00 | VC |
| 10 | HUNDLEY | 15.00 | VC |
| 11 | ZOSKY | 20.00 | VC |
| 12 | VAN POPPEL | 25.00 | VC |
| 13 | THOME | 20.00 | VC |
| 14 | FLEMING | 20.00 | VC |
| 15 | CLAYTON | 15.00 | VC |
| 16 | HARRIS | 15.00 | VC |
| 17 | CURTIS | 15.00 | VC |
| 18 | BELL | 15.00 | VC |

## 1992 SCORE PINNACLE ROOKIES

*Set: $10.00*

| 3 | LOFTON | 1.00 |
|-----|-------|-----|
| 5 | LISTACH | 2.25 |
| 11 | MAHOMES | .35 |
| 12 | VAN POPPEL | .35 |
| 13 | FLEMING | 1.00 |
| 20 | OSBORNE | .40 |
| 22 | SANDERS | .80 |
| 23 | WILLIAMS | .35 |
| 24 | KARROS | 1.75 |
| 26 | CLAYTON | .35 |
| 29 | CURTIS | .35 |

**1992 UPPER DECK.** Another nice set, but a big print run this time.

*Warning:* The Deion Sanders "football/baseball" card was short-printed but seems to be available in great quantity.

*Avoid:* The Bloodlines subset. It's fun to look at,

but just try selling these cards a few years from now.

*Tough Call:* The Ted Williams subset. There seem to be an awful lot of these cards in each box—including the header card. Why people are paying more for these cards than they are for cards from the 1991 Ryan subset is an utter mystery. The randomly inserted Williams hologram, however, looks like a keeper.

*Set: $30.00*
*Factory Set (includes extended series): $32.50*
*Commons: $ .005*

| | | | |
|---|---|---|---|
| 3 | JORDAN | .35 | VC |
| 4 | FLEMING | .75 | VC |
| 5 | THOME | .25 | VC |
| 18 | P. MARTINEZ | .35 | VC |
| 24 | KLESKO | .60 | VC |
| 27 | R. SANDERS | .30 | VC |
| 52 | PEREZ | .30 | VC |
| 55 | S. GREEN | .30 | VC |
| 58 | YOUNG | .30 | VC |
| 60 | MONDESI | .25 | VC |
| 63 | RAMIREZ | .60 | VC |
| 64 | NEWFIELD | .25 | VC |
| 65 | BURNITZ | .25 | VC |
| 66 | M. SMITH | .30 | VC |
| 67 | HAMILTON | .30 | VC |
| 68 | T. GREEN | .35 | VC |
| 73 | VITIELLO | .30 | VC |
| 75 | MCCARTY | 1.00 | VC |
| 85 | GRIFFEY | .30 | OTF |
| 166 | THOMAS | .75 | VC |
| 243 | GONZALES | .30 | VC |
| 245 | I. RODRIGUEZ | .50 | VC |
| 276 | BAGWELL | .40 | VC |
| 424 | GRIFFEY | .50 | OTF |
| 425 | PLANTIER | .25 | VC |
| 534 | KARROS | .35 | VC |
| 625 | GUZMAN | .75 | VC |
| 655 | RYAN | .35 | BC |
| 675 | MUSSINA | .40 | VC |
| 701 | NUNEZ | .30 | VC |
| 710 | TURNER | .35 | VC |
| 745 | SHEFFIELD | .25 | VC |
| 771 | BOONE | .40 | VC |
| 774 | CURTIS | .25 | VC |
| 775 | LISTACH | .60 | VC |
| 776 | MAHOMES | .25 | VC |
| 777 | OSBORNE | .25 | VC |
| 786 | STAIRS | .25 | VC |
| 794 | KELLY | .60 | VC |
| | MCCARTY HOLOGRAM | 1.00 | VC |
| | KELLY HOLOGRAM | 1.00 | VC |
| | MCDONALD HOLOGRAM | .60 | VC |
| H-6 | BROCK | 6.00 | VC |
| H-7 | FINGERS | 6.00 | VC |
| SP | SELLECK | 7.00 | VC |
| SP | D. SANDERS | 5.00 | VC |
| | WILLIAMS HOLOGRAM | 12.50 | BC |

# BUYING

Whatever buying strategy you embrace, in most cases you'll be executing that strategy with dealers. They are, for better or worse, your primary source for cards. Once you've accepted that, then you can use what you now know about them—who they are, how they approach the business, and the "inside" prices they use—to give yourself an important edge. All you need to remember is that buying from dealers requires three things: preparation, execution, and flexibility.

Sound simple? It is. But then how do you explain the fact that the average card buyer almost always screws up when he goes to a card shop or show? Why does he spend more money than he'd planned for cards he hadn't planned on buying in the first place? Because preparation, execution, and flexibility are intellectual skills that require a high degree of concentration, as well as a modicum of maturity. In short, the average card buyer in a typical buying situation is just too overwhelmed and excited to concentrate properly. And as for maturity, well, the average card buyer has a nasty tendency to revert back to his childhood the moment he comes face-to-face with a showcase full of cards. If these observations ring true in your case, take heart—you're definitely not alone. At one time or another, *everyone* has set out to buy a quality card for $30 only to return with three 1990 Donruss wax boxes or some other dreck! It happens, so just forget it. But before you do, think about why it happens and what you can do about it.

As stated, the genesis of buying mistakes is usually a slipup in preparation, execution, or flexibility. But there's a fourth element that comes into play—namely, the dealer. Just as you have your agenda, he has his. Obviously, he is in the business of selling cards; his job, as it were, is to make sure that you spend as much of your money with him as possible. But in his mind, there is a pecking order of cards he would like you to buy, and he will push his cards accordingly. Needless to say, the cards at the top of this pecking order are the ones he wants to get rid of: overproduced or overpriced cards, or cards that he hasn't been able to sell for one reason or the other. At the bottom are cards in high demand, or that have the greatest potential for increase in the near future. If he senses a chink in your armor—a hole in your agenda—you can bet he'll try, with varying degrees of subtlety, to make you purchase his least desirable cards.

Poor preparation is the major culprit in this scenario. If you go to a shop or show without a specific idea of what you want to buy, you are especially prone to suggestion. Admit it: you've gone to card shows with money in your pocket and no plan other than "to buy something." Did you ever come home with anything of substance? Probably not. You wouldn't go into a real estate deal just to buy a house, nor would you invest in stocks just to play the market—so why buy cards if you haven't got a plan? Preparation is, of course, a matter of doing your homework, but above all it is a complicated, four-step process of elimination:

1. Eliminate all of the cards you can't afford. If you have $200 to spend over the next couple of months, go through the price guide in Chapter 9 and simply eliminate all the cards listed at more than $200. (Obviously, if you have your eye on a card that's more expensive than that, you'll have to squirrel away that $200 until you have more).

2. Eliminate the cards you *don't* want—cards you feel are overpriced or that have little potential, or players you just don't like—so that a dealer doesn't manipulate you into buying them. This, by the way, is the step that most buyers ignore—and, not surprisingly, dealers count on it. If you go to a shop or show without having completely eliminated, say, the 1991 Fleer Set from your realm of possibilities, and a dealer offers it to you at a "bargain" price of $17.50, it's very likely that you'll come home with that set instead of the 1963 Billy Williams card you had planned on buying. Billy—and *you*, for that matter—will probably be long dead before that set ever pays off.

3. Of the cards that are left, make a detailed list of the ones you feel are worth buying immediately, eliminating those you feel won't be moving for a while. This list should have two sections. The first section should be a selection of players who you feel are "due"—either on the field or in the business itself. Next to each player, write down the years and sets in which his cards are available—not in chronological order, but from "best" to "worst." Finally, combining information from the price guide in this book with what

you can glean about demand from the monthly guides, come up with the price you'd be willing to pay for each card. (This price should be pretty close to what you believe the "inside" price to be, but if you're a real believer in a particular card, it's okay to pay a little more if you have to.) The second section should be developed much like the first, but this time start by selecting the *sets* you feel are "due." Then, pick out the players in those sets who fit into a category (Blue Chip, On the Fence, Volatile, etc.) that you find compelling. Next to those players, write down what you estimate the "inside" price to be.

4. Take a break—a day or more, if possible—and then come back to this "hit list" that you've created and see if it still makes sense. Do so with extreme prejudice, eliminating cards that don't seem to belong. Remember, any card that makes it past this point could end up in your collection, so be careful. Next, review the prices you've written net to the cards and see if there are any that rub you the wrong way. If a card seems too expensive to you, then eliminate it from the list. Don't attempt to rationalize buying it if your gut feeling is to give it a pass. At this point, approach the cards on your hit list from the other direction—do any stand out as real bargains? There should be a few. Go ahead and list these cards on a separate piece of paper—they are the ones for which the "execution" part of the buying process will be critical.

Armed with your A list (the bargain cards) and your B list (all the rest), you must determine as quickly as possible which dealers have what you want to buy. If you're buying at a show, it's a matter of walking the aisles. If you're buying at local shops, you'll have to visit them regularly. In either case, the actual buying process works the same.

Take particular note of the dealers who seem to have most or all of the cards you want, as it's easier to negotiate price on a large number of cards. By the way, don't worry about prices during this little scouting mission—dealers all pay roughly the same to purchase their cards, so you can't always tell from the marked prices which dealer will ultimately cut you the best deal.

While you make your initial run, be prepared to execute. If you see one of the cards on your A list and the price is right, don't hesitate—buy! That's what all the preparation was for! The mistake a lot of buyers make is to decide which cards they want to buy and go to shows or shops with the idea that they'll comparison-shop for the best price. They see a good price, walk away looking for a better one, and then when they return, the card has already been sold.

Once you've determined which dealers have the cards you want, it's time to start negotiating. Use what you know about dealers and inside pricing, and don't forget to review the dialogue back on pages 54–55. When you've got your price, execute.

The final thing a good buyer needs is flexibility. Don't haggle over the prices of individual cards— it's time-consuming for you and infuriating for a dealer. Instead, make offers on groups of cards. If you are negotiating the purchase of ten different cards and you know the total amount you want to pay, negotiate on that basis. If you and the dealer are close, but not in total agreement, try to determine which card (or cards) is (are) the sticking point. Come right out and tell him, "Look, I know what I want to pay, and I have an idea of what you have invested in these cards. I think my offer is fair, but obviously there's a card here that's holding up the deal. Which of these cards do you have the *least* room to work with? Maybe we can eliminate it and we'll both be happy." You'd be shocked at how effective this approach can be. Very often, a dealer has overpaid for a card and would rather wait until he gets full retail price.

When you're negotiating for newer, less expensive cards, flexibility comes into play in terms of the quantity you're willing to buy. If you want a card at 50 cents and a dealer won't budge from 75 cents, ask how many you'd have to buy to get the price down to your level. If that quantity is acceptable to you, then make the deal. Should a dealer not lower his price quite enough in this situation, take a look at some more expensive cards. If you can make up the difference with a good deal on a pricier card, you shouldn't care that the 50-cent cards actually cost you 65 cents.

Finally, you must be flexible enough to mix cards off your A list with cards off your B list. This is why thorough preparation is so important. If you allow a card you don't really want to make your B list—or worse, don't develop a B list at all—you'll end up paying for cards you *don't* want just in order to get the ones you *do.*

# CONCLUSION

What should you be looking for this season? Plenty. Keep your eyes on young players like Reggie Sanders, Eric Karros, Kenny Lofton, Dave Fleming, Travis Fryman, Juan Gonzales, Mike Mussina, Gary Sheffield, Cal Eldred, Arthur Rhodes, and Pat Listach. They all had breakthrough years in 1992, and all have the talent to remain stars for the next decade. If any should falter, watch for a sharp drop in prices and then go make your best deal—remember, each can afford an off-year or two.

As for up-and-coming youngsters like Pat Mahomes, Mel Nieves, Mike Kelley, Phil Nevin, Jeff Hammonds, Ryan Klesko, and Roger Salkeld, try not to pay top dollar for their cards if they get off to fast starts. If you haven't bought already, you might want to wait until the feeding frenzies subside.

There will, of course, be other flashy rookies this season, so be prepared to grab them if the price is right. Remember, you can save yourself a bundle if you stick to the buying guidelines in Chapter 8, "Picking a Winner".

Another trend to watch for is what happens to the super premium sets of 1991 and 1992 when the 1993 super premium sets are released. Demand for the older sets could drop like a rock, so don't get stuck holding the bag.

Finally, don't forget to use this book as your primary buying tool. That means getting involved—updating prices and moving players from category to category. It also means reading this book from cover to cover. If you don't understand something, read it again until you do. Hey, you already paid for it . . . why not get your money's worth?

*Houghton Mifflin*

# Mathematics

# Teacher Resource Book

- **Teaching Tools**
- **Family Letters**
- **Fast Facts Practice**
- **Just the Facts Worksheets**
  Includes Answer Key and
  Awards Certificates

**3**

## HOUGHTON MIFFLIN

BOSTON • MORRIS PLAINS, NJ

California • Colorado • Georgia • Illinois • New Jersey • Texas

# Contents

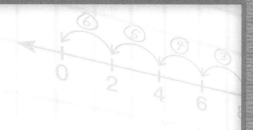

# Teaching
# Tools

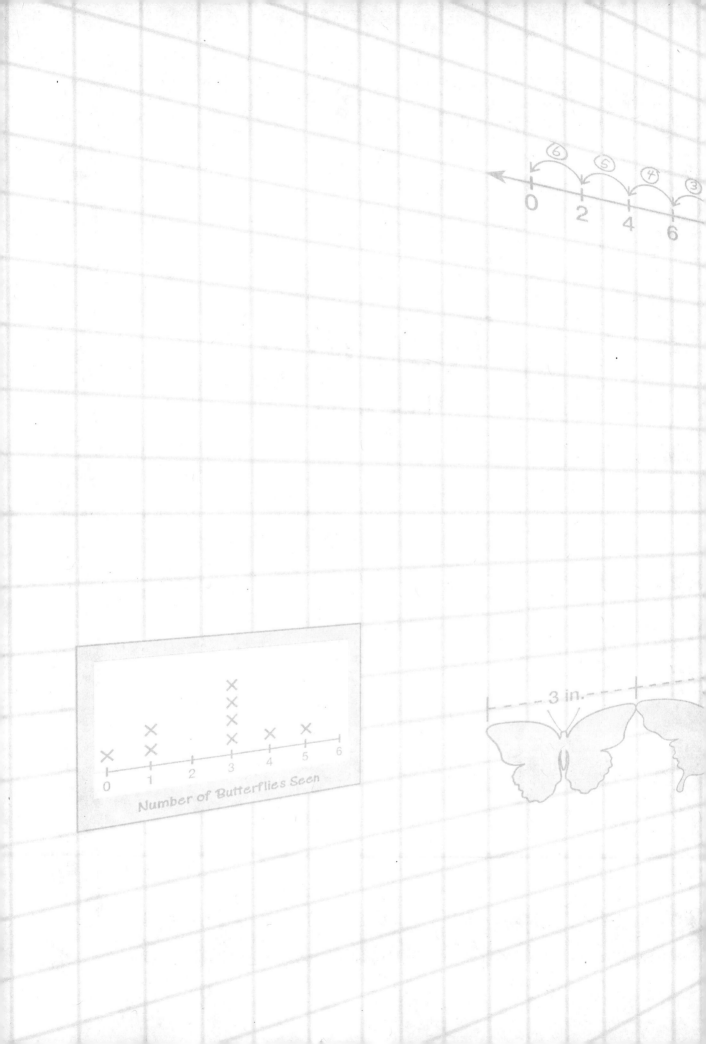

Number of Butterflies Seen

3 in.

Name _____

# *Match the Measure* Game Cards

| milk in a small carton | weight of a cat |
| juice in a glass | height of a third-grader |
| water in a pool | water in a sink |
| distance to the store | length of your classroom |
| distance to the moon | weight of a desk |
| feet | feet |
| pounds | pounds |
| miles | miles |
| cups | cups |
| gallons | gallons |

Name _____

## *Multiplying Dots* Game Board

Name _____

# Multiplication Table

| X | 1 | 2 | 3 | 4 | 5 | 6 | 7 | 8 | 9 | 10 |
|---|---|---|---|---|---|---|---|---|---|----|
| 0 | | | | | | | | | | |
| 1 | | | | | | | | | | |
| 2 | | | | | | | | | | |
| 3 | | | | | | | | | | |
| 4 | | | | | | | | | | |
| 5 | | | | | | | | | | |
| 6 | | | | | | | | | | |
| 7 | | | | | | | | | | |
| 8 | | | | | | | | | | |
| 9 | | | | | | | | | | |
| 10 | | | | | | | | | | |

Name _____

# Hundred Chart

| 1 | 2 | 3 | 4 | 5 | 6 | 7 | 8 | 9 | 10 |
|---|---|---|---|---|---|---|---|---|----|
| 11 | 12 | 13 | 14 | 15 | 16 | 17 | 18 | 19 | 20 |
| 21 | 22 | 23 | 24 | 25 | 26 | 27 | 28 | 29 | 30 |
| 31 | 32 | 33 | 34 | 35 | 36 | 37 | 38 | 39 | 40 |
| 41 | 42 | 43 | 44 | 45 | 46 | 47 | 48 | 49 | 50 |
| 51 | 52 | 53 | 54 | 55 | 56 | 57 | 58 | 59 | 60 |
| 61 | 62 | 63 | 64 | 65 | 66 | 67 | 68 | 69 | 70 |
| 71 | 72 | 73 | 74 | 75 | 76 | 77 | 78 | 79 | 80 |
| 81 | 82 | 83 | 84 | 85 | 86 | 87 | 88 | 89 | 90 |
| 91 | 92 | 93 | 94 | 95 | 96 | 97 | 98 | 99 | 100 |

Name _____

# Multiplication Table

| X | 0 | 1 | 2 | 3 | 4 | 5 | 6 | 7 | 8 | 9 | 10 | 11 | 12 |
|---|---|---|---|---|---|---|---|---|---|---|----|----|----|
| 0 | | | | | | | | | | | | | |
| 1 | | | | | | | | | | | | | |
| 2 | | | | | | | | | | | | | |
| 3 | | | | | | | | | | | | | |
| 4 | | | | | | | | | | | | | |
| 5 | | | | | | | | | | | | | |
| 6 | | | | | | | | | | | | | |
| 7 | | | | | | | | | | | | | |
| 8 | | | | | | | | | | | | | |
| 9 | | | | | | | | | | | | | |
| 10 | | | | | | | | | | | | | |
| 11 | | | | | | | | | | | | | |
| 12 | | | | | | | | | | | | | |

Name _____

# *Meet Your Match* Classifying Shapes

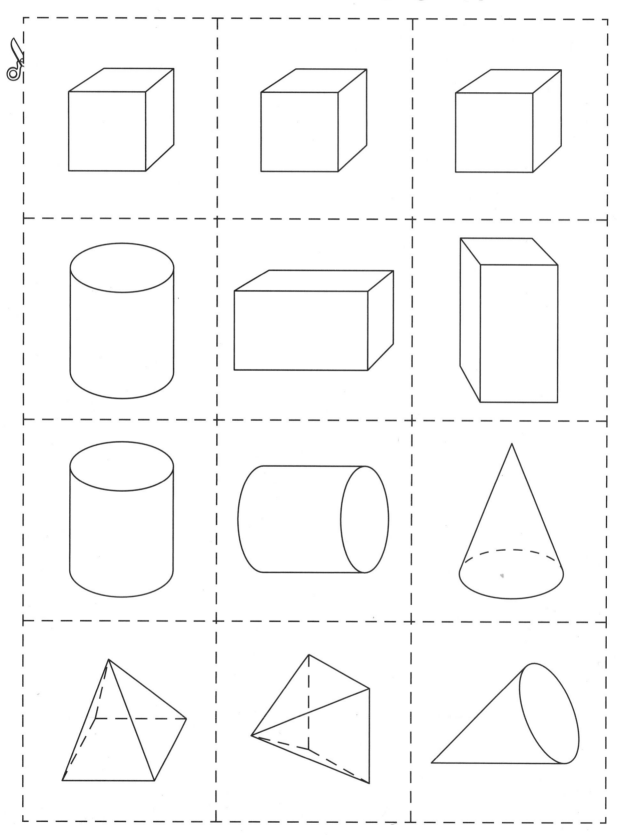

Name _____

## *Meet Your Match* Classifying Shapes

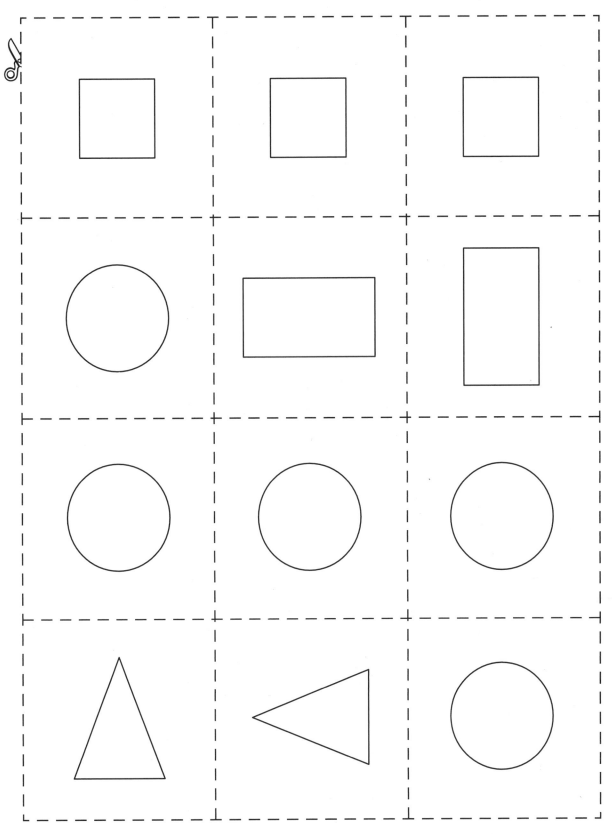

Name _____

# *Make a Match* Practice Game

| | | | | | | | |
|---|---|---|---|---|---|---|---|
| $12 \div 2$ | $18 \div 2$ | $18 \div 3$ | $27 \div 3$ | $24 \div 4$ | $36 \div 4$ | $30 \div 5$ | $45 \div 5$ |
| $10 \div 2$ | $16 \div 2$ | $15 \div 3$ | $24 \div 3$ | $20 \div 4$ | $32 \div 4$ | $25 \div 5$ | $40 \div 5$ |
| $8 \div 2$ | $14 \div 2$ | $12 \div 3$ | $21 \div 3$ | $16 \div 4$ | $28 \div 4$ | $20 \div 5$ | $35 \div 5$ |

Name _____

## *Math Scramble* Number Cards

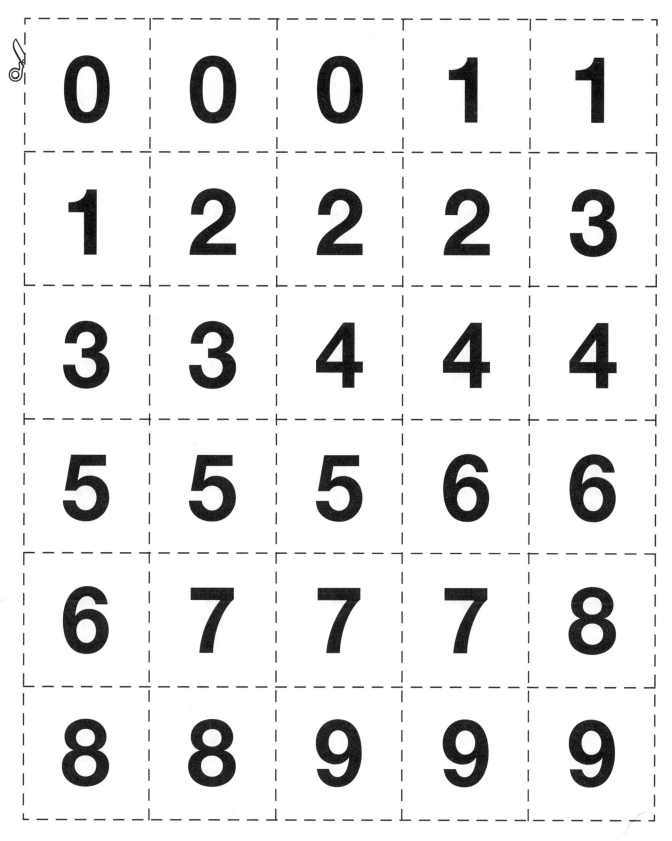

Name _____

# Math Scramble Symbols

| X | X | X | X | X |
| X | X | X | X | X |
| X | X | X | X | X |
| ÷ | ÷ | ÷ | ÷ | ÷ |
| ÷ | ÷ | ÷ | ÷ | ÷ |
| ÷ | ÷ | ÷ | ÷ | ÷ |

Name _____

## *Math Scramble* Symbols (continued)

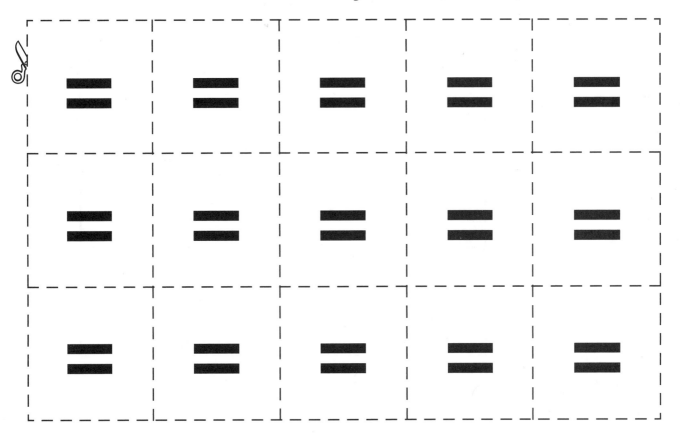

Name _____

## Recording Outcomes Chart

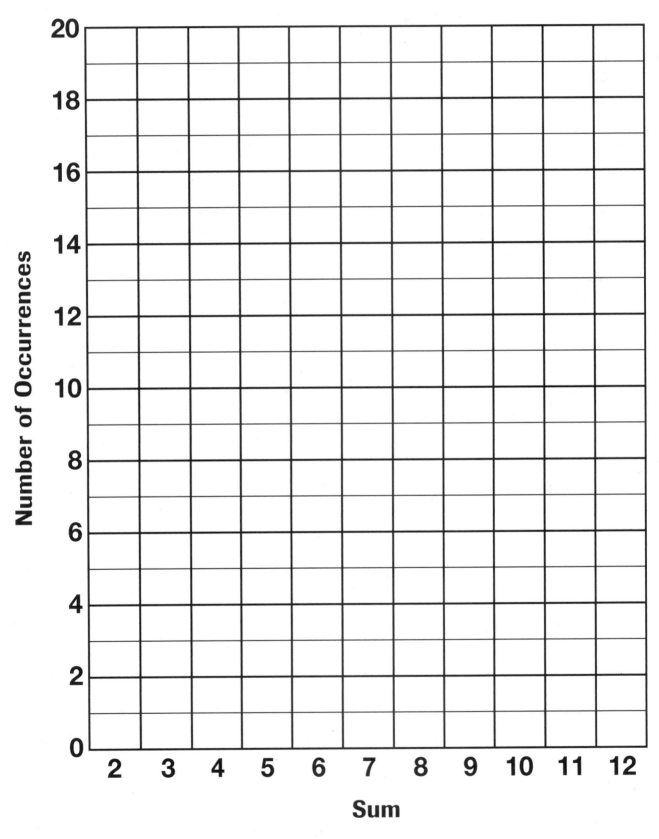

Name _____

# *Recording Outcomes* Spinner 1

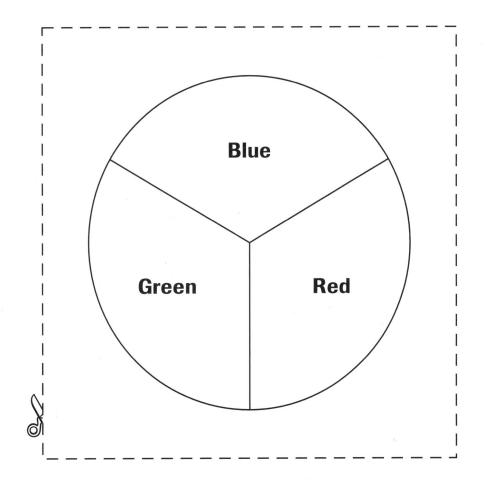

Name _____

## *Recording Outcomes* Spinner 2

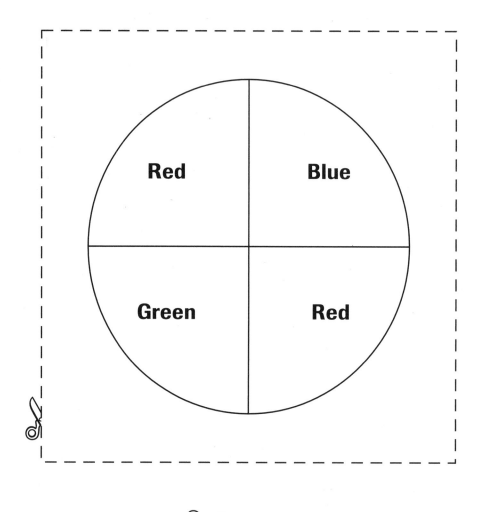

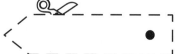

Name _____

# *Pick and Predict* Paper Squares

| | | | |
|---|---|---|---|
| **Red** | **Red** | **Blue** | **Blue** |
| **Red** | **Red** | **Blue** | **Blue** |
| **Red** | **Red** | **Blue** | **Blue** |
| **Red** | | **Blue** | |

Name _____

## *Make Predictions* Spinner

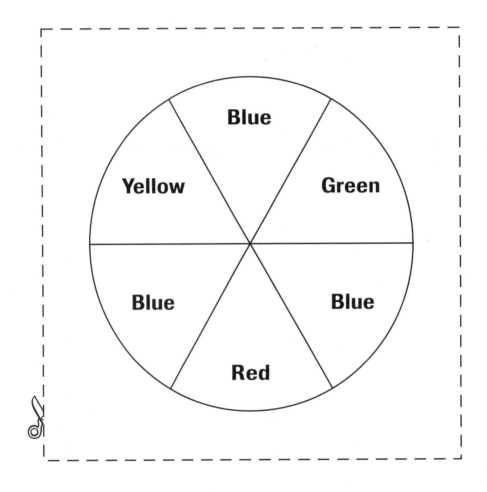

Name _____

# Paper Circle

Name _____

# *Fraction Bingo* Game Boards

| Player 2 | | | | |
|----------|-----|------|------|------|
| | 0 | $\frac{1}{2}$ | $\frac{2}{5}$ | $\frac{1}{8}$ |
| | $\frac{7}{10}$ | $\frac{7}{12}$ | $\frac{5}{8}$ | $\frac{1}{10}$ |
| | $\frac{5}{6}$ | $\frac{4}{5}$ | $\frac{1}{3}$ | $\frac{2}{3}$ |
| | $\frac{3}{4}$ | $\frac{7}{8}$ | 1 | $\frac{3}{8}$ |

| Player 1 | | | | |
|----------|-----|------|------|------|
| | $\frac{5}{6}$ | $\frac{2}{5}$ | $\frac{1}{10}$ | $\frac{1}{3}$ |
| | $\frac{5}{8}$ | $\frac{7}{8}$ | $\frac{1}{2}$ | $\frac{3}{8}$ |
| | 0 | $\frac{3}{4}$ | $\frac{1}{8}$ | $\frac{7}{12}$ |
| | $\frac{2}{3}$ | $\frac{7}{10}$ | $\frac{4}{5}$ | 1 |

Name _____

# *Fraction Bingo* Addition and Subtraction Problems

| | |
|---|---|
| $\dfrac{1}{4} + \dfrac{2}{4}$ | $\dfrac{1}{8} - \dfrac{1}{8}$ |
| $\dfrac{1}{4} + \dfrac{1}{4}$ | $\dfrac{6}{8} - \dfrac{1}{8}$ |
| $\dfrac{1}{2} + \dfrac{1}{2}$ | $\dfrac{9}{12} - \dfrac{2}{12}$ |
| $\dfrac{1}{8} + \dfrac{2}{8}$ | $1 - \dfrac{1}{8}$ |
| $\dfrac{2}{6} + \dfrac{2}{6}$ | $\dfrac{7}{8} - \dfrac{6}{8}$ |
| $\dfrac{1}{6} + \dfrac{1}{6}$ | $\dfrac{9}{10} - \dfrac{4}{10}$ |
| $\dfrac{1}{5} + \dfrac{1}{5}$ | $\dfrac{5}{10} - \dfrac{2}{10}$ |
| $\dfrac{1}{5} + \dfrac{3}{5}$ | $1 - \dfrac{1}{6}$ |

Name _____

# *Remainder Race* Game Board

| | | | |
|---|---|---|---|
| $4\overline{)4\square}$ | $2\overline{)8\square}$ | $3\overline{)6\square}$ | $5\overline{)5\square}$ |
| $3\overline{)3\square}$ | $2\overline{)4\square}$ | $4\overline{)4\square}$ | $4\overline{)8\square}$ |
| $2\overline{)2\square}$ | $3\overline{)9\square}$ | $4\overline{)8\square}$ | $2\overline{)4\square}$ |
| $5\overline{)5\square}$ | $3\overline{)6\square}$ | $2\overline{)8\square}$ | $3\overline{)9\square}$ |

Name _____

# Answer Sheet 1–50

| | | | | | | | | | |
|---|---|---|---|---|---|---|---|---|---|
| 1. | A | B | C | D | 26. | F | G | H | J |
| 2. | F | G | H | J | 27. | A | B | C | D |
| 3. | A | B | C | D | 28. | F | G | H | J |
| 4. | F | G | H | J | 29. | A | B | C | D |
| 5. | A | B | C | D | 30. | F | G | H | J |
| 6. | F | G | H | J | 31. | A | B | C | D |
| 7. | A | B | C | D | 32. | F | G | H | J |
| 8. | F | G | H | J | 33. | A | B | C | D |
| 9. | A | B | C | D | 34. | F | G | H | J |
| 10. | F | G | H | J | 35. | A | B | C | D |
| 11. | A | B | C | D | 36. | F | G | H | J |
| 12. | F | G | H | J | 37. | A | B | C | D |
| 13. | A | B | C | D | 38. | F | G | H | J |
| 14. | F | G | H | J | 39. | A | B | C | D |
| 15. | A | B | C | D | 40. | F | G | H | J |
| 16. | F | G | H | J | 41. | A | B | C | D |
| 17. | A | B | C | D | 42. | F | G | H | J |
| 18. | F | G | H | J | 43. | A | B | C | D |
| 19. | A | B | C | D | 44. | F | G | H | J |
| 20. | F | G | H | J | 45. | A | B | C | D |
| 21. | A | B | C | D | 46. | F | G | H | J |
| 22. | F | G | H | J | 47. | A | B | C | D |
| 23. | A | B | C | D | 48. | F | G | H | J |
| 24. | F | G | H | J | 49. | A | B | C | D |
| 25. | A | B | C | D | 50. | F | G | H | J |

Name _____

# 10 x 10 Grid Paper

Name _____

# Centimeter Grid

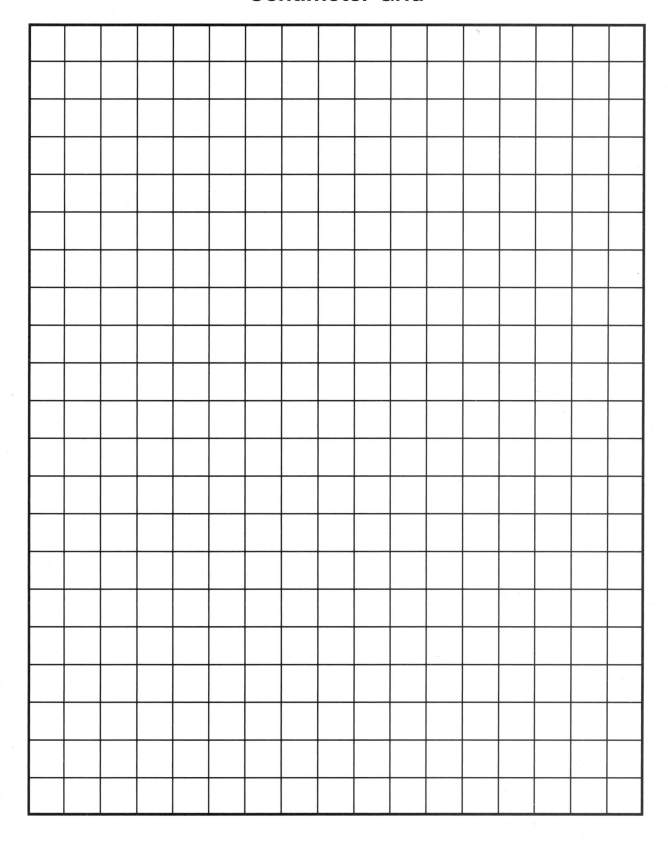

Name _____

# Dot Paper

Name _____

# Input-Output Tables

Rule:

| Input | Output |
|-------|--------|
|       |        |
|       |        |
|       |        |
|       |        |

Rule:

| Input | Output |
|-------|--------|
|       |        |
|       |        |
|       |        |
|       |        |

Rule:

| Input | Output |
|-------|--------|
|       |        |
|       |        |
|       |        |
|       |        |

Rule:

| Input | Output |
|-------|--------|
|       |        |
|       |        |
|       |        |
|       |        |

Rule:

| Input | Output |
|-------|--------|
|       |        |
|       |        |
|       |        |
|       |        |

Rule:

| Input | Output |
|-------|--------|
|       |        |
|       |        |
|       |        |
|       |        |

Rule:

| Input | Output |
|-------|--------|
|       |        |
|       |        |
|       |        |
|       |        |

Rule:

| Input | Output |
|-------|--------|
|       |        |
|       |        |
|       |        |
|       |        |

Rule:

| Input | Output |
|-------|--------|
|       |        |
|       |        |
|       |        |
|       |        |

Rule:

| Input | Output |
|-------|--------|
|       |        |
|       |        |
|       |        |
|       |        |

Rule:

| Input | Output |
|-------|--------|
|       |        |
|       |        |
|       |        |
|       |        |

Rule:

| Input | Output |
|-------|--------|
|       |        |
|       |        |
|       |        |
|       |        |

Rule:

| Input | Output |
|-------|--------|
|       |        |
|       |        |
|       |        |
|       |        |

Rule:

| Input | Output |
|-------|--------|
|       |        |
|       |        |
|       |        |
|       |        |

Rule:

| Input | Output |
|-------|--------|
|       |        |
|       |        |
|       |        |
|       |        |

Rule:

| Input | Output |
|-------|--------|
|       |        |
|       |        |
|       |        |
|       |        |

Rule:

| Input | Output |
|-------|--------|
|       |        |
|       |        |
|       |        |
|       |        |

Rule:

| Input | Output |
|-------|--------|
|       |        |
|       |        |
|       |        |
|       |        |

Rule:

| Input | Output |
|-------|--------|
|       |        |
|       |        |
|       |        |
|       |        |

Rule:

| Input | Output |
|-------|--------|
|       |        |
|       |        |
|       |        |
|       |        |

Name _____

# Addition Chart

| + | 1 | 2 | 3 | 4 | 5 | 6 | 7 | 8 | 9 | 10 |
|---|---|---|---|---|---|---|---|---|---|----|
| 0 | | | | | | | | | | |
| 1 | | | | | | | | | | |
| 2 | | | | | | | | | | |
| 3 | | | | | | | | | | |
| 4 | | | | | | | | | | |
| 5 | | | | | | | | | | |
| 6 | | | | | | | | | | |
| 7 | | | | | | | | | | |
| 8 | | | | | | | | | | |
| 9 | | | | | | | | | | |
| 10 | | | | | | | | | | |

Grade 3, Multi-Use

Name _____

# Hundred Chart

| 1 | 2 | 3 | 4 | 5 | 6 | 7 | 8 | 9 | 10 |
|---|---|---|---|---|---|---|---|---|----|
| 11 | 12 | 13 | 14 | 15 | 16 | 17 | 18 | 19 | 20 |
| 21 | 22 | 23 | 24 | 25 | 26 | 27 | 28 | 29 | 30 |
| 31 | 32 | 33 | 34 | 35 | 36 | 37 | 38 | 39 | 40 |
| 41 | 42 | 43 | 44 | 45 | 46 | 47 | 48 | 49 | 50 |
| 51 | 52 | 53 | 54 | 55 | 56 | 57 | 58 | 59 | 60 |
| 61 | 62 | 63 | 64 | 65 | 66 | 67 | 68 | 69 | 70 |
| 71 | 72 | 73 | 74 | 75 | 76 | 77 | 78 | 79 | 80 |
| 81 | 82 | 83 | 84 | 85 | 86 | 87 | 88 | 89 | 90 |
| 91 | 92 | 93 | 94 | 95 | 96 | 97 | 98 | 99 | 100 |

Name _____

## 0–99 Chart

| 0 | 1 | 2 | 3 | 4 | 5 | 6 | 7 | 8 | 9 |
|---|---|---|---|---|---|---|---|---|---|
| 10 | 11 | 12 | 13 | 14 | 15 | 16 | 17 | 18 | 19 |
| 20 | 21 | 22 | 23 | 24 | 25 | 26 | 27 | 28 | 29 |
| 30 | 31 | 32 | 33 | 34 | 35 | 36 | 37 | 38 | 39 |
| 40 | 41 | 42 | 43 | 44 | 45 | 46 | 47 | 48 | 49 |
| 50 | 51 | 52 | 53 | 54 | 55 | 56 | 57 | 58 | 59 |
| 60 | 61 | 62 | 63 | 64 | 65 | 66 | 67 | 68 | 69 |
| 70 | 71 | 72 | 73 | 74 | 75 | 76 | 77 | 78 | 79 |
| 80 | 81 | 82 | 83 | 84 | 85 | 86 | 87 | 88 | 89 |
| 90 | 91 | 92 | 93 | 94 | 95 | 96 | 97 | 98 | 99 |

Grade 3, Multi-Use

Name _____

# Whole-Number Place-Value Charts

| tens | ones |
|------|------|
|      |      |
|      |      |
|      |      |
|      |      |
|      |      |

| tens | ones |
|------|------|
|      |      |
|      |      |
|      |      |
|      |      |
|      |      |

| tens | ones |
|------|------|
|      |      |
|      |      |
|      |      |
|      |      |
|      |      |

| tens | ones |
|------|------|
|      |      |
|      |      |
|      |      |
|      |      |
|      |      |

| hundreds | tens | ones |
|----------|------|------|
|          |      |      |
|          |      |      |
|          |      |      |
|          |      |      |
|          |      |      |

| hundreds | tens | ones |
|----------|------|------|
|          |      |      |
|          |      |      |
|          |      |      |
|          |      |      |
|          |      |      |

| thousands | | | | ones | | |
|---|---|---|---|---|---|---|
| h | t | o | , | h | t | o |
|   |   |   |   |   |   |   |
|   |   |   |   |   |   |   |
|   |   |   |   |   |   |   |
|   |   |   |   |   |   |   |
|   |   |   |   |   |   |   |

| thousands | | | | ones | | |
|---|---|---|---|---|---|---|
| h | t | o | , | h | t | o |
|   |   |   |   |   |   |   |
|   |   |   |   |   |   |   |
|   |   |   |   |   |   |   |
|   |   |   |   |   |   |   |
|   |   |   |   |   |   |   |

Name _____

# Decimal Place-Value Charts

| ones | | tenths | hundredths |
|---|---|---|---|
| | . | | |
| | . | | |
| | . | | |
| | . | | |
| | . | | |

| ones | | tenths | hundredths |
|---|---|---|---|
| | . | | |
| | . | | |
| | . | | |
| | . | | |
| | . | | |

| ones | | tenths | hundredths |
|---|---|---|---|
| | . | | |
| | . | | |
| | . | | |
| | . | | |
| | . | | |

Name _____

# Decimal Models

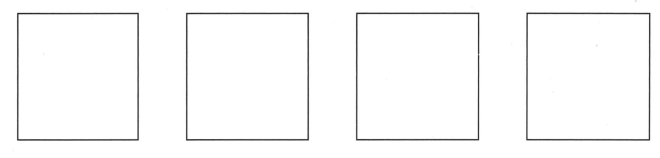

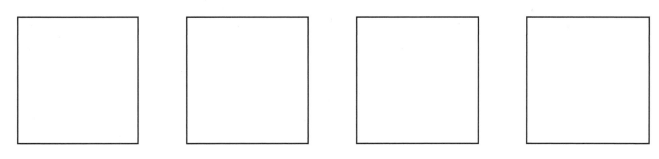

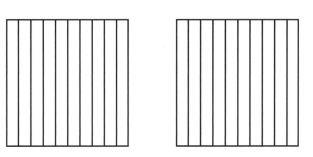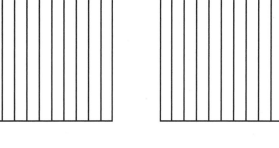

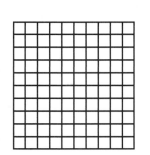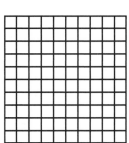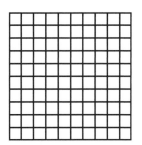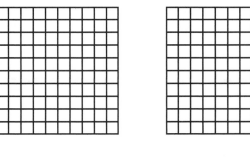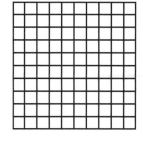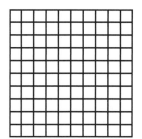

Name _____

# Number Lines

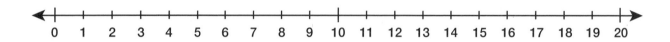

| 0 | 1 | 2 | 3 | 4 | 5 | 6 | 7 | 8 | 9 | 10 | 11 | 12 | 13 | 14 | 15 | 16 | 17 | 18 | 19 | 20 |

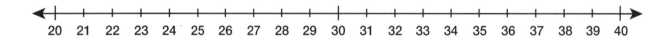

| 20 | 21 | 22 | 23 | 24 | 25 | 26 | 27 | 28 | 29 | 30 | 31 | 32 | 33 | 34 | 35 | 36 | 37 | 38 | 39 | 40 |

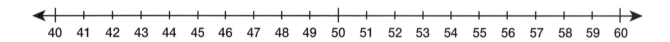

| 40 | 41 | 42 | 43 | 44 | 45 | 46 | 47 | 48 | 49 | 50 | 51 | 52 | 53 | 54 | 55 | 56 | 57 | 58 | 59 | 60 |

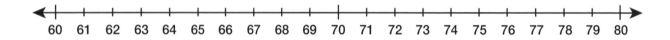

| 60 | 61 | 62 | 63 | 64 | 65 | 66 | 67 | 68 | 69 | 70 | 71 | 72 | 73 | 74 | 75 | 76 | 77 | 78 | 79 | 80 |

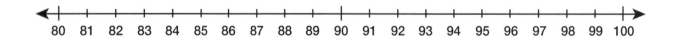

| 80 | 81 | 82 | 83 | 84 | 85 | 86 | 87 | 88 | 89 | 90 | 91 | 92 | 93 | 94 | 95 | 96 | 97 | 98 | 99 | 100 |

Name _____

# Bill and Coin Models

Name _____

# Base-Ten Blocks, Set 1

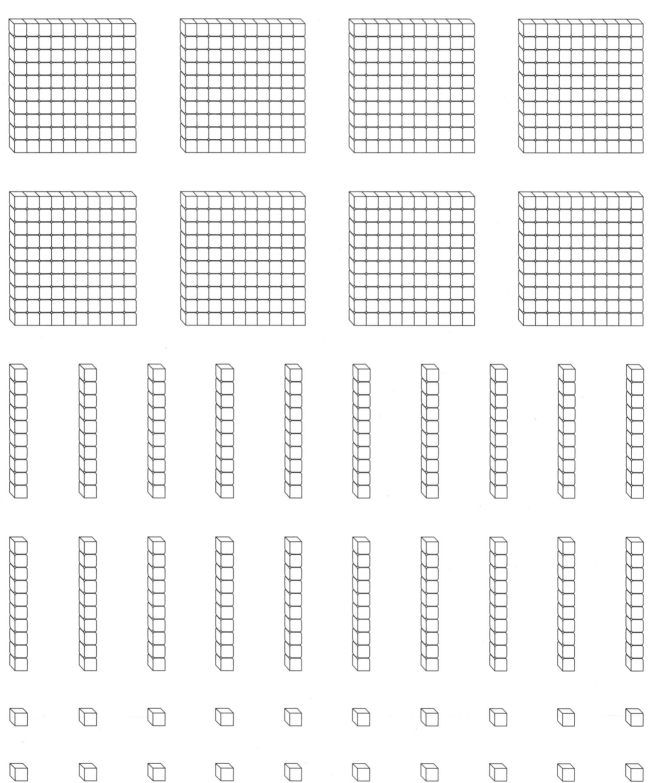

Name _____

# Base-Ten Blocks, Set 2

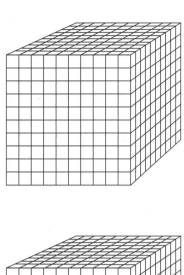
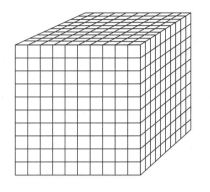
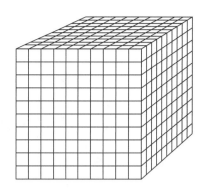

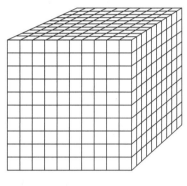
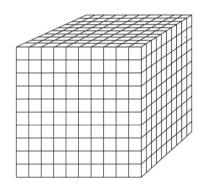
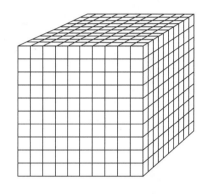

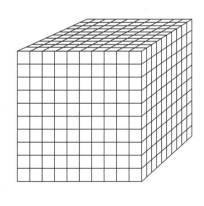
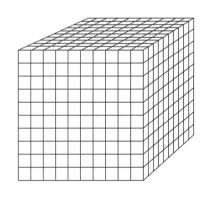
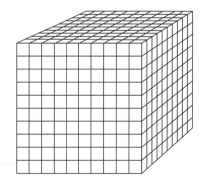

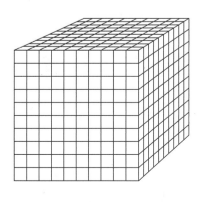
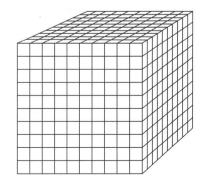
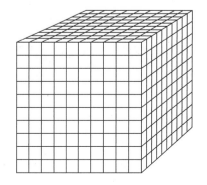

Name _____

# Clock Face

Minute Hand

Hour Hand

- Cut out the clock and the hour and minute hands
- Attach the hour hand and minute hand to the clock face with a paper fastner

Name _____

# Blank Clock Faces

Name _____

# Fraction Strips

| 1 |
|---|

| $\frac{1}{2}$ | |
|---|---|

| $\frac{1}{3}$ | | |
|---|---|---|

| $\frac{1}{4}$ | | | |
|---|---|---|---|

| $\frac{1}{5}$ | | | | |
|---|---|---|---|---|

| $\frac{1}{6}$ | | | | | |
|---|---|---|---|---|---|

| $\frac{1}{8}$ | | | | | | | |
|---|---|---|---|---|---|---|---|

| $\frac{1}{10}$ | | | | | | | | | |
|---|---|---|---|---|---|---|---|---|---|

| $\frac{1}{12}$ | | | | | | | | | | | |
|---|---|---|---|---|---|---|---|---|---|---|---|

Name _____

# Fraction Pieces

| 1 |
|---|

| $\frac{1}{2}$ | $\frac{1}{2}$ |
|---|---|

| $\frac{1}{3}$ | $\frac{1}{3}$ | $\frac{1}{3}$ |
|---|---|---|

| $\frac{1}{4}$ | $\frac{1}{4}$ | $\frac{1}{4}$ | $\frac{1}{4}$ |
|---|---|---|---|

| $\frac{1}{5}$ | $\frac{1}{5}$ | $\frac{1}{5}$ | $\frac{1}{5}$ | $\frac{1}{5}$ |
|---|---|---|---|---|

| $\frac{1}{6}$ | $\frac{1}{6}$ | $\frac{1}{6}$ | $\frac{1}{6}$ | $\frac{1}{6}$ | $\frac{1}{6}$ |
|---|---|---|---|---|---|

| $\frac{1}{8}$ | $\frac{1}{8}$ | $\frac{1}{8}$ | $\frac{1}{8}$ | $\frac{1}{8}$ | $\frac{1}{8}$ | $\frac{1}{8}$ | $\frac{1}{8}$ |
|---|---|---|---|---|---|---|---|

| $\frac{1}{10}$ | $\frac{1}{10}$ | $\frac{1}{10}$ | $\frac{1}{10}$ | $\frac{1}{10}$ | $\frac{1}{10}$ | $\frac{1}{10}$ | $\frac{1}{10}$ | $\frac{1}{10}$ | $\frac{1}{10}$ |
|---|---|---|---|---|---|---|---|---|---|

| $\frac{1}{12}$ | $\frac{1}{12}$ | $\frac{1}{12}$ | $\frac{1}{12}$ | $\frac{1}{12}$ | $\frac{1}{12}$ | $\frac{1}{12}$ | $\frac{1}{12}$ | $\frac{1}{12}$ | $\frac{1}{12}$ | $\frac{1}{12}$ | $\frac{1}{12}$ |
|---|---|---|---|---|---|---|---|---|---|---|---|

Name _____

# Fraction Circles

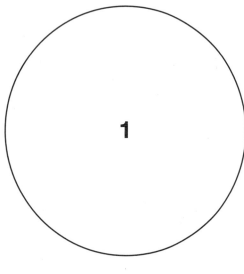

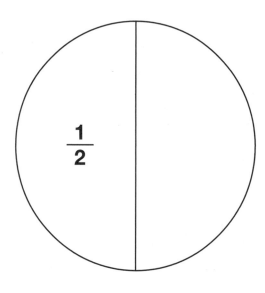

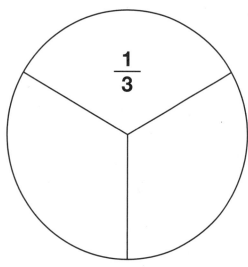

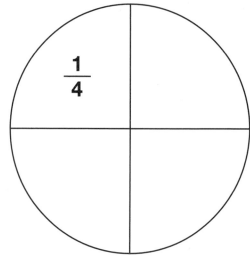

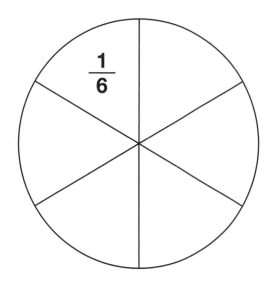

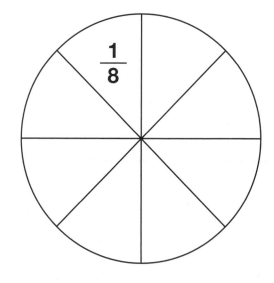

**Grade 3, Multi-Use**

Name _____

# Rulers

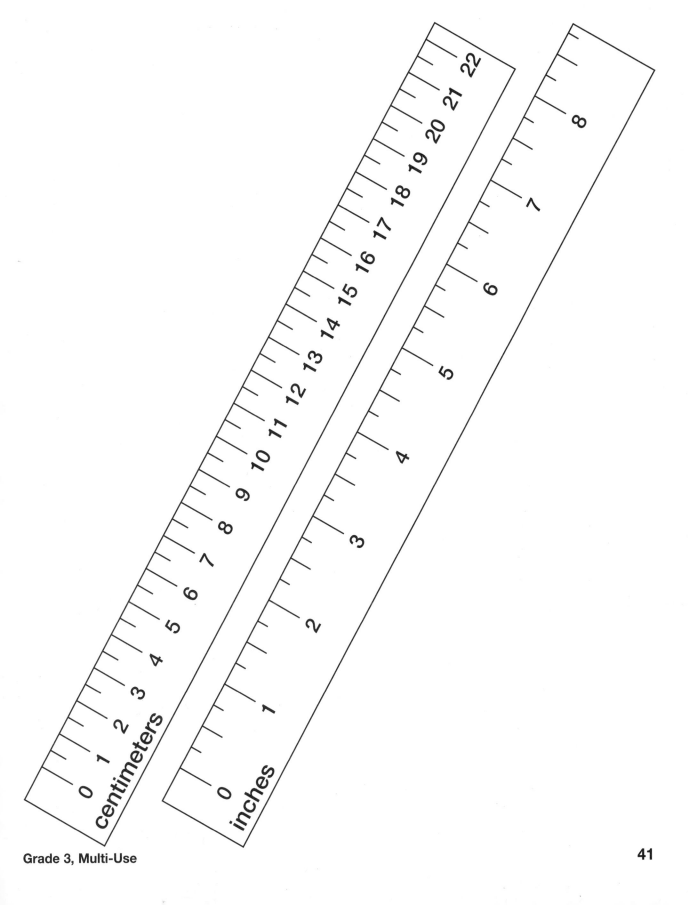

Name _____

# Monthly Calendar

| Year | Sunday | Monday | Tuesday | Wednesday | Thursday | Friday | Saturday |
|---|---|---|---|---|---|---|---|
| Month | | | | | | | |
| | | | | | | | |
| | | | | | | | |
| | | | | | | | |
| | | | | | | | |
| | | | | | | | |

Name _____

# Tangram Pieces

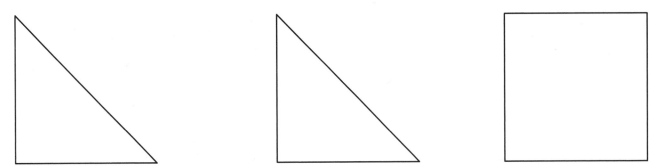

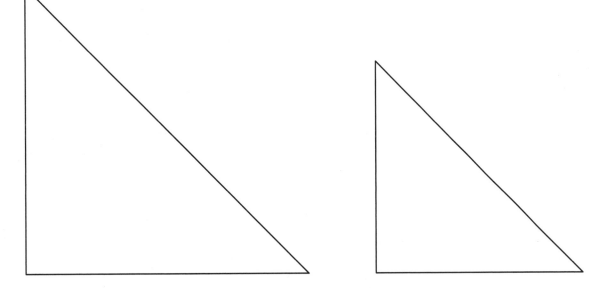

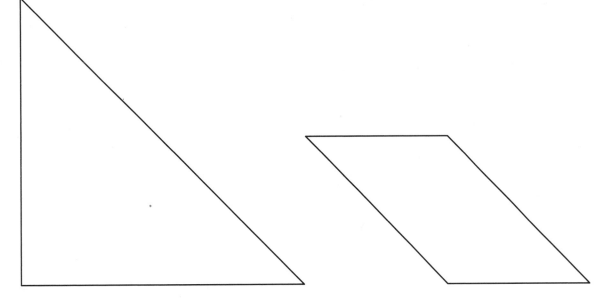

Name _____

# Spinners

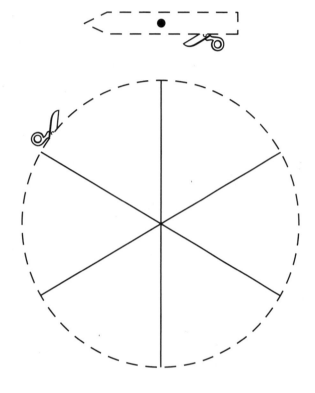

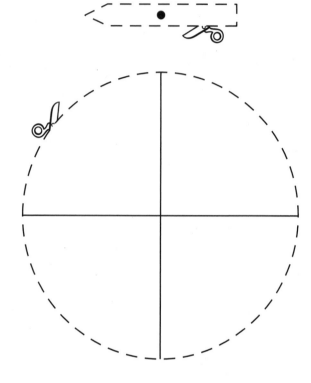

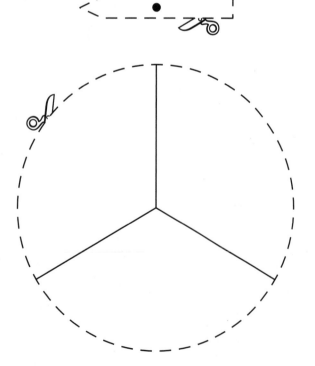

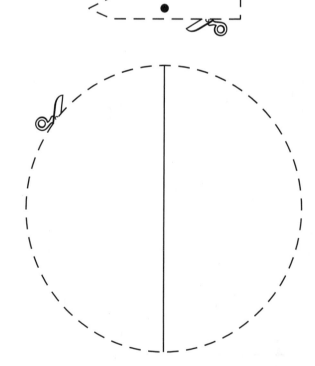

**Grade 3, Multi-Use**

Name _____

# First-Quadrant Grids

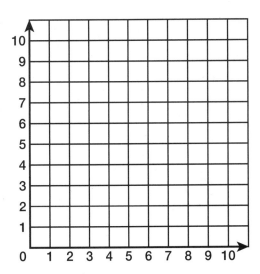

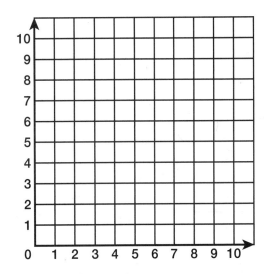

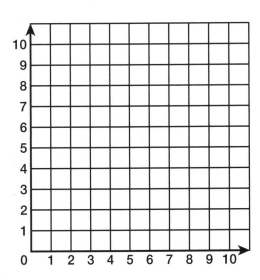

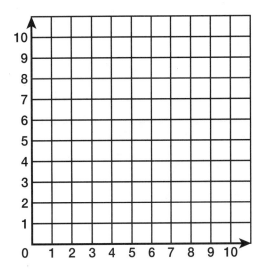

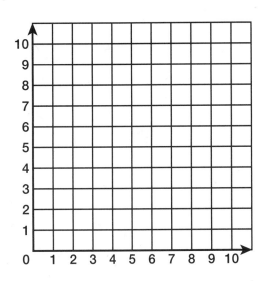

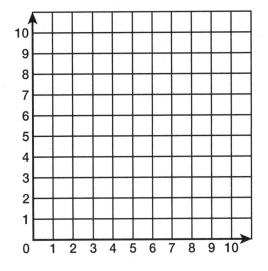

Name _____

# Cube Net

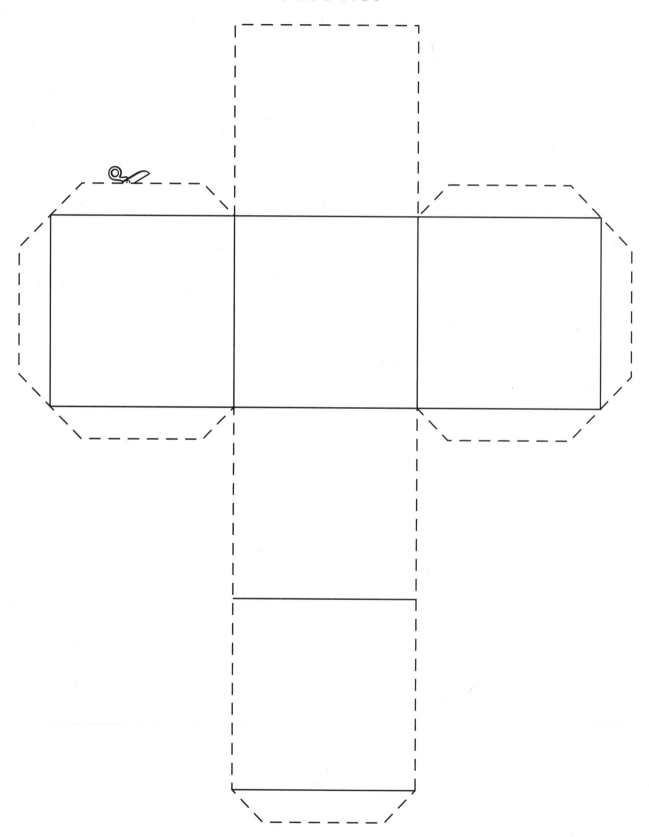

Name _____

# Rectangular Prism Net

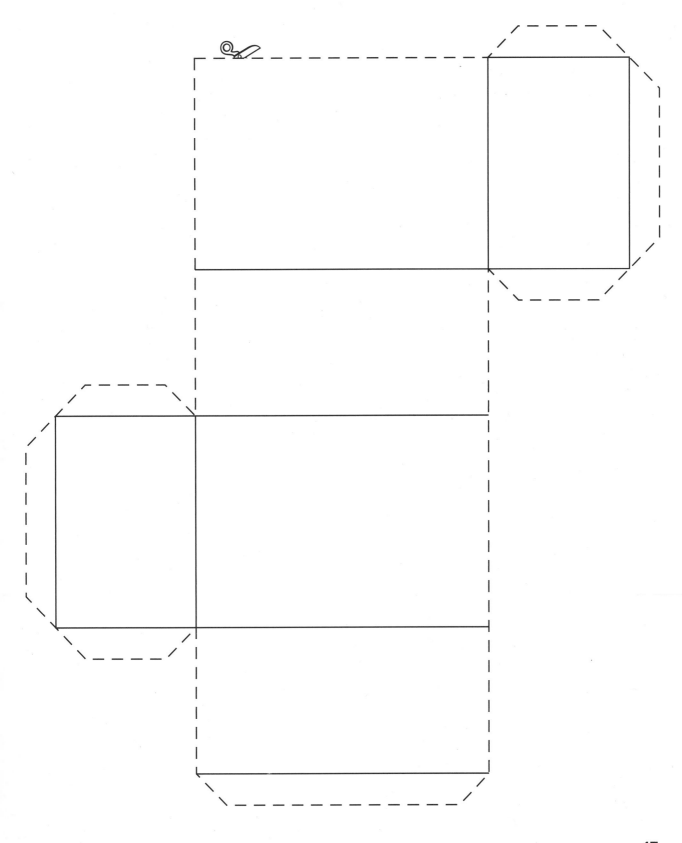

Name _____

# Square Pyramid Net

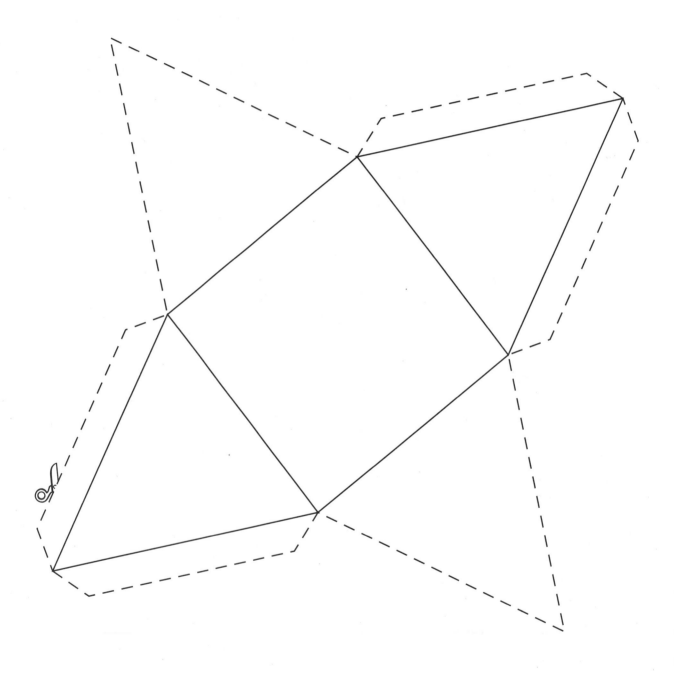

Name _____

# Cone Net

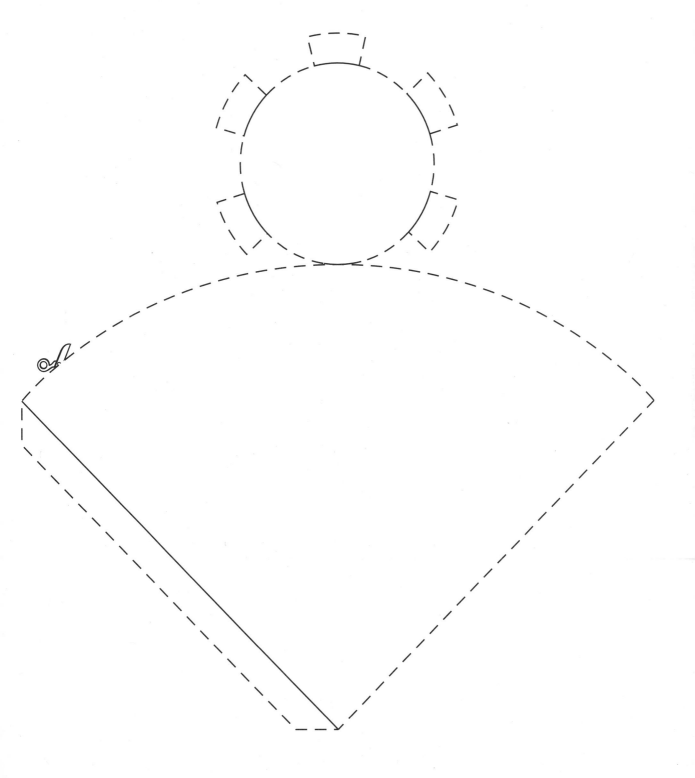

Name _____

# Cylinder Net

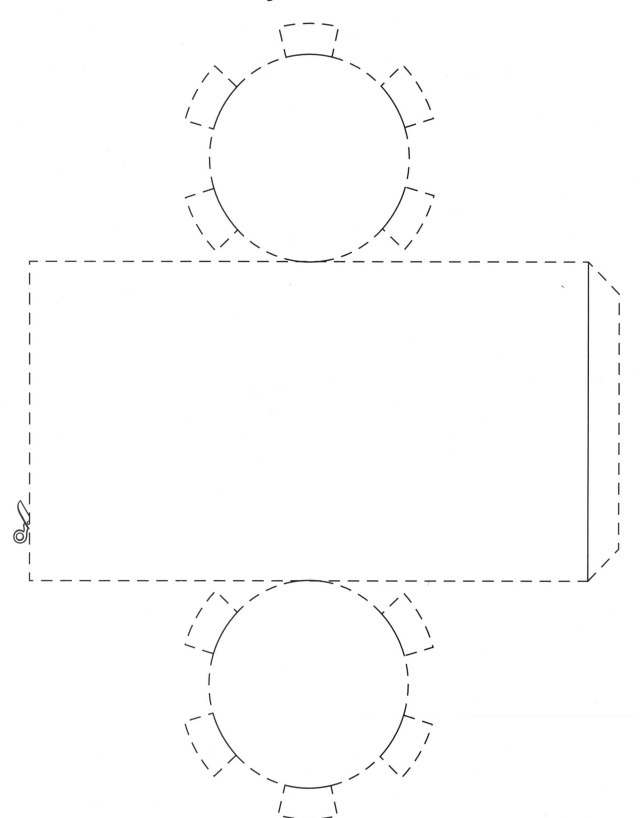

# Family
# Letters

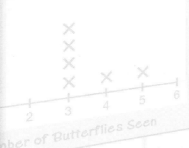

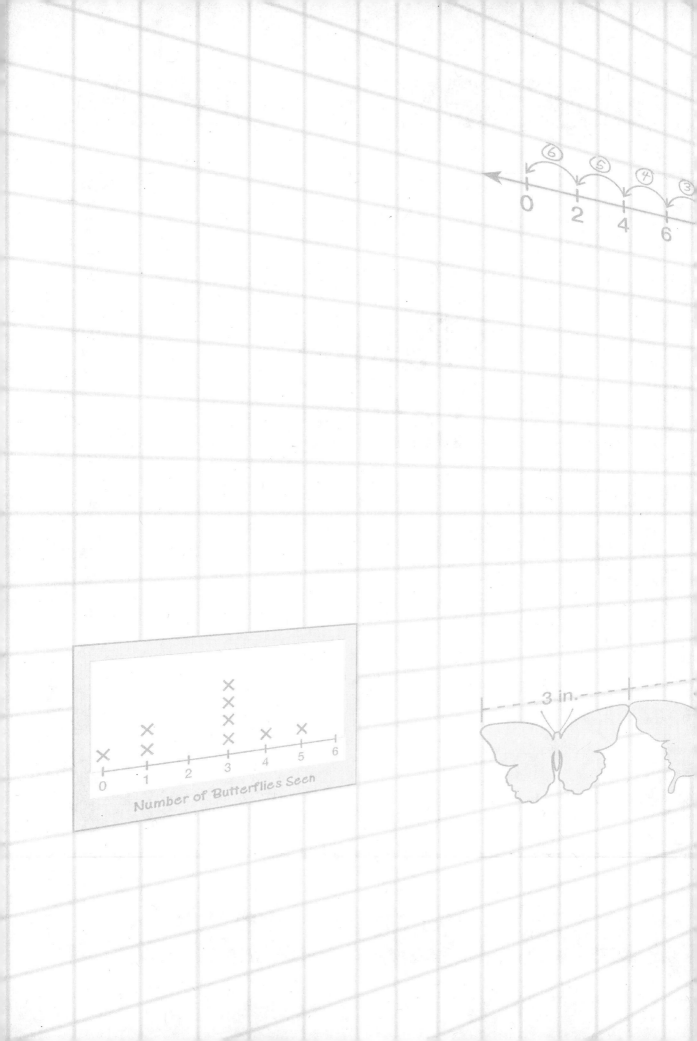

# Family Letter

## Vocabulary

**estimate** A number close to an exact amount.

**expanded form** A way to write a number that shows the value of each digit.

**standard form** A way to write a number by using only digits.

**word form** A way to write a number by using only words.

Dear Family,

During the next few weeks, our math class will be learning about place value. We will be learning how to read and write numbers up to 999,999.

We will also be comparing, ordering, and rounding these numbers. As we learn how to compare and order greater numbers, you may wish to use the following sample as a guide.

### Order Three 4-Digit Numbers

To order 4,569, 4,280, and 4,100 from least to greatest, write the numbers one above the other in a place-value chart.

1. Compare the thousands digits. Since all the digits are 4, look at the hundreds digits.

2. Compare the hundreds digits.

| Thousands | Hundreds | Tens | Ones |
|-----------|----------|------|------|
| 4 | 5 | 6 | 9 |
| 4 | 2 | 8 | 0 |
| 4 | 1 | 0 | 0 |

Since 1 hundred is less than 2 hundreds, 4,100 < 4,280.

Since 2 hundreds is less than 5 hundreds, 4,280 < 4,569.

So the numbers in order from least to greatest are

4,100    4,280    4,569.

Knowing about place value can help students understand numbers through 999,999 and use them to solve problems.

Sincerely,

Your Child's Teacher

# Family Letter

Dear Family,

During the next few weeks, our math class will be learning about money and time.

You can expect to see work that provides practice with counting and comparing collections of coins and bills as well as with reading analog and digital clocks.

As we learn how to count money to make change using the fewest coins and bills, you may wish to use the following sample as a guide.

## Vocabulary

**ordinal numbers** Numbers used to show order or position, such as *first, second, third, fourth,* and *fifth.*

**decade** A unit of time equal to 10 years.

**century** A unit of time equal to 100 years.

**Count to Make Change**

You can follow these steps to find the change you should receive if you use a $10 bill to buy an item that costs $8.64.

**1.** Start with the amount the item costs.

**2.** Count on coins and bills until you reach the amount you paid.

**3.** Then find the value of the coins and bills used to make the change.

$8.64 ⇨ $8.65 ⇨ $8.75 ⇨ $9.00 ⇨ $10.00

$ 8.64     1¢     10¢     25¢     1 $ 1 / 1 1

You should receive $1.36 in change.

Knowing about money and time concepts will help students understand how to use money and time in real-life situations.

Sincerely,

Your Child's Teacher

# Family Letter

Dear Family,

Our math class will be spending the next few weeks learning to add and subtract greater numbers. We will also round numbers to estimate sums and differences.

You can expect to see work that provides practice in adding and subtracting numbers with up to four digits, using regrouping.

As we learn to subtract across zeros, you may wish to use the following sample as a guide.

## Vocabulary

**Commutative Property** The property that states that the order of addends does not change the sum. It is also called the *Order Property*.

**Associative Property** The property that states that the way in which addends are grouped does not change the sum. It is also called the *Grouping Property*.

**Zero Property** The property that states that the sum of any number and 0 is that number.

### Subtracting Across Zeros

| Since there are no ones or tens to subtract from, you have to regroup 4 hundreds as 3 hundreds 10 tens. | Then you can regroup the 10 tens as 9 tens 10 ones. | Finally, you can subtract ones, tens, and hundreds. |
|---|---|---|
| $\begin{array}{r}400\\-169\end{array}$  $\begin{array}{r}3\ 10\\\cancel{400}\\-169\end{array}$ | $\begin{array}{r}9\\3\ \cancel{10}\,10\\\cancel{400}\\-169\end{array}$ | $\begin{array}{r}9\\3\ \cancel{10}\,10\\\cancel{400}\\-169\\\hline 231\end{array}$ |

During this chapter, students should continue to memorize basic addition and subtraction facts.

Sincerely,

Your Child's Teacher

# Family Letter

Dear Family,

During the next few weeks, our math class will be learning how to estimate and measure in customary and metric units.

You can expect to see work that provides practice in measuring length to the nearest inch, half inch, and centimeter.

As we learn how to convert one customary or metric unit to another, you may wish to keep the following equivalents in mind.

## Vocabulary

**mile (mi), yard (yd)** Customary units used to measure length.

**ounce (oz)** A customary unit used to measure weight.

**kilometer (km), decimeter (dm)** Metric units used to measure length.

**milliliter (mL)** A metric unit used to measure capacity.

**gram (g)** A metric unit used to measure mass.

## Measurement Equivalents

| Customary Units of Length | Customary Units of Capacity | Customary Units of Weight |
|---|---|---|
| 12 inches = 1 foot | 2 cups = 1 pint | 16 ounces = 1 pound |
| 3 feet = 1 yard | 2 pints = 1 quart | |
| 36 inches = 1 yard | 4 quarts = 1 gallon | |
| 5,280 feet = 1 mile | 16 cups = 1 gallon | |

| Metric Units of Length | Metric Units of Capacity | Metric Units of Mass |
|---|---|---|
| 100 centimeters = 1 meter | 1,000 milliliters = 1 liter | 1,000 grams = 1 kilogram |
| 10 decimeters = 1 meter | | |
| 10 centimeters = 1 decimeter | | |
| 1,000 meters = 1 kilometer | | |
| 100 decimeters = 1 kilometer | | |

Knowing about measurement will help students estimate and use length, capacity, weight or mass, and temperature in everyday life.

Sincerely,

Your Child's Teacher

# Family Letter

Dear Family,

During the next few weeks, our math class will be learning about multiplication of whole numbers.

You can expect to see work that provides practice in multiplying with 2, 5, 10, 3, and 4. We will also be learning about the special multiplication properties of 0 and 1.

As we learn how to represent multiplication sentences by using arrays, you may wish to use the following sample as a guide.

## Vocabulary

**array** An arrangement of objects, pictures, or numbers in equal columns and equal rows.

**factor** A number that divides evenly into a given number.

**Commutative Property** The property that states that the order of the factors does not change the product. It is also called the *Order Property*.

### Using Arrays

An array shows objects arranged in equal rows and equal columns.

$3 \times 4$ can be represented using an array with 3 rows and 4 columns.

There are 12 squares in the array, so $3 \times 4 = 12$.

$4 \times 3$ can be represented using an array with 4 rows and 3 columns.

There are 12 squares in the array, so $4 \times 3 = 12$

During this chapter, students should continue to practice and memorize basic multiplication facts.

Sincerely,

Your Child's Teacher

# Family Letter

Dear Family,

During the next few weeks, our math class will be learning more about multiplication of whole numbers.

You can expect to see work that provides practice in multiplying with 6, 8, 7, and 9.

As we learn about the Associative Property, you may wish to keep the following sample in mind.

## Vocabulary

**multiple** A number that is the product of the given number and a number.

**square number** A whole number multiplied by itself.

**Associative Property** The property that states that the order in which factors are grouped does not change the product. It is also called the *Grouping Property*.

## The Associative Property of Multiplication

The way factors are grouped does not change the product. Do the operations in parentheses first.

| | |
|---|---|
| $6 \times 3 \times 3 = n$ | $6 \times 3 \times 3 = n$ |
| $(6 \times 3) \times 3 = n$ | $6 \times (3 \times 3) = n$ |
| $18 \times 3 = 54$ | $6 \times 9 = 54$ |

Using the Associative Property can make finding the product of three factors easier. Look at the examples above.

- If you find $6 \times 3$ first, you have to then find $18 \times 3$ which is not a basic fact.

- If you find $3 \times 3$ first, you have to then find $6 \times 9$ which is a basic fact.

As you can see in the examples above, we will be introducing the variable $n$ in this chapter. You may wish to remind your child that $n$ is just a symbol used to show a missing number.

Sincerely,

Your Child's Teacher

# Family Letter

Dear Family,

During the next few weeks, our math class will be learning about geometry and measurement.

You can expect to see work that provides practice with identifying and classifying plane figures and solid figures as well as with finding area, perimeter, and volume.

As we learn about area and perimeter, you may wish to use the following sample as a guide.

### Finding the Perimeter and Area of a Figure

Look at the figures on the right.

To find the **perimeter** of Figure A, add the lengths of the sides:
$2 + 4 + 2 + 4 = 12$ cm

The perimeter is 12 cm.

To find the **area** of Figure B, count the square units:
There are 16 whole square units.
There are 4 half square units.
$16 + 2 = 18$

The area is 18 square units.

Knowing about geometric figures will help students understand the geometry that is all around them.

Sincerely,

Your Child's Teacher

## Vocabulary

**line** A straight path that goes on forever in opposite directions.

**angle** A figure formed by two rays with the same endpoint.

**polygon** A simple closed plane figure made up of three or more line segments.

**quadrilateral** A polygon with four sides.

**similar figures** Figures that have the same shape, but not the same size.

**volume** The number of cubic units that fit inside a solid figure.

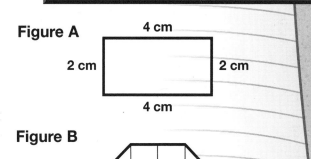

**Figure A**

4 cm

2 cm   2 cm

4 cm

**Figure B**

# Family Letter

Dear Family,

During the next few weeks, our math class will be learning about division of whole numbers.

You can expect to see work that provides practice with dividing 2-digit numbers by 2, 5, 3, and 4 and with finding unit cost.

As we learn how to find unit cost, you may wish to use the following sample as a guide.

## Vocabulary

**dividend** The number that is divided in a division problem.

**divisor** The number by which a number is divided in a division problem.

**unit cost** The price of one item.

### Finding Unit Cost

Look at the table on the right. Which item costs the least?

To find which item costs the least, you can find the unit cost. To find the unit cost of each item, divide the cost of the items by the number of items.

| Item | Cost |
|------|------|
| Books | 4 for $20 |
| Notebooks | 5 for $15 |
| Disks | 3 for $12 |

The cost of 1 book: $20 ÷ 4 = $5
The cost of 1 notebook: $15 ÷ 5 = $3
The cost of 1 disk: $12 ÷ 3 = $4

A notebook costs the least.

During this chapter, students should continue to memorize basic multiplication and division facts.

Sincerely,

Your Child's Teacher

# Family Letter

Dear Family,

During the next few weeks, our math class will be learning more about division of whole numbers.

You can expect to see work that provides practice with dividing by 10, 6, 7, and 9. Students will learn about fact families and how to use a multiplication table to divide.

As we learn about fact families, you may wish to use this sample as a guide.

## Vocabulary

**dividend** The number that is divided in a division problem.

**divisor** The number by which a number is divided in a division problem.

**array** An arrangement of objects, pictures, or numbers in equal columns and equal rows.

## Writing Fact Families for Multiplication and Division

Since multiplication and division are related operations, we can write groups of number sentences called fact families. The number sentences in a fact family are mathematically related to each other.

The fact family for this array is

$5 \times 6 = 30$      $30 \div 5 = 6$
$6 \times 5 = 30$      $30 \div 6 = 5$

During this chapter, students should continue to memorize basic multiplication and division facts.

Sincerely,
Your Child's Teacher

# Family Letter

Dear Family,

During the next few weeks, our math class will be learning about data and probability.

You can expect to see work that provides practice with line plots, bar graphs, and pictographs. Students will also find the likelihood of events, list the outcomes of probability experiments, and make predictions.

As we learn about probability, you may wish to use the following as a guide.

## A Probability Experiment

There are 20 red marbles, 5 blue marbles, and 1 green marble in a bag. You pick a marble out of the bag, note its color, and put it back in the bag. What can we say about this experiment?

- There are 3 possible **outcomes.** You can pick a red marble, a blue marble, or a green marble.

- It is **likely** that you will pick a red marble. It is **unlikely** that you will pick a green marble. It is **impossible** that you will pick an orange marble.

- If this experiment is repeated 100 times, these are some of the predictions you might make: a red marble is likely to be picked most often; a green marble is likely to be picked least often.

Understanding data and how it is displayed will help students evaluate the information they encounter in the real world.

Sincerely,

Your Child's Teacher

## Vocabulary

**line plot** A diagram that organizes data by using a number line.

**range** The difference between the greatest number and the least number in a set of data.

**mode** The number or numbers that occur most often in a set of data.

**ordered pair** A pair of numbers in which one number is named as the first and the other number is named as the second.

**probability** The chance that a given event will occur.

**outcome** A result in a probability experiment.

# Family Letter

Dear Family,

During the next few weeks, our math class will be learning about fractions and decimals.

You can expect to see work that provides practice with comparing and ordering fractions, mixed numbers, and decimals.

As we learn how to compare and order fractions, you may wish to use these samples as a guide.

## Vocabulary

**numerator** The number above the bar in a fraction.

**denominator** The number below the bar in a fraction.

**equivalent fractions** Fractions that show the same amount.

**improper fraction** A fraction whose numerator is greater than or equal to its denominator.

**mixed number** A number that has a whole number part and a fraction part.

### Ordering Fractions

To order unit fractions, compare denominators. Fractions with greater denominators are the lesser fractions.

$$\frac{1}{6} < \frac{1}{4} < \frac{1}{2}$$

To order fractions with the same denominators, compare numerators. Fractions with greater numerators are the greater fractions.

$$\frac{1}{6} < \frac{3}{6} < \frac{5}{6}$$

Knowing about fractions and decimals will help students solve problems involving these kinds of numbers.

Sincerely,

Your Child's Teacher

# Family Letter

## Vocabulary

**remainder** The number left over after one number is divided by another.

Dear Family,

During the next few weeks, our math class will be learning and practicing multiplication and division.

You can expect to see work that provides practice in multiplying with greater numbers and dividing with 2- and 3-digit dividends as well as with money amounts.

As we divide greater numbers, you may wish to use the following sample as a guide.

### Two-Digit Quotients

To find 51 ÷ 3 follow these steps.

| First, divide the tens. | Next, regroup leftover tens as ones. | Then divide the ones. |
|---|---|---|
| **Think:** 5 tens ÷ 3. <br> $\begin{array}{r} 1 \\ 3\overline{)51} \\ -3 \\ \hline 2 \end{array}$   Write 1 in the tens place. <br><br> Multiply. 3 × 1 ten <br> Subtract. 5 − 3 <br> Compare. 2 < 3 | **Think:** 2 tens 1 one = 21 ones. <br> $\begin{array}{r} 1 \\ 3\overline{)51} \\ -3\downarrow \\ \hline 21 \end{array}$ <br><br> Bring down 1 one. <br> Regroup 2 tens 1 one as 21 ones. | **Think:** 21 ones ÷ 3. <br> $\begin{array}{r} 17 \\ 3\overline{)51} \\ -3 \\ \hline 21 \\ -21 \\ \hline 0 \end{array}$   Write 7 in the ones place. <br><br> Multiply. 3 × 7 ones <br> Subtract. 21 − 21 <br> Compare. 0 < 3 |

Knowing how to multiply and divide with greater numbers and money amounts will allow students to solve more complex problems.

Sincerely,

Your Child's Teacher

# Fast Facts
# Practice

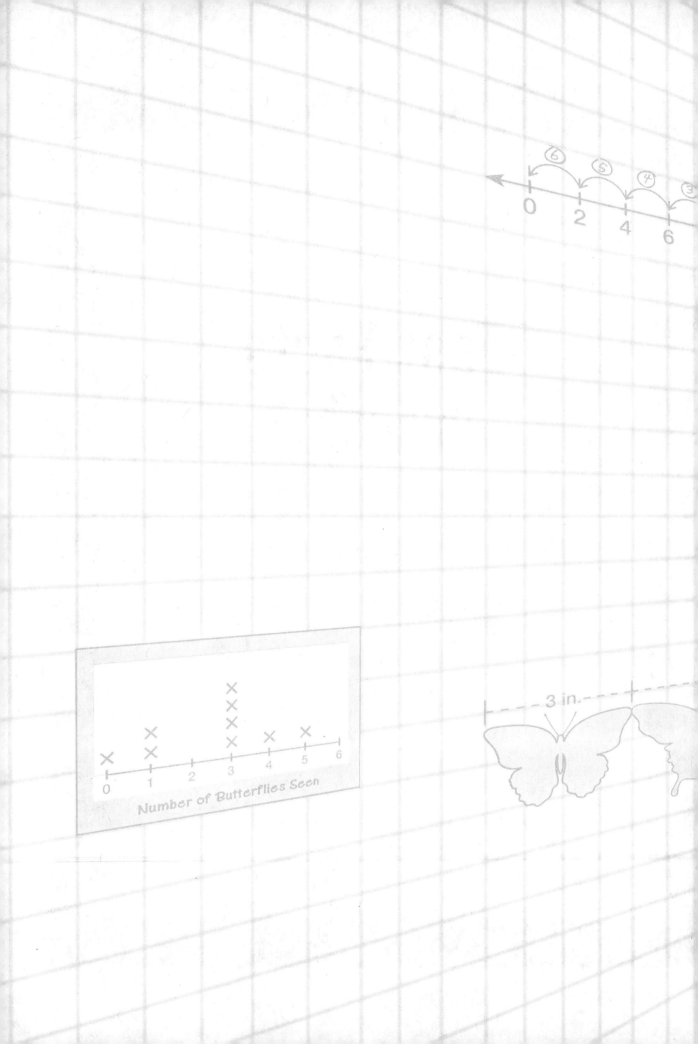

0   2   4   6

Number of Butterflies Seen
0   1   2   3   4   5   6

3 in.

Name _____

# FAST FACTS PRACTICE

**Add as fast as you can.**

**1.** $0 + 8 =$ _____   $4 + 5 =$ _____   $1 + 6 =$ _____   $9 + 2 =$ _____

**2.** $6 + 4 =$ _____   $6 + 6 =$ _____   $1 + 9 =$ _____   $3 + 6 =$ _____

**3.** $7 + 2 =$ _____   $5 + 3 =$ _____   $9 + 3 =$ _____   $3 + 8 =$ _____

**4.** $5 + 6 =$ _____   $4 + 4 =$ _____   $7 + 3 =$ _____   $5 + 7 =$ _____

**5.** $5 + 5 =$ _____   $7 + 4 =$ _____   $3 + 4 =$ _____   $2 + 8 =$ _____

**6.** $8 + 4 =$ _____   $2 + 9 =$ _____   $6 + 3 =$ _____   $3 + 7 =$ _____

**7.** $2 + 5 =$ _____   $4 + 7 =$ _____   $4 + 8 =$ _____   $6 + 5 =$ _____

**8.** $3 + 9 =$ _____   $8 + 3 =$ _____   $7 + 5 =$ _____   $4 + 6 =$ _____

Name _____

# FAST FACTS PRACTICE

**Subtract as fast as you can.**

1.  10 − 4 = _____     9 − 6 = _____     12 − 6 = _____     11 − 7 = _____

2.  7 − 1 = _____     11 − 9 = _____     9 − 5 = _____     10 − 6 = _____

3.  9 − 3 = _____     8 − 4 = _____     11 − 6 = _____     12 − 7 = _____

4.  10 − 5 = _____     12 − 3 = _____     11 − 5 = _____     10 − 7 = _____

5.  9 − 1 = _____     8 − 0 = _____     12 − 8 = _____     11 − 3 = _____

6.  12 − 5 = _____     7 − 3 = _____     11 − 4 = _____     9 − 2 = _____

7.  10 − 3 = _____     11 − 8 = _____     12 − 4 = _____     7 − 5 = _____

8.  11 − 2 = _____     9 − 7 = _____     10 − 8 = _____     12 − 9 = _____

Name _____

# FAST FACTS PRACTICE

## Add as fast as you can.

**1.** 5 + 9 = ____    7 + 7 = ____    4 + 8 = ____    9 + 5 = ____

**2.** 6 + 7 = ____    9 + 3 = ____    9 + 8 = ____    4 + 9 = ____

**3.** 8 + 9 = ____    6 + 6 = ____    9 + 4 = ____    6 + 8 = ____

**4.** 7 + 5 = ____    8 + 7 = ____    7 + 9 = ____    5 + 6 = ____

**5.** 8 + 6 = ____    9 + 7 = ____    8 + 4 = ____    5 + 8 = ____

**6.** 5 + 7 = ____    6 + 9 = ____    8 + 3 = ____    7 + 8 = ____

**7.** 8 + 5 = ____    9 + 9 = ____    7 + 4 = ____    2 + 9 = ____

**8.** 9 + 6 = ____    7 + 6 = ____    8 + 8 = ____    3 + 9 = ____

Name _____

# FAST FACTS PRACTICE

**Subtract as fast as you can.**

**1.** 16 − 9 = _____   13 − 4 = _____   15 − 9 = _____   14 − 9 = _____

**2.** 18 − 9 = _____   16 − 8 = _____   17 − 9 = _____   14 − 7 = _____

**3.** 17 − 8 = _____   14 − 6 = _____   13 − 9 = _____   13 − 5 = _____

**4.** 14 − 5 = _____   12 − 8 = _____   16 − 7 = _____   12 − 9 = _____

**5.** 12 − 6 = _____   13 − 6 = _____   11 − 3 = _____   15 − 7 = _____

**6.** 12 − 3 = _____   11 − 5 = _____   15 − 8 = _____   12 − 7 = _____

**7.** 13 − 8 = _____   11 − 7 = _____   14 − 8 = _____   11 − 8 = _____

**8.** 12 − 5 = _____   13 − 7 = _____   15 − 6 = _____   12 − 4 = _____

Name _____

# FAST FACTS PRACTICE

**Multiply as fast as you can.**

**1.** $3 \times 5 =$ _____     $2 \times 4 =$ _____     $4 \times 3 =$ _____     $0 \times 10 =$ _____

**2.** $3 \times 4 =$ _____     $8 \times 4 =$ _____     $9 \times 10 =$ _____     $6 \times 3 =$ _____

**3.** $7 \times 2 =$ _____     $6 \times 5 =$ _____     $6 \times 2 =$ _____     $9 \times 4 =$ _____

**4.** $1 \times 5 =$ _____     $7 \times 3 =$ _____     $9 \times 5 =$ _____     $8 \times 5 =$ _____

**5.** $9 \times 3 =$ _____     $8 \times 10 =$ _____     $7 \times 1 =$ _____     $5 \times 5 =$ _____

**6.** $6 \times 4 =$ _____     $7 \times 5 =$ _____     $4 \times 4 =$ _____     $10 \times 3 =$ _____

**7.** $9 \times 2 =$ _____     $8 \times 3 =$ _____     $2 \times 10 =$ _____     $7 \times 4 =$ _____

**8.** $3 \times 3 =$ _____     $4 \times 5 =$ _____     $8 \times 2 =$ _____     $6 \times 0 =$ _____

Name _____

# FAST FACTS PRACTICE

**Multiply as fast as you can.**

**1.** $10 \times 8 =$ _____     $10 \times 7 =$ _____     $4 \times 9 =$ _____     $8 \times 9 =$ _____

**2.** $3 \times 8 =$ _____     $3 \times 9 =$ _____     $5 \times 6 =$ _____     $9 \times 7 =$ _____

**3.** $5 \times 9 =$ _____     $2 \times 6 =$ _____     $2 \times 7 =$ _____     $6 \times 8 =$ _____

**4.** $7 \times 9 =$ _____     $3 \times 7 =$ _____     $8 \times 8 =$ _____     $7 \times 7 =$ _____

**5.** $7 \times 6 =$ _____     $6 \times 9 =$ _____     $6 \times 6 =$ _____     $4 \times 7 =$ _____

**6.** $4 \times 6 =$ _____     $5 \times 7 =$ _____     $4 \times 8 =$ _____     $9 \times 8 =$ _____

**7.** $5 \times 8 =$ _____     $9 \times 6 =$ _____     $7 \times 8 =$ _____     $6 \times 7 =$ _____

**8.** $9 \times 9 =$ _____     $8 \times 7 =$ _____     $3 \times 6 =$ _____     $8 \times 6 =$ _____

Name _____

# FAST FACTS PRACTICE

**Multiply as fast as you can.**

**1.** $6 \times 5 =$ _____     $7 \times 7 =$ _____     $4 \times 6 =$ _____     $8 \times 3 =$ _____

**2.** $9 \times 9 =$ _____     $7 \times 6 =$ _____     $5 \times 8 =$ _____     $10 \times 0 =$ _____

**3.** $6 \times 6 =$ _____     $3 \times 7 =$ _____     $8 \times 9 =$ _____     $5 \times 5 =$ _____

**4.** $3 \times 9 =$ _____     $9 \times 6 =$ _____     $8 \times 1 =$ _____     $7 \times 4 =$ _____

**5.** $8 \times 7 =$ _____     $4 \times 4 =$ _____     $8 \times 6 =$ _____     $9 \times 4 =$ _____

**6.** $3 \times 6 =$ _____     $8 \times 4 =$ _____     $6 \times 7 =$ _____     $5 \times 3 =$ _____

**7.** $9 \times 5 =$ _____     $8 \times 8 =$ _____     $7 \times 9 =$ _____     $10 \times 10 =$ _____

**8.** $6 \times 2 =$ _____     $7 \times 8 =$ _____     $9 \times 7 =$ _____     $7 \times 5 =$ _____

Name _____

# FAST FACTS PRACTICE

**Divide as fast as you can.**

1. $15 \div 3 =$ _____    $8 \div 2 =$ _____    $12 \div 4 =$ _____    $7 \div 1 =$ _____

2. $20 \div 5 =$ _____    $32 \div 4 =$ _____    $3 \div 1 =$ _____    $18 \div 3 =$ _____

3. $14 \div 2 =$ _____    $4 \div 1 =$ _____    $18 \div 2 =$ _____    $36 \div 4 =$ _____

4. $5 \div 5 =$ _____    $21 \div 3 =$ _____    $45 \div 5 =$ _____    $6 \div 3 =$ _____

5. $27 \div 3 =$ _____    $10 \div 2 =$ _____    $8 \div 4 =$ _____    $25 \div 5 =$ _____

6. $24 \div 4 =$ _____    $35 \div 5 =$ _____    $16 \div 4 =$ _____    $16 \div 2 =$ _____

7. $40 \div 5 =$ _____    $24 \div 3 =$ _____    $0 \div 2 =$ _____    $20 \div 4 =$ _____

8. $9 \div 3 =$ _____    $28 \div 4 =$ _____    $30 \div 5 =$ _____    $9 \div 1 =$ _____

Name _____

# FAST FACTS PRACTICE

**Divide as fast as you can.**

**1.** 24 ÷ 6 = _____     40 ÷ 10 = _____     48 ÷ 8 = _____     18 ÷ 3 = _____

**2.** 36 ÷ 6 = _____     32 ÷ 8 = _____     90 ÷ 10 = _____     24 ÷ 8 = _____

**3.** 21 ÷ 7 = _____     30 ÷ 6 = _____     49 ÷ 7 = _____     36 ÷ 9 = _____

**4.** 10 ÷ 10 = _____     40 ÷ 8 = _____     45 ÷ 9 = _____     42 ÷ 7 = _____

**5.** 27 ÷ 9 = _____     80 ÷ 8 = _____     56 ÷ 7 = _____     60 ÷ 10 = _____

**6.** 12 ÷ 6 = _____     35 ÷ 7 = _____     16 ÷ 8 = _____     72 ÷ 9 = _____

**7.** 70 ÷ 10 = _____     54 ÷ 6 = _____     20 ÷ 10 = _____     28 ÷ 7 = _____

**8.** 48 ÷ 6 = _____     63 ÷ 9 = _____     56 ÷ 8 = _____     81 ÷ 9 = _____

Name _____

# FAST FACTS PRACTICE

**Divide as fast as you can.**

**1.** 8 ÷ 1 = ____     40 ÷ 5 = ____     48 ÷ 8 = ____     21 ÷ 3 = ____

**2.** 36 ÷ 6 = ____     32 ÷ 4 = ____     18 ÷ 2 = ____     36 ÷ 9 = ____

**3.** 21 ÷ 7 = ____     30 ÷ 6 = ____     70 ÷ 10 = ____     24 ÷ 3 = ____

**4.** 50 ÷ 10 = ____     20 ÷ 5 = ____     45 ÷ 9 = ____     8 ÷ 2 = ____

**5.** 27 ÷ 9 = ____     80 ÷ 8 = ____     40 ÷ 4 = ____     24 ÷ 6 = ____

**6.** 90 ÷ 10 = ____     35 ÷ 5 = ____     16 ÷ 2 = ____     72 ÷ 8 = ____

**7.** 49 ÷ 7 = ____     54 ÷ 9 = ____     12 ÷ 4 = ____     28 ÷ 7 = ____

**8.** 48 ÷ 6 = ____     27 ÷ 3 = ____     56 ÷ 8 = ____     63 ÷ 7 = ____

Name _____

# FAST FACTS PRACTICE
..................................................

**Multiply and divide as fast as you can.**

**1.** $3 \times 5 =$ _____     $5 \times 7 =$ _____     $6 \times 3 =$ _____     $0 \times 10 =$ _____

**2.** $2 \times 7 =$ _____     $4 \times 8 =$ _____     $10 \times 9 =$ _____     $8 \times 9 =$ _____

**3.** $5 \times 5 =$ _____     $9 \times 9 =$ _____     $7 \times 9 =$ _____     $2 \times 10 =$ _____

**4.** $1 \times 6 =$ _____     $3 \times 8 =$ _____     $9 \times 5 =$ _____     $6 \times 7 =$ _____

**5.** $15 \div 3 =$ _____     $10 \div 1 =$ _____     $24 \div 4 =$ _____     $72 \div 8 =$ _____

**6.** $35 \div 5 =$ _____     $40 \div 10 =$ _____     $42 \div 6 =$ _____     $27 \div 3 =$ _____

**7.** $18 \div 2 =$ _____     $5 \div 5 =$ _____     $54 \div 9 =$ _____     $49 \div 7 =$ _____

**8.** $0 \div 4 =$ _____     $21 \div 7 =$ _____     $56 \div 8 =$ _____     $60 \div 10 =$ _____

Name _____

# FAST FACTS PRACTICE
..............................................................

**Multiply and divide as fast as you can.**

**1.** $3 \times 7 =$ _____     $4 \times 8 =$ _____     $6 \times 10 =$ _____     $10 \times 10 =$ _____

**2.** $3 \times 9 =$ _____     $1 \times 9 =$ _____     $9 \times 7 =$ _____     $8 \times 8 =$ _____

**3.** $7 \times 6 =$ _____     $8 \times 7 =$ _____     $2 \times 8 =$ _____     $5 \times 6 =$ _____

**4.** $10 \times 8 =$ _____     $4 \times 4 =$ _____     $6 \times 9 =$ _____     $9 \times 4 =$ _____

**5.** $0 \div 7 =$ _____     $81 \div 9 =$ _____     $72 \div 8 =$ _____     $6 \div 6 =$ _____

**6.** $35 \div 7 =$ _____     $12 \div 3 =$ _____     $48 \div 6 =$ _____     $25 \div 5 =$ _____

**7.** $56 \div 8 =$ _____     $70 \div 10 =$ _____     $45 \div 5 =$ _____     $24 \div 3 =$ _____

**8.** $32 \div 4 =$ _____     $10 \div 2 =$ _____     $90 \div 10 =$ _____     $54 \div 9 =$ _____

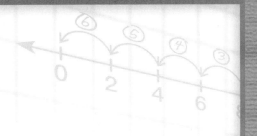

# Just the Facts
# Worksheets

Number of Butterflies Seen

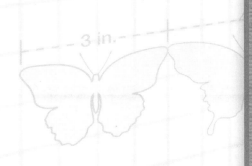

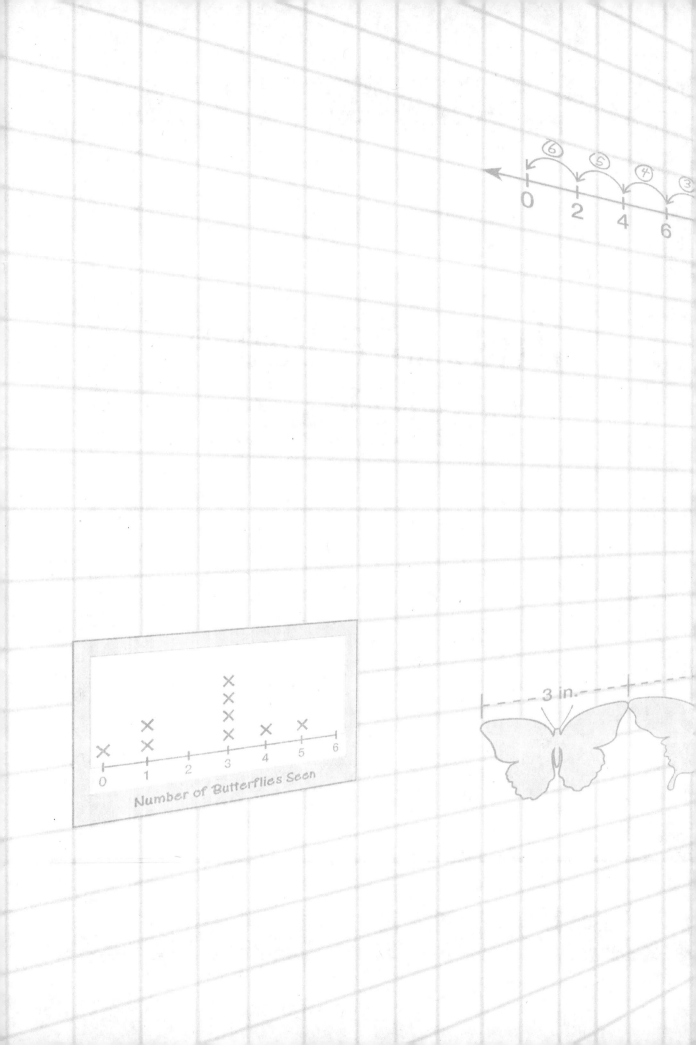

Number of Butterflies Seen

3 in.

Name_____  Date _____

# 1A BASIC FACTS

## Addition and Subtraction Facts

**Add.**

| | | | | |
|---|---|---|---|---|
| **1.** $\begin{array}{r} 2 \\ +\ 4 \\ \hline \end{array}$ | **2.** $\begin{array}{r} 3 \\ +\ 5 \\ \hline \end{array}$ | **3.** $\begin{array}{r} 8 \\ +\ 1 \\ \hline \end{array}$ | **4.** $\begin{array}{r} 3 \\ +\ 4 \\ \hline \end{array}$ | **5.** $\begin{array}{r} 7 \\ +\ 2 \\ \hline \end{array}$ |
| **6.** $\begin{array}{r} 1 \\ +\ 0 \\ \hline \end{array}$ | **7.** $\begin{array}{r} 2 \\ +\ 6 \\ \hline \end{array}$ | **8.** $\begin{array}{r} 2 \\ +\ 8 \\ \hline \end{array}$ | **9.** $\begin{array}{r} 7 \\ +\ 1 \\ \hline \end{array}$ | **10.** $\begin{array}{r} 0 \\ +\ 6 \\ \hline \end{array}$ |

**Add or subtract. Find a pattern. Write the next number sentence.**

**11.** 1 + 6 = _____

2 + 6 = _____

3 + 6 = _____

_____ + _____ = _____

**12.** 3 + 3 = _____

4 + 3 = _____

5 + 3 = _____

_____ + _____ = _____

**13.** 7 − 2 = _____

8 − 2 = _____

9 − 2 = _____

_____ − _____ = _____

**14.** 9 − 5 = _____

9 − 6 = _____

9 − 7 = _____

_____ − _____ = _____

**Grade 3, Just the Facts**

Name_____     Date _____

# 1B BASIC FACTS

## Addition and Subtraction Facts

**Find the greater number. Count on to add.**

**1.** 6 + 1 = _____        **2.** 3 + 4 = _____        **3.** 5 + 2 = _____

**4.** 3 + 7 = _____        **5.** 6 + 2 = _____        **6.** 1 + 8 = _____

**7.** 2 + 9 = _____        **8.** 3 + 5 = _____        **9.** 4 + 2 = _____

## Find the difference.

| **10.** 5<br>− 3 | **11.** 7<br>− 4 | **12.** 8<br>− 6 | **13.** 10<br>− 7 | **14.** 4<br>− 0 |
|---|---|---|---|---|
| **15.** 6<br>− 5 | **16.** 4<br>− 2 | **17.** 9<br>− 6 | **18.** 6<br>− 4 | **19.** 7<br>− 6 |
| **20.** 5<br>− 2 | **21.** 6<br>− 3 | **22.** 8<br>− 5 | **23.** 7<br>− 3 | **24.** 6<br>− 0 |
| **25.** 9<br>− 3 | **26.** 8<br>− 2 | **27.** 9<br>− 5 | **28.** 4<br>− 3 | **29.** 7<br>− 5 |

**Grade 3, Just the Facts**

Name_____  Date _____

# 2A BASIC FACTS

## Doubles, Near Doubles Addition and Subtraction Facts

**Write a double that helps. Add.**

**1.** 6
 + 5  + _____

**2.** 8
 + 9  + _____

**3.** 7
 + 6  + _____

**4.** 6
 + 5  + _____

**5.** 8
 + 9  + _____

**6.** 7
 + 6  + _____

**Find the difference.**

**7.** 5
 − 3

**8.** 7
 − 4

**9.** 8
 − 6

**10.** 10
 − 5

**11.** 4
 − 0

**12.** 16
 − 8

**13.** 4
 − 2

**14.** 12
 − 6

**15.** 8
 − 4

**16.** 7
 − 6

**Look for doubles first. Then add.**

**17.** $2 + 3 + 4 =$ _____

**18.** $3 + 3 + 5 =$ _____

**19.** $4 + 5 + 5 =$ _____

**20.** $2 + 7 + 3 =$ _____

Name_____ Date _____

## 2B BASIC FACTS

### Doubles, Near Doubles Addition and Subtraction Facts

**Add.**

| | | | | |
|---|---|---|---|---|
| **1.**  4<br>+ 4 | **2.**  7<br>+ 6 | **3.**  2<br>+ 8 | **4.**  6<br>+ 3 | **5.**  4<br>+ 5 |
| **6.**  9<br>+ 9 | **7.**  5<br>+ 5 | **8.**  3<br>+ 3 | **9.**  5<br>+ 6 | **10.**  8<br>+ 7 |
| **11.**  8<br>+ 8 | **12.**  1<br>+ 2 | **13.**  6<br>+ 6 | **14.**  7<br>+ 7 | **15.**  3<br>+ 7 |

## Draw a line to match. Subtract.

**16.** $16 - 8 =$ _____     **A.**  18<br>              $- 9$

**17.** $9 - 5 =$ _____     **B.**  16<br>              $- 8$

**18.** $18 - 9 =$ _____     **C.**  9<br>              $- 5$

Name_____ Date _____

## 3A ▶ BASIC FACTS

### Using Ten to Add and Subtract

**Add. Make a ten to help.**

**1.** $9 + 5 = $ _____     **2.** $4 + 7 = $ _____     **3.** $5 + 8 = $ _____

**4.** $6 + 8 = $ _____     **5.** $4 + 9 = $ _____     **6.** $7 + 9 = $ _____

**7.** $8 + 9 = $ _____     **8.** $4 + 8 = $ _____     **9.** $9 + 6 = $ _____

## Subtract.

**10.** $\begin{array}{r} 10 \\ -\ 3 \\ \hline \end{array}$   **11.** $\begin{array}{r} 6 \\ -\ 4 \\ \hline \end{array}$   **12.** $\begin{array}{r} 7 \\ -\ 5 \\ \hline \end{array}$   **13.** $\begin{array}{r} 9 \\ -\ 6 \\ \hline \end{array}$   **14.** $\begin{array}{r} 8 \\ -\ 3 \\ \hline \end{array}$

**15.** $\begin{array}{r} 6 \\ -\ 2 \\ \hline \end{array}$   **16.** $\begin{array}{r} 10 \\ -\ 2 \\ \hline \end{array}$   **17.** $\begin{array}{r} 11 \\ -\ 1 \\ \hline \end{array}$   **18.** $\begin{array}{r} 10 \\ -\ 8 \\ \hline \end{array}$   **19.** $\begin{array}{r} 11 \\ -\ 9 \\ \hline \end{array}$

**20.** $\begin{array}{r} 8 \\ -\ 5 \\ \hline \end{array}$   **21.** $\begin{array}{r} 7 \\ -\ 4 \\ \hline \end{array}$   **22.** $\begin{array}{r} 7 \\ -\ 6 \\ \hline \end{array}$   **23.** $\begin{array}{r} 8 \\ -\ 2 \\ \hline \end{array}$   **24.** $\begin{array}{r} 9 \\ -\ 7 \\ \hline \end{array}$

**25.** $\begin{array}{r} 11 \\ -\ 3 \\ \hline \end{array}$   **26.** $\begin{array}{r} 10 \\ -\ 7 \\ \hline \end{array}$   **27.** $\begin{array}{r} 8 \\ -\ 6 \\ \hline \end{array}$   **28.** $\begin{array}{r} 10 \\ -\ 4 \\ \hline \end{array}$   **29.** $\begin{array}{r} 8 \\ -\ 4 \\ \hline \end{array}$

Name_____  Date _____

# ◣3B ▶ BASIC FACTS

## Using Ten to Add and Subtract

### Subtract. Make a ten to help.

**1.** $13 - 8 =$ _____  **2.** $15 - 9 =$ _____  **3.** $16 - 8 =$ _____

**4.** $12 - 9 =$ _____  **5.** $14 - 8 =$ _____  **6.** $17 - 8 =$ _____

### Add or subtract.

**7.** $9 + 6 =$ _____  **8.** $16 - 8 =$ _____  **9.** $4 + 9 =$ _____

**10.** $18 - 9 =$ _____  **11.** $13 - 5 =$ _____  **12.** $7 + 7 =$ _____

**13.** $11 - 6 =$ _____  **14.** $14 - 8 =$ _____  **15.** $7 + 8 =$ _____

**16.** $12 - 7 =$ _____  **17.** $6 + 6 =$ _____  **18.** $10 - 6 =$ _____

**19.** $17 - 9 =$ _____  **20.** $9 + 7 =$ _____  **21.** $13 - 8 =$ _____

**22.** $15 - 8 =$ _____  **23.** $5 + 6 =$ _____  **24.** $7 + 9 =$ _____

### Find the missing number.

**25.** $12 -$ _____ $= 3$  **26.** $14 -$ _____ $= 7$  **27.** $11 -$ _____ $= 9$

**28.** $16 -$ _____ $= 7$  **29.** $13 -$ _____ $= 5$  **30.** $12 -$ _____ $= 7$

Name_____ Date _____

# BASIC FACTS
......................................................................................................

## Naming and Using Arrays in Multiplication

**Write one addition sentence and one multiplication sentence to describe each array.**

1. • • • • •
   • • • • •
   • • • • •

   _____ = _____

   _____ = _____

2. • • • • • •
   • • • • • •

   _____ = _____

   _____ = _____

## Solve.

**3.** $2 + 2 =$ _____

   $2 \times 2 =$ _____

**4.** $2 + 2 + 2 =$ _____

   $3 \times 2 =$ _____

**5.** $2 + 2 + 2 + 2 =$ _____

   $4 \times 2 =$ _____

**6.** $2 + 2 + 2 + 2 + 2 =$ _____

   $5 \times 2 =$ _____

**7.** $9 \times 2 =$ _____

**8.** $8 \times 2 =$ _____

**Draw counters to show the array. Then write the product.**

9. 

   $2 \times 7 =$ _____

10. 

   $6 \times 2 =$ _____

11. 

   $4 \times 2 =$ _____

Name_____  Date _____

## ◣4B BASIC FACTS
### Naming and Using Arrays in Multiplication

**Draw counters to show the array. Then find the product.**

1.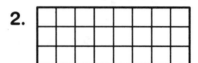
   3 × 6 = _____

2. 3 × 8 = _____

3. 3 × 5 = _____

**Multiply. Think of doubles or the order property.**

4. 2 × 7 = _____      5. 6 × 2 = _____      6. 2 × 9 = _____

7. 4 × 2 = _____      8. 2 × 8 = _____      9. 2 × 5 = _____

10. 2 × 3 = _____     11. 9 × 2 = _____     12. 2 × 2 = _____

13. 5 × 3 = _____     14. 4 × 3 = _____     15. 3 × 7 = _____

**Use estimation. Write < or >.**

16. 4 × 3 = 12, so 3 × 3 _____ 12      17. 7 × 2 = 14, so 7 × 3 _____ 14

18. 3 × 2 = 6, so 4 × 2 _____ 6        19. 8 × 3 = 24, so 9 × 3 _____ 24

20. 3 × 3 = 9, so 4 × 3 _____ 9        21. 6 × 3 = 18, so 7 × 3 _____ 18

Name_____  Date _____

 **BASIC FACTS**
................................................................................

## Multiplying by 1 and 2

**Multiply.**

| | | | | |
|---|---|---|---|---|
| **1.** 1<br>$\times$ 2 | **2.** 2<br>$\times$ 3 | **3.** 4<br>$\times$ 1 | **4.** 1<br>$\times$ 7 | **5.** 6<br>$\times$ 2 |
| **6.** 1<br>$\times$ 1 | **7.** 7<br>$\times$ 1 | **8.** 9<br>$\times$ 2 | **9.** 1<br>$\times$ 8 | **10.** 1<br>$\times$ 5 |
| **11.** 4<br>$\times$ 2 | **12.** 1<br>$\times$ 6 | **13.** 2<br>$\times$ 2 | **14.** 1<br>$\times$ 4 | **15.** 1<br>$\times$ 3 |
| **16.** 2<br>$\times$ 5 | **17.** 2<br>$\times$ 7 | **18.** 6<br>$\times$ 1 | **19.** 2<br>$\times$ 4 | **20.** 1<br>$\times$ 9 |

## Use mental math. Write just the answer.

**21.** $5 \times 1 \times 2 = $ _____      **22.** $7 \times 0 \times 2 = $ _____

**23.** $1 \times 2 \times 8 = $ _____      **24.** $3 \times 2 \times 1 = $ _____

**25.** $4 \times 2 \times 1 = $ _____      **26.** $2 \times 2 \times 1 = $ _____

Name_____ Date _____

## 5B ◢ BASIC FACTS

### Multiplying by 1 and 2

**Multiply. Think of doubles.**

**1.** $2 \times 3 = $ _____     **2.** $2 \times 5 = $ _____     **3.** $2 \times 4 = $ _____

**4.** $2 \times 9 = $ _____     **5.** $2 \times 2 = $ _____     **6.** $2 \times 8 = $ _____

**Multiply.**

**7.** $1 \times 4 = $ _____     **8.** $1 \times 8 = $ _____     **9.** $6 \times 2 = $ _____

**10.** $9 \times 1 = $ _____     **11.** $1 \times 3 = $ _____     **12.** $2 \times 2 = $ _____

**13.** $1 \times 5 = $ _____     **14.** $7 \times 2 = $ _____     **15.** $2 \times 9 = $ _____

| | | | | |
|---|---|---|---|---|
| **16.** $\begin{array}{r} 1 \\ \times 2 \\ \hline \end{array}$ | **17.** $\begin{array}{r} 7 \\ \times 1 \\ \hline \end{array}$ | **18.** $\begin{array}{r} 5 \\ \times 2 \\ \hline \end{array}$ | **19.** $\begin{array}{r} 1 \\ \times 9 \\ \hline \end{array}$ | **20.** $\begin{array}{r} 2 \\ \times 1 \\ \hline \end{array}$ |
| **21.** $\begin{array}{r} 1 \\ \times 1 \\ \hline \end{array}$ | **22.** $\begin{array}{r} 1 \\ \times 6 \\ \hline \end{array}$ | **23.** $\begin{array}{r} 8 \\ \times 2 \\ \hline \end{array}$ | **24.** $\begin{array}{r} 1 \\ \times 4 \\ \hline \end{array}$ | **25.** $\begin{array}{r} 2 \\ \times 6 \\ \hline \end{array}$ |
| **26.** $\begin{array}{r} 8 \\ \times 1 \\ \hline \end{array}$ | **27.** $\begin{array}{r} 1 \\ \times 3 \\ \hline \end{array}$ | **28.** $\begin{array}{r} 3 \\ \times 2 \\ \hline \end{array}$ | **29.** $\begin{array}{r} 2 \\ \times 7 \\ \hline \end{array}$ | **30.** $\begin{array}{r} 4 \\ \times 2 \\ \hline \end{array}$ |

Name_____ Date _____

## 6A ▸ BASIC FACTS

### Multiplying by 4

Write one addition sentence and one
multiplication sentence to describe each array.

1. • • • •
 • • • •

2. • • •
 • • •
 • • •
 • • •

_____ = _____

_____ = _____

_____ = _____

_____ = _____

## Multiply.

**3.** $4 \times 3 =$ _____      **4.** $4 \times 8 =$ _____      **5.** $7 \times 4 =$ _____

**6.** $5 \times 4 =$ _____      **7.** $4 \times 2 =$ _____      **8.** $4 \times 4 =$ _____

**9.**  $\begin{array}{r} 4 \\ \times 7 \\ \hline \end{array}$    **10.**  $\begin{array}{r} 4 \\ \times 4 \\ \hline \end{array}$    **11.**  $\begin{array}{r} 4 \\ \times 3 \\ \hline \end{array}$    **12.**  $\begin{array}{r} 9 \\ \times 4 \\ \hline \end{array}$    **13.**  $\begin{array}{r} 5 \\ \times 4 \\ \hline \end{array}$

**14.**  $\begin{array}{r} 4 \\ \times 6 \\ \hline \end{array}$    **15.**  $\begin{array}{r} 3 \\ \times 4 \\ \hline \end{array}$    **16.**  $\begin{array}{r} 7 \\ \times 4 \\ \hline \end{array}$    **17.**  $\begin{array}{r} 4 \\ \times 8 \\ \hline \end{array}$    **18.**  $\begin{array}{r} 2 \\ \times 4 \\ \hline \end{array}$

Name_____ Date _____

**BASIC FACTS**

## Multiplying by 4

**Multiply. Think of doubles or the order property.**

**1.** $2 \times 7 = $ _____

**2.** $6 \times 2 = $ _____

**3.** $2 \times 9 = $ _____

**4.** $4 \times 2 = $ _____

**5.** $2 \times 8 = $ _____

**6.** $2 \times 5 = $ _____

**7.** $2 \times 3 = $ _____

**8.** $9 \times 2 = $ _____

**9.** $2 \times 2 = $ _____

## Multiply.

**10.** $4 \times 3 = $ _____

**11.** $4 \times 8 = $ _____

**12.** $7 \times 4 = $ _____

**13.** $5 \times 4 = $ _____

**14.** $4 \times 2 = $ _____

**15.** $4 \times 4 = $ _____

**16.** $9 \times 4 = $ _____

**17.** $4 \times 6 = $ _____

**18.** $8 \times 4 = $ _____

**19.** $1 \times 4 = $ _____

**20.** $2 \times 4 = $ _____

**21.** $6 \times 4 = $ _____

**22.** $4 \times 7 = $ _____

**23.** $4 \times 1 = $ _____

**24.** $4 \times 9 = $ _____

**25.** $3 \times 4 = $ _____

**26.** $4 \times 5 = $ _____

**27.** $4 \times 6 = $ _____

**28.** $4 \times 8 = $ _____

**29.** $4 \times 2 = $ _____

**30.** $7 \times 4 = $ _____

Name_____  Date _____

 **BASIC FACTS**
.......................................................................................

## Multiplying by 3

**Multiply.**

| 1.  2 | 2.  5 | 3.  6 | 4.  4 |
|---|---|---|---|
| × 3 | × 3 | × 3 | × 3 |

| 5.  9 | 6.  8 | 7.  7 | 8.  3 |
|---|---|---|---|
| × 3 | × 3 | × 3 | × 3 |

| 9.  3 | 10.  3 | 11.  3 | 12.  3 |
|---|---|---|---|
| × 9 | × 5 | × 6 | × 2 |

## Think of multiplication facts. Complete the tables.

| | x | 2 |
|---|---|---|
| 13. | 6 | 12 |
| 14. | 7 | |
| 15. | 3 | |
| 16. | 4 | |
| 17. | 5 | |

| | x | 3 |
|---|---|---|
| 18. | | 27 |
| 19. | 6 | |
| 20. | | 12 |
| 21. | | 24 |
| 22. | | 15 |

Name_____ Date _____

## 7B BASIC FACTS

### Multiplying by 3

**Match.**

1. $3 \times 4 = $ _____
2. $3 \times 5 = $ _____
3. $3 \times 6 = $ _____
4. $7 \times 3 = $ _____
5. $3 \times 2 = $ _____
6. $3 \times 3 = $ _____
7. $3 \times 1 = $ _____

a. $9 \times 1$
b. $9 \times 2$
c. $6 \times 2$
d. $5 \times 3$
e. $1 \times 3$
f. $3 \times 7$
g. $6 \times 1$

**Write pairs of factors for each product.**

8. _____ $\times$ _____ $= 4$

9. _____ $\times$ _____ $= 8$

10. _____ $\times$ _____ $= 3$

11. _____ $\times$ _____ $= 5$

12. _____ $\times$ _____ $= 6$

13. _____ $\times$ _____ $= 10$

14. _____ $\times$ _____ $= 7$

15. _____ $\times$ _____ $= 9$

16. _____ $\times$ _____ $= 12$

17. _____ $\times$ _____ $= 15$

Name_____  Date _____

## 8A BASIC FACTS

### Multiplying by 6

**Multiply.**

| | | | | |
|---|---|---|---|---|
| **1.** $3 \times 6$ | **2.** $5 \times 6$ | **3.** $6 \times 2$ | **4.** $4 \times 6$ | **5.** $0 \times 6$ |

| | | | | |
|---|---|---|---|---|
| **6.** $1 \times 6$ | **7.** $6 \times 4$ | **8.** $9 \times 6$ | **9.** $8 \times 6$ | **10.** $6 \times 2$ |

**Compare. Write <, >, or =.**

**11.** $5 \times 6$ _____ $3 \times 6$      **12.** $4 \times 3$ _____ $2 \times 6$

**13.** $3 \times 3$ _____ $6 \times 2$      **14.** $3 \times 2$ _____ $6 \times 1$

**Multiply.**

**15.** $6 \times 3 =$ _____      **16.** $6 \times 0 =$ _____      **17.** $9 \times 6 =$ _____

**18.** $5 \times 6 =$ _____      **19.** $6 \times 1 =$ _____      **20.** $7 \times 6 =$ _____

**21.** $2 \times 6 =$ _____      **22.** $6 \times 4 =$ _____      **23.** $6 \times 6 =$ _____

**24.** $6 \times 8 =$ _____      **25.** $3 \times 6 =$ _____      **26.** $6 \times 5 =$ _____

Name_____ Date _____

## 8B ▶ BASIC FACTS

### Multiplying by 6

**Draw an array for each multiplication sentence.
Find the product.**

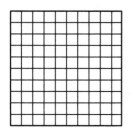    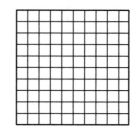

**1.** $6 \times 3 =$ _____        **2.** $2 \times 6 =$ _____

## Multiply.

| | | | | |
|---|---|---|---|---|
| **3.**  6<br>$\times\,6$ | **4.**  6<br>$\times\,4$ | **5.**  9<br>$\times\,6$ | **6.**  3<br>$\times\,6$ | **7.**  6<br>$\times\,2$ |
| **8.**  7<br>$\times\,6$ | **9.**  8<br>$\times\,6$ | **10.**  4<br>$\times\,6$ | **11.**  0<br>$\times\,6$ | **12.**  6<br>$\times\,8$ |
| **13.**  2<br>$\times\,9$ | **14.**  5<br>$\times\,6$ | **15.**  8<br>$\times\,3$ | **16.**  6<br>$\times\,1$ | **17.**  3<br>$\times\,2$ |

Name_____ Date _____

# 9A BASIC FACTS

## Multiplying by 5

**Multiply.**

| 1. | 3<br>× 5 | 2. | 5<br>× 6 | 3. | 7<br>× 5 | 4. | 2<br>× 5 | 5. | 5<br>× 8 |

| 6. | 5<br>× 4 | 7. | 9<br>× 5 | 8. | 6<br>× 5 | 9. | 8<br>× 5 | 10. | 5<br>× 9 |

**Compare. Write < or >.**

11. $5 \times 6$ _____ $3 \times 6$      12. $5 \times 7$ _____ $9 \times 5$

13. $5 \times 8$ _____ $5 + 8$      14. $5 \times 9$ _____ $4 \times 8$

**Complete the multiplication table.**

|     | x | 6 |
|-----|---|---|
| 15. | 6 |   |
| 16. | 2 |   |
| 17. | 8 |   |
| 18. | 7 |   |
| 19. | 9 |   |

Name_____  Date _____

# 9B BASIC FACTS

## Multiplying by 5

**Multiply.**

**1.** $5 \times 2 =$ _____      **2.** $3 \times 5 =$ _____      **3.** $4 \times 5 =$ _____

$2 \times 5 =$ _____         $5 \times 3 =$ _____         $5 \times 4 =$ _____

**Find the products. Write whether each product is _greater than_, _less than_, or _equal to_ 40.**

**4.** $8 \times 5 =$ _____      _____

**5.** $5 \times 6 =$ _____      _____

**6.** $2 \times 5 =$ _____      _____

**7.** $9 \times 5 =$ _____      _____

**8.** $5 \times 10 =$ _____      _____

**Multiply.**

**9.** $8 \times 5 =$ _____      **10.** $5 \times 3 =$ _____      **11.** $8 \times 2 =$ _____

**12.** $9 \times 5 =$ _____      **13.** $4 \times 5 =$ _____      **14.** $6 \times 5 =$ _____

**15.** $0 \times 5 =$ _____      **16.** $7 \times 5 =$ _____      **17.** $5 \times 2 =$ _____

Name_____ Date _____

 **10A** # BASIC FACTS

·····································································································

## Multiplying by 9

Complete the multiplication table. Use the table
to complete the number sentences.

| x | 9 |
|---|---|
| **1.** 1 | |
| **2.** 2 | |
| **3.** 3 | |
| **4.** 4 | |
| **5.** 5 | |

**6.**    9
    × 2
    ☐

**7.**    4
    × 9
    ☐

**8.**    1
  × ☐
    9

**9.**    ☐
    × 9
    36

## Multiply.

**10.**    9
    × 7

**11.**    9
    × 4

**12.**    9
    × 3

**13.**    9
    × 2

**14.**    4
    × 9

**15.**    8
    × 9

**16.**    5
    × 9

**17.**    9
    × 9

**18.**    3
    × 9

**19.**    2
    × 9

**Grade 3, Just the Facts**

Name_____  Date _____

## 10B  BASIC FACTS

### Multiplying by 9

Complete the chart below, using what you know
about nines facts.

| | | | |
|---|---|---|---|
| **1.** | $1 \times 9$ | = | |
| **2.** | $2 \times 9$ | = | |
| **3.** | $3 \times 9$ | = | |
| **4.** | $4 \times 9$ | = | |
| **5.** | $5 \times 9$ | = | |
| **6.** | $6 \times 9$ | = | |
| **7.** | $7 \times 9$ | = | |
| **8.** | $8 \times 9$ | = | |
| **9.** | $9 \times 9$ | = | |

## Multiply.

**10.**  $9 \times 4$  **11.**  $9 \times 6$  **12.**  $4 \times 5$  **13.**  $7 \times 6$  **14.**  $7 \times 9$

**15.** $9 \times 5 =$ _____   **16.** $9 \times 1 =$ _____   **17.** $0 \times 9 =$ ___

## Fill in the blanks.

**18.** $2 \times$ ___ $= 18$   **19.** $3 \times 9 =$ ___   **20.** $9 \times$ ___ $= 9$

**21.** ___ $\times 9 = 36$   **22.** ___ $\times 9 = 9$   **23.** $9 \times$ ___ $= 45$

Name_____ Date _____

# 11A BASIC FACTS

## Multiplying by 7

**Find the products. Write whether each product is**
*greater than*, *less than*, or *equal to* 30.

**1.** $7 \times 3 =$ _____

**2.** $7 \times 8 =$ _____

**3.** $6 \times 7 =$ _____

**4.** $5 \times 7 =$ _____

## Multiply.

| 5. 3<br>$\times\,7$ | 6. 4<br>$\times\,7$ | 7. 7<br>$\times\,6$ | 8. 5<br>$\times\,7$ | 9. 7<br>$\times\,5$ |
|---|---|---|---|---|

| 10. 8<br>$\times\,7$ | 11. 2<br>$\times\,7$ | 12. 1<br>$\times\,7$ | 13. 0<br>$\times\,7$ | 14. 9<br>$\times\,7$ |
|---|---|---|---|---|

## Use estimation. Write < or >.

**15.** $7 \times 3 = 21$, so $7 \times 4$ ____ 21          **16.** $7 \times 2 = 14$, so $7 \times 1$ ____ 14

**17.** $7 \times 5 = 35$, so $7 \times 4$ ____ 35          **18.** $7 \times 6 = 42$, so $7 \times 7$ ____ 42

Name_____   Date _____

## ◢ 11B BASIC FACTS

## Multiplying by 7

**Multiply.**

| x | 7 |
|---|---|
| **1.** 8 | |
| **2.** 3 | |
| **3.** 9 | |
| **4.** 6 | |
| **5.** 7 | |

**6.** $7 \times 7 =$ _____   **7.** $6 \times 8 =$ _____   **8.** $1 \times 7 =$ _____

**9.** $8 \times 7 =$ _____   **10.** $7 \times 4 =$ _____   **11.** $7 \times 3 =$ _____

**12.** $4 \times 7 =$ _____   **13.** $6 \times 7 =$ _____   **14.** $7 \times 9 =$ _____

**15.** $7 \times 8 =$ _____   **16.** $3 \times 9 =$ _____   **17.** $2 \times 7 =$ _____

**Multiply and add using mental math. Work from left to right. Write just the answer.**

**18.** $7 \times 8 + 3 =$ _____         **19.** $7 \times 4 + 2 =$ _____

**20.** $2 \times 7 + 4 =$ _____         **21.** $3 \times 7 + 3 =$ _____

Name_____     Date _____

# 12A ◢ BASIC FACTS
## Multiplying by 8

**Multiply.**

| | | | | |
|---|---|---|---|---|
| 1. $\begin{array}{r} 8 \\ \times 6 \end{array}$ | 2. $\begin{array}{r} 8 \\ \times 7 \end{array}$ | 3. $\begin{array}{r} 8 \\ \times 3 \end{array}$ | 4. $\begin{array}{r} 6 \\ \times 8 \end{array}$ | 5. $\begin{array}{r} 5 \\ \times 8 \end{array}$ |
| 6. $\begin{array}{r} 7 \\ \times 8 \end{array}$ | 7. $\begin{array}{r} 8 \\ \times 4 \end{array}$ | 8. $\begin{array}{r} 0 \\ \times 8 \end{array}$ | 9. $\begin{array}{r} 8 \\ \times 8 \end{array}$ | 10. $\begin{array}{r} 1 \\ \times 8 \end{array}$ |

**Complete the table.**

| | x | 8 |
|---|---|---|
| 11. | 2 | |
| 12. | | 64 |
| 13. | 7 | |
| 14. | 4 | |
| 15. | | 40 |

**Multiply and add using mental math. Work from left to right. Write just the answer.**

16. $5 \times 8 + 2 =$ _____

17. $1 \times 8 + 4 =$ _____

18. $8 \times 2 + 2 =$ _____

19. $3 \times 8 + 1 =$ _____

Name_____  Date _____

# 12B BASIC FACTS

## Multiplying by 8

**Multiply.**

1. $8 \times 7 =$ _____

2. $8 \times 5 =$ _____

3. $8 \times 3 =$ _____

4. $1 \times 8 =$ _____

5. $4 \times 8 =$ _____

6. $8 \times 2 =$ _____

7. $8 \times 4 =$ _____

8. $8 \times 1 =$ _____

9. $6 \times 8 =$ _____

**Complete the table with the facts you have learned. One column has been completed for you.**

|        | x | 2 | 3 | 4  | 5 | 6 | 7 | 8 | 9 |
|--------|---|---|---|----|---|---|---|---|---|
| 10.    | 2 |   |   | 8  |   |   |   |   |   |
| 11.    | 3 |   |   | 12 |   |   |   |   |   |
| 12.    | 4 |   |   | 16 |   |   |   |   |   |
| 13.    | 5 |   |   | 20 |   |   |   |   |   |
| 14.    | 6 |   |   | 24 |   |   |   |   |   |
| 15.    | 7 |   |   | 28 |   |   |   |   |   |
| 16     | 8 |   |   | 32 |   |   |   |   |   |
| 17.    | 9 |   |   | 36 |   |   |   |   |   |

**Compare. Write <, >, or =.**

18. $2 \times 8$ ___ $3 \times 5$

19. $3 \times 8$ ___ $4 \times 8$

20. $8 \times 4$ ___ $5 \times 9$

21. $4 \times 6$ ___ $3 \times 8$

22. $2 \times 8$ ___ $3 \times 5$

23. $1 \times 8$ ___ $1 + 8$

Name_____  Date _____

 **BASIC FACTS**
............................................................................................

### Fact Families

## Write two multiplication facts.

1. • • • •
   • • • •
   • • • •
   _____

   _____

2. • • • • • •
   • • • • • •
   • • • • • •
   _____

   _____

3. • • • • •
   • • • • •
   • • • • •
   _____

   _____

## Use the order property. Complete.

**4.** $4 \times 5 =$ _____ $\times$ _____

**5.** $2 \times 6 =$ _____ $\times$ _____

**6.** $7 \times 3 =$ _____ $\times$ _____

**7.** $8 \times 2 =$ _____ $\times$ _____

## Write a multiplication fact.

**8.** 3 sevens = _____

**9.** 5 fives = _____

## Write a division number sentence.

10. • • • • • •
    • • • • • •

    _____

11. • • • • •
    • • • • •
    • • • • •

    _____

Name_____  Date _____

## 1B  BASIC FACTS

### Fact Families

**Draw an array. Then multiply.**

**1.**  2
$\times$ 3

**2.**  4
$\times$ 4

**3.**  3
$\times$ 6

**4.**  2
$\times$ 8

**5.**  5
$\times$ 3

**6.**  4
$\times$ 2

**7.**  2
$\times$ 7

**8.**  3
$\times$ 4

**9.**  5
$\times$ 2

**10.**  2
$\times$ 6

**11.**  3
$\times$ 3

**12.**  5
$\times$ 4

**Draw an array. Then divide.**

**13.** $8 \div 2 =$ _____

**14.** $15 \div 3 =$ _____

**15.** $6 \div 3 =$ _____

**16.** $18 \div 3 =$ _____

**17.** $6 \div 2 =$ _____

**18.** $18 \div 2 =$ _____

**19.** $10 \div 2 =$ _____

**20.** $12 \div 3 =$ _____

**21.** $16 \div 2 =$ _____

**Grade 3, Just the Facts**

Name_____ Date _____

# 2A ▶ BASIC FACTS
....................................................................................................................
## Multiplying and Dividing by 2

**Look at the multiplication sentences below. Write a related division fact for each.**

**1.** $2 \times 2 = 4$ _____

**2.** $2 \times 5 = 10$ _____

**3.** $2 \times 6 = 12$ _____

**List the first ten multiples.**

**4.** of 2 ____ ____ ____ ____ ____ ____ ____ ____ ____ ____

**Draw a picture of the groups in the division fact.**

**5.** $8 \div 2$                              **6.** $14 \div 2$

**Write the correct sign. Choose +, ×, or ÷.**

**7.** 45     5 = 9             **8.** 4     3 = 12             **9.** 9     9 = 18

**Write a multiplication sentence. Then solve.**

**10.** $8 \div 4 =$ ____ _____         **11.** $5 \div 5 =$ ____ _____

**12.** $2 \div 1 =$ ____ _____         **13.** $14 \div 7 =$ ____ _____

Name_____  Date _____

# 2B BASIC FACTS

## Multiplying and Dividing by 2

**Multiply. Think of doubles or the order property.**

**1.** $2 \times 7 =$ _____     **2.** $6 \times 2 =$ _____     **3.** $2 \times 9 =$ _____

**4.** $4 \times 2 =$ _____     **5.** $2 \times 8 =$ _____     **6.** $2 \times 5 =$ _____

**7.** $2 \times 3 =$ _____     **8.** $1 \times 2 =$ _____     **9.** $2 \times 2 =$ _____

| **10.** | **11.** | **12.** | **13.** | **14.** | **15.** |
|---|---|---|---|---|---|
| 2 | 2 | 8 | 9 | 2 | 2 |
| $\times 5$ | $\times 3$ | $\times 2$ | $\times 2$ | $\times 4$ | $\times 6$ |

**Divide.**

**16.** $8 \div 2 =$ _____     **17.** $6 \div 2 =$ _____     **18.** $18 \div 2 =$ _____

**19.** $10 \div 2 =$ _____     **20.** $16 \div 2 =$ _____     **21.** $12 \div 2 =$ _____

**22.** $14 \div 2 =$ _____     **23.** $2 \div 1 =$ _____     **24.** $4 \div 2 =$ _____

**Write a division sentence. Then solve.**

**25.** $2 \times 7 =$ ____ _____     **26.** $2 \times 3 =$ ____ _____

**27.** $2 \times 4 =$ ____ _____     **28.** $2 \times 8 =$ ____ _____

Name_____   Date _____

# 3A BASIC FACTS

## Multiplying and Dividing by 4

**Find the missing factor. Complete.**

**1.** $9 \times$ _____ $= 36$    **2.** $4 \times$ _____ $= 32$    **3.** $4 \times$ _____ $= 12$

**4.** $7 \times 4 = 4 \times$ _____    **5.** $4 \times 5 = 5 \times$ _____    **6.** _____ $\times 7 = 28$

**7.** $4 \times$ _____ $= 16$    **8.** $2 \times$ _____ $= 4 \times 2$    **9.** $4 \times$ _____ $= 24$

**List the first ten multiples.**

**10.** of 4 _____ _____ _____ _____ _____ _____ _____ _____ _____ _____

**Write a related multiplication fact. Then divide.**

**11.** $10 \div 2 =$ _____    **12.** $8 \div 4 =$ _____    **13.** $16 \div 4 =$ _____

_____   _____   _____

**14.** $14 \div 2 =$ _____    **15.** $24 \div 4 =$ _____    **16.** $20 \div 4 =$ _____

_____   _____   _____

**17.** $32 \div 4 =$ _____    **18.** $18 \div 2 =$ _____    **19.** $28 \div 4 =$ _____

_____   _____   _____

# 3B ▸ BASIC FACTS

## Multiplying and Dividing by 4

**Divide. Check by multiplying.**

**1.** 4)8̄

**2.** 4)3̄2̄

**3.** 4)2̄4̄

_____

_____

_____

**4.** 4)1̄6̄

**5.** 4)3̄6̄

**6.** 4)1̄2̄

_____

_____

_____

**7.** 28 ÷ 4 = _____

**8.** 20 ÷ 4 = _____

**9.** 12 ÷ 4 = _____

_____

_____

_____

**Multiply.**

**10.** 6 × 4

**11.** 5 × 4

**12.** 7 × 4

**13.** 4 × 8

**14.** 4 × 9

**15.** 3 × 4

**16.** 4 × 4

**17.** 9 × 4

**18.** 8 × 4

**19.** 4 × 5

**20.** 4 × 3 = _____

**21.** 2 × 7 = _____

**22.** 6 × 4 = _____

Name_____    Date _____

# 4A BASIC FACTS

................................................................................

## Multiplying and Dividing by 5

## Multiply.

**1.** $5 \times (1 \times 8) =$ _____    **2.** $(3 \times 5) \times 1 =$ _____    **3.** $5 \times 2 =$ _____

**4.** $5 \times 5 =$ _____    **5.** $5 \times 8 =$ _____    **6.** $5 \times 9 =$ _____

## Complete.

**7.** $6 \times (1 \times 5) =$ _____    **8.** $1 \times 5 \times 6 =$ _____

## List the first ten multiples.

**9.** of 5 ____ ____ ____ ____ ____ ____ ____ ____ ____ ____

## Divide. Think of multiplication.

**10.** $40 \div 5 =$ ____    **11.** $35 \div 5 =$ ____    **12.** $25 \div 5 =$ ____

**13.** $10 \div 5 =$ ____    **14.** $20 \div 5 =$ ____    **15.** $30 \div 5 =$ ____

**16.** $15 \div 5 =$ ____    **17.** $45 \div 5 =$ ____    **18.** $5 \div 1 =$ ____

**19.** $40 \div 8 =$ ____    **20.** $35 \div 7 =$ ____    **21.** $45 \div 9 =$ ____

Name_____ Date _____

## 4B ▸ BASIC FACTS

### Multiplying and Dividing by 5

**What is the quotient? Think of multiplication.**

1. $5\overline{)25}$    2. $5\overline{)30}$    3. $5\overline{)45}$    4. $5\overline{)40}$

5. $5\overline{)35}$    6. $5\overline{)50}$    7. $5\overline{)15}$    8. $5\overline{)20}$

**List the multiples**

9. of 4 up to 50

_____

**Complete the number sentence.**

10. $45 = $ ____ $\times$ ____      11. $25 \div 5 = $ ____      12. ____ $= 7 \times 5$

13. $5 \times 8 = $ ____      14. $3 \times 7 = $ ____      15. $18 = $ ____ $\times 2$

16. $54 = $ ____ $\times$ ____      17. $20 = $ ____ $\times$ ____      18. $50 \div $ ____ $= 10$

19. $30 = $ ____ $\times$ ____      20. $10 \div 2 = $ ____      21. ____ $\div 5 = 9$

22. $15 \div 5 = $ ____      23. $6 \times 4 = $ ____      24. $9 \div 3 = $ ____

Name_____ Date _____

## 5A ◢ BASIC FACTS

### Multiplying and Dividing by 1

**Use multiplication and division properties to complete.**

**1.** $8 \div$ _____ $= 1$

**2.** $(6 \times 2) \times 1 = 1 \times$ _____

**3.** $(3 \times$ _____$) \times 5 = 1 \times (3 \times 5)$

**4.** _____ $\div 1 = 10$

**Multiply.**

**5.** $\begin{array}{r} 1 \\ \times\, 2 \\ \hline \end{array}$
**6.** $\begin{array}{r} 7 \\ \times\, 1 \\ \hline \end{array}$
**7.** $\begin{array}{r} 5 \\ \times\, 1 \\ \hline \end{array}$
**8.** $\begin{array}{r} 1 \\ \times\, 9 \\ \hline \end{array}$
**9.** $\begin{array}{r} 2 \\ \times\, 1 \\ \hline \end{array}$
**10.** $\begin{array}{r} 1 \\ \times\, 1 \\ \hline \end{array}$

**11.** $\begin{array}{r} 1 \\ \times\, 6 \\ \hline \end{array}$
**12.** $\begin{array}{r} 8 \\ \times\, 1 \\ \hline \end{array}$
**13.** $\begin{array}{r} 1 \\ \times\, 4 \\ \hline \end{array}$
**14.** $\begin{array}{r} 6 \\ \times\, 1 \\ \hline \end{array}$
**15.** $\begin{array}{r} 1 \\ \times\, 7 \\ \hline \end{array}$
**16.** $\begin{array}{r} 1 \\ \times\, 3 \\ \hline \end{array}$

**Write a multiplication sentence. Then solve.**

**17.** $5 \div 5 =$ ____ _____

**18.** $3 \div 1 =$ ____ _____

**What is the quotient? Think of multiplication.**

**19.** $1\overline{)5}$

**20.** $1\overline{)1}$

**21.** $1\overline{)8}$

**22.** $1\overline{)3}$

Name_____    Date _____

## 5B BASIC FACTS

## Multiplying and Dividing by 1

## Multiply.

**1.** $1 \times 4 =$ _____     **2.** $1 \times 8 =$ _____     **3.** $6 \times 2 =$ _____

**4.** $9 \times 1 =$ _____     **5.** $1 \times 3 =$ _____     **6.** $2 \times 4 =$ _____

**7.** $1 \times 5 =$ _____     **8.** $7 \times 1 =$ _____     **9.** $2 \times 9 =$ _____

**10.**  2      **11.**  1      **12.**  5      **13.**  1      **14.**  2
$\underline{\times 2}$       $\underline{\times 7}$       $\underline{\times 4}$       $\underline{\times 9}$       $\underline{\times 1}$

**15.**  1      **16.**  1      **17.**  8      **18.**  4      **19.**  2
$\underline{\times 2}$       $\underline{\times 6}$       $\underline{\times 4}$       $\underline{\times 1}$       $\underline{\times 7}$

## Divide.

**20.** $4 \div 1 =$ _____     **21.** $6 \div 1 =$ _____     **22.** $2 \div 1 =$ _____

**23.** $18 \div 2 =$ _____    **24.** $12 \div 1 =$ _____    **25.** $24 \div 3 =$ _____

**26.** $25 \div 5 =$ _____    **27.** $24 \div 4 =$ _____    **28.** $8 \div 1 =$ _____

**29.** $40 \div 5 =$ _____    **30.** $11 \div 1 =$ _____    **31.** $16 \div 4 =$ _____

Name_____ Date _____

## 6A BASIC FACTS

......................................................................................................

## Multiplying and Dividing by 3

**Complete each fact family.**

**1.** 3 × 2 = _____          6 ÷ 2 = _____

   2 × 3 = _____          6 ÷ 3 = _____

**2.** 6 × 3 = _____          18 ÷ 6 = _____

   3 × 6 = _____          18 ÷ 3 = _____

**3.** 8 × 3 = _____          24 ÷ 3 = _____

   3 × 8 = _____          24 ÷ 8 = _____

**4.** 3 × 9 = _____          27 ÷ 9 = _____

   9 × 3 = _____          27 ÷ 3 = _____

**5.** 5 × 3 = _____          15 ÷ 3 = _____

   3 × 5 = _____          15 ÷ 5 = _____

**Write four number sentences for each fact family.**

**6.** 3, 4, 12 _____  _____  _____  _____

**7.** 3, 7, 21 _____  _____  _____  _____

Name_____ Date _____

## 6B BASIC FACTS

### Multiplying and Dividing by 3

**Write a related multiplication fact. Then divide.**

**1.** $6 \div 3 =$ ____

____ $\times$ ____ = ____

**2.** $21 \div 3 =$ ____

____ $\times$ ____ = ____

**3.** $12 \div 3 =$ ____

____ $\times$ ____ = ____

**4.** $3 \div 3 =$ ____

____ $\times$ ____ = ____

**5.** $9 \div 3 =$ ____

____ $\times$ ____ = ____

**6.** $24 \div 3 =$ ____

____ $\times$ ____ = ____

**7.** $15 \div 3 =$ ____

____ $\times$ ____ = ____

**8.** $0 \div 3 =$ ____

____ $\times$ ____ = ____

**9.** $18 \div 3 =$ ____

____ $\times$ ____ = ____

**10.** $27 \div 3 =$ ____

____ $\times$ ____ = ____

**Check by multiplying. Correct any mistakes.**

**11.** $12 \div 3 = 6$

_____

**12.** $9 \div 3 = 3$

_____

**14.** $15 \div 3 = 4$

_____

Name_____  Date _____

# BASIC FACTS

## Reviewing 1's - 5's and 0's

**Multiply.**

**1.** $0 \times 4 =$ _____    **2.** $1 \times 8 =$ _____    **3.** $6 \times 0 =$ _____

**4.** $9 \times 1 =$ _____    **5.** $0 \times 3 =$ _____    **6.** $2 \times 0 =$ _____

**7.** $1 \times 5 =$ _____    **8.** $7 \times 0 =$ _____    **9.** $0 \times 9 =$ _____

**10.**  $\begin{array}{r} 7 \\ \times\,1 \\ \hline \end{array}$    **11.**  $\begin{array}{r} 5 \\ \times\,5 \\ \hline \end{array}$    **12.**  $\begin{array}{r} 3 \\ \times\,0 \\ \hline \end{array}$    **13.**  $\begin{array}{r} 2 \\ \times\,1 \\ \hline \end{array}$    **14.**  $\begin{array}{r} 1 \\ \times\,0 \\ \hline \end{array}$

**15.**  $\begin{array}{r} 8 \\ \times\,0 \\ \hline \end{array}$    **16.**  $\begin{array}{r} 1 \\ \times\,4 \\ \hline \end{array}$    **17.**  $\begin{array}{r} 1 \\ \times\,3 \\ \hline \end{array}$    **18.**  $\begin{array}{r} 6 \\ \times\,2 \\ \hline \end{array}$    **19.**  $\begin{array}{r} 2 \\ \times\,7 \\ \hline \end{array}$

**20.**  $\begin{array}{r} 3 \\ \times\,3 \\ \hline \end{array}$    **21.**  $\begin{array}{r} 3 \\ \times\,7 \\ \hline \end{array}$    **22.**  $\begin{array}{r} 8 \\ \times\,3 \\ \hline \end{array}$    **23.**  $\begin{array}{r} 3 \\ \times\,5 \\ \hline \end{array}$    **24.**  $\begin{array}{r} 4 \\ \times\,3 \\ \hline \end{array}$

**25.**  $\begin{array}{r} 2 \\ \times\,5 \\ \hline \end{array}$    **26.**  $\begin{array}{r} 5 \\ \times\,4 \\ \hline \end{array}$    **27.**  $\begin{array}{r} 2 \\ \times\,4 \\ \hline \end{array}$    **28.**  $\begin{array}{r} 4 \\ \times\,4 \\ \hline \end{array}$    **29.**  $\begin{array}{r} 5 \\ \times\,0 \\ \hline \end{array}$

Name_____    Date _____

## 7B BASIC FACTS

### Reviewing 1's - 5's and 0's

**Find the quotient. Think of multiplication.**

1. $1\overline{)5}$        2. $5\overline{)0}$        3. $1\overline{)4}$        4. $8\overline{)0}$

5. $7\overline{)14}$       6. $9\overline{)0}$        7. $1\overline{)9}$        8. $8\overline{)8}$

9. $3\overline{)15}$       10. $1\overline{)8}$       11. $1\overline{)3}$       12. $6\overline{)0}$

13. $6\overline{)6}$       14. $2\overline{)0}$       15. $4\overline{)16}$      16. $1\overline{)7}$

**Write a multiplication sentence. Then solve.**

17. $0 \div 4 =$ _____  _____    18. $5 \div 5 =$ _____  _____

19. $3 \div 1 =$ _____  _____    20. $10 \div 2 =$ _____  _____

21. $6 \div 3 =$ _____  _____    22. $0 \div 3 =$ _____  _____

23. $8 \div 1 =$ _____  _____    24. $14 \div 2 =$ _____  _____

25. $4 \div 1 =$ _____  _____    26. $9 \div 3 =$ _____  _____

27. $3 \div 3 =$ _____  _____    28. $16 \div 1 =$ _____  _____

Name_____ Date _____

 **8A** BASIC FACTS
·································································································································

## Multiplying and Dividing by 9

**Find two multiplication facts.**

1. • • • • • • • • • •
   • • • • • • • • • •
   • • • • • • • • • •
   _____

   _____

2. • • • • • • • • • •
   • • • • • • • • •
   _____

   _____

**Find the missing factor. Complete.**

3. ____ $\times$ 3 = 27     4. 9 $\times$ ____ = 72     5. 6 $\times$ 9 = 9 $\times$ ____

**Complete the number sentence.**

6. 36 = ____ $\times$ ____     7. 18 = ____ $\times$ ____     8. 45 = ____ $\times$ ____

**Multiply.**

9.    5     10.    7     11.    3     12.    4     13.    9
   $\times 9$       $\times 9$       $\times 9$       $\times 9$       $\times 9$

14.    6     15.    9     16.    2     17.    1     18.    8
   $\times 9$       $\times 5$       $\times 9$       $\times 9$       $\times 9$

Name_____ Date _____

# 8B BASIC FACTS
## Multiplying and Dividing by 9

**Divide.**

**1.** $0 \div 9 = $ _____   **2.** $9 \div 1 = $ _____   **3.** $5 \div 1 = $ _____

**4.** $9 \div 9 = $ _____   **5.** $54 \div 6 = $ _____   **6.** $27 \div 9 = $ _____

**7.** $9 \div 3 = $ _____   **8.** $18 \div 9 = $ _____   **9.** $45 \div 9 = $ _____

**10.** $63 \div 9 = $ _____   **11.** $36 \div 9 = $ _____   **12.** $81 \div 9 = $ _____

**13.** $72 \div 9 = $ _____   **14.** $27 \div 9 = $ _____   **15.** $54 \div 9 = $ _____

**Compare. Write >, <, or =.**

**16.** $18 \div 2$ ____ $18 \div 9$   **17.** $9 \div 9$ ____ $3 \div 3$

**18.** $27 \div 9$ ____ $25 \div 5$   **19.** $24 \div 6$ ____ $36 \div 4$

**Divide.**

**20.** $2\overline{)18}$   **21.** $9\overline{)81}$   **22.** $9\overline{)27}$   **23.** $9\overline{)9}$

**24.** $9\overline{)36}$   **25.** $6\overline{)54}$   **26.** $5\overline{)45}$   **27.** $8\overline{)72}$

Name_____  Date _____

# 9A BASIC FACTS

## Multiplying and Dividing by 6

**Multiply.**

**1.** $3 \times 3 =$ ____   $6 \times 3 =$ ____      **2.** $3 \times 2 =$ ____   $6 \times 2 =$ ____

**3.** $3 \times 7 =$ ____   $6 \times 7 =$ ____      **4.** $3 \times 4 =$ ____   $6 \times 4 =$ ____

**5.** $3 \times 9 =$ ____   $6 \times 9 =$ ____      **6.** $3 \times 5 =$ ____   $6 \times 5 =$ ____

**7.** $3 \times 8 =$ ____   $6 \times 8 =$ ____      **8.** $3 \times 6 =$ ____   $6 \times 6 =$ ____

| **9.** $\begin{array}{r} 4 \\ \times 6 \\ \hline \end{array}$ | **10.** $\begin{array}{r} 3 \\ \times 6 \\ \hline \end{array}$ | **11.** $\begin{array}{r} 5 \\ \times 6 \\ \hline \end{array}$ | **12.** $\begin{array}{r} 7 \\ \times 6 \\ \hline \end{array}$ | **13.** $\begin{array}{r} 6 \\ \times 6 \\ \hline \end{array}$ |
|---|---|---|---|---|
| **14.** $\begin{array}{r} 6 \\ \times 1 \\ \hline \end{array}$ | **15.** $\begin{array}{r} 2 \\ \times 6 \\ \hline \end{array}$ | **16.** $\begin{array}{r} 6 \\ \times 0 \\ \hline \end{array}$ | **17.** $\begin{array}{r} 9 \\ \times 6 \\ \hline \end{array}$ | **18.** $\begin{array}{r} 8 \\ \times 6 \\ \hline \end{array}$ |
| **19.** $\begin{array}{r} 6 \\ \times 5 \\ \hline \end{array}$ | **20.** $\begin{array}{r} 6 \\ \times 7 \\ \hline \end{array}$ | **21.** $\begin{array}{r} 6 \\ \times 4 \\ \hline \end{array}$ | **22.** $\begin{array}{r} 6 \\ \times 3 \\ \hline \end{array}$ | **23.** $\begin{array}{r} 7 \\ \times 3 \\ \hline \end{array}$ |
| **24.** $\begin{array}{r} 6 \\ \times 2 \\ \hline \end{array}$ | **25.** $\begin{array}{r} 6 \\ \times 8 \\ \hline \end{array}$ | **26.** $\begin{array}{r} 6 \\ \times 9 \\ \hline \end{array}$ | **27.** $\begin{array}{r} 5 \\ \times 5 \\ \hline \end{array}$ | **28.** $\begin{array}{r} 8 \\ \times 2 \\ \hline \end{array}$ |

Name_____ Date _____

## 9B ▸ BASIC FACTS
......................................................................
### Multiplying and Dividing by 6

Write four number sentences for each fact family.

**1.** 6, 7, 42

_____ × _____ = _____

_____ × _____ = _____

_____ ÷ _____ = _____

_____ ÷ _____ = _____

**2.** 5, 6, 30

_____ × _____ = _____

_____ × _____ = _____

_____ ÷ _____ = _____

_____ ÷ _____ = _____

**3.** 6, 8, 48

_____ × _____ = _____

_____ × _____ = _____

_____ ÷ _____ = _____

_____ ÷ _____ = _____

**4.** 6, 9, 54

_____ × _____ = _____

_____ × _____ = _____

_____ ÷ _____ = _____

_____ ÷ _____ = _____

**5.** 4, 6, 24

_____ × _____ = _____

_____ × _____ = _____

_____ ÷ _____ = _____

_____ ÷ _____ = _____

**Grade 3, Just the Facts**

Name_____  Date _____

## 0A ▼ BASIC FACTS
..................................................................................

### Multiplying and Dividing by 7

**Write a related multiplication fact. Then divide.**

**1.** 7 ÷ 7 = ___

___ × ___ = ___

**2.** 21 ÷ 7 = ___

___ × ___ = ___

**3.** 35 ÷ 7 = ___

___ × ___ = ___

**4.** 56 ÷ 7 = ___

___ × ___ = ___

**5.** 42 ÷ 7 = ___

___ × ___ = ___

**6.** 63 ÷ 7 = ___

___ × ___ = ___

**7.** 14 ÷ 7 = ___

___ × ___ = ___

**8.** 28 ÷ 7 = ___

___ × ___ = ___

**9.** 49 ÷ 7 = ___

___ × ___ = ___

**Write four number sentences for each fact family.**

**10.** 7, 9, 63

_____ × _____ = _____

_____ × _____ = _____

_____ ÷ _____ = _____

_____ ÷ _____ = _____

**11.** 7, 8, 56

_____ × _____ = _____

_____ × _____ = _____

_____ ÷ _____ = _____

_____ ÷ _____ = _____

Name_____ Date _____

## 10B BASIC FACTS

### Multiplying and Dividing by 7

**Multiply.**

**1.** $7 \times 2 =$ _____  **2.** $7 \times 5 =$ _____  **3.** $7 \times 7 =$ _____

**4.** $7 \times 4 =$ _____  **5.** $7 \times 3 =$ _____  **6.** $7 \times 8 =$ _____

**7.** $7 \times 9 =$ _____  **8.** $7 \times 6 =$ _____  **9.** $7 \times 1 =$ _____

**10.**  $\begin{array}{r} 7 \\ \times\,0 \\ \hline \end{array}$
**11.**  $\begin{array}{r} 2 \\ \times\,7 \\ \hline \end{array}$
**12.**  $\begin{array}{r} 6 \\ \times\,7 \\ \hline \end{array}$
**13.**  $\begin{array}{r} 8 \\ \times\,7 \\ \hline \end{array}$

**14.**  $\begin{array}{r} 4 \\ \times\,7 \\ \hline \end{array}$
**15.**  $\begin{array}{r} 1 \\ \times\,7 \\ \hline \end{array}$
**16.**  $\begin{array}{r} 9 \\ \times\,7 \\ \hline \end{array}$
**17.**  $\begin{array}{r} 5 \\ \times\,7 \\ \hline \end{array}$

**18.**  $\begin{array}{r} 7 \\ \times\,7 \\ \hline \end{array}$
**19.**  $\begin{array}{r} 3 \\ \times\,7 \\ \hline \end{array}$
**20.**  $\begin{array}{r} 0 \\ \times\,7 \\ \hline \end{array}$
**21.**  $\begin{array}{r} 7 \\ \times\,1 \\ \hline \end{array}$

**Divide.**

**22.** $63 \div 7 =$ ____  **23.** $21 \div 7 =$ ____  **24.** $7 \div 7 =$ ____

**25.** $14 \div 7 =$ ____  **26.** $56 \div 7 =$ ____  **27.** $42 \div 7 =$ ____

**28.** $28 \div 7 =$ ____  **29.** $49 \div 7 =$ ____  **30.** $35 \div 7 =$ ____

**Grade 3, Just the Facts**

Name_____ Date _____

## 11A ▸ BASIC FACTS
∙∙∙∙∙∙∙∙∙∙∙∙∙∙∙∙∙∙∙∙∙∙∙∙∙∙∙∙∙∙∙∙∙∙∙∙∙∙∙∙∙∙∙∙∙∙∙∙∙∙∙∙∙∙∙∙∙∙∙∙∙∙∙∙∙∙∙∙∙∙∙∙∙∙∙

### Multiplying and Dividing by 8

**Find two multiplication facts.**

1. • • • • • • • •
   • • • • • • • •
   • • • • • • • •

   _____

   _____

2. • • • • • • • •
   • • • • • • • •

   _____

   _____

3. • • • • • • • •
   • • • • • • • •
   • • • • • • • •
   • • • • • • • •

   _____

   _____

**Write a multiplication fact.**

4. 6 eights = _____

5. 5 eights = _____

6. 7 eights = _____

7. 9 eights = _____

8. 4 eights = _____

9. 8 eights = _____

**Draw an array. Find the product.**

10. $6 \times 8 =$ _____

11. $3 \times 8 =$ _____

**Multiply.**

12.  6
    $\times 8$

13.  8
    $\times 5$

14.  7
    $\times 8$

15.  8
    $\times 4$

Name_____ Date _____

# 11B BASIC FACTS

## Multiplying and Dividing by 8

**Write the missing numbers.**

1. ___ × 8 = 40          2. ___ × 8 = 56          3. ___ × 8 = 24

4. ___ × 8 = 64          5. ___ × 8 = 48          6. ___ × 8 = 72

7. 72 = ___ × ___        8. 56 = ___ × ___        9. 24 = ___ × ___

**Divide.**

10. 8)32          11. 8)16          12. 8)40          13. 8)24

14. 8)48          15. 8)8          16. 8)56          17. 8)64

**Check by multiplying. Correct any quotients that are wrong.**

18. 40 ÷ 8 = 6          19. 16 ÷ 8 = 3          20. 64 ÷ 8 = 7

_____        _____        _____

21. 24 ÷ 8 = 4          22. 56 ÷ 8 = 6          23. 32 ÷ 8 = 5

_____        _____        _____

Name_____ Date _____

 **BASIC FACTS**

## Review 6, 7, 8, and 9

**Multiply.**

| 1.  4<br>× 8 | 2.  9<br>× 2 | 3.  5<br>× 8 | 4.  9<br>× 4 | 5.  8<br>× 8 |
|---|---|---|---|---|
| 6.  9<br>× 3 | 7.  9<br>× 7 | 8.  1<br>× 8 | 9.  5<br>× 9 | 10.  7<br>× 9 |
| 11.  9<br>× 9 | 12.  8<br>× 6 | 13.  9<br>× 8 | 14.  3<br>× 9 | 15.  8<br>× 7 |
| 16.  6<br>× 8 | 17.  9<br>× 5 | 18.  2<br>× 8 | 19.  7<br>× 7 | 20.  8<br>× 5 |
| 21.  7<br>× 8 | 22.  3<br>× 8 | 23.  4<br>× 9 | 24.  7<br>× 4 | 25.  9<br>× 6 |
| 26.  6<br>× 7 | 27.  3<br>× 9 | 28.  4<br>× 6 | 29.  6<br>× 6 | 30.  2<br>× 7 |

Name_____ Date _____

# 12B BASIC FACTS

## Review 6, 7, 8, and 9

**Divide.**

1. $9\overline{)36}$  2. $6\overline{)30}$  3. $8\overline{)8}$  4. $8\overline{)64}$  5. $6\overline{)24}$

6. $6\overline{)54}$  7. $7\overline{)42}$  8. $9\overline{)9}$  9. $8\overline{)56}$  10. $9\overline{)72}$

11. $7\overline{)21}$  12. $8\overline{)72}$  13. $9\overline{)45}$  14. $8\overline{)0}$  15. $6\overline{)12}$

16. $9\overline{)0}$  17. $9\overline{)54}$  18. $6\overline{)0}$  19. $7\overline{)49}$  20. $9\overline{)81}$

21. $6\overline{)36}$  22. $6\overline{)48}$  23. $7\overline{)35}$  24. $7\overline{)7}$  25. $7\overline{)28}$

26. $8\overline{)16}$  27. $9\overline{)18}$  28. $8\overline{)48}$  29. $8\overline{)32}$  30. $7\overline{)63}$

31. $6\overline{)18}$  32. $7\overline{)56}$  33. $5\overline{)30}$  34. $3\overline{)21}$  35. $8\overline{)24}$

Name_____  Date _____

# 13A BASIC FACTS

......................................................................................

## Review Multiplication and Division Facts

**Write the fact family for each of the arrays.**

1.
• • • • • • •
• • • • • • •
• • • • • • •
• • • • • • •

_____ × _____ = _____

_____ × _____ = _____

_____ ÷ _____ = _____

_____ ÷ _____ = _____

2.
• • • • • • • •
• • • • • • • •
• • • • • • • •

_____ × _____ = _____

_____ × _____ = _____

_____ ÷ _____ = _____

_____ ÷ _____ = _____

## Multiply.

3.

| x | 7 |
|---|---|
| 8 | 56 |
| 3 | |
| 9 | |
| 6 | |
| 7 | |

4.

| x | 9 |
|---|---|
| 3 | |
| | 63 |
| | 54 |
| | 45 |
| 9 | |

5.  9
   × 3

6.  4
   × 9

7.  8
   × 9

8.  5
   × 9

9.  9
   × 9

Name_____  Date _____

# 13B BASIC FACTS

## Review Multiplication and Division Facts

**Write four number sentences for each fact family.**

**1.** 5, 7, 35 _____ _____ _____ _____

**2.** 6, 8, 48 _____ _____ _____ _____

**Complete.**

**3.** $4 \times 8 =$ _____   $32 \div 8 =$ _____

$8 \times 4 =$ _____   $32 \div 4 =$ _____

**4.** $6 \times 7 =$ _____   $42 \div 7 =$ _____

$7 \times 6 =$ _____   $42 \div 6 =$ _____

**5.** $8 \times 5 =$ _____   $40 \div 5 =$ _____

$5 \times 8 =$ _____   $40 \div 8 =$ _____

**6.** $4 \times 9 =$ _____   $36 \div 9 =$ _____

$9 \times 4 =$ _____   $36 \div 4 =$ _____

**Divide.**

**7.** $9\overline{)45}$     **8.** $5\overline{)40}$     **9.** $6\overline{)54}$     **10.** $7\overline{)28}$

Name_____    Date _____

# BASIC FACTS: ADDITION

Find the sum. Use strategies to help you.

| | | | | | |
|---|---|---|---|---|---|
| **1.**  4<br>  + 5 | **2.**  2<br>  + 4 | **3.**  0<br>  + 7 | **4.**  6<br>  + 1 | **5.**  8<br>  + 2 | **6.**  1<br>  + 4 |
| **7.**  5<br>  + 4 | **8.**  8<br>  + 9 | **9.**  6<br>  + 5 | **10.**  9<br>  + 2 | **11.**  7<br>  + 8 | **12.**  5<br>  + 3 |
| **13.**  9<br>  + 9 | **14.**  1<br>  + 0 | **15.**  3<br>  + 5 | **16.**  6<br>  + 4 | **17.**  5<br>  + 9 | **18.**  6<br>  + 7 |
| **19.**  1<br>  + 9 | **20.**  8<br>  + 4 | **21.**  1<br>  + 5 | **22.**  3<br>  + 3 | **23.**  8<br>  + 8 | **24.**  6<br>  + 2 |
| **25.**  5<br>  + 7 | **26.**  3<br>  + 7 | **27.**  3<br>  + 9 | **28.**  5<br>  + 8 | **29.**  7<br>  + 5 | **30.**  2<br>  + 8 |

I need more practice with these facts:

Name_____  Date _____

# BASIC FACTS: ADDITION

Find the sum. Use strategies to help you.

| | | | | | |
|---|---|---|---|---|---|
| **1.**  0<br>+ 4 | **2.**  9<br>+ 6 | **3.**  7<br>+ 3 | **4.**  4<br>+ 5 | **5.**  1<br>+ 8 | **6.**  3<br>+ 6 |
| **7.**  5<br>+ 0 | **8.**  2<br>+ 1 | **9.**  9<br>+ 8 | **10.**  7<br>+ 6 | **11.**  7<br>+ 4 | **12.**  4<br>+ 9 |
| **13.**  4<br>+ 1 | **14.**  8<br>+ 5 | **15.**  5<br>+ 6 | **16.**  4<br>+ 7 | **17.**  1<br>+ 3 | **18.**  7<br>+ 9 |
| **19.**  3<br>+ 4 | **20.**  2<br>+ 2 | **21.**  8<br>+ 7 | **22.**  9<br>+ 3 | **23.**  9<br>+ 2 | **24.**  7<br>+ 0 |
| **25.**  1<br>+ 1 | **26.**  6<br>+ 8 | **27.**  5<br>+ 2 | **28.**  0<br>+ 6 | **29.**  3<br>+ 2 | **30.**  0<br>+ 0 |

**I need more practice with these facts:**

Name_____  Date _____

# BASIC FACTS: ADDITION

Find the sum. Use strategies to help you.

| | | | | | |
|---|---|---|---|---|---|
| **1.** 4 <br> + 3 | **2.** 6 <br> + 1 | **3.** 8 <br> + 9 | **4.** 2 <br> + 5 | **5.** 2 <br> + 0 | **6.** 2 <br> + 7 |
| **7.** 0 <br> + 3 | **8.** 7 <br> + 2 | **9.** 5 <br> + 5 | **10.** 9 <br> + 4 | **11.** 8 <br> + 0 | **12.** 3 <br> + 1 |
| **13.** 6 <br> + 6 | **14.** 2 <br> + 3 | **15.** 8 <br> + 3 | **16.** 4 <br> + 2 | **17.** 6 <br> + 9 | **18.** 0 <br> + 5 |
| **19.** 4 <br> + 8 | **20.** 4 <br> + 6 | **21.** 2 <br> + 9 | **22.** 0 <br> + 1 | **23.** 9 <br> + 1 | **24.** 1 <br> + 2 |
| **25.** 5 <br> + 1 | **26.** 9 <br> + 5 | **27.** 7 <br> + 7 | **28.** 4 <br> + 0 | **29.** 9 <br> + 7 | **30.** 8 <br> + 1 |

I need more practice with these facts:

Name_____ Date _____

# BASIC FACTS: SUBTRACTION

Find the difference. Use strategies to help you.

| | | | | | |
|---|---|---|---|---|---|
| **1.** 9<br>− 3 | **2.** 16<br>− 8 | **3.** 3<br>− 1 | **4.** 7<br>− 6 | **5.** 12<br>− 5 | **6.** 14<br>− 9 |
| **7.** 8<br>− 5 | **8.** 4<br>− 0 | **9.** 10<br>− 7 | **10.** 11<br>− 2 | **11.** 6<br>− 3 | **12.** 1<br>− 1 |
| **13.** 7<br>− 1 | **14.** 8<br>− 8 | **15.** 9<br>− 4 | **16.** 5<br>− 5 | **17.** 16<br>− 7 | **18.** 10<br>− 6 |
| **19.** 11<br>− 2 | **20.** 9<br>− 2 | **21.** 14<br>− 5 | **22.** 13<br>− 6 | **23.** 7<br>− 2 | **24.** 1<br>− 0 |
| **25.** 9<br>− 8 | **26.** 5<br>− 4 | **27.** 18<br>− 9 | **28.** 12<br>− 8 | **29.** 6<br>− 2 | **30.** 15<br>− 8 |

**I need more practice with these facts:**

**Grade 3, Just the Facts**

Name_____ Date _____

# BASIC FACTS: SUBTRACTION

Find the difference. Use strategies to help you.

| | | | | | |
|---|---|---|---|---|---|
| **1.** 5<br>− 1 | **2.** 3<br>− 3 | **3.** 9<br>− 0 | **4.** 15<br>− 7 | **5.** 11<br>− 3 | **6.** 8<br>− 2 |
| **7.** 9<br>− 7 | **8.** 3<br>− 2 | **9.** 14<br>− 8 | **10.** 2<br>− 1 | **11.** 6<br>− 4 | **12.** 7<br>− 7 |
| **13.** 10<br>− 5 | **14.** 13<br>− 5 | **15.** 8<br>− 0 | **16.** 13<br>− 4 | **17.** 8<br>− 4 | **18.** 17<br>− 8 |
| **19.** 2<br>− 0 | **20.** 11<br>− 4 | **21.** 16<br>− 9 | **22.** 10<br>− 2 | **23.** 7<br>− 3 | **24.** 2<br>− 1 |
| **25.** 9<br>− 9 | **26.** 5<br>− 3 | **27.** 12<br>− 7 | **28.** 7<br>− 5 | **29.** 12<br>− 6 | **30.** 15<br>− 6 |

I need more practice with these facts:

Name_____   Date _____

# BASIC FACTS: SUBTRACTION

Find the difference. Use strategies to help you.

| | | | | | |
|---|---|---|---|---|---|
| **1.**   7<br>  − 0 | **2.**   4<br>  − 3 | **3.** 13<br>  − 8 | **4.** 17<br>  − 9 | **5.**   4<br>  − 4 | **6.** 11<br>  − 7 |
| **7.**   8<br>  − 3 | **8.** 14<br>  − 6 | **9.** 10<br>  − 1 | **10.**   0<br>  − 0 | **11.** 13<br>  − 7 | **12.**   9<br>  − 5 |
| **13.**   6<br>  − 1 | **14.** 11<br>  − 5 | **15.**   4<br>  − 1 | **16.** 10<br>  − 9 | **17.** 12<br>  − 4 | **18.**   3<br>  − 0 |
| **19.**   7<br>  − 4 | **20.** 12<br>  − 9 | **21.**   6<br>  − 5 | **22.**   8<br>  − 1 | **23.** 14<br>  − 7 | **24.** 10<br>  − 4 |
| **25.**   5<br>  − 0 | **26.** 12<br>  − 3 | **27.**   8<br>  − 6 | **28.**   4<br>  − 2 | **29.** 15<br>  − 9 | **30.**   8<br>  − 7 |

**I need more practice with these facts:**

Name_____   Date _____

# BASIC FACTS: MULTIPLICATION

Find the product. Use strategies to help you.

| | | | | | |
|---|---|---|---|---|---|
| **1.** 2<br>$\times 5$ | **2.** 4<br>$\times 1$ | **3.** 8<br>$\times 7$ | **4.** 2<br>$\times 0$ | **5.** 4<br>$\times 3$ | **6.** 6<br>$\times 3$ |
| **7.** 6<br>$\times 9$ | **8.** 6<br>$\times 6$ | **9.** 0<br>$\times 6$ | **10.** 2<br>$\times 7$ | **11.** 6<br>$\times 8$ | **12.** 6<br>$\times 5$ |
| **13.** 5<br>$\times 7$ | **14.** 3<br>$\times 5$ | **15.** 4<br>$\times 7$ | **16.** 2<br>$\times 9$ | **17.** 2<br>$\times 8$ | **18.** 3<br>$\times 3$ |
| **19.** 6<br>$\times 2$ | **20.** 0<br>$\times 4$ | **21.** 7<br>$\times 9$ | **22.** 7<br>$\times 5$ | **23.** 3<br>$\times 4$ | **24.** 7<br>$\times 6$ |
| **25.** 3<br>$\times 7$ | **26.** 4<br>$\times 6$ | **27.** 8<br>$\times 5$ | **28.** 4<br>$\times 8$ | **29.** 9<br>$\times 1$ | **30.** 9<br>$\times 5$ |

**I need more practice with these facts:**

Name_____ Date _____

# BASIC FACTS: MULTIPLICATION

**Find the product. Use strategies to help you.**

| | | | | | |
|---|---|---|---|---|---|
| **1.** 0 <br> × 8 | **2.** 9 <br> × 7 | **3.** 5 <br> × 5 | **4.** 3 <br> × 6 | **5.** 2 <br> × 1 | **6.** 8 <br> × 3 |
| **7.** 4 <br> × 3 | **8.** 7 <br> × 0 | **9.** 1 <br> × 7 | **10.** 6 <br> × 1 | **11.** 8 <br> × 8 | **12.** 5 <br> × 9 |
| **13.** 9 <br> × 2 | **14.** 9 <br> × 3 | **15.** 1 <br> × 9 | **16.** 2 <br> × 3 | **17.** 0 <br> × 0 | **18.** 4 <br> × 1 |
| **19.** 7 <br> × 7 | **20.** 5 <br> × 4 | **21.** 5 <br> × 1 | **22.** 7 <br> × 3 | **23.** 9 <br> × 6 | **24.** 3 <br> × 0 |
| **25.** 3 <br> × 6 | **26.** 3 <br> × 1 | **27.** 6 <br> × 7 | **28.** 9 <br> × 8 | **29.** 2 <br> × 6 | **30.** 9 <br> × 4 |

**I need more practice with these facts:**

Name_____ Date _____

# BASIC FACTS: MULTIPLICATION

Find the product. Use strategies to help you.

| | | | | | |
|---|---|---|---|---|---|
| **1.** 1 <br> × 1 | **2.** 7 <br> × 8 | **3.** 4 <br> × 5 | **4.** 9 <br> × 2 | **5.** 0 <br> × 7 | **6.** 2 <br> × 4 |
| **7.** 8 <br> × 9 | **8.** 8 <br> × 1 | **9.** 1 <br> × 6 | **10.** 5 <br> × 2 | **11.** 7 <br> × 4 | **12.** 9 <br> × 0 |
| **13.** 5 <br> × 6 | **14.** 7 <br> × 3 | **15.** 8 <br> × 6 | **16.** 3 <br> × 4 | **17.** 5 <br> × 8 | **18.** 8 <br> × 4 |
| **19.** 9 <br> × 9 | **20.** 0 <br> × 1 | **21.** 4 <br> × 4 | **22.** 0 <br> × 5 | **23.** 3 <br> × 8 | **24.** 6 <br> × 2 |
| **25.** 2 <br> × 2 | **26.** 5 <br> × 3 | **27.** 8 <br> × 0 | **28.** 3 <br> × 9 | **29.** 9 <br> × 6 | **30.** 4 <br> × 9 |

I need more practice with these facts:

Name_____ Date _____

# BASIC FACTS: DIVISION

Find the quotient. Use strategies to help you.

**1.** $1\overline{)6}$      **2.** $7\overline{)28}$      **3.** $4\overline{)12}$      **4.** $5\overline{)45}$      **5.** $3\overline{)0}$      **6.** $6\overline{)36}$

**7.** $3\overline{)27}$      **8.** $2\overline{)10}$      **9.** $8\overline{)8}$      **10.** $9\overline{)63}$      **11.** $3\overline{)21}$      **12.** $6\overline{)12}$

**13.** $5\overline{)25}$      **14.** $7\overline{)56}$      **15.** $2\overline{)2}$      **16.** $4\overline{)36}$      **17.** $5\overline{)15}$      **18.** $1\overline{)3}$

**19.** $5\overline{)35}$      **20.** $3\overline{)9}$      **21.** $1\overline{)9}$      **22.** $2\overline{)4}$      **23.** $6\overline{)0}$      **24.** $8\overline{)48}$

**25.** $9\overline{)27}$      **26.** $4\overline{)24}$      **27.** $2\overline{)14}$      **28.** $6\overline{)24}$      **29.** $4\overline{)20}$      **30.** $2\overline{)18}$

**I need more practice with these facts:**

Name_____ Date _____

# BASIC FACTS: DIVISION

**Find the quotient. Use strategies to help you.**

**1.** 6)42    **2.** 4)32    **3.** 5)0    **4.** 1)2    **5.** 3)15    **6.** 8)64

**7.** 3)3    **8.** 6)18    **9.** 7)49    **10.** 3)6    **11.** 1)5    **12.** 8)40

**13.** 9)72    **14.** 5)30    **15.** 9)0    **16.** 4)16    **17.** 5)10    **18.** 7)21

**19.** 3)18    **20.** 6)6    **21.** 6)54    **22.** 2)16    **23.** 9)45    **24.** 7)14

**25.** 5)20    **26.** 1)0    **27.** 6)48    **28.** 4)28    **29.** 5)5    **30.** 7)35

**I need more practice with these facts:**

Name_____ Date _____

# BASIC FACTS: DIVISION

Find the quotient. Use strategies to help you.

**1.** 1$\overline{)4}$ **2.** 7$\overline{)42}$ **3.** 8$\overline{)24}$ **4.** 7$\overline{)7}$ **5.** 2$\overline{)12}$ **6.** 8$\overline{)32}$

**7.** 6$\overline{)30}$ **8.** 4$\overline{)8}$ **9.** 2$\overline{)0}$ **10.** 5$\overline{)40}$ **11.** 7$\overline{)0}$ **12.** 3$\overline{)24}$

**13.** 1$\overline{)7}$ **14.** 8$\overline{)72}$ **15.** 2$\overline{)16}$ **16.** 9$\overline{)9}$ **17.** 9$\overline{)54}$ **18.** 2$\overline{)6}$

**19.** 7$\overline{)63}$ **20.** 4$\overline{)0}$ **21.** 9$\overline{)81}$ **22.** 1$\overline{)1}$ **23.** 9$\overline{)36}$ **24.** 8$\overline{)0}$

**25.** 5$\overline{)45}$ **26.** 3$\overline{)12}$ **27.** 9$\overline{)18}$ **28.** 2$\overline{)8}$ **29.** 8$\overline{)56}$ **30.** 4$\overline{)4}$

**I need more practice with these facts:**

# Practice Minutes Record

**30 Minutes**

**Name** _____

Dear Family,

Please help me practice my _____ facts.

...................................................................................

| **I practiced:** | **Date** | **Helper** |
|---|---|---|
| 5 minutes | _____ | _____ |
| 5 minutes | _____ | _____ |
| 5 minutes | _____ | _____ |
| 5 minutes | _____ | _____ |
| 5 minutes | _____ | _____ |
| 5 minutes | _____ | _____ |

**Return completed record to your teacher.**

# Practice Minutes Record

**60 Minutes**

**Name** _____

Dear Family,

Please help me practice my _____ facts.

························································································································································

## New Facts

| I practiced: | Date | Helper |
|---|---|---|
| 5 minutes | _____ | _____ |
| 5 minutes | _____ | _____ |
| 5 minutes | _____ | _____ |
| 5 minutes | _____ | _____ |
| 5 minutes | _____ | _____ |
| 5 minutes | _____ | _____ |

## Review Facts

| I practiced: | Date | Helper |
|---|---|---|
| 5 minutes | _____ | _____ |
| 5 minutes | _____ | _____ |
| 5 minutes | _____ | _____ |
| 5 minutes | _____ | _____ |
| 5 minutes | _____ | _____ |
| 5 minutes | _____ | _____ |

**Return completed record to your teacher.**

# Practice Minutes Record

**100 Minutes**

**Name** _____

Dear Family,

Please help me practice my _____ facts.

........................................................................................................

## New Facts

| I practiced: | Date | Helper |
|---|---|---|
| 10 minutes | _____ | _____ |
| 10 minutes | _____ | _____ |
| 10 minutes | _____ | _____ |
| 10 minutes | _____ | _____ |
| 10 minutes | _____ | _____ |

## Review Facts

| I practiced: | Date | Helper |
|---|---|---|
| 10 minutes | _____ | _____ |
| 10 minutes | _____ | _____ |
| 10 minutes | _____ | _____ |
| 10 minutes | _____ | _____ |
| 10 minutes | _____ | _____ |

**Return completed record to your teacher.**

# Practice Minutes Record

120 Minutes

**Name** _____

Dear Family,

Please help me practice my _____ facts.

...........................................................................................................

## New Facts

| I practiced: | Date | Helper |
|---|---|---|
| 10 minutes | _____ | _____ |
| 10 minutes | _____ | _____ |
| 10 minutes | _____ | _____ |
| 10 minutes | _____ | _____ |
| 10 minutes | _____ | _____ |
| 10 minutes | _____ | _____ |

## Review Facts

| I practiced: | Date | Helper |
|---|---|---|
| 10 minutes | _____ | _____ |
| 10 minutes | _____ | _____ |
| 10 minutes | _____ | _____ |
| 10 minutes | _____ | _____ |
| 10 minutes | _____ | _____ |
| 10 minutes | _____ | _____ |

**Return completed record to your teacher.**

# Just the Facts

**30 Minutes**

# CONGRATULATIONS

on your hard work practicing your _____ facts.

_____
Teacher's Signature

Practice Award

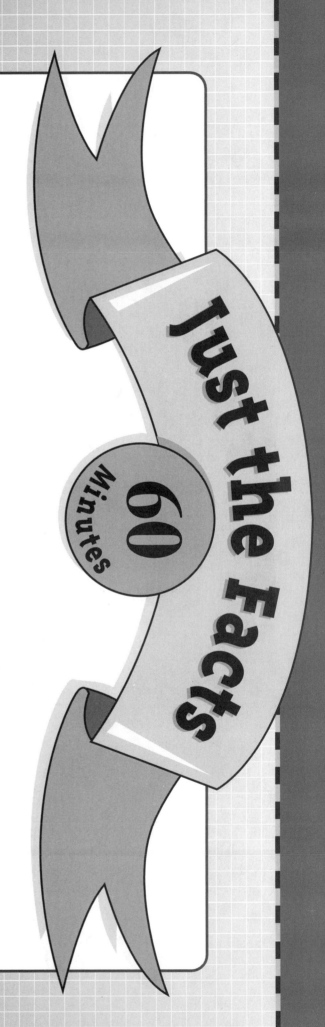

Practice Award

CONGRATULATIONS

on your hard work practicing your

_____

Student's Name

_____ facts.

_____

Teacher's Signature

Just the Facts

60 Minutes

# Just the Facts

## 100 Minutes

# CONGRATULATIONS

on your hard work practicing your _____ facts.

_____
Teacher's Signature

Practice Award

Practice Award

CONGRATULATIONS

on your hard work practicing your _____ facts.

Student's Name

Teacher's Signature

Just the Facts

120 Minutes

150

# Just the Facts
# Answers

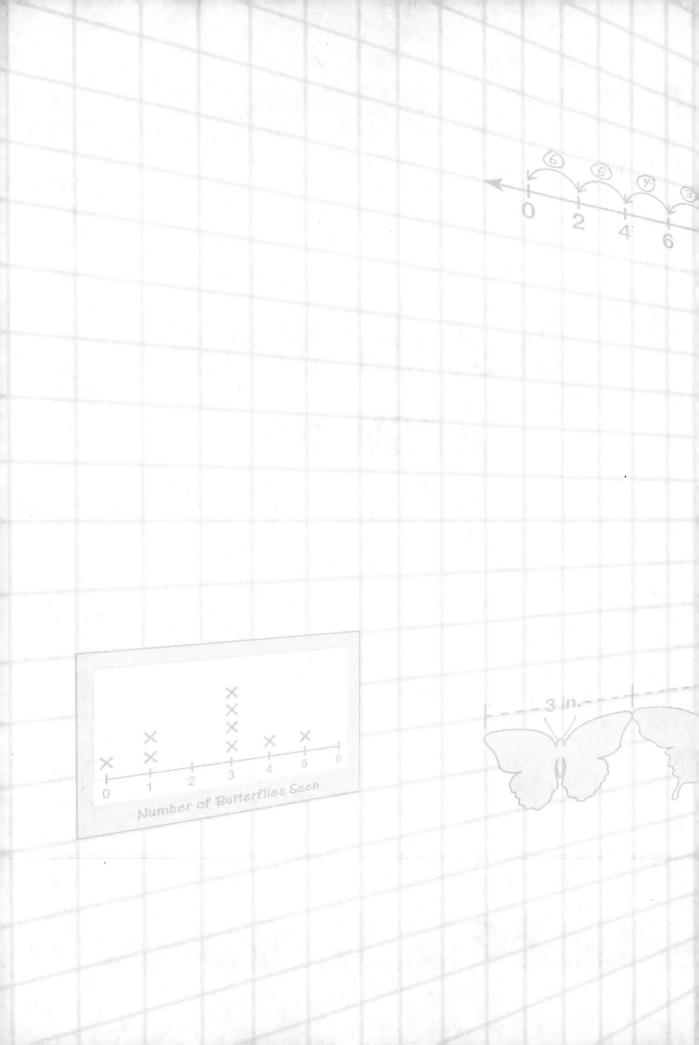

0   2   4   6

Number of Butterflies Seen

3 in.

# Answers

**Level 3**  **Worksheet 1A: 1.** 6 **2.** 8 **3.** 9 **4.** 7 **5.** 9 **6.** 1 **7.** 8 **8.** 10 **9.** 8 **10.** 6 **11.** 7, 8, 9, 4 + 6 = 10 **12.** 6, 7, 8, 6 + 3 = 9 **13.** 5, 6, 7, 10 − 2 = 8 **14.** 4, 3, 2, 9 − 8 = 1 **Worksheet 1B: 1.** 7 **2.** 7 **3.** 7 **4.** 10 **5.** 8 **6.** 9 **7.** 11 **8.** 8 **9.** 6 **10.** 2 **11.** 3 **12.** 2 **13.** 3 **14.** 4 **15.** 1 **16.** 2 **17.** 3 **18.** 2 **19.** 1 **20.** 3 **21.** 3 **22.** 3 **23.** 4 **24.** 6 **25.** 6 **26.** 6 **27.** 4 **28.** 1 **29.** 2 **Worksheet 2A:** Answers will vary for doubles. **1.** 11 **2.** 17 **3.** 13 **4.** 11 **5.** 17 **6.** 13 **7.** 2 **8.** 3 **9.** 2 **10.** 5 **11.** 4 **12.** 8 **13.** 2 **14.** 6 **15.** 4 **16.** 1 **17.** 9 **18.** 11 **19.** 14 **20.** 12 **Worksheet 2B: 1.** 8 **2.** 13 **3.** 10 **4.** 9 **5.** 9 **6.** 18 **7.** 10 **8.** 6 **9.** 11 **10.** 15 **11.** 16 **12.** 3 **13.** 12 **14.** 14 **15.** 10 **16.** B; 8 **17.** C; 4 **18.** A; 9 **Worksheet 3A: 1.** 14 **2.** 11 **3.** 13 **4.** 14 **5.** 13 **6.** 16 **7.** 17 **8.** 12 **9.** 15 **10.** 7 **11.** 2 **12.** 2 **13.** 3 **14.** 5 **15.** 4 **16.** 8 **17.** 10 **18.** 2 **19.** 2 **20.** 3 **21.** 3 **22.** 1 **23.** 6 **24.** 2 **25.** 8 **26.** 3 **27.** 2 **28.** 6 **29.** 4 **Worksheet 3B: 1.** 5 **2.** 6 **3.** 8 **4.** 3 **5.** 6 **6.** 9 **7.** 15 **8.** 8 **9.** 13 **10.** 9 **11.** 8 **12.** 14 **13.** 5 **14.** 6 **15.** 15 **16.** 5 **17.** 12 **18.** 4 **19.** 8 **20.** 16 **21.** 5 **22.** 7 **23.** 11 **24.** 16 **25.** 9 **26.** 7 **27.** 2 **28.** 9 **29.** 8 **30.** 5 **Worksheet 4A:** Answers will vary. Possible answers are given. **1.** 10 + 5 = 15, 5 × 3 = 15 **2.** 7 + 7 = 14, 7 × 2 = 14 **3.** 4, 4 **4.** 6, 6 **5.** 8, 8 **6.** 10, 10 **7.** 18 **8.** 16 Drawings will vary. **9.** 14 **10.** 12 **11.** 8 **Worksheet 4B:** Drawings will vary. **1.** 18 **2.** 24 **3.** 15 **4.** 14 **5.** 12 **6.** 18 **7.** 8 **8.** 16 **9.** 10 **10.** 6 **11.** 18 **12.** 4 **13.** 15 **14.** 12 **15.** 21 **16.** < **17.** > **18.** > **19.** > **20.** > **21.** > **Worksheet 5A: 1.** 2 **2.** 6 **3.** 4 **4.** 7 **5.** 12 **6.** 1 **7.** 7 **8.** 18 **9.** 8 **10.** 5 **11.** 8 **12.** 6 **13.** 4 **14.** 4 **15.** 3 **16.** 10 **17.** 14 **18.** 6 **19.** 8 **20.** 9 **21.** 10 **22.** 0 **23.** 16 **24.** 6 **25.** 8 **26.** 4 **Worksheet 5B: 1.** 6 **2.** 10 **3.** 8 **4.** 18 **5.** 4 **6.** 16 **7.** 4 **8.** 8 **9.** 12 **10.** 9 **11.** 3 **12.** 4 **13.** 5 **14.** 14 **15.** 18 **16.** 2 **17.** 7 **18.** 10 **19.** 9 **20.** 2 **21.** 1 **22.** 6 **23.** 16 **24.** 4 **25.** 12 **26.** 8 **27.** 3 **28.** 6 **29.** 14 **30.** 8 **Worksheet 6A:** Answers will vary. Possible answers are given. **1.** 4 + 4 = 8, 4 × 2 = 8 **2.** 4 + 4 + 4 = 12, 4 × 3 = 12 **3.** 12 **4.** 32 **5.** 28 **6.** 20 **7.** 8 **8.** 16 **9.** 28 **10.** 16 **11.** 12 **12.** 36 **13.** 20 **14.** 24 **15.** 12 **16.** 28 **17.** 32 **18.** 8 **Worksheet 6B: 1.** 14 **2.** 12 **3.** 18 **4.** 8 **5.** 16 **6.** 10 **7.** 6 **8.** 18 **9.** 4 **10.** 12 **11.** 32 **12.** 28 **13.** 20 **14.** 8 **15.** 16 **16.** 36 **17.** 24 **18.** 32 **19.** 4 **20.** 8 **21.** 24 **22.** 28 **23.** 4 **24.** 36 **25.** 12 **26.** 20 **27.** 24 **28.** 32 **29.** 8 **30.** 28 **Worksheet 7A: 1.** 6 **2.** 15 **3.** 18 **4.** 12 **5.** 27 **6.** 24 **7.** 21 **8.** 9 **9.** 27 **10.** 15 **11.** 18 **12.** 6 **13.** Answer given. **14.** 14 **15.** 6 **16.** 8 **17.** 10 **18.** 9 **19.** 18 **20.** 4 **21.** 8 **22.** 5 **Worksheet 7B: 1.** c. **2.** d. **3.** b. **4.** f. **5.** g. **6.** a. **7.** e. Answers will vary. Possible answers are given. **8.** 2 × 2 **9.** 4 × 2 **10.** 3 × 1 **11.** 1 × 5 **12.** 2 × 3 **13.** 5 × 2 **14.** 1 × 7 **15.** 3 × 3 **16.** 6 ×

2 **17.** 5 × 3 **Worksheet 8A: 1.** 18 **2.** 30 **3.** 12 **4.** 24 **5.** 0 **6.** 6 **7.** 24 **8.** 54 **9.** 48 **10.** 12 **11.** > **12.** = **13.** < **14.** = **15.** 18 **16.** 0 **17.** 54 **18.** 30 **19.** 6 **20.** 42 **21.** 12 **22.** 24 **23.** 36 **24.** 48 **25.** 18 **26.** 30 **Worksheet 8B:** Drawings will vary. **1.** 18 **2.** 12 **3.** 36 **4.** 24 **5.** 54 **6.** 18 **7.** 12 **8.** 42 **9.** 48 **10.** 24 **11.** 0 **12.** 48 **13.** 18 **14.** 30 **15.** 24 **16.** 6 **17.** 6 **Worksheet 9A: 1.** 15 **2.** 30 **3.** 35 **4.** 10 **5.** 40 **6.** 20 **7.** 45 **8.** 30 **9.** 40 **10.** 45 **11.** > **12.** < **13.** > **14.** > **15.** 36 **16.** 12 **17.** 48 **18.** 42 **19.** 54 **Worksheet 9B: 1.** 10, 10 **2.** 15, 15 **3.** 20, 20 **4.** 40, equal to **5.** 30, less than **6.** 10, less than **7.** 45, greater than **8.** 50, greater than **9.** 40 **10.** 15 **11.** 16 **12.** 45 **13.** 20 **14.** 30 **15.** 0 **16.** 35 **17.** 10 **Worksheet 10A: 1.** 9 **2.** 18 **3.** 27 **4.** 36 **5.** 45 **6.** 18 **7.** 36 **8.** 9 **9.** 4 **10.** 63 **11.** 36 **12.** 27 **13.** 18 **14.** 36 **15.** 72 **16.** 45 **17.** 81 **18.** 27 **19.** 18 **Worksheet 10B: 1.** 9 **2.** 18 **3.** 27 **4.** 36 **5.** 45 **6.** 54 **7.** 63 **8.** 72 **9.** 81 **10.** 36 **11.** 54 **12.** 20 **13.** 42 **14.** 63 **15.** 45 **16.** 9 **17.** 0 **18.** 9 **19.** 27 **20.** 1 **21.** 4 **22.** 1 **23.** 5 **Worksheet 11A: 1.** 21, less than **2.** 56, greater than **3.** 42, greater than **4.** 35, greater than **5.** 21 **6.** 28 **7.** 42 **8.** 35 **9.** 35 **10.** 56 **11.** 14 **12.** 7 **13.** 0 **14.** 63 **15.** > **16.** < **17.** < **18.** > **Worksheet 11B: 1.** 56 **2.** 21 **3.** 63 **4.** 42 **5.** 49 **6.** 49 **7.** 48 **8.** 7 **9.** 56 **10.** 28 **11.** 21 **12.** 28 **13.** 42 **14.** 63 **15.** 56 **16.** 27 **17.** 14 **18.** 59 **19.** 30 **20.** 18 **21.** 24 **Worksheet 12A: 1.** 48 **2.** 56 **3.** 24 **4.** 48 **5.** 40 **6.** 56 **7.** 32 **8.** 0 **9.** 64 **10.** 8 **11.** 16 **12.** 8 **13.** 56 **14.** 32 **15.** 5 **16.** 42 **17.** 12 **18.** 18 **19.** 25 **Worksheet 12B: 1.** 56 **2.** 40 **3.** 24 **4.** 8 **5.** 32 **6.** 16 **7.** 32 **8.** 8 **9.** 48 **10.** 4, 6, 10, 12, 14, 16, 18 **11.** 6, 9, 15, 18, 21, 24, 27 **12.** 8, 12, 20, 24, 28, 32, 36 **13.** 10, 15, 25, 30, 35, 40, 45 **14.** 12, 18, 30, 36, 42, 48, 54 **15.** 14, 21, 35, 42, 49, 56, 63 **16.** 16, 24, 40, 48, 56, 64, 72 **17.** 18, 27, 45, 54, 63, 72, 81 **18.** > **19.** < **20.** < **21.** = **22.** > **23.** <

**Level 4**  **Worksheet 1A: 1.** 3 × 4 = 12; 4 × 3 = 12 **2.** 3 × 6 = 18; 6 × 3 = 18 **3.** 3 × 5 = 15; 5 × 3 = 15 **4.** 5; 4 **5.** 6; 2 **6.** 3; 7 **7.** 2; 8 **8.** 3 × 7 = 21 **9.** 5 × 5 = 25 **10.** 12 ÷ 2 = 6 **11.** 15 ÷ 3 = 5 **Worksheet 1B:** Models will vary. **1.** 6 **2.** 16 **3.** 18 **4.** 16 **5.** 15 **6.** 8 **7.** 14 **8.** 12 **9.** 10 **10.** 12 **11.** 9 **12.** 20 Drawings will vary. **13.** 4 **14.** 5 **15.** 2 **16.** 6 **17.** 3 **18.** 9 **19.** 5 **20.** 4 **21.** 8 **Worksheet 2A: 1.** 4 ÷ 2 = 2 **2.** 10 ÷ 5 = 2 **3.** 12 ÷ 6 = 2 **4.** 2, 4, 6, 8, 10, 12, 14, 16, 18, 20 **5.** Drawings will vary. **6.** Drawings will vary. **7.** ÷ **8.** × **9.** + **10.** 2; 4 × 2 = 8 or 2 × 4 = 8 **11.** 1; 5 × 1 = 5 or 1 × 5 = 5 **12.** 2; 2 × 1 = 2 or 1 × 2 = 2 **13.** 2; 2 × 7 = 14 or 7 × 2 = 14 **Worksheet 2B: 1.** 14 **2.** 12 **3.** 18 **4.** 8 **5.** 16 **6.** 10 **7.** 6 **8.** 2 **9.** 4 **10.** 10 **11.** 6 **12.** 16 **13.** 18 **14.** 8 **15.** 12 **16.** 4 **17.** 3 **18.** 9 **19.** 5 **20.** 8 **21.** 6 **22.** 7 **23.** 2 **24.** 2 **25.** 14; 14 ÷ 7 = 2 or 14 ÷ 2 = 7 **26.** 6; 6 ÷ 3 = 2 or 6 ÷ 2 = 3 **27.** 8; 8 ÷ 4 = 2 or 8 ÷ 2 = 4 **28.** 16; 16 ÷ 8 = 2 or 16 ÷ 2 = 8 **Worksheet 3A: 1.** 4 **2.** 8 **3.** 3 **4.** 7

5. 4 6. 4 7. 4 8. 4 9. 6 10. 4, 8, 12, 16, 20, 24, 28, 32, 36, 40 11. 5; 5 × 2 = 10 or 2 × 5 = 10 12. 2; 2 × 4 = 8 or 4 × 2 = 8 13. 4; 4 × 4 = 16 14. 7; 7 × 2 = 14 or 2 × 7 = 14 15. 6; 6 × 4 = 24 or 4 × 6 = 24 16. 5; 5 × 4 = 20 or 4 × 5 = 20 17. 8; 8 × 4 = 32 or 4 × 8 = 32 18. 9; 9 × 2 = 18 or 2 × 9 = 18 19. 7; 7 × 4 = 28 or 4 × 7 = 28 **Worksheet 3B: 1.** 2; 2 × 4 = 8 **2.** 8; 8 × 4 = 32 **3.** 6; 6 × 4 = 24 **4.** 4; 4 × 4 = 16 **5.** 9; 9 × 4 = 36 **6.** 3; 4 × 3 = 12 **7.** 7; 7 × 4 = 28 **8.** 5; 5 × 4 = 20 **9.** 3; 3 × 4 = 12 **10.** 24 **11.** 20 **12.** 28 **13.** 32 **14.** 36 **15.** 12 **16.** 16 **17.** 36 **18.** 32 **19.** 20 **20.** 12 **21.** 14 **22.** 24 **Worksheet 4A: 1.** 40 **2.** 15 **3.** 10 **4.** 25 **5.** 40 **6.** 45 **7.** 30 **8.** 30 **9.** 5, 10, 15, 20, 25, 30, 35, 40, 45, 50 **10.** 8 **11.** 7 **12.** 5 **13.** 2 **14.** 4 **15.** 6 **16.** 3 **17.** 9 **18.** 5 **19.** 5 **20.** 5 **21.** 5 **Worksheet 4B: 1.** 5 **2.** 6 **3.** 9 **4.** 8 **5.** 7 **6.** 10 **7.** 3 **8.** 4 **9.** 4, 8, 12, 16, 20, 24, 28, 32, 36, 40, 44, 48 **10.** 9; 5 **11.** 5 **12.** 35 **13.** 40 **14.** 21 **15.** 9 **16.** 9; 6 **17.** 4; 5 **18.** 5 **19.** 5; 6 **20.** 5 **21.** 45 **22.** 3 **23.** 24 **24.** 3 **Worksheet 5A: 1.** 8 **2.** 12 **3.** 1 **4.** 10 **5.** 2 **6.** 7 **7.** 5 **8.** 9 **9.** 2 **10.** 1 **11.** 6 **12.** 8 **13.** 4 **14.** 6 **15.** 7 **16.** 3 **17.** 1; 1 × 5 = 5 **18.** 3; 1 × 3 = 3 **19.** 5 **20.** 1 **21.** 8 **22.** 3 **Worksheet 5B: 1.** 4 **2.** 8 **3.** 12 **4.** 9 **5.** 3 **6.** 8 **7.** 5 **8.** 7 **9.** 18 **10.** 4 **11.** 7 **12.** 20 **13.** 9 **14.** 2 **15.** 2 **16.** 6 **17.** 32 **18.** 4 **19.** 14 **20.** 4 **21.** 6 **22.** 2 **23.** 9 **24.** 12 **25.** 8 **26.** 5 **27.** 6 **28.** 8 **29.** 8 **30.** 11 **31.** 4 **Worksheet 6A: 1.** 6; 3; 6; 2 **2.** 18; 3; 18; 6 **3.** 24; 8; 24; 3 **4.** 27; 3; 27; 9 **5.** 15; 5; 15; 3 **6.** 3 × 4 = 12; 4 × 3 = 12; 12 ÷ 3 = 4; 12 ÷ 4 = 3 **7.** 3 × 7 = 21; 7 × 3 = 21; 21 ÷ 3 = 7; 21 ÷ 7 = 3 **Worksheet 6B: 1.** 2; 2, 3, 6 **2.** 7; 7, 3, 21 **3.** 4; 4, 3, 12 **4.** 1; 1, 3, 3 **5.** 3; 3, 3, 9 **6.** 8; 8, 3, 24 **7.** 5; 5, 3, 15 **8.** 0; 0,3,0 **9.** 6; 6, 3, 18 **10.** 9; 9, 3, 27 **11.** incorrect; corrections will vary. **12.** correct; 3 × 3 = 9 **13.** incorrect; corrections will vary. **Worksheet 7A: 1.** 0 **2.** 8 **3.** 0 **4.** 9 **5.** 0 **6.** 0 **7.** 5 **8.** 0 **9.** 0 **10.** 7 **11.** 25 **12.** 0 **13.** 2 **14.** 0 **15.** 0 **16.** 4 **17.** 3 **18.** 12 **19.** 14 **20.** 9 **21.** 21 **22.** 24 **23.** 15 **24.** 12 **25.** 10 **26.** 20 **27.** 8 **28.** 16 **29.** 0 **Worksheet 7B: 1.** 5 **2.** 0 **3.** 4 **4.** 0 **5.** 2 **6.** 0 **7.** 9 **8.** 1 **9.** 5 **10.** 8 **11.** 3 **12.** 0 **13.** 1 **14.** 0 **15.** 4 **16.** 7 **17.** 0, 0 × 4 = 0 **18.** 1, 1 × 5 = 5 **19.** 3, 3 × 1 = 3 **20.** 5, 5 × 2 = 10 **21.** 2, 2 × 3 = 6 **22.** 0, 0 × 3 = 0 **23.** 8, 8 × 1 = 8 **24.** 7, 7 × 2 = 14 **25.** 4, 4 × 1 = 4 **26.** 3, 3 × 3 = 9 **27.** 1, 1 × 3 = 3 **28.** 16, 16 × 1 = 16 **Worksheet 8A: 1.** 9 × 3 = 27; 3 × 9 = 27 **2.** 9 × 2 = 18; 2 × 9 = 18 **3.** 9 **4.** 8 **5.** 6 **6.** 6, 6 or 9, 4 **7.** 2, 9 or 3, 6 **8.** 9, 5 **9.** 45 **10.** 63 **11.** 27 **12.** 36 **13.** 81 **14.** 54 **15.** 40 **16.** 18 **17.** 9 **18.** 72 **Worksheet 8B: 1.** 0 **2.** 9 **3.** 5 **4.** 1 **5.** 9 **6.** 3 **7.** 3 **8.** 2 **9.** 5 **10.** 7 **11.** 4 **12.** 9 **13.** 8 **14.** 3 **15.** 6 **16.** > **17.** = **18.** < **19.** < **20.** 9 **21.** 9 **22.** 3 **23.** 1 **24.** 4 **25.** 9 **26.** 9 **27.** 9 **Worksheet 9A: 1.** 9; 18 **2.** 6; 12 **3.** 21; 42 **4.** 12; 24 **5.** 27; 54 **6.** 15; 30 **7.** 24; 48 **8.** 18; 36 **9.** 24 **10.** 18 **11.** 30 **12.** 42 **13.** 36 **14.** 6 **15.** 12 **16.** 0 **17.** 54 **18.** 48 **19.** 30 **20.** 42 **21.** 24 **22.** 18 **23.** 21 **24.** 12 **25.** 48 **26.** 54

**27.** 25 **28.** 16 **Worksheet 9B: 1.** 6, 7, 42; 7, 6, 42; 42, 7, 6; 42, 6, 7 **2.** 5, 6, 30; 6, 5, 30; 30, 6, 5; 30, 5, 6 **3.** 6, 8, 48; 8, 6, 48; 48, 8, 6; 48, 6, 8 **4.** 6, 9, 54; 9, 6, 54; 54, 9, 6; 54, 6, 9 **5.** 6, 4, 24; 4, 6, 24; 24, 4, 6; 24, 6, 4 **Worksheet 10A: 1.** 1; 1, 7, 7 **2.** 3; 3, 7, 21 **3.** 5; 5, 7, 35 **4.** 8; 8, 7, 56 **5.** 6; 6, 7, 42 **6.** 9; 9, 7, 63 **7.** 2; 2, 7, 14 **8.** 4; 4, 7, 28 **9.** 7; 7, 7, 49 **10.** 7, 9, 63; 9, 7, 63; 63, 9, 7; 63, 7, 9 **11.** 7, 8, 56; 8, 7, 56; 56, 8, 7; 56, 7, 8 **Worksheet 10B: 1.** 14 **2.** 35 **3.** 49 **4.** 28 **5.** 21 **6.** 56 **7.** 63 **8.** 42 **9.** 7 **10.** 0 **11.** 14 **12.** 42 **13.** 56 **14.** 28 **15.** 7 **16.** 63 **17.** 35 **18.** 49 **19.** 21 **20.** 0 **21.** 7 **22.** 9 **23.** 3 **24.** 1 **25.** 2 **26.** 8 **27.** 6 **28.** 4 **29.** 7 **30.** 5 **Worksheet 11A: 1.** 3 × 8 = 24; 8 × 3 = 24 **2.** 2 × 8 = 16; 8 ×2 = 16 **3.** 4 × 8 = 32; 8 × 4 = 32 **4.** 6 × 8 = 48 **5.** 5 × 8 = 40 **6.** 7 × 8 = 56 **7.** 9 × 8 = 72 **8.** 4 × 8 = 32 **9.** 8 × 8 = 64 **10.** Models will vary; 48 **11.** Models will vary; 24 **12.** 48 **13.** 40 **14.** 56 **15.** 32 **Worksheet 11B: 1.** 5 **2.** 7 **3.** 3 **4.** 8 **5.** 6 **6.** 9 **7.** 8, 9 **8.** 7, 8 **9.** 3, 8 **10.** 4 **11.** 2 **12.** 5 **13.** 3 **14.** 6 **15.** 1 **16.** 7 **17.** 8 **18. - 23.** incorrect; corrections will vary. **Worksheet 12A: 1.** 32 **2.** 18 **3.** 40 **4.** 36 **5.** 64 **6.** 27 **7.** 63 **8.** 8 **9.** 45 **10.** 63 **11.** 81 **12.** 48 **13.** 72 **14.** 27 **15.** 56 **16.** 48 **17.** 45 **18.** 16 **19.** 49 **20.** 40 **21.** 56 **22.** 24 **23.** 36 **24.** 28 **25.** 54 **26.** 42 **27.** 27 **28.** 24 **29.** 36 **30.** 14 **Worksheet 12B: 1.** 4 **2.** 5 **3.** 1 **4.** 8 **5.** 4 **6.** 9 **7.** 6 **8.** 1 **9.** 7 **10.** 8 **11.** 3 **12.** 9 **13.** 5 **14.** 0 **15.** 2 **16.** 0 **17.** 6 **18.** 0 **19.** 7 **20.** 9 **21.** 6 **22.** 8 **23.** 5 **24.** 1 **25.** 4 **26.** 2 **27.** 2 **28.** 6 **29.** 4 **30.** 9 **31.** 3 **32.** 8 **33.** 6 **34.** 7 **35.** 3 **Worksheet 13A: 1.** 7, 4, 28; 4, 7, 28; 28, 4, 7; 28, 7, 4 **2.** 8, 3, 24; 3, 8, 24; 24, 3, 8; 24, 8, 3 **3.** 21; 63; 42; 49 **4.** 27; 7; 6; 5; 81 **5.** 27 **6.** 36 **7.** 72 **8.** 45 **9.** 81 **Worksheet 13B: 1.** 5 × 7 = 35; 7 × 5 = 35; 35 ÷ 7 = 5; 35 ÷ 5 = 7 **2.** 6 × 8 = 48; 8 × 6 = 48; 48 ÷ 8 = 6; 48 ÷ 6 = 8 **3.** 32; 4; 32; 8 **4.** 42; 6; 42; 7 **5.** 40; 8; 40; 5 **6.** 36; 4; 36; 9 **7.** 5 **8.** 8 **9.** 9 **10.** 4

**Cumulative Practice** **Practice 1 : 1.** 9 **2.** 6 **3.** 7 **4.** 7 **5.** 10 **6.** 5 **7.** 9 **8.** 17 **9.** 11 **10.** 11 **11.** 15 **12.** 8 **13.** 18 **14.** 1 **15.** 8 **16.** 10 **17.** 14 **18.** 13 **19.** 10 **20.** 12 **21.** 6 **22.** 6 **23.** 16 **24.** 8 **25.** 12 **26.** 10 **27.** 12 **28.** 13 **29.** 12 **30.** 10 **Practice 2: 1.** 4 **2.** 15 **3.** 10 **4.** 9 **5.** 9 **6.** 9 **7.** 5 **8.** 3 **9.** 17 **10.** 13 **11.** 11 **12.** 13 **13.** 5 **14.** 13 **15.** 11 **16.** 11 **17.** 4 **18.** 16 **19.** 7 **20.** 4 **21.** 15 **22.** 12 **23.** 11 **24.** 7 **25.** 2 **26.** 14 **27.** 7 **28.** 6 **29.** 5 **30.** 0 **Practice 3: 1.** 7 **2.** 7 **3.** 17 **4.** 7 **5.** 2 **6.** 9 **7.** 3 **8.** 9 **9.** 10 **10.** 13 **11.** 8 **12.** 4 **13.** 12 **14.** 5 **15.** 11 **16.** 6 **17.** 15 **18.** 5 **19.** 12 **20.** 10 **21.** 11 **22.** 1 **23.** 10 **24.** 3 **25.** 6 **26.** 14 **27.** 14 **28.** 4 **29.** 16 **30.** 9 **Practice 4: 1.** 6 **2.** 8 **3.** 2 **4.** 1 **5.** 7 **6.** 5 **7.** 3 **8.** 4 **9.** 3 **10.** 9 **11.** 3 **12.** 0 **13.** 6 **14.** 0 **15.** 5 **16.** 0 **17.** 9 **18.** 4 **19.** 9 **20.** 7 **21.** 9 **22.** 7 **23.** 5 **24.** 1 **25.** 1 **26.** 1 **27.** 9 **28.** 9 **29.** 4 **30.** 7 **Practice 5: 1.** 4 **2.** 0 **3.** 9 **4.** 8 **5.** 8 **6.** 6 **7.** 2 **8.** 1 **9.** 6 **10.** 1 **11.** 2 **12.** 0 **13.** 5 **14.** 8 **15.** 8 **16.** 9 **17.** 4 **18.** 9 **19.** 2 **20.** 7 **21.** 7 **22.** 8 **23.** 4 **24.** 1 **25.** 0 **26.** 2 **27.** 5 **28.** 2 **29.** 6 **30.** 9 **Practice 6: 1.** 7 **2.** 1 **3.** 5 **4.** 8 **5.** 0 **6.**

4 **7.** 5 **8.** 8 **9.** 9 **10.** 0 **11.** 6 **12.** 4 **13.** 5 **14.** 6 **15.** 3 **16.** 1 **17.** 8 **18.** 3 **19.** 3 **20.** 3 **21.** 1 **22.** 7 **23.** 7 **24.** 6 **25.** 5 **26.** 9 **27.** 2 **28.** 2 **29.** 6 **30.** 1 **Practice 7: 1.** 10 **2.** 4 **3.** 56 **4.** 0 **5.** 12 **6.** 18 **7.** 54 **8.** 36 **9.** 0 **10.** 14 **11.** 48 **12.** 30 **13.** 35 **14.** 15 **15.** 28 **16.** 18 **17.** 16 **18.** 9 **19.** 12 **20.** 0 **21.** 63 **22.** 35 **23.** 12 **24.** 42 **25.** 21 **26.** 24 **27.** 40 **28.** 32 **29.** 9 **30.** 45 **Practice 8: 1.** 0 **2.** 63 **3.** 25 **4.** 18 **5.** 2 **6.** 24 **7.** 12 **8.** 0 **9.** 7 **10.** 6 **11.** 64 **12.** 45 **13.** 18 **14.** 27 **15.** 9 **16.** 6 **17.** 0 **18.** 4 **19.** 49 **20.** 20 **21.** 5 **22.** 21 **23.** 54 **24.** 0 **25.** 18 **26.** 3 **27.** 42 **28.** 72 **29.** 12 **30.** 36 **Practice 9: 1.** 1 **2.** 56 **3.** 20 **4.** 18 **5.** 0 **6.** 8 **7.** 72 **8.** 8 **9.** 6 **10.** 10 **11.** 28 **12.** 0 **13.** 30 **14.** 21 **15.** 48 **16.** 12 **17.** 40 **18.** 32 **19.**

81 **20.** 0 **21.** 16 **22.** 0 **23.** 24 **24.** 12 **25.** 4 **26.** 15 **27.** 0 **28.** 27 **29.** 54 **30.** 36 **Practice 10: 1.** 6 **2.** 4 **3.** 3 **4.** 9 **5.** 0 **6.** 6 **7.** 9 **8.** 5 **9.** 1 **10.** 7 **11.** 7 **12.** 2 **13.** 5 **14.** 8 **15.** 1 **16.** 9 **17.** 3 **18.** 3 **19.** 7 **20.** 3 **21.** 9 **22.** 2 **23.** 0 **24.** 6 **25.** 3 **26.** 6 **27.** 7 **28.** 4 **29.** 5 **30.** 9 **Practice 11: 1.** 7 **2.** 8 **3.** 0 **4.** 2 **5.** 5 **6.** 8 **7.** 1 **8.** 3 **9.** 7 **10.** 2 **11.** 5 **12.** 5 **13.** 8 **14.** 6 **15.** 0 **16.** 4 **17.** 2 **18.** 3 **19.** 6 **20.** 1 **21.** 9 **22.** 8 **23.** 5 **24.** 2 **25.** 4 **26.** 0 **27.** 8 **28.** 7 **29.** 1 **30.** 5 **Practice 12: 1.** 4 **2.** 6 **3.** 3 **4.** 1 **5.** 6 **6.** 4 **7.** 5 **8.** 2 **9.** 0 **10.** 8 **11.** 0 **12.** 8 **13.** 7 **14.** 9 **15.** 8 **16.** 1 **17.** 6 **18.** 3 **19.** 9 **20.** 0 **21.** 9 **22.** 1 **23.** 4 **24.** 0 **25.** 9 **26.** 4 **27.** 2 **28.** 4 **29.** 7 **30.** 1